MAKING SENSE OF MESSAGES:
A CRITICAL APPRENTICESHIP IN RHETORICAL CRITICISM

Making Sense of Messages: A Critical Apprenticeship in Rhetorical Criticism

Mark Stoner
California State University, Sacramento

Sally Perkins
California State University, Sacramento

Houghton Mifflin Company   Boston   New York

To my husband, Jim, who has patiently endured this process, and to my children, Kendra and Elliott, whose education I hope will be advanced by this work.

–S.P.

To my wife, Daria, who has been so patient and supportive, and to my children, Ian and Heather.

–M.S.

Editor-in-Chief: Patricia Coryell
Sponsoring Editor: Mary Finch
Development Editor: Julia Casson
Senior Project Editor: Claudine Bellanton
Editorial Assistant: Lisa Goodman
Art and Design Coordinator: Jill Haber
Senior Composition Buyer: Sarah L. Ambrose
Senior Manufacturing Coordinator: Marie Barnes
Marketing Manager: Elinor Gregory

Cover Image: © The Image Bank

TEXT CREDITS: page 145, Excerpt from "A Time for Peace" by Kendra Creasy. Reprinted by permission of the author.; pages 145–146, From Wil A. Linkugel, R.R. Allen, and Richard L. Johannesen, eds. *Contemporary American Speeches: A Sourcebook of Speech Forms and Principles,* 5/e, p. 309. Copyright © 1982. Published by Kendall/Hunt Publishing Company.; page 201, "Fantasy and Rhetorical Vision: The Rhetorical Criticism of Social Reality," by Ernest Bormann, *Quarterly Journal of Speech* 58, 1972, pp. 396–402. Reprinted by permission of Taylor & Francis Ltd. Visit us at http://www.tandf.co.uk/journals; page 271, "Jewel Tones Return for the Holidays," by Linda Pliagas from HispanicMagazine.com, December 2002. Reprinted with permission from Hispanic Magazine.

PHOTO CREDITS: page 10, © Center for Creative Freedom; page 30, Courtesy of the National Smokers Alliance; page 43, Courtesy of the National Smokers Alliance; page 185, © Zits Partnership. Reprinted with special permission of King Features Syndicate.; page 302, © Painet, Inc.; page 304, ©Afghanistan Online (www.afghan-web.com); page 305, © University of California, Davis: Information Center for the Environment (ICE); page 305, © Enron; page 307, © Ron English; page 308, © 1999 California Deparment of Health Services, used with permission.; page 309, © Franco Vogt/Corbis; page 310, © Arkidata, Inc.; page 311, © Sami Sarkis/Getty Images; page 312, © Charles Phillip/Corbis; page 312, © Patti Murray/Animals, Animals/Earth Sciences; page 313, Courtesy of the author; page 314, Courtesy Devito/Verdi, NY.

Printed in the U.S.A.
Library of Congress Control Number: 2002109681
ISBN: 0-618-14488-9

123456789-MP-08 07 06 05 04

CONTENTS

VISUAL APPROACHES

PREFACE

In this "Age of Information," communication in all its forms is foundational to the quality of life we all experience. Communication is no longer understood as just one of many tools used for producing goods. Today, much of our gross national product is communication—everything from books and movies to websites, wireless communication systems and gadgets to human services of all sorts. In the early 1990s, the value of information systems alone was seven percent of the gross national product. That represents twice as much value as the Department of Defense budget! Factoring in the value of telecommunications, publishing, video and film production, and a host of communication services such as public relations, training and education, technical and popular writing, and so on, it becomes clear that communication is central to our economy.

Rather than becoming less important to each of us individually, "speech" is becoming more important. Whether coming from candidates for office, commentators, bureaucrats, military or business leaders, the talk of public speakers is important in our complex, globalized society. For example, the messages of political candidates are increasingly related to those of political action committees acting in support of or in opposition to the candidates.

The media plays an increasingly important role in shaping and massaging information about legislators and candidates, initiatives and policies. The interface of traditional rhetoric and new communication channels allowing those with a message to tailor that message to you makes it important for you to be able to analyze those messages.

Every dimension of our lives from entertainment to religion is affected by what, how, and why people communicate with each other. Understanding the communication processes that underlie a complex society is essential if we are to make the best possible use of rhetoric for social development while avoiding the dangers that accompany the use of powerful tools of persuasion. Given the need for all of us to be critical consumers and creators of messages, this text is designed to explain and model how communication critics identify how messages do and do not work.

As the title notes, this book is designed as an apprenticeship in rhetorical criticism. An apprenticeship is built upon two principles: sequencing and modeling. Just as a carpenter learns his or her trade through an apprenticeship in which an expert carpenter instructs the novice carpenter in a graduated sequence of skills and models, we have structured this book to help you learn in that fashion. Sequencing has to do with providing instruction in a way that evolves your skills.

Part I begins with an introduction to rhetorical messages and criticism. In Part II, Process to Product, we have sequenced the four kinds of critical thinking critics use to conduct a complete analysis. We describe each kind of thinking to help you recognize the thought process you would use as a rhetorical critic. We augment the sequencing of the critical process by modeling our own thought process for you. Using a two-column format, we show you what a critic thinks and why. In Part III, Analytical Tools, we present a number of critical theories, and with each we provide models for how those theories can be applied. Finally, we provide student essays that model both the thought processes of a critic and the critical product.

This book will assist you in developing critical skills that you can effectively apply in a variety of professional and personal contexts. Our focus is on the thought processes a critic employs before writing or presenting a critical response to a message. To be sure, we do instruct you on writing the critical response, but we believe that the thought process that precedes writing deserves the bulk of our attention. As you focus on the process of critically analyzing messages, you will develop valuable, transferable analytical skills, and you will learn to present your findings through written and oral channels.

With the help of our students, we have designed a text that "fits" you as a newcomer to criticism. We begin where you are as a critical analyst and writer of criticism, and we help you develop your knowledge and skills. The text operates from the following set of assumptions:

1) you learn best by working directly and immediately with material to be learned;

2) you already possess some of the cognitive skills that facilitate criticism, and you can learn new ones;

3) you increase control of your critical-thinking skills by learning to think about your own thought processes in order to monitor and evaluate your own progress as critics;

4) you deepen your insights into communication and rhetoric by focusing on the process of criticism before focusing on the product of criticism;

5) you must be exposed to the vocabulary, theories, and mental habits of expert critics.

Our approach is intended to make the process of rhetorical criticism understandable without unduly simplifying it. The text is designed to help you increase your critical competence, but you will find that there is no algorithm or formula for achieving critical insight. Reaching that goal requires systematic thinking, creativity, and research. This text will help you do these things.

Criticism is often understood by the general public—maybe even by you at this point—as just pointing out perceived errors in a message. Sometimes it is understood as giving your opinion about something. For example, movie reviews typically are centered around whether or not critics liked the movie — "Two thumbs up!" or "Two thumbs down!" Message analysis goes far beyond deciding what you like about a message. As future communication professionals, you'll need to do more than say whether you like a message or not. This book will teach you how to make clear to other people the elements of the message that work or fail as persuasion or argument.

Once you have grasped the readings, it is our hope that you will then creatively apply what you've learned. As you master the foundational skills, procedures, and theory of rhetorical criticism, we invite you to explore the fascinating, almost magical process of communication with an eye to understanding it in new, insightful, and powerful ways.

ACKNOWLEDGEMENTS

We wish to thank our students, who have been patient in the development of this text, for providing guidance as to the most useful and sensible presentation of these ideas to people who are new to rhetorical criticism. Thanks to Professor Steve Jenkins for his commentary and direction early in the development of the book, and to Professor Pam Sanger for her faithful support of the project in using the text and providing "notes from the field." We also thank our former students Casey Frye, Amy Inman, and Rachel Mayse, who read manuscript drafts in search of errors and in search of statements that needed clarification from a student perspective.

We extend our sincere thanks to Ernest Cox, University of Arkansas, Little Rock; Dayle Hardy-Short, Northern Arizona University; John Mckay, Bowling Green State University; Bernard Armada, University of St. Thomas; Mary Triece, University of Akron; Deanna Fassett, San Jose State University; David Beard, University of Minnesota; Catherine Hastings, Susquehanna University; and Stephanie Kelly-Romano, who reviewed the text and have provided excellent ideas for development and revision. We appreciate the kind and constructive reviews that came from thoughtful, open-minded readings of the text. We also thank our Development Editor, Julia Casson, who saw this project to its completion. We are grateful for the careful editing of Claudine Bellanton and Lisa Goodman of Houghton Mifflin.

Finally, we thank our best friends, Daria Stoner and Jim Obermaier, for their endless patience, encouragement, and support over the last three years.

M.S. and S.P.

WORK CITED

Saunders, Carol Stoak and Jack William Jones. "Measuring Performance of the Information Systems Function." *Journal of Management Information Systems* 8 (1992): 63+.

Making Sense of Messages:
A Critical Apprenticeship in Rhetorical Criticism

WHAT ARE RHETORICAL MESSAGES?

CHARACTERISTICS OF RHETORIC

In an article about parenting in *Newsweek* magazine, an author writes, "Like so many other American cities, Hampton, Va., is full of parents who need help. But instead of settling for easy denunciations, the town is trading rhetoric for action" (Wingert 1997, 88).

When you hear the word *rhetoric,* what comes to mind? If you're like most people, you think of flowery language with no real substance, politicians blowing hot air, or language that manipulates emotions but lacks substance. You may have heard or may yourself have used the phrase "Oh, that's just rhetoric," suggesting that you're hearing words without real meaning or substance. Most people believe action is real work that gets things done, whereas rhetoric is mere talk about action that doesn't, itself, accomplish anything.

Unfortunately, rhetoric has carried this negative connotation for thousands of years. In the fifth century B.C. in ancient Greece, citizens who were constructing the first known democracy suddenly found themselves in need of instruction in public oratory in order to function effectively in the newfound legislative and judicial systems. Ancient philosophical teachers known as *Sophists* came from Italy to teach rhetoric or oratory, among other subjects. The great philosopher Plato (1952) argued in his treatise *Gorgias* that the rhetoric being taught by the Sophists was mere "cookery." The study of rhetoric was empty by contrast to the study of biology, for example. The discipline of biology has content, substance to be learned, whereas the discipline of rhetoric is all about learning how to speak the content or substance from other disciplines like biology. Thus, said Plato, rhetoric itself has no substance as a discipline of study. For him, rhetoric was a matter of making substantial or sometimes insubstantial ideas taste or sound good, just as the art of cooking involves making a real substance taste good though the cooking itself is not real substance. For Plato, where chemistry would be considered the substantive discipline of understanding the elements of temperature, water, and food substances involved in cooking, cookery was the mere knack of being able to make food taste good. The discipline was of more value to Plato than the knack. As cookery, rhetoric was also seen as an act of merely assembling prefabricated ideas, much as a cook might assemble ingredients already processed by others. For a long time, Plato believed rhetoricians mixed together other people's ideas rather than deriving truth themselves through logic.

Although Plato's criticisms of rhetoric have persisted throughout the years, many scholars and philosophers have disputed the notion that rhetoric is merely cookery, hot air, or flowery language. Plato's student Aristotle wrote a treatise, *The Rhetoric,* that remains to this day an influential legitimization of the subject. Aristotle defined rhetoric as "the faculty of observing in any given case the available means of persuasion" (1984, 3). Specifically, he was interested in the intentional application of "all the available means of persuasion" in political speeches, courtroom speeches, and ceremonial speeches. Aristotle disagreed with Plato's view that rhetoric was mere cookery. He saw it as a necessary, legitimate tool of democracy, worthy of study.

What was available only in the form of oratory in ancient Greece is created in many different forms today. Take a look at the following list of messages.

A comic book memorializing the victims of 9/11/01

The "Free Kobe" website arguing for basketball pro Kobe Bryant's innocence

Vietnam War Memorial

A presidential campaign speech

A closing argument in a murder trial

The AIDS quilt

A speech by a U.S. senator to the Senate supporting a tax cut

A controversial episode of the television show *The West Wing*

An editorial in the newspaper

A website by the Susan G. Komen Breast Cancer Foundation

A eulogy at a funeral

One might say that a presidential campaign speech is merely cookery, that candidates often do not speak the truth, but instead try to make things sound good so they can get elected. One might say that a trial attorney who knows she has a losing case might use rhetoric merely to make her client look good, even when the client is guilty. Although both illustrations, indeed, may be cases of cookery, they may also be more than that. We'd like to suggest several functions of rhetoric that help us delineate our focus of study.

RHETORIC TYPICALLY ADDRESSES PUBLIC AUDIENCES

Each of the messages in our list is directed toward a listener, a viewer, a reader. The AIDS quilt addresses the public viewer who sees part of the quilt wherever it may be displayed. The editorial addresses readers of the newspaper. The Vietnam War Memorial addresses tourists, schoolchildren, and others who visit the historical, commemorative monuments in Washington, D.C. The "Free Kobe" website for Kobe Bryant addresses interested readers surfing for information on the NBA player (freekobe.com). None of these messages was created merely for its own sake. They were all created to address audiences, more or less clearly defined.

RHETORIC IS PURPOSEFUL

Each of the messages in our list seeks to affect its audiences' beliefs, values, or actions. It is more than merely the sharing of information for information's sake or the expression of emotion for emotion's sake. For example, the comic book, to some degree, raises questions in its readers' minds about the terrorist attacks of September 11, 2001. The Vietnam War Memorial affects viewers' attitudes, emotions, and beliefs about the Vietnam War and its soldiers. Some say it causes the viewer to critique the value of the war, as the memorial is black and descends into the ground, in contrast to surrounding memorials like the Washington Monument and Lincoln Memorial. Others say it causes the viewer to valorize and respect the soldiers who received little respect upon their return home from the war (Blair, Jeppeson, and Pucci 1991, 274–77). No matter what the actual effect, we know that the rhetorical message of the Vietnam War Memorial seeks to impact its viewers' attitudes and beliefs. By the same token, the infomercial seeks to affect its viewers' behaviors, persuading them to call a toll-free number and purchase a product, while the eulogy seeks to affect mourners by helping them accept the death of a loved one and transform their physical relationship with the deceased to a spiritual relationship. So, in each case, the message is purposeful.

That said, we must also recognize that some messages are more or less intentional in their persuasive purpose. Communication scholar Roderick Hart writes that rhetorical messages might be viewed on a continuum with more obviously persuasive messages being at one end and less obviously persuasive messages being at the other (1997, 12). For example, the persuasive purpose of a speech by a politician running for office is obvious: to convince its audience to vote for the politician. However, on the other end of the scale we might place messages that function rhetorically without necessarily intending to do so. For example, on an audiocassette tape of children's songs produced by Walt Disney Productions, male voices are used to sing all the songs ("Ring Around the Rosie," "One-Two Buckle My Shoe," "The Itsy Bitsy Spider," and "Pat-a-Cake") except "I'm a Little Teapot," which is sung by a female (*Disney Songtape*). The stated purpose of the audiocassette tape is to entertain children and teach them common childhood songs. Without necessarily intending to, however, the producers of the music reinforce a stereotype that domestic activities and items are for girls and women, whereas sticks, shoes, and spiders are for boys and men. Because authors of rhetorical messages may or may not intentionally seek to affect audiences as they do, intentionality is not a necessary characteristic of rhetoric. Messages are purposeful insofar as they are deliberately crafted by some author or authors, but the authors' apparent purposes may or may not necessarily be related to the rhetorical functions of their messages.

What is *not* rhetoric, you might wonder? A table reporting statistical data is not rhetorical. Numerical data are simply numbers without meaning, unless explained. It is how a scientist interprets the data or how a politician presents that data in the context of a persuasive speech that is rhetorical. In a sense, the data are meaningless unless accompanied by other symbols (in this case, words) that assign meaning to the data. So raw information on its own does not necessarily meet the criteria for what constitutes rhetoric.

RHETORIC RESPONDS TO AND CREATES MORE OR LESS OBVIOUS SOCIAL CONCERNS

In some cases rhetorical messages respond overtly to existing social concerns. For example, the Susan G. Komen Breast Cancer Foundation website is a response to the lack of awareness of breast cancer problems among women and a response to the need for money to support breast cancer research (*Power of Promise* 2003). A speech by a senator supporting a bill (on gun control, e.g.) may be a response to a social concern about violence. These cases are what Lloyd Bitzer called "rhetorical situations," social problems that humans attempt to resolve through rhetoric. Bitzer argues that situations, like the death of the *Columbia* space shuttle astronauts, are exigencies, "imperfection[s] marked by urgency . . . something waiting to be done" (Bitzer 1968, 6). When Americans and Israelis learned that the shuttle exploded, they awaited a response from President Bush. In some cases, however, we come across situations in which we must use physical force rather than symbolic discourse to respond to problems. For example, if Mark has ants in his kitchen, he must respond with brute force rather than language. He doesn't get the ants to leave by talking to them. Hence, such a situation would not be rhetorical in nature. The use of force or other sorts of leverage involve power imbalances whereby one party has significant power over another, typically by being able to punish the other party physically or materially. In such instances, influence or impact is not brought about through symbols that people can choose to respond to or ignore. But rhetorical messages presume that audiences have some degree (more or less) of choice in their responses.

It is, however, naïve to think that situations themselves exist apart from rhetoric, for as much as rhetoric responds to social concerns it is also instrumental in the creation of social concerns (Vatz 1973, 158–59). In fact, Richard Vatz argued that Lloyd Bitzer's notion of an "exigence" is erroneous because no sense of imperfection or urgency exists apart from rhetoric (159). For example, Hitler's speeches to the Germans in the 1930s and 1940s created social concerns about the German economy and beliefs about the Jewish people, which, in turn, demanded other rhetorical responses. Recently, at a university graduation in northern California, the commencement speaker responded to the events of September 11, 2001, articulating her concerns about the preservation of civil rights post 9/11. The members of the audience had such a negative reaction that the speaker was unable to complete her speech because of their stomping and hissing. Both the audience's reaction and the content of the speech created a wild controversy and national debate (hence more rhetoric) about the speaker's views, about what is appropriate subject matter for a commencement speech, and the meaning of the audience's intolerance of her viewpoints. This speech both responded to and created social concerns.

RHETORIC RELIES ON VERBAL AND NONVERBAL SYMBOLS

Whether rhetorical messages respond to or create rhetorical situations, they are strategically constructed by author(s) through verbal and nonverbal symbols. Aristotle's definition of rhetoric was narrower than ours because he lived in an oral culture whose primary medium for the exchange of ideas was public oratory. Today, however, we would include television images, the verbal and nonverbal symbols on the Internet, music, and architecture, for example, as variations of the forms of discourse that respond to social problems and seek to affect public audiences. A speech or editorial relies on linguistic symbols (language), whereas the Vietnam War Memorial relies heavily on visual, nonverbal symbols such as its color, shape, and location. A eulogist uses verbal symbols (language) to respond to the situation of death, but the civil rights protester might use the nonverbal symbol of a sit-in or a march. An episode of *The West Wing* or a television commercial might shape its viewers' beliefs or opinions through the use of camera angles, which essentially are nonverbal symbols that affect audiences' responses to characters, actions, and ideas. The close-up shots of an elderly woman with a tear streaming down her face while reading a Hallmark card from her grandson might be just enough to motivate a viewer to swing by a Hallmark shop the next day and buy a card for Grandma. The author of a university website relies on words and visual and auditory images to cause the surfer to imagine the university in a particular, positive manner. Symbols of all sorts are used in rhetorical messages.

RHETORIC SHAPES THE WAY PEOPLE THINK, ACT, BELIEVE, AND FEEL

No matter how objective and critically astute we pride ourselves on being or how much control we presume to have over our own thoughts, all of us are influenced by rhetoric. The books we read, the news we listen to, the movies we watch, the advertisements we see, the architecture we encounter, the religions we practice—all of these shape our ideas of what is true and good. This is not to suggest that we are controlled by some malicious force out there or that we all allow ourselves to be defined by others. It is, however, to suggest that all of these enterprises (advertising, religion, education, entertainment, education) ultimately rely on rhetoric (public symbol use) to accomplish their ends. Symbols (words, signs, images) are our only mechanism of making sense of our environment in an abstract way, so how we make use of those symbols will affect the way we make sense of our environment. Whether a president refers to a foreign country as "our neighbor," "our ally," or an "evil empire" will impact how others will shape foreign policy. Whether a movie portrays the heroes in a successful war battle or the rebellious soldiers arguing with one another while in battle will help shape the way audiences conceptualize a war. Whether a teacher uses positive or negative adjectives to describe a theorist will affect how students conceive of that theorist. In other words, no matter how hard we try to be independent thinkers, we never think outside the influence of rhetoric.

Because rhetorical messages are more or less intentional and their purposes more or less obvious, their impact may be more or less related to the message makers' intentions. For example, after 9/11, the Department of National Homeland Security began using color codes to warn people of the level of danger and precautions being taken against possible terrorist attacks. A green level means the risk is low, blue means guarded, yellow means elevated, orange means high, and red means severe (*Homeland Security* 2003). Although the intent of the color-coded messages was to help people make decisions and inform them of the level of government security they should expect, it also initially raised people's fears unnecessarily. Messages as simple as a single color can shape the way people think, act, believe, and feel, so the sender's intention may not always be the best indicator of whether a message is successful in achieving its purpose.

DEFINITION OF RHETORIC

Knowing the preceding five characteristics, we could now define **rhetoric** as *messages that rely on verbal and nonverbal symbols that more or less intentionally influence social attitudes, values, beliefs, and actions.* According to this definition, political speeches you might consider merely hot air are rhetorical, but so are those messages that make important, substantive arguments about consequential matters of public concern. Inasmuch as politicians might use "mere rhetoric" by talking about something they will never act upon, Abraham Lincoln used rhetoric to persuade Americans of the injustices of slavery; Susan B. Anthony used rhetoric to persuade Americans that women were entitled to the right to vote; the Susan G. Komen Breast Cancer Foundation uses rhetoric to persuade people to run, walk, and sing to raise money for breast cancer research; President George W. Bush used rhetoric to comfort the nation after the attacks of 9/11; popular singers and actors used rhetoric to persuade Americans to raise funds for disaster relief in New York City after 9/11; President Roosevelt used rhetoric to relieve Americans' fears about the Great Depression; and Martin Luther King Jr. used rhetoric to change white Americans' attitudes about black Americans. As you can see, rhetoric is a necessary tool of a democratic society, not something we can easily dismiss as mere flowery language.

Throughout Western history, changes in communication media brought changes to the definition and understanding of rhetoric. During the Medieval period, scholars like St. Augustine defined rhetoric primarily in terms of its use in the Christian church for preaching and proselytizing. During the Renaissance, with the invention of the printing press, people began to employ written rhetoric in the form of letters and pamphlets. During the Enlightenment, scholars came to think about rhetoric in terms of its ability to help people systematically debate truth. In the early twentieth century, scholars defined rhetoric as a tool for argumentation and, later, the construction of meaning. The advent of mass media in the twentieth century changed our understanding of rhetoric even further. An influential twentieth-century scholar by the name of Kenneth Burke (1969) defined rhetoric far more broadly than Aristotle and his scholarly successors, expanding the traditional association of the term *rhetoric* with oratory. Burkeian scholar Joseph Gusfield describes Burke's definition of rhetoric this way:

> *All communication, whether Shakespeare, Dashiell Hammett, income-tax returns, deodorant ads, or* The American Sociological Review, *is both socio-logical and artistic. They are analyzable as documents in relation to a time, a place, an institution, an audience. They are analyzable as texts whose style and form are placed within a culture of writing and speaking, of a literary context. As performances they share with all documents a rhetorical function. (1989, 44)*

In other words, where Aristotle limited the definition of rhetoric to include only speeches, Burke expanded the definition to include any form of symbol use that addresses others at some level. By Burke's definition, then, cartoons, art, poetry, flags, and demonstrations can be considered rhetorical messages. This conception of rhetoric along with the changes in media opened the door for rhetorical scholars to study less obviously intentional rhetorical messages and messages that were not necessarily responses to obvious, explicit social problems (e.g., the Vietnam War Memorial, a Disney film, *The West Wing*).

Whether one relies on Aristotle's definition or Burke's definition, it is most important to note that neither source defines rhetoric as "flowery language" that substitutes for real action or substance. Instead, for Aristotle, Burke, and many others, rhetoric *is* action. It is the means by which social truth is established and decisions are made.

RHETORICAL TERMINOLOGY

It is important to point out that in this text several words are used to refer to rhetoric. Rhetorical messages are often referred to as **rhetorical acts, rhetorical artifacts, rhetorical texts,** or **rhetorical discourse.** The Vietnam War Memorial, the breast cancer website, the audiocassette tape of children's music, and the trial attorney's closing argument may all be referred to as texts, for example. You will find these terms used interchangeably throughout this textbook.

Each of those texts exists within a **context:** *events, time periods, settings, audiences, authors, social attitudes, and more, which influence the construction of the message.* Rhetorical scholars often refer to the *author of a message* as the **rhetor.**

WHY STUDY RHETORICAL MESSAGES?

Now that you perhaps have a different connotation of the term *rhetoric,* you may be wondering why someone thinks you need to study it. We offer two reasons.

First, rhetoric abounds in our daily life experience. Reflect for a moment on your day today, taking stock of the many rhetorical messages you have encountered. A typical student, Rita, might experience a day something like this:

> She wakes up and turns on the morning news or opens the newspaper and reads an editorial that criticizes a recent school board decision. In the car on the way to school, Rita hears eight to ten commercials persuading her to buy various products. Those commercials also shape her beliefs about how she should behave as a female, an American, a professional on the rise. She then arrives on campus and attends a lecture by her history professor who works to convince her class that the Vietnam War caused the decline of American idealism. While on campus, she notices that the old, Gothic architecture of the buildings gives her a very different feeling about being at school than the feeling she has about being at work in the contemporary architecture of the mall. She heads to the computer lab where she goes online for an hour surfing the Web for information on Iraq. She is confronted with dozens of websites offering various opinions on American-Iraqi relations and Islamic beliefs as they relate to the regime of Saddam Hussein.
>
> When driving to her apartment from campus that afternoon, she notices a billboard that reads "Got Milk?" Above the words sits a picture of a half-eaten chocolate chip cookie surrounded by crumbs. As she turns into the parking lot of the grocery store, she passes a cluster of employees holding up picket signs and parading around the property's edge. Once she is home, Rita opens her e-mail where she reads a letter from the CEO of the company she works for, justifying a recent decision by the board of directors to change the company policy on telecommuting. The memo ends with a request for employees to support their immediate supervisors in this decision. Finally, she sits down to watch her favorite reality TV show, The Bachelorette. The episode portrays a gender conflict that reveals the participants' negative attitudes toward homosexuality.

Rita's day is not in any way unusual or atypical. Indeed, her frequent encounters with rhetorical messages probably are much like ours, though we don't often think about it. Because rhetoric is so central to our daily lives, it is worth studying. Imagine all the decisions Rita is asked to make and beliefs she is asked to buy into. Rita needs to understand how the authors of these messages craft their messages so that she can respond wisely to their ideas.

A second reason for studying rhetorical messages is that they profoundly influence how human beings perceive and respond to their worlds. The rhetoric we see and hear influences who we are as human beings: for whom we vote; how we prioritize our time; what we purchase; what and how we eat; what we believe about ourselves as creatures of the earth; what we believe about spirituality; what we believe about being male or female; what we believe about our ethnicity; what we believe is truth; what laws we pass; whether we believe someone is guilty or innocent. Osama Bin Laden used rhetoric to shape many people's attitudes about Americans. Martin Luther King Jr., Malcolm X, and the Black Panthers all used rhetoric to affect American attitudes about civil rights, and each presented a different way of understanding racial problems and solutions. Tobacco companies use rhetoric to develop in consumers positive attitudes toward smoking and to defend themselves in smoking-related legislation. Billy Graham uses rhetoric to convince his audiences of their need for God. Leaders of Israel and leaders of Palestine both use rhetoric to convince their people of the morality of their position against the opposing nation.

As you can see, people use rhetoric for good and bad, moral and immoral, democratic and autocratic reasons. The more we know about the tools people use to make such significant impacts on human lives, the more we can become cautious and discerning consumers of rhetoric. Perhaps thousands of Jewish lives could have been saved had more people understood the power of rhetoric. Perhaps racial discrimination could be more easily eliminated if people understood the rhetorical tools used to advance *and* dismantle it. Perhaps terrorism more often could be replaced with discourse if people understood the power of rhetoric for creating and solving social ills. Because rhetoric engulfs us it has enormous influence, positive and negative, on our beliefs, attitudes, values, and behaviors. Thus, we need to understand how it works, how it affects us, and what it is worth to us. We need to study rhetoric. This book is designed to help you learn how to study rhetoric so that you can respond wisely to the ideas you confront every day. In subsequent chapters you will learn about different ways to think about messages, and you will be given a variety of theoretical perspectives that will help you understand how messages rely on verbal and nonverbal symbols in a manner that shapes human thought and behavior.

SUMMARY

Many people have negative connotations of the word *rhetoric*. Although often these connotations are merited, to categorize all rhetorical acts as "hot air" and "mere rhetoric" is to misunderstand rhetoric. Indeed, if we view rhetoric only as that which uses flowery language to substitute for substance, we ignore the subtle and thus powerful ways rhetoric shapes the substance of human experience, both positively and negatively. Furthermore, for you to "make sense of messages," as the book's title implies, you may need to erase any preconceptions you might have about rhetoric. We have offered you a substitute definition: messages that use verbal and nonverbal symbols that more or less intentionally influence social attitudes, values, beliefs, and actions. You will find that this understanding of the term *rhetoric* will open for you a new way of experiencing your everyday life.

Scholars from many disciplines provide insight into the human experience. Sociologists study how humans behave in relation to one another in social organizations; psychologists study the mind and behavior of humans as individuals; and anthropologists study humans in relation to their environment, origin, classification, and culture. Rhetorical scholars also provide insight into the human experience, but they do so by studying the messages human beings exchange with one another. To ignore these messages would be to miss an important dimension of the human experience. But to study these messages is to enrich our understanding and augment our chances of improving that experience.

EXERCISES

1 List three messages you think are rhetorical. Use the five characteristics of rhetoric to explain your choices.

2 Explain why it might prove useful to study the three messages you just named.

3 Skip ahead to page 73 in Chapter 5 where you will find a nationally televised address that President Clinton delivered to the nation, confessing his affair with Monica Lewinsky. The speech is what scholars Linkugel and Ware call an *apologia,* or a speech of self-defense in which a leader must reclaim credibility by admitting guilt, denying responsibility, or blaming others (Ware and Linkugel 1973, 275). After reading the President Clinton speech, study the political cartoon at the bottom of the page. Then answer the following questions:

- Who are the rhetors? Who is the audience? What is the apparent purpose of each message? How do you know?
- Which of the five characteristics of rhetoric do these messages exhibit?

© 2003 Center for Consumer Freedom

WORKS CITED

Aristotle. *The Rhetoric and the Poetics of Aristotle.* Translated by W. Rhys Roberts and Edward P. J. Corbett. New York: McGraw-Hill, 1984.

Bitzer, Lloyd. "The Rhetorical Situation." *Philosophy and Rhetoric* 1 (1968): 1–14.

Blair, Carole, Marsha S. Jeppeson, and Enrico Pucci Jr. "Public Memorializing in Postmodernity: The Vietnam Veterans Memorial as Prototype." *Quarterly Journal of Speech* 77 (1991): 263–88.

Burke, Kenneth. *A Rhetoric of Motives.* Berkeley: University of California Press, 1969.

Disney Songtape: Disney's Children's Favorites. Vol. II. Walt Disney Productions, 1979.

freekobe.com. Romadel, LLC. http://www.freekobe.com (accessed September 5, 2003).

Gusfield, Joseph, ed. *Kenneth Burke: On Symbols and Society.* Chicago: University of Chicago Press, 1989.

Hart, Roderick. *Modern Rhetorical Criticism.* 2nd ed. Boston: Allyn and Bacon, 1997.

Homeland Security. The White House. http://whitehouse.gov/homeland/ (accessed September 5, 2003).

Plato. *Gorgias.* Translated by W. C. Helmbold. Indianapolis: Bobbs-Merrill, 1952.

The Power of Promise. The Susan G. Komen Breast Cancer Foundation. http://www.susangkomen.com/ (accessed September 5, 2003).

Vatz, Richard E. "The Myth of the Rhetorical Situation." *Philosophy and Rhetoric* 6 (1973): 154–61.

Ware, B. L., and Wil A. Linkugel. "They Spoke in Defense of Themselves: On the Generic Criticism of Apologia." *Quarterly Journal of Speech* 59 (1973): 273–83.

Wingert, Pat. "Helping Families Help Themselves." *Newsweek,* Special Edition, Spring/Summer (1997): 88.

CRITICISM: WHAT CRITICS DO WITH RHETORICAL MESSAGES

Now that you know what rhetorical messages are, you may be wondering what you will do with those messages. In a word, you will learn to be a *message analyst*. A message analyst responds to a rhetorical message differently than does a typical audience member to that message. Where an audience member responds with a *reaction,* the analyst responds with a *critique.* Our task now is to help you understand the difference between those two responses and help you develop expertise in responding with a critique.

REACTION VERSUS CRITIQUE

Edwin Black, an influential scholar of rhetorical messages, once wrote that one who responds to a message with a reaction speaks from his or her "glands" (1965, 7). Imagine your sweat glands responding to heat. They instantly pour out moisture to cool the body. They do not engage in careful deliberation; they simply react to your body's temperature. Likewise, a **glandular reaction** to a message is *spontaneous, without careful thought or deliberation.* One might say a glandular reaction is a gut reaction. Imagine, for example, watching a television news report in which a reporter interviews people off the street as they exit a new ride at a local amusement park. Typically, the interviewees make comments like, "Wow! That's one mean ride!" or "That was really scary," or "It was just OK," or "I was disappointed. I had expected more." These phrases are statements of preference or reaction. They indicate what the respondent prefers or feels, based on his or her personal tastes, interests, agendas, or expectations. These are valid preferences and responses that are useful particularly to market researchers, but they cannot be called critiques. They do not explain how the ride works; they are simply spontaneous, glandular reactions.

We often give such reactions to movies. For example, a few years ago Sally and her nephew were talking about the film *Titanic.* Sally said, "Wow! That was a great movie!" Jeremy retorted, "Except for the special effects, I thought it was the worst, most overrated movie I've ever seen. The acting was terrible." Neither person had much of anything substantial to say about why he or she liked it or disliked it, neither person taught the other anything about the film, and neither person persuaded the other to change his or her opinion of the film. In sum, neither of them reached their conclusions as the result of having studied films, the film industry, or even *Titanic* specifically. Instead, both responses were based on personal preferences. Jeremy's response is worth noting, however. He observed two distinct qualities of the film: the special effects and the acting. The very act of naming these qualities and drawing conclusions about them is the essence of a critique. Although he probably had never studied acting and had no theoretical knowledge of filmmaking or special effects, Jeremy's response indicates that we all conduct critiques at some level. But if we want our critiques to be convincing and useful to others, we must refine the skills we already possess.

Reactions also run rampant at sporting events. Imagine two fans watching a Monday Night Football game between the San Francisco 49ers and the Denver Broncos. The 49ers win 35 to 17. The Bronco fan walks away saying, "That was a terrible game. The referees were unfair. The 49ers got away with murder. The poor Broncos were victims of unfair treatment all the way around." In contrast, the 49ers fan says, "What a great game! We beat 'em fair and square. That game really proved where the talent lies this year!" Both fans respond from their glands, relying primarily on their personal preferences and biases, making little effort to see the game from any other point of view. This point of view is legitimate. We would expect no less from a fan and, in fact, it's what the players need. But we would expect something different from a sports analyst. In fact, with some training, one of these fans could learn to take her initial critical observations of refereeing and develop a more systematic analysis of how the refereeing impacted the game.

We're all critics at some level. The terms *reaction* and *critique* can be thought of as two ends of a continuum. Both are legitimate, important responses. Most people are capable of offering a reaction, but to offer a more carefully considered and potentially more persuasive critique requires a different sort of response, one that comes from considerably more effort.

CHARACTERISTICS OF CRITICS

In contrast to the person who responds to a message with a glandular reaction, a **message analyst**, or **critic**, *responds to messages in a more deliberative, sophisticated way through the eyes of his or her professional knowledge about communication.* The person responding with a glandular reaction typically wants others to share his or her preferences. But the critic intends more than that. Critics intend to understand how the message works and why in order to teach others how we are impacted by rhetorical messages, thus arming others to be careful consumers of rhetorical messages. Unlike a glandular reaction, a **critique** is *the process of coming to understand how a message works in relation to those who encounter it.* To conduct a critique, critics do two things with the message that the average reactor doesn't do: (1) study messages systematically and (2) teach others about the messages they study.

CRITICS STUDY MESSAGES SYSTEMATICALLY

People who are experts in their fields do their work in some **systematic** way. That is, *they use their knowledge of the subject at hand to proceed in a deliberative, purposeful order.* Expert mechanics know precisely the parts of automobile engines and how those parts work together, so when they are presented with a problem in a car, they are conscious of the systematic process they use to examine the engine. The average car owner, in contrast, might look randomly at different parts of the engine, hopelessly trying to detect the source of the problem. Like expert mechanics, critics of rhetorical messages use theoretical knowledge, expertise, and deliberate methods as a way of studying messages systematically. Message analysts must know something about the parts of a message and how those parts may work together. Thus, they must study rhetorical theories and other rhetorical messages in order to know what to look for in a message. For example, a rhetorical critic who knows of various persuasion techniques and types of evidence and argumentation would be able to classify the persuasion and argumentation strategies used in a series of presidential campaign advertisements. The average viewer of those ads likely would not know what details and nuances to look for. The act of classifying the strategies enables the critic to explain how the ads are conveyed, not just say whether he or she liked the ads. Critics use their knowledge to generate questions to ask about messages. Ultimately, knowledge about communication or rhetoric enables them to proceed systematically rather than randomly in their analysis, helping critics see all there is to see in a message from a particular point of view. Subsequent chapters of this book will offer you some of that knowledge.

Studying messages systematically has two results. First, because critics study messages systematically, they see more than what the average person can see in the message. If you have ever been to a national forest, you may have encountered rangers whose jobs were to "interpret" the forest to the visitors. Because of their expertise in botany and forestry, rangers see things in the forest that the average passerby is likely to overlook. Similarly, because message analysts study messages regularly and have expertise in communication and rhetoric, they have insight into messages that the average viewer lacks. *Critics respond to a message not as an audience member or "fan" of the rhetor, but as somewhat removed, expert viewers who sit (metaphorically) in the press box or the balcony.* From this **balcony stance**, experts have a broader perspective than do the fans and the players. And because of their expertise, analysts can point out what an average audience member would likely miss.

Second, critics are likely to see *patterns* within and across messages that the average person cannot see. Perhaps a critic will notice patterns of language use in a message, patterns of organization, patterns of argumentation and evidence use, patterns of color or imagery, or patterns of camera angles. Becoming conscious of patterns is key to understanding how messages work and why they affect audiences as they do. By explaining these patterns to consumers, the message analyst helps them become more critical and cautious in their own responses to the many messages competing for their attention. Indeed, seeing patterns is a marker of expertise in many fields. A colleague of ours, for example, is a nationally ranked, expert Scrabble player who memorizes words, studies Scrabble strategy books, and has years of experience playing the game. When he looks at a Scrabble board and a collection of letter tiles, he sees patterns of words and word combinations that most of us would never see. His ability to detect these patterns not only separates him from the average, casual Scrabble player, it is critical to his success with the game. So too, the critic's ability to see rhetorical patterns in messages is essential to the second goal of teaching others (Black 1965, 6).

CRITICS HAVE A RESPONSIBILITY TO TEACH OTHERS

Critics are most valuable when they share their insights (typically in a written or oral presentation) so others can learn. To study an important, influential rhetorical message systematically and understand it better than others, but never share those insights with others, is most unfortunate for consumers. Critics' work has the most utility when it is shared. Yet one critic's insights on a message may not be the same as another's. Because there are many ways to see a message, no single critic has *the* single, correct perspective. So critics must help their audiences see a message as they do by providing their audiences with sufficient evidence from theory, research, and the message itself to lead their audiences out of their seats in the "stands" and up to the "balcony" with the critic. Having multiple perspectives on a message deepens consumers' understanding, enabling them to study the message more carefully themselves.

As you refine your ability to respond to messages with a systematic critique, you will begin as a novice (one who typically reacts and critiques with little expertise) and gradually become an expert (one who skillfully critiques from expertise and consciousness). With practice and some knowledge, you will learn to study messages systematically and consciously, identifying patterns within and across messages, and teaching others to be critical consumers of messages.

A CRITICAL STANCE: IN THE BALCONY

So what is the first step in developing expertise as a critic? How does one start seeing beyond what the average person sees? How does one learn how to study messages systematically and to see patterns? We believe that one must start by learning to take a different stance, a **critical stance** or a balcony position in relation to a rhetorical message. In taking a critical stance, a person *consciously looks at a message from a more emotionally distant, broader, and theoretically informed point of view, rather than from the position of the rhetor or audience members*. This is not a purely objective point of view, but it is a point of view that takes more into consideration, sees the bigger picture, and is informed by the critic's expert knowledge. It is much like the position of a family therapist who must remain emotionally distant from the family members, never take sides, identify the patterns of interaction in the family, and use her theoretical knowledge to interpret those interactions. The family therapist can never shed all of her biases from her training and personal experience, but she can work to be as conscious as possible of her procedures and her biases.

To experience this stance, join us in a little exercise. Although you may be inclined to skip over the tasks we ask of you, resist the temptation, pick up a pen and paper, and follow the instructions. You'll be glad you did.

You have three small writing tasks. Begin by recalling a recent interpersonal interaction you have had that involved some sort of conflict. Think of a particular occasion and interaction, not just a general conflicting relationship. Your first task is to recount that occasion on paper in a paragraph or two. Here's an example from Sally's experience.

> *Recently I attended a conference at Lake Tahoe. Each day I had to commute from the south shore of the lake to the north shore, about a forty-minute drive. On the last day I was running a little late. As I turned out of the south shore area, I saw a patrol car parked on the opposite side of the road. I slowed down immediately, but in the rearview mirror I saw the police car do a U-turn and flash its red lights. Butterflies filled my stomach and throat as I pulled over. The cop walked up, gruffly announced how severely I was violating the speed limit, and requested to see my vehicle registration. I nervously searched through my glove box that was overstuffed with napkins and pens. I finally found the registration and the cop took it back to his car. Once he learned that I had no other tickets on my record, he returned and said he'd give me a slight break on the fine, but he added that if I wanted the ticket off my record I'd have to go to traffic school. I retorted in disbelief, "You're kidding? I have to go to TRAFFIC SCHOOL?" Clearly he didn't get the fact that I am a professor attending a professional conference on teaching, not just some tourist zipping around Lake Tahoe for a good time. He impatiently clarified that I'd have to go if I didn't want the ticket on my record and if I didn't want it to affect my insurance. He acted as if I was a real idiot and he had the nerve to walk away saying, "Have a safe drive." I was furious at his attitude and the fact that I was speeding and he was right.*

Now you write a paragraph about your conflicting interaction.

Your second task is to write about the same episode, but to write it from the perspective of the other person involved in the conflict. In the following example, Sally attempts to tell the story from the officer's perspective.

> *I was on speeding patrol duty around the lake the other day. Around 8:00 a.m. I was sitting in my car, bored, looking for speeders. The speed limit coming around the bend out of South Shore is 35 mph. But people get carried away, which is really dangerous this time of year with so many vacationing pedestrians and all. Like most mornings, a car finally came whipping around the curve and blew past me doing 50, according to the radar. I saw the taillights flash in my rearview mirror, so I knew the driver saw me and slowed down. Too late. I did a quick U-turn to head north, turned on my lights, and pulled the car over. The driver was a nervous young woman who couldn't even find her registration*

> *card. I'm not even sure she knew what she was looking for. After I finally pointed it out to her, I checked her record, found it clean, and figured I'd give her a break. I told her she'd owe eighty bucks and that traffic school was the way to go if she wanted to keep it off her record. She went ballistic when I mentioned traffic school. I thought, gimme a goddamn break lady. You're the one who was speeding. This is your problem, not mine. I'm just doin' my job. But I didn't say that. I just told her what I tell every speeder I catch: "Drive safely."*

Now you write a paragraph about your interaction, from the other party's perspective.

Your third and final task is to recount the episode one last time, this time from the perspective of someone in the balcony, watching the interaction from above. Here's an example.

> *From where I sit, I can see the lake, the perimeter road, and all the traffic that circles the lake each day. I see lots of curves on that perimeter road and lots of vacationers walking near the road, especially around the north and south shores. I see traffic accidents daily as drivers quickly wind their way through the mountainous roads. One morning a cop was planted near the south shore, watching for speeders heading north. A car came along going about 50 mph or so. The cop caught the driver, turned on his lights, and did a U-turn heading north to pull the driver over. The cop got out of his car and went to the driver, a young woman, asking for her vehicle registration. I saw that she had to search through some papers to find it and the cop pointed it out to her once he saw it. The cop took the registration back to his car and ran it through his computer. Since he looked pretty relaxed going back to his car, he apparently discovered that she had no tickets on her record. He returned to the driver, asked her if she knew how fast she was driving, told her that he clocked her doing 50 in a 35, and said that because of her record he would only issue her an $80 ticket. He mentioned traffic school and the woman, apparently feeling embarrassed, asked if she really had to go. The officer answered that she would have to go only if she wanted the ticket off of her record and if she did not want her insurance rates to go up. He then told her to have a safe drive before he returned to his car and headed back to his post. The woman drove off slowly, obeying the speed limit all the way up the north side of the lake.*

Now you write a paragraph about your interaction, from the third party's or balcony perspective.

As you reflect on your paragraphs, what do you notice about the three versions? How do they differ? When we run this exercise in our classes, most students notice that the first version is typically the most reactionary. They feel strong emotions when writing it and they read it as being biased and one-sided. They also find this version the easiest of the three to write, and in many cases this is their longest version. Typically, students find the second version difficult to write. Because it is a perspective other than their own, it is usually a bit less reactionary, but it is still one-sided and somewhat emotional. Students notice a significant difference, however, in the third version. Admittedly this version is not purely objective. After all, it's still *Sally* with all her subjectivities trying to be the third party, and if the third party had spoken, he or she would have been his or her own subjective self. Nonetheless, this version is the most distant and least emotional because it is told with a broader perspective. The third story of the speeder and the police officer begins with a broader, factual description of the context (Lake Tahoe, the perimeter road, the winding roads, and frequent traffic accidents), a perspective not immediately apparent to the two main characters.

The perspective gained from the balcony position is the perspective the critic takes when examining a rhetorical message. This is the kind of perspective we demand of a sports reporter who is assigned to write an analysis of a sporting event for a newspaper. Although the writer never completely rids himself of allegiances to a particular team, while acting as a sports reporter, he cannot write from the perspective of a fan, a player, or a coach. In fact, the writer must be willing to see more than the average person by setting aside his allegiance to a particular team. The writer must sit in the press box above the field where he can see more than the others. In that stance, the writer sees the context for the game: the city, the field, the weather, the team roster, and data from previous games. Furthermore, a particular writer would be given the assignment, in part because of his knowledge of the game, the teams playing, other teams, season statistics, and so forth. Indeed, since no two writers have all the same knowledge in their heads or the same data available to them, each writer will offer a different perspective from the press box, neither of which is purely objective or absolutely accurate. In fact, by being in the balcony, the writer might miss something that a fan sitting in the first row near the 10-yard line sees. Nonetheless, the balcony offers a point of view necessary for good critical consideration.

Like the sports analyst, the message analyst must take a balcony stance. The following two columns demonstrate the difference between how an audience member might respond to two messages differently than a critic does. The two messages refer to the 1998 speech that President Bill Clinton gave to religious leaders and the nation after he was caught having an affair with Monica Lewinsky and the 1988 speech Reverend Jimmy Swaggart gave to the Assemblies of God Church and the nation after he was caught having an affair with a prostitute. Notice the two different types of responses in the two columns.

AUDIENCE MEMBER'S RESPONSE	CRITIC'S RESPONSE
Wow. President Clinton's speech was insulting. Here he just confessed that he had an affair with a twenty-five-year-old intern and he doesn't even have it within him to apologize to his wife and daughter. I was pretty uncomfortable with all the emotional gobbledygook in Swaggart's speech, but at least	President Clinton and the Reverend Jimmy Swaggart took radically different approaches to their apologia speeches, even though the events leading to their speeches were quite similar. Both Swaggart and President Clinton needed to confess their adulterous acts and somehow

AUDIENCE MEMBER'S RESPONSE (cont.)	CRITIC'S RESPONSE (cont.)
he said he was sorry—to his wife and the people he leads. President Clinton sounded hard as a brick. I wasn't convinced that he had any real remorse for what he'd done. He might as well have said, "This is what my advisers told me to say." I will have to give it to President Clinton, though. At least he kept his speech short and sweet—to the point. I thought Swaggart's speech would never end. It went on and on. After a while, I thought to myself, "Come on, pal. Get over it and get on with it." I also think President Clinton was lying when he said, "Nothing is more important to me personally," than his family. If his family were that important, his affair wouldn't have gone on as long as it did. Swaggart probably does care about his family a lot, but it sounded a little like he was kissing up, especially when he went on and on about how wonderful they were and how "God never gave a man a better wife and family. . . ." He probably embarrassed the reporter (John Camp) when he told him, "I love you, John."	restore their personal credibility and the credibility of the positions they held. Yet their specific contexts demanded different rhetorical responses. Swaggart's audience consisted primarily of fellow believers (though also the members of the mass media): his family, his church and Bible College, and the Church at large. President Clinton's audience consisted of the American public. His wife and daughter were not present and his audience did not share a single moral code regarding sexuality, as did Swaggart's. Because of his audience's shared belief system, it was necessary for Swaggart to use several rhetorical strategies. He confessed his "sin" and sought the forgiveness of his people, yet he also quoted Scripture to proclaim that God has "saved," "washed," and "cleansed" him. By proclaiming God's forgiveness, Swaggart required his audience to forgive him. For if God can forgive, who are they not to? Also, Swaggart's emotional tone was consistent with the typical emotional tone of weekly services in the charismatic Assemblies of God Church. Had he been unemotional, he likely would have appeared insincere to his people. Clinton, on the other hand, used different strategies. Like Swaggart, he confessed his wrongdoing, saying his relationship with Lewinsky was "inappropriate" and "wrong." He admitted "regret" at having misled his wife. His tone was more matter of fact, yet to have been too emotional was to risk losing credibility as the president, commander in chief, leader of the "strongest" nation in the world. Clinton also used the strategy of differentiation (Ware and Linkugel 1973, 278). That is, he differentiated between his sexual wrongdoing and his "justifiable" motives for lying: to protect his family and to avoid a lawsuit. He also differentiated the issues of his sexual wrongdoing from the matter of privacy, focusing the second half of his speech on the wrongdoing of others

AUDIENCE MEMBER'S RESPONSE (cont.)	CRITIC'S RESPONSE (cont.)
	who have violated his privacy. In his conclusion he stated, "We have important work to do— real opportunities to seize, real problems to solve, real security matters to face," thus imply- ing that his affair was not a "real problem." So, where Swaggart positioned his audience to *for- give* his sin, President Clinton positioned his audience to *forget* his sin.

Notice that the audience member's commentary in the left-hand column contains emotional, reactionary language. The author uses phrases like "I was uncomfortable," "It looked fake to me," and "It was insulting." The audience member argues with Clinton (saying his family must not be that important to him) and expresses his feelings about the speech. These reactions are legiti- mate and useful in helping the audience member sort out her responses to these two leaders, but their value differs from those of the critic's comments. Because she sits in the balcony, the critic sees each speech in its own context. She recognizes that the different audiences and belief systems require different rhetorical responses from the two leaders. The critic does not position herself as an audience member of either speech, though she could have been an audi- ence member of both. The critic names each rhetor's rhetorical choices, explaining how those choices function in their particular context. She cites evidence from the speeches and uses a theoretical construct called *differentia- tion* to understand each rhetor's strategies. By taking a balcony stance, the ana- lyst is able to study the messages more systematically, see beyond what the average person sees in the messages, observe relevant patterns in the messages, and teach others.

HOW THIS BOOK CAN HELP

The ensuing chapters of this book are designed to equip you to take a bal- cony stance in relation to rhetorical messages. Part II, "Process to Product" focuses on the *thinking processes* you must go through to examine a message systematically. You will learn different ways to become conscious of your thinking when you encounter a rhetorical message. Part III, "Analytical Tools," provides you with introductory theoretical knowledge you will need to exe- cute the thinking processes described in Part II. Each chapter in Part III offers a different theoretical perspective that will suggest different dimensions to look for in a message. Some theories will invite you to look at the stories in a message, others will ask you to look at the evidence and arguments in a message, and still others will ask you to look at the language or visual imagery in a message. Chapter 8 of Part II focuses on the *product* (oral or written) you may create in order to report your thinking to others whom you will teach. This chapter also will help you learn to argue your perspective to your audience. Since analysts are never fully objective, they must learn to convince others to see messages from their particular balcony perspectives. If a critic wishes to evaluate a message, for example, he or she must provide criteria and rationale to cause the critic's audience to draw the same inference (not an absolute conclusion) about the message. Inferences may be more or less certain, and each critic bears the burden of proving that his or her inference is more certain than not. The critic's audience then has the option of accepting or rejecting the criteria, the evidence, or the critic's rationale for the evaluation (Brockriede 1974, 167–68). Because criticism is more than reporting facts, you must learn how to present your arguments in the most convincing and reasonable manner.

MESSAGE ANALYSIS MATTERS!

At this point you may be wondering why you should learn to be a message analyst. What good will it do, you ask? We believe the world is in need of more people with the ability to critique rather than react to rhetorical messages. As explained in Chapter 1, rhetorical messages are everywhere, influencing our perceptions, behaviors, attitudes, values, and beliefs. Most people do not have the time or energy to process critically all the rhetorical messages that come their way, nor are they equipped to do so. Yet because rhetorical messages are so pervasive and profoundly influential, the world needs people who can help audiences sort out those messages, helping us understand how they work, what they mean, and what they're worth to us. The average football fan doesn't have the time or skill necessary to keep up on all the games, statistics, scores, rules, and strategies. Fans must rely on the expertise of good sports analysts. Yet rhetorical communication is probably far more influential and complex than sports. Surely we need the expertise of good message analysts since their work may impact the quality of our lives. By refining your skills as a critic, you empower yourself to become your own decision maker about what is true and right and good. You also empower yourself to become a more ethical, effective, and critically minded maker of messages. People will notice your skill and find value in the leadership you will be able to offer.

Specifically, a number of social contexts require the expertise of message analysts. Juries need critics to help them understand how they are being persuaded by attorneys. Voters need critics to help them understand the rhetorical messages regarding political candidates and referendums. Parents need the help of critics in sorting out rhetorical messages about their responsibilities in rearing their children. Members of religious organizations need critics to help them understand how they are being affected by religious messages. Employees need the help of critics to understand how rhetorical messages (e.g., memos, proposals, speeches, videos) function in their workplace. Students need critics to help them understand how the rhetorical messages of their professors and academic institutions work.

Even specific professions require the skills of message analysts. Trial consultants use their knowledge of rhetorical messages to critically analyze the opponent's arguments and to advise their own clients. Public relations professionals use their knowledge of rhetorical messages to advise corporations on how to attack PR problems. Many politicians and government workers use their knowledge of rhetorical messages to understand how they are being persuaded by constituents or colleagues to take particular actions. They also use their expertise as message analysts in constructing persuasive messages of their own.

As you can see, message analysts are needed both in professional and social settings. As a communication expert, you will set yourself apart from the average person by refining your natural skill in analyzing rhetorical messages. As your skills develop you will find yourself offering critiques from the balcony rather than glandular reactions, even when among friends and family. You will have opportunities, formal and informal, to teach others and, thus, help them to be more critical consumers of rhetorical communication. You will be making valuable contributions to your own life and the lives of those around you.

SUMMARY

As human beings, our immediate responses to messages are important, but our studied, controlled responses are potentially instructive to ourselves and others. Critics monitor their responses and consciously adopt a balcony stance in relation to messages that merit analysis. The effort required to examine a message from the "balcony" is necessary to get past purely personal preferences for the purpose of learning something about communication.

Looking at any text from the metaphorical balcony changes what we know about a message and how we know it. It provides a broader perspective (outside our own skin) that other people can share; it provides a way of teaching others how the invisible dynamics of rhetoric influence (or fail to influence) audiences.

The knowledge and skills of message analysts are important in a society that is saturated daily with messages from many sources using a variety of media for a variety of purposes, not all of which are constructive. Developing your ability to look at messages in systematic ways is important for you as an individual but even more important for those with whom you live and work. Rhetoric is powerful and capable critics serve to ensure that the power of rhetoric is used properly.

EXERCISES

1 Reread the two different responses to President Clinton and Jimmy Swaggart's speeches. Then do the following tasks and answer the following questions:

■ In what ways is the Audience Member's Response column like your first-person reaction in the balcony exercise you did earlier?

■ Underline the language in the Critic's Response column that indicates to you that she is responding from a perspective other than her own personal preferences.

■ What is the value of the critic's response to Reverend Swaggart's and President Clinton's message for herself? For other people who may hear or read it?

2 In 2003, the state of California held a special election to recall the governor, Gray Davis. The recall passed and Arnold Schwarzenegger was elected as the new governor. Read the material on Schwarzenegger's campaign website (http://www.joinarnold.com/en/aboutarnold); then write your gut reaction. In a paragraph, express your feelings as an audience member of the site. Then, try to put yourself in a balcony position. Write a second paragraph that is a more distanced response to what you see happening in the website. Compare your two paragraphs.

WORKS CITED

Black, Edwin. *Rhetorical Criticism: A Study in Method.* New York: Macmillan, 1965.

Brockriede, Wayne. "Rhetorical Criticism as Argument." *Quarterly Journal of Speech* 60 (1974): 165–74.

Join Arnold. Californians for Schwarzenegger. http://www.joinarnold.com/en/aboutarnold/ (accessed September 5, 2003).

Ware, B. L., and Wil A. Linkugel. "They Spoke in Defense of Themselves: On the Generic Criticism of Apologia." *Quarterly Journal of Speech* 59 (1973): 273–83.

3

FOUR KINDS OF CRITICAL THINKING

Thinking critically doesn't happen naturally. How we think is a matter of training and choice. We can think quickly, slowly, systematically, haphazardly, critically, creatively, for a long time or short time—we decide whether or not to control our thinking. In the following paragraph Mark describes a film he saw about the great twentieth-century inventor, architect, and philosopher Buckminster Fuller, in which Fuller demonstrates systematic thinking.

Fuller was handed a small, sealed wooden box. There was an object inside the box and it was "Bucky's" job to figure out what it was. What I found striking was, as Fuller began to consciously and purposefully focus his mind on the task, his facial expression changed. Taking the box in his hand, he looked at it carefully for what seemed to be a long time. Then, he slowly began to heft it, feeling its weight, estimating how much of the weight was attributable to the box—the balance being the weight of the object. Next, he tilted the box slowly forward and backward, side to side; each time he noted the sound of the object and its feel as it moved (or didn't move) with each tilt of the box. He talked aloud about what in his experience was like the sound or the feel of each movement saying things like, "This feels like . . ." or "This resembles. . . ." Gradually, he narrowed the possible universe of objects that fit the data and his experience. He determined it was of a single piece, weighed just a few ounces, and was neither round nor rectangular in cross section. It tended to move along the short axis but not along the long axis. Finally, he correctly concluded that the object was a machine bolt.

What was impressive about Fuller was not only that he correctly deduced the object, but how he visibly shifted into a highly focused thinking mode that exhibited both a plan and a kind of playfulness. Fuller's habits of mind are an excellent example for us because he modeled good thinking skills that are useful to anyone in any field, be it physics, architecture, philosophy, medicine, law, business, or message analysis.

As you learned in Chapter 2, effectively analyzing messages requires that you approach messages in ways that are different from natural thinking patterns or habits. That doesn't mean that now, when you come out of a movie, for instance, you cannot say, "That was the worst (or best) action movie I've ever seen!" We still respond like everyone else. But what makes a trained critic different from other folks is that the critic realizes the response was glandular, and he or she has the ability, when necessary, to look at the movie from a variety of perspectives and think systematically about it. The fact is you already possess the thinking skills of a message analyst even though you may not consciously use them. You regularly *describe* events you've seen; sometimes you divide the event into segments in particular ways as you *analyze* them; you *interpret* the events by giving them meaning, and sometimes you *evaluate* or judge their quality.

Those are the kinds of thinking an expert message analyst consciously engages in as a critic. This chapter explains how to think as a critic by learning to recognize the four kinds of critical thinking: description, analysis, interpretation, and evaluation (Andrews 1983, 49–66; Cathcart 1981, 22–26). You will learn how these kinds of thinking differ, what function each plays, and how, when used together, they help you make sense of the significant messages you encounter each day. Finally, you'll see a brief example of the four kinds of critical thinking in action, and then you'll practice thinking like a critic. Mastery of the ideas presented in this chapter is essential for your development as a message analyst, so pay particular attention to the model and the explanation accompanying it. Now, let's begin looking at what it means to think like a critic.

CREATIVE AND CRITICAL THINKING

M essage analysis, or rhetorical criticism, is not an easy job because it requires you to think not only about the message that you want to analyze but also about your thinking processes while you are doing the analysis. *Thinking about your thinking* is called **metacognition**. As in any job, a message analyst or rhetorical critic uses certain tools to get the job done. The tools of message analysis happen to be various kinds of thinking processes used along with information about a message and knowledge acquired from rhetorical theory. We'll be talking about research and theory in later chapters, but now we need to focus on the thinking tools of criticism.

Two primary categories of thinking we can identify are creative and critical thinking. Often people talk about these as if they are not related to each other. For example, creative artists are seldom portrayed as rigorous thinkers. We often talk as if creative people are born that way, are eccentric, absent-minded, or flaky. On the other hand, critical thinkers are often portrayed as serious decision makers, people who are judgmental and immediately perceive mistakes in arguments. Most likely your schooling up to now has taught you that in an art class or creative writing course, you think creatively—just letting your mind do what it wants. But in your debate class or math class, you think systematically—not being sloppy in your thinking. Schooling tends to separate creative and critical thinking, leading us to think we are one or the other (or sometimes neither). However, we believe the best thinking is both creative *and* critical. To be an insightful critic, you must, like Buckminster Fuller, learn to consciously make use of both types of thinking. Let's look at these more closely and see how they work together.

Creative thinking has been defined as *"the ability to form new combinations of ideas to fulfill a need,"* and as *"thinking [that is] patterned in a way that tends to lead to creative results"* (Marzano et al. 1988, 23–24). Powerful examples of creative thinking can be found in the space program. One particularly interesting story springs from the ill-fated *Apollo 13* mission. After the explosion that disabled the spacecraft, the life-support system was damaged and the crew had to fix the system in space with the material they had in hand. Ground control was faced with finding a creative and functional solution to the problem the astronauts faced. Collecting only the materials they knew the astronauts had available, they began systematically working their way through the problem in an effort to devise necessary equipment for the life-support system. The intent was to form new combinations of materials to fulfill a need. Through thinking that was systematic (or patterned) the engineers developed a device that saved the lives of the three *Apollo* astronauts. Creative thinking is not just fooling around but is goal oriented and systematic. A critic analyzes messages for lots of reasons, as we saw in Chapter 2, but even those who are just appreciating a message have a purpose in mind and usually take a systematic approach to appreciation. So your work as a message analyst will produce an interesting and valuable analysis through a rigorous creative process.

Even if you don't see yourself as creative per se, you *are* creative, but you need to exercise your creativity in the search for insight into how messages work. Message analysis is not a process that follows a recipe, but at the same time, it is not haphazard. The balance between establishing a system or pattern for thinking and discovering new and unique combinations of persuasive strategies is a difficult one to find, but you will find it with practice.

Creative thinking is only one side of the coin. The process of opening up new possibilities is closely connected with the cognitive process of critical thinking.

Critical thinking has been defined as *"reasonable, reflective thinking that is focused on deciding what to believe or do"* (Ennis 1985, 54). This tells us that critical thinking gets you somewhere—to a decision or behavior. Notice that the central term in the definition is *reasonable*. As Marzano states, "thinking is 'reasonable' when the thinker strives to analyze arguments carefully, looks for valid evidence, and reaches sound conclusions" (1988, 18). Thinking critically is specifically related to message analysis or rhetorical criticism. The earliest teachers of rhetoric learned their craft through careful observation and analysis of effective and ineffective speeches observed in the courts, legislatures, and civic gatherings. Socrates, for example, modeled critical thinking skills that are still in use today. Just as creative thinking is systematic, so is critical thinking. What marks critical thinking are the skills of classification and questioning (Marzano 1988, 18). We can take an example of critical thinking from the groundbreaking medical studies of William Harvey (1578–1657). Harvey's interest was in the nature of the human circulatory system. Until Harvey began his studies, scholars believed that the body's blood collected between the liver and lungs, pulsing back and forth, gaining what he called "nourishing natural spirits," seeping through a permeable wall in the heart, which then pushed the blood on to the rest of the body. Harvey, beginning with Galen's ancient classification of the parts of the circulation system, asked why the valves observed in the circulation system only allowed blood to flow in one direction. (The body's valves wouldn't permit blood moving back and forth between the liver and lungs.) His question led him to pressure-test a heart to discover that the heart walls were not, in fact, permeable. This finding led him to reason that the blood must flow in a circuitous fashion from the body into the right atrium, then right ventricle, to the lungs, then to the left atrium, left ventricle, to the body, and back again. Harvey's breakthrough was due to his practice of classification and questioning which led him to new insights that overturned 1,400 years of mistaken belief about this central body function (Franklin 1963, 15–20).

People who study messages encounter many of the same problems faced by Harvey: due to the nature of his interest, it was extremely difficult for him to observe the circulatory system in action since he couldn't cut open a live person and the blood did not circulate in a cadaver! The problem you face is that what you observe as a critic is not concrete like the body's systems, but completely abstract. Since you cannot do an experiment on a message you want to analyze, you must exercise your critical thinking skills of classification and questioning even more rigorously, at times, than scientists. It is only through such critical thinking that fifty years ago, critic Kenneth Burke unmasked the persuasive strategies of Hitler's book, *Mein Kampf*; or how, today, communication scholar and political analyst Kathleen Jamieson provides insightful analyses of political campaign rhetoric, helping audiences make sense of the candidates' speeches, advertisements, and actions. Jamieson is a particularly important model because her regular commentaries on National Public Radio each election season teach a large audience about how political communication works as persuasion. In both examples, creative and critical thinking provide a valuable product—useful knowledge about communication.

By combining critical and creative thinking, we have learned much about how the often mysterious process of communication works. In sum, expert critics think systematically about the communication phenomena they observe, and that leads them to new knowledge about communication or rhetoric. They draw upon existing theories of rhetoric, which essentially are classification schemes, to begin their analysis, then push their knowledge further through their creative application of theory and their own inferences drawn from careful study of messages (Black 1965, 9).

THE PROCESS OF CRITICAL ANALYSIS OF MESSAGES

We can't emphasize enough the usefulness of the *process* of message analysis. Your confrontation of the message in the process of message analysis is where you discover your insights about how the message works as rhetoric. This, after all, is where your skills as a critic are most exercised and where the value of your skill is realized. Remember, your work is not about writing papers for a class, or even writing reports for clients—those are important, but the value of such writing is substantially diminished if you have little insight to share from the process of message analysis. Keep in mind the twofold nature of what you are doing: first, thinking critically, and second, explaining and arguing your discoveries. Keep the process first and foremost in your mind as we move through this chapter and the following chapters. Otherwise, there will be little reason to write about or make a presentation on a text if you haven't first attended to the process of analysis.

Thinking like a rhetorical critic is a process that is marked by certain habits of mind. That is, critics think like critics using identifiable and recognizable ways of approaching a message. The key to being an insightful critic is controlling your thinking processes and using them as tools, choosing the right thinking tool for the right purpose at the appropriate time. The balance of this chapter gives an overview of four kinds of critical thinking: description, analysis, interpretation, and evaluation. Chapters 4, 5, 6, and 7 will elaborate on each kind of thinking. It is important at this point that you examine each kind of critical thinking and how they all work together. Experienced critics use these four kinds of thinking to accomplish whatever kind of analysis they choose to complete. You will learn that each kind of thinking yields certain kinds of information, and depending on your goal(s) you may use different types of thinking at different times. Now let's take a look at each kind of thinking.

DESCRIPTION

Describing a message is an important first step for discovering and understanding how a message works as rhetoric. **Description**, as a process, amounts to *characterizing the message under analysis.* That is, as you look long and hard at a message, you want to be able to grasp the message in such a way that you can present to another person the essential characteristics and patterns within the message. Describing is not "retelling" the message, but bringing to the foreground the most important dimensions of the particular message you are examining. For example, think about the last time you described one friend to another friend. Since you cannot retell your friend, you characterize her to another. Your description may be like this: "You should meet my other friend Karen. She's got a great sense of humor; she has the most interesting perspective where she can see the silliness in things most people take seriously. Not only is Karen funny, but she's got this infectious confidence. After I've been with Karen, I always feel like the future possibilities of life are unlimited! She's a lot of fun to be around." This description doesn't attempt to retell the other person by getting stuck in recounting superficial details; rather, it points out what makes Karen a distinctive personality—it recounts the features that make Karen unique and important.

Your description process may begin with you talking through all the details of the message, but each time you examine the message, your description will become less a retelling and more a characterization of essential elements—those elements or dimensions of the message that make it worth examining. Remember that at this point description is a way of thinking about a message; you are working on discovering an insight about a message. Description, in this phase, will be different in purpose and structure from the description you will present in a report of your analytical findings.

When you describe a message, taking notes on what you see, you begin to think systematically about it, which often helps you overcome prior expectations or beliefs you had about the message. Assumptions and expectations, if not recognized, can blind you to the effective dynamics of the message. That is, until you describe or characterize a message, you often are responding to it like an untrained consumer—you are affected by it, but you don't know why; or you think you know based on a quick judgment that has no support. That is what Black (1965) called *glandular criticism*, and it indicates what you felt at a particular time, but it reveals nothing about how a message worked as an effort to communicate (7). When you describe a message, you make a decision to open yourself to what is actually there; description helps you stay in the balcony, so to speak.

To see clearly you must be as precise and as personally removed as possible as you characterize the message and its context (Black 1965, 4). Description is an important activity because, through the process of a rigorous characterization, you often begin to see patterns within the message that were not immediately evident, for example, argument structures, organizational patterns, shifts in point of view, word choice, and so on. Also, when you finally report your findings, a written or oral description provides consumers of your criticism the information necessary to mentally construct the message so that the analysis of it will make sense to them. So, in doing description you must pay close attention to internal characteristics of the message: form, style, organization, and lines of argument, for example. You must also attend to the environment of the message: the social and political context, the nature of the audience(s), similar messages in the environment, and so on. You must draw from all the knowledge you possess about the communication process in order to accomplish this task with rigor, depth, and precision.

Not only do you need to be precise in your description, but you should be as fair as possible. We all encounter messages that we accept or reject enthusiastically. For those messages with which we agree, the temptation is to see only what we think is best or to portray the message to others in ways that predispose them to interpret the message positively or uncritically. The converse is true for those messages we reject. It's easy to find yourself arguing *with* message content (just as fans side with their own team), rather than making an argument *about* the message as rhetoric. If you aren't fair in examining the message, the work you do to analyze the message is, at best, mindless confirmation of it; or worse, manipulation of your audience into drawing a negative conclusion about the message. In either case, such an approach only serves to diminish our knowledge of communication rather than enhance it.

You can monitor yourself regarding the degree to which you are, in fact, describing a message by checking for language in your notes that marks description, or in your writing when you are producing a final critical product. Specifically, your description should exhibit neutral terms that present what the message looks or sounds like while avoiding words that indicate what it *should* look or sound like. Examine the advertisement in Figure 3.1 by the

FIGURE 3.1

National Smokers Alliance run in a large, urban newspaper. Then, read the critical model that follows. The left column presents each kind of critical thinking we will discuss. The right column is our explanation of each kind of thinking in operation.

No doubt, after you have read this description, if you were given a series of advertisements produced by the National Smokers Alliance, you could pick this particular one out of the group. Notice the lack of commentary in the description of the message—we attempted to provide sufficient detail to help you envision the message, but we did not attempt to report every detail of the piece.[1] At no point do we use language that says if the ad is good or bad, right or wrong, effective or ineffective. The final paragraph of the description, you notice, provides an abstract of the copy rather than the copy itself. Such

DESCRIPTION OF ADVERTISEMENT	COMMENTARY ON DESCRIPTIVE THINKING
Over the past few years, cigarette manufacturers have been encountering an increasingly less tolerant public and legislatures. In California, many municipalities are enacting tough antismoking ordinances; the state government has banned smoking from all state offices. In response to this increasingly hostile atmosphere, in June 1995 a full-page advertisement for smokers' rights appeared in the *Sacramento Bee*. The advertisement presents a cartoon that occupies the left third of the page and runs the length of it. The cartoon consists of a stack of blocks, all tenuously piled one upon another, with labels such as "The right to eat bacon and eggs!" "The right to enjoy coffee!" "The right to make your own choices!" and "The right to speak your mind!" On top of the teetering pile is a group of distressed citizens who are anticipating a long and painful fall should the "lifestyle police" at the bottom manage to dislodge a foundational block, "The right to smoke!" The right half of the page is composed of copy that is headlined, "Defending smokers' rights protects everyone's." The copy consists of about 75 words that identify the lifestyle police as a self-appointed group of extremists, and it invites readers to call the National Smokers Alliance. In sum, the advertisement exhibits patterns of juxtaposition and mimicry. That is, it verbally equates basic civil rights such as thinking and speaking freely with personal preferences such as drinking coffee and smoking by placing them next to each other on the blocks. It mimics an argument by making a claim ("Defending smokers' rights protects everyone's"), then using vague terms, such as "Big Government" and "a group of extremists" to support the claim.	We began by describing the *context* in which the message was found. In this case, we described the attitudes of the audience and the legislative activity surrounding the right to smoke debate. We were able to do this easily because it was for us a current event. Sometimes, however, you may be describing the context of a message that is very old or from such a different culture than the one in which you operate that you may need to research the context in which the message exists. We systematically described the message, first by dividing it into recognizable sections, describing each, beginning with the left side, then moving to the right side. Description of the message itself often entails giving some samples of the message in an effort to portray the message as precisely and as fairly as possible. Notice that we didn't attempt to replay all that was written, but described, as precisely and fairly as possible, the essence of the ideas presented in the written portion of the advertisement. You want to describe the essential elements of the message, not reproduce it verbatim; that is, characterize the message, rather than retell it. The final paragraph characterizes the message by bringing to the foreground the most important patterns or elements of the message discovered in the process of describing it. Notice that the level of abstraction is raised at this point—we shift from the details of the message to what patterns those details present when clustered together. Notice, too, how the characterization begins the process of analysis. You know you have managed to characterize the message when you are able to point out the central patterns or devices that the details of your observation suggest like we did in the paragraph to the left.

abstracting is necessary to avoid having the description be nothing more than a mindless reproduction of the message. Description requires the critic to think about the message in a deep and attentive fashion, if done correctly. However, when characterizing, you must be particularly careful to present precisely and fairly the essence of the message to others, even if you strongly disagree with it. Although description and analysis are different ways of thinking about a message, you will find that, in practice, they are related. To describe a message, you must identify specific elements of the message that you see as important. The descriptive process leads naturally to analysis.

ANALYSIS

Analysis, as a way of thinking, is *the process of systematically discovering, identifying, and articulating the various parts of the message and the relationship of those parts to one another.* Analysis serves to make visible the key elements of the message and the interactions of those parts that create specific effects in audiences. Since messages are human creations in the same way radios, cars, or buildings are human creations, messages are assembled by people, and the parts of a message interact with one another to make it work, just like the parts of a building, for example, work together to make the structure function as it was designed to function. The first goal of a message analyst is to identify the parts of messages and look for relationships between the parts.

A second goal of analysis is to uncover the choices message creators made when constructing the message. Rhetoric is a process of adapting ideas to audiences (Bryant 1953, 413). To do that, message makers of all kinds must choose how to construct the messages. For example, when the president prepares to speak on policies regarding the powers of the presidency, he must carefully consider his audience, and the context of the message, and decide what his purpose is, what topics he needs to discuss, what tone to adopt, what sorts of support to provide, and how it should be organized. He usually has many choices available to him and when we hear his speech, we can infer a great deal about the president as a thinker, his perception of his audiences, and his values and priorities by looking at the choices he made when preparing the speech. When critics focus attention on the potential choices available to speakers and the specific choices ultimately made by the speaker, we learn much about specific rhetorical events and the people (both speakers and audiences) involved in them. By examining lots of messages, we begin to see patterns of human behavior that become useful, general knowledge about how people communicate.

To be systematic in analysis, it is generally useful to consciously adopt a particular point of view toward the message. Without a point of view, our approach to the message tends to be random, which lessens the validity of our conclusions; lest we end up comparing apples and oranges, we need a consistent way of looking at a message. In the field of rhetorical criticism, the point of view may also be called a theory, a method or methodology for analyzing a message. However, to keep our focus on the process of message analysis, we will use the term *search model*. A **search model** is *an organized set of related con-*

cepts that provide a critic with a ready-made set of topics to examine or questions to ask about a message. Since the concepts in a search model are logically related to one another, using a search model helps us avoid the apples and oranges mistakes we would be prone to make otherwise. For practical purposes, a search model provides a critic starting points for excavating, or digging into a message. However, it is important to note that different points of view, or search models, will bring different elements of a message to our attention, which, of course, will lead us to draw quite different conclusions about any particular message. (Chapters 9 through 17 in this textbook provide an introduction to a number of different search models to assist you in your analyses.) Since different search models name the parts of messages differently, they cause us to experience messages in different ways. It is like looking at an ant using a magnifying glass or looking at the same ant using a spectrometer. The subject remains the same, but the conclusions you can draw about that ant based on what you see will be very different to say the least. Each search model facilitates seeing something about a message while masking other things about it. That's why it is often valuable to examine the same message using different search models—we understand more about how any message works when we do that. Let's take a look at a search model in operation. We've decided to use the classical search model, which is one of many possible models or theories we could have chosen. As you will learn when you read Chapter 9, the classical model is very complicated; however, we want you to note in the following example how we selected only those concepts that were most relevant to our study. At this point, don't worry about how you would do this; just read the model analysis and the commentary explaining why we did what we did.

The left column is our working analysis of the advertisement "Defending smokers' rights protects everyone's," which was reproduced in Figure 3.1. The right column explains our thinking and decision making as critics. You can read these pages in different ways. For example, you can read only the left columns straight through to get a sense for the four kinds of thinking critics do. You can then read the commentary to help you check your own thoughts about how the study proceeded. Or you can read part of the left column and the related parts of the commentary as you go. Use the model in whatever way helps you best understand how to use a search model to assist a systematic analysis of a text.

The goal of the analysis was to take the message apart, to discover what elements made the advertisement. In this case, based on the concepts available in the chosen search model, we used the terms *argument strategy, logic, enthymeme,* and *organizational structure,* and we pointed out how they functioned in the message. In essence, we took the message apart to see how it works. We used those terms from our search model because the process of describing the message caused us to see something interesting about the pictures, the words, and their relationships to one another. The process of describing the message was related to our analysis. Notice that the analysis raised an important question about whether or not the argument (in the form of an enthymeme) was spurious. The answer to that question will help us give meaning to the

ANALYSIS OF ADVERTISEMENT	COMMENTARY ON ANALYTICAL THINKING
Inasmuch as this advertisement relies on visual impact due to the dominance of the cartoon, what is striking about the cartoon is its organizational and logical structure.	These are two important concepts we draw from our knowledge of Aristotle's ideas; organization is a basic element of Aristotle's description of rhetoric; logic was central to the canon of invention. Based on our study of Aristotle, we are choosing only those concepts that we feel help us the most. (In the process of analysis, we play with many different concepts as we analyze the message. Don't let the finished nature of the example lead you to believe we picked these ideas right away.)
The eye of the reader is taken from its natural starting point in the upper-left corner of the page and is pulled immediately down that side of the page. One first sees the image of numerous and various characters who are obviously distressed—mouths are opened in shock, arms are flailing about, and eyes are all cast downward—which the reader follows, leading one to wonder what is causing their distress.	
The list of "rights" moves from least important to most important: from "The right to eat bacon and eggs!" at the top, to "The right to think for yourself!" at the bottom. This *organizational* structure mimics the classic *argumentation* strategy of presenting the least important argument first, then moving to the most important strategy to build a case. . . . "The right to smoke!" is placed immediately above "thinking for yourself," and the inference may be made that if the right to smoke is removed, the rights of free speech and free choice will come crashing down, injuring all who stand upon those rights. The *argument* is constructed in a way that invites the reader of the advertisement to complete the argument for the author, drawing the conclusion intended by the message's creator: My rights are threatened by antismoking laws, whether or not I smoke. An argument that has most of the parts, but lacks the conclusion is what Aristotle calls an *enthymeme*. Enthymemes are powerful because the audience delights in completing the argument mentally—we value closure and sensibility. However, Aristotle also noted that a rhetor may also present spurious enthymemes that invite completion, but lack	Here, we are pointing out that the organization of the parts of the picture is similar to spoken or written arguments. Comparison is a common form of analysis; sometimes, creative thinking allows us to make new comparisons that provide new insights. Comparing the organization of a picture to the organization of an oral argument gives us a way of talking about the picture that we didn't have before.

We point out here how the concepts of "organization" and "argument" work together to cause a reader to draw the conclusion the rhetor wants. Useful analysis usually does more than categorize the message parts; it looks further to discover the relationships of the parts.

We use precise terminology like "spurious enthymeme" to deepen and elaborate our analysis of the argument structure in the message. It is important to be as precise in your analysis as you can be. Precision leads to greater control of the message and more significant |

ANALYSIS OF ADVERTISEMENT (cont.)	COMMENTARY ON ANALYTICAL THINKING (cont.)
logical validity. This may lead us to ask if the enthymeme in the ad is spurious. The ad draws upon the same mental predispositions toward closure as an enthymeme, but the ad does not present a logical, coherent, and rigorous set of connections between the concepts. By seeing the minor concerns of "The right to eat bacon and eggs!" and "The right to think for yourself!" in proximity to "The right to smoke!" the audience is led to equate each of these in value and conclude that loss of smokers' rights will mean the loss of basic rights of freedom of thought and speech. The copy in the ad serves to provide direction to readers in how to understand the cartoon. It names the lifestyle police as "self-styled" or self-appointed (not requested or elected) and "extremist." The copy asserts, "If they succeed, we lose our basic rights to free choice." So, if the reader didn't manage to make the implicit connections presented in the cartoon, the copy reinforces and makes explicit the intent of the cartoon.	The question we generate in the analysis leads us to interpret the message; since we aren't finished with the analysis we leave the question for now, but will explore it later in our study. Being aware of the specific kind of critical thinking we are doing helps us not to leave the task of analysis before we are done. We are explaining further how the parts of the message relate to each other, elaborating and broadening our analysis. This reflects an *inference* we are making about the effects of the interaction of the organizational and logical parts of the message. An inference is knowledge we create by "putting two and two together." This section explains how the two elements of the message identified earlier, the picture in cartoon form and the copy next to it, work together to cause the reader to fear the consequences of smoking limitations suggested in the message. Our conclusions here are inferences about how the parts of the message work. You will find that you will quickly jump to a conclusion about how the message works once you see with some precision the parts and their relationships.

to the message makers' use of message makers' use of a potentially spurious argument; saying what the choice means is interpretation.

The temptation to interpret before we have thoroughly completed our analysis is powerful. Analysis and interpretation are very closely related ways of thinking, and you can easily move into interpretation without knowing it unless you consciously monitor your thinking. As you analyze a message, either orally or in writing notes, you can check your thinking by reviewing the words you are using at the moment. When analyzing a message, you should use the terms of whatever search model you selected. In our case, we used such terms as *organization, argument,* and *enthymeme* to name the parts of the message. Analysis is marked by the dominance of such terms. When you are engaged in the process of analysis, first, play with the concepts of your search model, then, as precisely and completely as possible, apply those you find most helpful to the message. You need to learn as much about the components of the message as possible before interpreting the message. If you allow yourself to jump to interpretation before completing your analysis, the interpretation may very well be flawed. You or others may find that with a bit more probing, an important, but undiscovered dynamic is at work in the message, and the interpretation will be quite different as a result. Human beings are driven to make sense of their experience so critics are compelled to interpret their findings, especially if the analysis turns up things we didn't expect. Now, let's take a look at interpretation as a kind of critical thinking.

INTERPRETATION

We define **interpretation** as *drawing conclusions about the rhetorical patterns you discover in the analysis so that something significant is learned from the analysis; the process of deciding what it means that the rhetor used the particular devices you discovered in the analysis phase.* In other words, interpretation is the process of making sense of the findings of the analysis. Interpretation answers the "So what?" question that naturally flows from the analysis. For example, you may ask what it matters that, in the preceding example, we discovered that the same organizational structure typical of oral arguments was used in the cartoon portion of the National Smokers Alliance advertisement. You may also want to know what it suggests about the rhetors if spurious enthymemes were used. Figuring out the answers to these questions teaches us something significant about how communication works, generally, and how persuasion works, specifically.

We believe that your most important task as a critic is interpretation. It is also the most difficult kind of thinking we've discussed so far because it requires you to exercise critical and creative thinking in an integrated way. Finally, interpretation requires you to balance voicing your personal feelings or conclusions about what you discover in your analysis with your balcony stance as a critic. In other words, your responses as a human being who has experienced the message become important information in interpretation, but you cannot allow your critical study to become just another editorial. As mentioned, you have a natural tendency to make interpretations as soon as you have *some* analysis done because you want to make sense of what you found. This is the same force, for example, that leads you to make instantaneous judgments about how interpersonally compatible you are with someone you just met. We know from the research that we create an initial judgment of the person and that judgment is very difficult to change, even when we get more information that indicates we were wrong (Dailey 1952, 149–51). Expert critics develop the ability to remain tentative about any interpretations they make until they have as much information as they can gather about a message. A

INTERPRETATION OF FINDINGS	COMMENTARY ON INTERPRETIVE THINKING
The brief analysis of the smokers' rights advertisement uncovered the organizational and logical structures of the message as they interact to persuade the audience to support the concept of smokers' rights. Both the cartoon and the copy in the ad function to invite the audience to participate in the creation of the message. By presenting elements of the message as a cartoon, which is incomplete as logical thought, the sentences within the pictures that serve to relate other sentences to each other ("The right to eat bacon and eggs!" must somehow be connected to "The right to speak your mind!") are implicit and must be supplied by the audience.	We are reviewing and summarizing the findings of our analysis, which we will use as support for our argument about what the message's organizational structure and logical appeals may mean.
This form of argument, providing part of the argument in such a way that the audience will complete it as the rhetor predicts, is called an *enthymeme*. As was shown earlier, the message mimics logical arguments rather than presenting rigorous, well-formed ones. The choices made by the message makers suggest at least two possible conclusions: one is that the rhetors realized that a straightforward argument would be impossible to make, based strictly on the "pleasures" of smoking; a second is that the rhetors believe that the audience is either unable to detect the rhetors' efforts to distract the audience from the real issues, or they don't really care about the issues underlying the efforts of the tobacco industry to promote consumption of its products.	NOTE: We assume all reasonable people who see the message understand the basic meaning of it. However, what is not so clear to the average message consumer is that the presence of certain rhetorical devices have meaning beyond the content of the message.

Here is the heart of the interpretation:

(1) presentation of possible meanings of the findings,

and . . . |
| In any case, the analysis suggests less than positive assumptions by the rhetors about their audience. The rhetors seem to be cynically attempting to make an impossible argument by distracting what they see as a dull and uncritical audience. Although one can explain why the message creators chose the | (2) explanation of what the choices mean. We drew an inference or conclusion from what we found in the analysis. Coupled with our understanding of the context, and our understanding of Aristotle's ideas, we drew a consis- We drew an inference or conclusion from what we found in the analysis. Coupled with our understanding of the context, and our understanding of Aristotle's ideas, we drew a consis- |

INTERPRETATION OF FINDINGS (cont.)	COMMENTARY ON INTERPRETIVE THINKING (cont.)
forms evident in this ad, one cannot excuse the unethical use of rhetoric presented herein.	tent conclusion about the rhetors' view of the audience. This conclusion cannot be derived from a naive reading of the message; it required us to describe and analyze the message before we could uncover this important finding.

mark of your increasing expertise will be the ability to resist jumping to conclusions; you will find yourself thinking through all the possible interpretations of your findings, and then making a reasoned case for the implications of the rhetor's choices. The interpretive phase of the process is exciting because here your self becomes an important resource in sense making, and your voice begins to be heard. When you read the interpretative section in the example, look for the places where the critic's personal response to the message gets more obvious.

Interpretation, as a way of thinking, requires you to reasonably go beyond the concrete evidence you have collected. To make any progress in developing our knowledge in any discipline, we must learn to interpret information, making reasonable inferences about what the data mean. For example, astronomer Percival Lowell suspected that "Planet X" (later named Pluto) existed before it was ever observed. After closely examining the subtle shifts in light coming from deep space, and by carefully noting slight movements in other distant planets, Lowell interpreted the data in the most reasonable way ("Percival Lowell" 2003). Given that light and other bodies were behaving like others previously observed to be near a planet, there had to be a planet in the vicinity, Lowell reasoned. Visual confirmation of the suspected planet was provided by Clyde Tombaugh who had been systematically photographing the night sky over a ten-month period. On February 18, 1930, Tombaugh took the first picture of Pluto, which was where Lowell thought it should be. Together, these scientists expanded our knowledge of the solar system. In a similar fashion, critics expand knowledge about communication processes by making reasonable inferences grounded in careful analyses of messages.

Interpretation is usually where your study of messages pays off. In the process of interpretation, you push your reasoning skills to wring from the data the insights that give you new knowledge about communication. Interpretation is marked by "case making" or arguing your conclusions. As you monitor your thinking, you should find yourself saying or writing such things as claims, reasons, evidence, and qualifiers, all of which indicate you are making a case for the conclusions you've drawn. In other words, your interpretation is marked by the language of argumentation.

Just as description leads to analysis, and just as analysis leads to interpretation, you will find that you want to make a judgment about the rhetorical event. Reread the last sentence in the example interpretation—what does it suggest? As you can see, we drew the conclusion that the message was unethical. That statement is different from the interpretive statements we made because it goes beyond suggesting meanings for the choices of the rhetor; it makes a judgment about the message. Evaluative thinking requires some different mental work than description, analysis, or interpretation. Let's examine those differences.

EVALUATION

Evaluation is *the critic's use of stated criteria to determine the merit, worth, significance, or effectiveness of the rhetorical strategies in a message.* Sometimes the standards for judging a message are explicit or implicit in the theory (search model) you have used to analyze the message as were the standards we drew from Aristotle; sometimes you may have to construct appropriate, relevant standards from a variety of sources. The difficulty you face in evaluating messages is articulating your criteria for your judgment. If you evaluate a message without articulated standards, your evaluation will be arbitrary. Arbitrary decisions invite others to dismiss your ideas, so judging without standards will diminish the value of all the work you did in the message analysis up to the point of evaluation.

Standards for evaluation come from a variety of sources: rhetorical theory, culture, professional codes of ethics, or community standards, to name a few. Which source or sources of standards you choose will depend on the nature of the message and your purposes in analyzing it. For example, if you are examining proposed legislation for your boss, the state representative, your standards for judgment will be drawn from legal standards if your boss wants to ensure that the law won't be nullified by the courts. Or your standards for judgment will be based on the ethics of social policy if your boss, by wording the law in specific ways, is attempting to change how people live their lives. Whatever your reason for doing your analysis, the best judgments are well grounded in articulated standards relevant to the purposes of the criticism.

As always, you can monitor your thinking by attending to the words you are using to talk or write about a message. Evaluation is marked by terms such as *good, bad, right, wrong, appropriate, inappropriate, effective, ineffective, ethical, unethical, better,* or *worse.* When those kinds of words emerge, you are most likely engaging in evaluation. The question you constantly ask yourself is: Do I intend to be doing this kind of thinking about this message at this time? If you are describing the message to yourself or others, and mixed in with the description are evaluative terms, you probably have jumped to an arbitrary judgment since you know little about the message at that point in your study, and you haven't articulated any standards. Your evaluation is glandular. Take a look at the example that follows and see if you can identify the language of evaluation in it.

EVALUATION OF RHETORICAL CHOICES	COMMENTARY ON THE EVALUATION
The message creators, in the case of smokers' rights, were faced with a difficult task: How to advocate *for* behavior that is a known threat to human life and health. Aristotle suggests that persuasion ought to be undertaken for good outcomes, with "good" being defined as "that which ought to be chosen for its own sake." Health and life ought to be chosen over illness and death. In order for the rhetor to avoid having the reader immediately dismiss the rhetor's ostensible goal—having people continue to choose illness and death by continuing to smoke—the message creators have opted to shift the reader's attention to personal rights by presenting a spurious enthymematic argument. The message serves to distract the reader to a false concern over basic rights.	Since we have been using Aristotle's concepts for the analysis, we felt that we would be most consistent by using his standards for rhetoric as well.
This is a false concern because we know that certain carefully drawn limitations on conduct can be in the interest of everyone. For example, we already have limited the ability of makers of beer, hard liquors, and fortified wines to advertise on television; advertisements for cigarettes have long been banned from television with no negative effects on the general rights of citizens to speak their minds. The same would be true of antismoking ordinances and laws: limitations in certain public areas and thoroughfares would be implemented, but no one would be unable to smoke if they desired to do so, in their own homes, for example.	Here, we apply Aristotle's concept of the "good" to the message we are analyzing, creating a specific standard: people should be encouraged to pursue what is healthy for them.
	Our analysis brought us to the realization that purposely flawed arguments were used by the rhetors. Now, we can explain that the rhetors had to use flawed arguments to confuse the audience because the motive of the rhetoric was flawed—getting people to choose something bad (smoking) rather than something good.
	This portion illustrates an argument offered to support our evaluation; we must argue our judgment just as we argued our interpretation.
	NOTE: We drew upon our knowledge of First Amendment limitations on commercial speech to make this argument. You must draw upon or develop your knowledge of communication as broadly as possible to do your best criticism.
The use of spurious enthymemes embedded in a subtle organizational pattern within a cartoon format makes detection of the intent of the rhetor more difficult.	We identify the message dynamics in message structure that were used to mask the truth of the matter, causing unnecessary confusion and fear in the audience. Using the tools of rhetoric to cause others to choose bad behavior is wrong and, therefore, unethical.

EVALUATION OF RHETORICAL CHOICES (cont.)	COMMENTARY ON THE EVALUATION (cont.)
Although the psychological impact of the message is probably quite effective, the message itself violates the ethics of persuasion by attempting to get audiences to believe, advocate, or behave in ways that are not good for them. Defending smokers' rights, in fact, diminishes all citizens' lives and only serves the interests of the cigarette industry. The ethical failure of this message is as clear as is its cleverness and creativity in avoiding the real issues behind the message.	Our conclusion is clearly stated: the message is clever and creative in its design, but the criterion that matters most is grounded in the effect of the message on the audience.

As you can see, the most important task we had in judging the message was creating appropriate standards. Since Aristotle's discussion of "the available means of persuasion" also includes a discussion of ethical uses of rhetoric, we were able to take our standards directly from that source. The fortunate result is that our evaluative standards are directly related to the analytical concepts we employed. If you use other search models, you may need to create and test appropriate standards to ensure consistency. We discuss this further in Chapter 7. You also were alerted to the fact that a portion of our support in our argument was drawn from our knowledge of the rules concerning regulation of speech. To complete a rigorous evaluation of some messages, you may need to do research in order to construct appropriate evaluative criteria. Research is discussed further in Chapters 4 and 8.

Evaluation is a way of thinking about messages that is quite different from the other three forms of thinking because it often requires you to look outside the message for standards. It requires you to take a perspective on the message in a way that permits you to draw conclusions about the merits. Evaluation is challenging since you must have a clear sense of standards and what they judge, and you must know if the standards you choose are appropriate for the evaluation you wish to make.

SUMMARY

This chapter has presented you with an overview of the kinds of thinking that an expert critic draws upon to complete an insightful analysis of any significant message. Each kind of thinking is related to the others, and all four are enlivened by the essential characteristics of both critical and creative ways of thinking and problem solving. Figure 3.2 provides a visual representation of the relationships of the thinking tools available to you.

The goal of this chapter was to show you that message analysis requires you to think about messages in particular ways. Expert message analysts or critics monitor and control their thinking so as to accomplish the specific critical task they have in mind. Understanding, monitoring, and applying specific critical-thinking skills make critics different from other professionals and the average consumer of messages. The ability to think about messages systematically leading to insight about a message makes a message analyst valuable in a wide variety of professional and civic roles as we've suggested.

In the following chapters we take an in-depth look at each kind of critical thinking previewed in this chapter and practice each. As you move through each chapter, you will become increasingly aware of, and in control of, your thinking processes. With each step you will acquire the mental skills and habits of mind that mark effective message analysts.

FIGURE 3.2

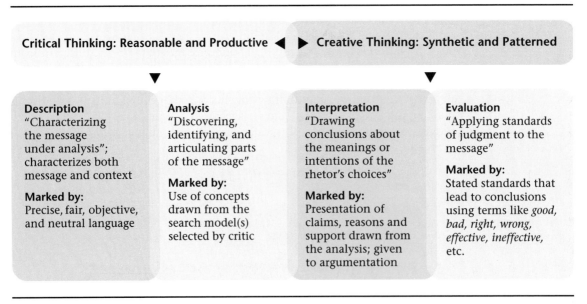

Critical Thinking: Reasonable and Productive ◀		▶ Creative Thinking: Synthetic and Patterned	
▼		▼	
Description "Characterizing the message under analysis"; characterizes both message and context	**Analysis** "Discovering, identifying, and articulating parts of the message"	**Interpretation** "Drawing conclusions about the meanings or intentions of the rhetor's choices"	**Evaluation** "Applying standards of judgment to the message"
Marked by: Precise, fair, objective, and neutral language	**Marked by:** Use of concepts drawn from the search model(s) selected by critic	**Marked by:** Presentation of claims, reasons and support drawn from the analysis; given to argumentation	**Marked by:** Stated standards that lead to conclusions using terms like *good, bad, right, wrong, effective, ineffective,* etc.

EXERCISES

Practicing the thinking habits of a critic is essential for your growth as a communication professional. The following exercises are designed to help you increase your consciousness about your thinking processes. It is important that when you review your work, you concentrate on the specific language you use in the exercise and concentrate on the characteristics of each kind of thinking.

1. Carefully (and slowly) examine the advertisement "Restricting choices little by little can add up to a big problem." Then, answer the questions that follow.

FIGURE 3.3

- Write a description of the advertisement in three hundred words or less concluding with a characterization of the message. (Review our model description of "Defending smokers' rights protects everyone's." Pay special attention to the final paragraph that models characterization.)
- Reflect on how the process of description and characterization affected what you see in the message that you hadn't seen before doing the exercise.

2. If you have some knowledge of rhetorical theory already, try applying one of the search models in Chapters 9 through 16. If you are new to the critical process, we suggest you try applying some of the elements of style from the classical search model (Chapter 9).

- Write a brief analysis of the advertisement using some of the concepts you selected from the model. Make sure you focus attention on how the rhetorical elements work together within the message. What does your analysis reveal about how the message works as rhetoric?

3. Choose a message that you think is important and interesting.

- Using a tape recorder, describe, analyze, interpret, and evaluate the message you selected. (Try to confine your thinking and talk to each specific kind of thinking in each phase. Feel free to turn the recorder off if you get confused, and start again.)
- Listen to the tape and check your thinking process, listening carefully to the specific language you used when you were at each stage of the process. (Figure 3.2 provides some descriptors of what sort of language is appropriate to each kind of thinking.)
- Write the best examples of each kind of thinking that you produced. How is what you say about messages different from what you *would* have said about the message before using this process? What is valuable about how you are learning to think about messages?

NOTES

1 The goal of the description is to help another person envision the message that is being examined. Sometimes the others haven't seen the message before, and oftentimes it is not possible to reproduce the message with the critical analysis due to its size or nature. So the description must be extensive enough to create a basic understanding of the message while avoiding replicating it.

WORKS CITED

Andrews, James. *The Practice of Rhetorical Criticism.* New York: Macmillan, 1983.

Black, Edwin. "The Meaning of Criticism." *Rhetorical Criticism: A Study Method.* New York: Macmillan, 1965.

Bryant, Donald C. "Rhetoric: Its Functions and Its Scope." *Quarterly Journal of Speech* 39 (1953): 401–24.

Cathcart, Robert. *Post Communication.* 2nd ed. Indianapolis: Bobbs-Merrill, 1981.

Dailey, C. A. "The Effects of Premature Conclusions upon the Acquisition of Understanding of a Person." *Journal of Psychology* 33 (1952): 133–52.

Ennis, Robert H. "Goals for a Critical Thinking Curriculum." *In Developing Minds: A Resource Book for Teaching Thinking,* edited by Arthur L. Costa, 54–57. Alexandria, VA: Association for Supervision and Curriculum Development, 1985.

Franklin, Kenneth J. *The Circulation of the Blood and Other Writings.* Translated by William Harvey. London: Dent, 1963.

Marzano, Robert J., Ronald S. Brandt, Carolyn Sue Hughes, Beau Fly Jones, Barbaran Z. Presseisen, Stuart C. Rankin, and Charles Suhor. *Dimensions of Thinking: A Framework for Curriculum and Instruction.* Alexandria, VA: Association for Supervision and Curriculum Development, 1988.

"Percival Lowell." *Lowell Observatory.* http://www.lowell.edu/AboutLowell/plowell.html (accessed September 5, 2003).

4

The Process
of Description

Vocabulary

➤ description

➤ planned survey

➤ context

➤ visible Web

➤ invisible Web

➤ conformity

➤ non-participation

➤ desecration

➤ contextual
   reconstruction

Scientist Samuel Scudder (1917) tells a fascinating story regarding his training as a scientist by Louis Agassiz. Agassiz's first lesson for Scudder was to "Take this fish, and look at it; we call it a haemulon: by and by I will ask you what you have seen." Scudder dutifully did as he was told by looking at the smelly specimen as carefully as he knew how. "In ten minutes," Scudder writes, "I had seen all that could be seen in that fish, and started in search of the Professor." He found that Agassiz had left the building and would not return for some time, so Scudder went back to his bench and bent over the fish for the rest of the morning, examining it from every possible angle. After lunch, he found that Agassiz would be gone for several more hours. He writes, "Slowly I drew forth that hideous fish, and with a feeling of desperation again looked at it. I might not use a magnifying-glass; instruments of all kinds were interdicted. My two hands, my two eyes, and the fish: it seemed a most limited field." Scudder pushed his finger in the mouth, felt the teeth, counted scales, and even drew a sketch of the specimen. Finally Agassiz returned and asked, "Well, what is it like?" After outlining in detail all the discrete observations made over the previous six hours, Agassiz replied, "You have not looked very carefully; why, you haven't even seen one of the most conspicuous features of the animal, which is as plainly before your eyes as the fish itself; look again, look again!" (Scudder 1917, 58).

Scudder persisted and began to discover "one new thing after another, until I saw how just the Professor's criticism had been." At the end of the day, Agassiz sent him home with the promise of "an examination" regarding the fish before looking at it again. Scudder spent a troubled evening thinking about what he saw, and the next morning, in response to his teacher's question said, "Do you perhaps mean that the fish has symmetrical sides with paired organs?" "Of course! Of course!" exclaimed the professor. When Scudder asked what he should do next, Agassiz said, "Oh, look at your fish!" and left. The lesson went on for three days, with Scudder making new discoveries each day. Then, "on the fourth day, a second fish of the same group was placed beside the first, and [Scudder] was bidden to point out the resemblances and differences between the two; another and another followed until the entire family lay before [him]." Scudder concluded that given "the description of the various parts, Agassiz's training in the method of observing facts and their orderly arrangement was ever accompanied by the urgent exhortation not to be content with them." "Facts are stupid things," he would say, "until brought into connection with some general law" (1917, 61).

Given Scudder's success on his first exam, he learned how important it is to see precisely and in detail all the parts of what one is observing. The task assigned to Scudder was what we call the first phase of a critique: description. Two important lessons can be learned from Scudder's experience. First, to see anything significant in an object (in our case, a rhetorical message), you must focus your attention on that object for a long time, longer than you think you can or need, so that you can describe precisely those elements that are relevant and important. Second, to see anything of significance in an object you must examine that object against other things. Each new fish added to Scudder's tray served to define and expand a context for the facts Scudder had collected. In our case as message analysts, we must look at messages against the context in which they were constructed, as well as against other messages and theory. Once you begin connecting what you see in a message with theories of rhetoric, you have entered the phases of analysis and interpretation, but first you must begin, like Scudder, by looking at (listening to or reading, as the case may be) your message and its context slowly and deliberately for a long time.

Description, as one kind of critical thinking, helps discipline your approach to any message. Description helps you slow down and consciously think about what you observe in the message, which helps you move beyond your first "glandular" reaction. By consciously describing a message, you do what Scudder did—take your time, and carefully look at what you can in the message, asking questions about what comes to your attention. Description helps you take a "balcony" stance, seeing the message with more distance, though not purely objectively. Just as Sally was able to get a new perspective on her encounter with the highway patrol officer by describing the event as if she were looking at it from a balcony nearby, you will be moved beyond your initial response to a message by consciously describing the message as precisely and fairly as possible. This chapter presents ways for you to work through the descriptive process of message analysis. First, we'll look at how you can describe the *content* of a message (sometimes referred to as the *text*). As you engage in description, you will need to record your thinking, so we will show you two systems for doing that. Next, we'll look at how you can describe the *context* of a message and we'll demonstrate how the examination of context affects your understanding of a message. Let's take a look at some tools that will help you get started on your description more easily and effectively.

APPROACHES TO DESCRIBING A TEXT

As we defined it in Chapter 3, **description**, *as a process, amounts to characterizing the message under analysis.* As you describe a message carefully, systematically, and thoughtfully, you will become aware of features of the message that were not immediately evident when you first encountered or experienced it. For example, when we first saw the National Smokers Alliance ad that we discussed in Chapter 3, the relationship between the cartoon and the copy was not evident. However, as we reviewed the message a number of times and talked through what we were seeing, relationships between images and copy began to emerge. We found something we didn't expect, which was interesting to us. By describing messages, finding the essential characteristics that make messages noteworthy, we become mindful and careful to see them in ways that we don't normally see them in daily life.

To think descriptively and critically, you must be able to monitor your thinking. Although you have a natural ability to describe a message, you can maximize your chances of finding something interesting about how a message is crafted if you adhere to some structure in your thinking. Samuel Scudder, the novice scientist, did not begin his observation very systematically. He had no plan for how to observe the fish, but a plan unfolded with the discipline of continuing the observation. He not only looked at the fish, but he began to feel it, inside and out. Moreover, his professor, Agassiz, planned an approach for how Scudder's observation would proceed. Once Scudder saw as many details as possible by looking at that fish alone, Agassiz put before him another fish each day, for comparison. Agassiz had a plan for which fish to add first, second, and so on. The next time Scudder went to observe a different species, he no doubt used the strategy Agassiz taught him for making initial observations. The principle is true for message analysts. In order to "see what's there" we must design appropriate methods to search out the significant characteristics of a message. Let's look at two procedures you might use to refine the ways you naturally describe messages.

PLANNED SURVEY

One way to organize your description is to create a **planned survey** of the message, just as explorers survey the land. That is, *make a plan for how you will initially observe the message and what dimensions of the message you will pay attention to; then follow through with that plan.* For example, when we encountered the smokers rights advertisement, we made a plan to survey first the cartoon, then survey the accompanying copy, and finally to look at both as a unit. Let's say you are analyzing an advocacy website. A planned survey of the website might be as follows:

- Read the website slowly and carefully several times to get a sense of the entire message.
- Note your initial "glandular" reactions so you can then ask what in the text may have contributed to those reactions. Make a notation, however, that these are glandular reactions and not deliberative critical responses.
- Lay out a concept map of the website, or outline it, to discover the specific topics treated in it and how they are organized.
- Taking each section of the website, look for specific devices used to cause the presumed audience to think in particular ways about the message and list them out or mark each in the message. If you have taken other communication classes, use what you know from those studies to help you look for specific devices.
- Note what arguments, devices, or points of view are *not* present in the message.

- Going over the same material, highlight all the material you did *not* account for in the previous step; create categories for that material.
- Reread the chapter at your regular rate to experience the message as a whole.

By doing all that in a workerlike fashion, you lead yourself through the message in a way that prevents a haphazard approach that may miss important but not immediately evident message components. If we examine a message in another medium, say, a television ad, program, or music video, the planned survey would have to change. A reasonable approach might be something like this:

- Watch the entire message a few times through.
- Look at the message without sound to focus attention on the images on the screen; note how they were cut together, the kinds of cuts, the lengths of cuts, and the content of each.
- Listen to the message without the pictures or images to focus attention on what is said, the quality of the sound, length of various segments, specific sounds or rhythms in the track, and how they are ordered.
- Lay out a concept map or outline of the contents of the message.
- List the topics treated and the order in which they appear.
- Look for specific devices (words or visual images) used to cause the presumed audience to think in particular ways about the message and list those devices.
- Note what images, words, ideas, or devices are *not* present in the message.
- Look at the message again as a whole to discover other images and sounds you did *not* notice before.

We look for something interesting and we note what we find. All we did was decide on a sensible plan for looking at the message to ensure that we saw the central features of the message. If we were examining a song, we would have a different plan; nevertheless, the plan would ensure that we attended to all that was important in the particular message we were examining. What would be your approach to describing a speech? Take a few minutes to recall the most recent classroom lecture you have experienced. Design a plan for describing the lecture; then implement the plan to see how it affects your ability to fairly and clearly see the rhetorical dynamics of the lecture.

QUESTIONS

A second way to organize your description involves *asking yourself questions* designed to make you take a closer look at the message. Your goal is to design questions that purposely cause you to think about a message in ways that are different from those you habitually use. For example, here's a list of possible questions that might facilitate descriptive thinking about any message:

- What do I immediately recall about the message?
- What did I *expect* to see or hear?

- What was *unexpected* or surprising to me? Why?
- What topics were treated?
- How were those topics addressed by the rhetor?
- What devices were used by the message maker(s) to get the audience to view the topics in the way he/she desired?
- What other messages does this *resemble?* How? In what ways, specifically?
- How does this message *differ* from similar messages? Do the differences matter?
- What questions did the message make me ask?

This is not a "magic" list; you can and should add your own questions to it. Each of the preceding questions forces us to look more closely at a message, and look at it from a slightly different angle. The questions act like polarizing filters in cameras or eyeglasses. Different filters allow different parts of the light spectrum to reach the film or your eyes, causing you to see the same object in different ways. Questions, like those just listed, help you to think about messages with more emotional distance because they disrupt your familiar response patterns; you become more aware of how the message is affecting you as a consumer. Practice using questions now. Think about a familiar television advertisement that you find interesting and describe it. Now, apply some of the preceding questions, or any new questions you designed, to that ad. Once you have answered the questions, describe the ad again. What new perceptions do you have as a result of thinking differently about the ad? You may have made a notable discovery about the message, or you may not have changed your description at all. However, you have accomplished the task of taking a long, hard look at the message and you have done it intentionally and consciously; you have controlled your thinking to promote precision and fairness.

RECORDING YOUR THINKING

Keep in mind that description at this point in the process is the first step toward analysis.[1] When you have completed your work and report it to others, "description" has a different function, which we discuss later when we talk about the *product* of criticism. As you conduct the descriptive process, you will want to take careful notes of what you observe in the message. One very simple means of noting your thoughts as you describe a message is essentially brainstorming or, in this case, brain-writing.[2] Using a blank piece of paper and your planned survey or questions, start talking your way through the description. As you note particular characteristics of the message, write them in any available space. You can use single words or phrases, whatever you prefer. When you finish, your page may look like Figure 4.1.

As you talk through the description multiple times, as we have suggested, and your page is full, you will then need to start organizing your findings in

FIGURE 4.1

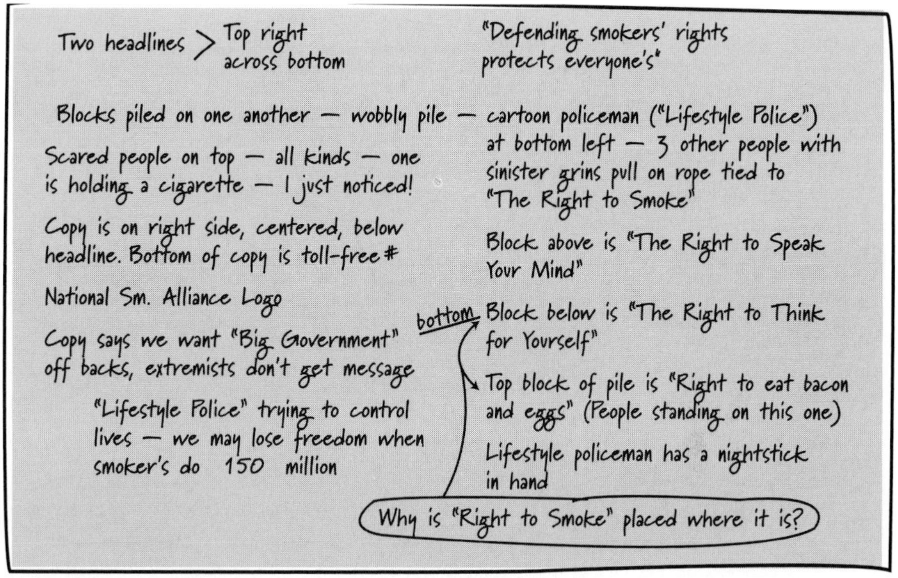

Two headlines > Top right across bottom

"Defending smokers' rights protects everyone's"

Blocks piled on one another — wobbly pile — cartoon policeman ("Lifestyle Police") at bottom left — 3 other people with sinister grins pull on rope tied to "The Right to Smoke"

Scared people on top — all kinds — one is holding a cigarette — I just noticed!

Copy is on right side, centered, below headline. Bottom of copy is toll-free #

Block above is "The Right to Speak Your Mind"

National Sm. Alliance Logo

bottom Block below is "The Right to Think for Yourself"

Copy says we want "Big Government" off backs, extremists don't get message

Top block of pile is "Right to eat bacon and eggs" (People standing on this one)

"Lifestyle Police" trying to control lives — we may lose freedom when smoker's do   150   million

Lifestyle policeman has a nightstick in hand

Why is "Right to Smoke" placed where it is?

some fashion. There is no single best way to do that, but some ideas include the following:

- Number or letter all the ideas that are related with the same number or letter.
- Connect similar or related ideas with lines.
- Color-code related ideas using a variety of highlighters.
- On a fresh page, recopy related concepts in groups creating concept maps.

We use concept maps in our work and find them particularly handy because they invite a user to change them at will. This is extremely important because we have found that students often get stuck in their critique when they try to put their ideas in writing too quickly. Students who write even a few pages have difficulty changing what they have written—their writing becomes a barrier to new ideas or approaches. Maps are also valuable because they provide a visual structure of ideas that is easily converted to a traditional outline, if necessary. Figure 4.2 is a sample map of the material in Figure 4.1.

The map is a visual representation of message elements we saw as we described the message. This method allows addition of ideas quickly; new connections between ideas or concepts not originally noted are quickly established simply by drawing lines between them. Keep your map handy as you move to description of the context of the message because, as you expand your field of vision to the context, you will most likely see new elements in the text you had previously overlooked.

FIGURE 4.2

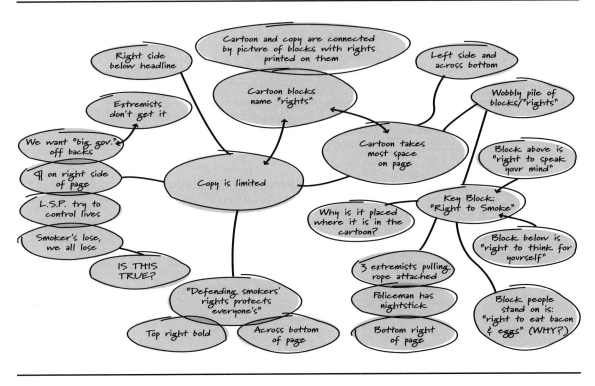

At this point, you should have a sense of the value in describing a message. However, the message itself is not all we must describe. Describing the context of the message is important as well.

APPROACHES TO DESCRIBING CONTEXT

No message exists without a context. Rhetoric is context bound because it is a response to some set of conditions that need a response (Bitzer 1968, 6). Any rhetorical message is what it is because of its context; it is a response to the context, which, as you learned in Chapter 2, may be an endless mass of rhetorical messages that influence one another (Vatz 1973, 159). So if you want to understand the nature of any message, you'll have to investigate its context.

As times have changed, much of the public discourse we encounter is in a form that *seems* discrete or without context. That is, we read speeches, pamphlets, or editorials that have a clear beginning, middle, and end; they seem complete in and of themselves. The same is true of television or radio programs. Even webpages, although hypertextually linked, give us a feeling that we leave one and go to another, each standing alone. In fact, since we can move from a webpage on a specific topic to a page on a completely different topic with a click of our mouse, the medium powerfully masks the importance and value of context for understanding the message. Unlike in earlier generations, today we don't often stand in a crowd that has gathered to hear a speaker, feeling the tensions and needs of the audience, or knowing the policies or concerns that are immediately important to the audience members. Because we often watch speeches on television in the isolation of our own homes, we don't get to talk to one another about why we've come; we don't get to hang around and help one another make sense of the speeches we've heard. If we could do that, we would certainly analyze them in relation to their context. However, many of the messages we examine today are taken out of context, or the context is not immediately apparent to us. As a result, we may forget how important context is to the message.

Imagine this scenario: You are a member of Senator Smith's public relations staff and you are assigned the task of writing the senator's upcoming speech on the problem of age discrimination. To prepare, you look at some historic speeches on discrimination in a variety of forms, starting with Frederick Douglass's speech, "What to the Slave is the Fourth of July?" You look at Carrie Chapman Catt's pamphlet, "Do You Know?" (1915) regarding women's suffrage, and finally you look at the 1908 Socialist Party presidential candidate Eugene Debs's speech "The Issue" regarding labor discrimination. Since these messages are greatly separated from you in time, and since you can only examine the discourse in print (so that Douglass's and Debs's speeches look more like essays), the tendency is to focus your critical attention only on the texts themselves. If, however, you do not learn about the context of the messages, your discoveries about the rhetors' approaches toward the topic of discrimination may be quite faulty. If you fail to examine the contexts but still borrow the old rhetorical strategies, you risk writing a speech that will turn off Senator Smith's contemporary audience.

Professional critic Michael McGee argued that, today, critics need to understand texts as *fragments* of a larger chain of messages (1990, 279). By understanding that larger chain of messages, critics will more accurately understand the rhetorical dynamics of any particular message (or fragment) of interest to them. For example, in 1999, The Partnership for a Drug-Free America, a private, nonprofit, nonpartisan coalition of professionals from the communications industry, began an advertising campaign featuring information for parents on how to talk with their children about drugs. The campaign was composed of television commercials, print ads, and a website. Any one of the messages may merit analysis; however, if any single message is treated as a fragment of the overall campaign, as well as a fragment from the larger body of discourse about illegal drug use, the message makers' choices in constructing any single message will make more sense and tell us more about how such persuasive communication works.

Contexts help to guide message consumers in giving meaning to a message. For example, if you are having an argument with your roommate who shouts, "Out! Out!" the context cues you to your roommate's meaning. You've had or observed similar events in the past and when you experience similar behaviors in the present, you use your memory, triggered by the message "Out! Out!" to attribute meaning to your roommate's ranting. That is, your past experience was connected to words, and use of the words now evokes the context. The context acts as a rule of interpretation of the message (Langer 1959, 121–24). Let's elaborate the example: If you are playing with a toddler in your living room and the toddler shouts, "Out! Out!" you probably will not immediately walk through the door, get in your car, and drive away. You draw upon the context as a guide to understand the toddler's exclamation. The context has limited your choices in attributing meaning as a message consumer. Conversely, contexts serve to limit the choices of a message maker in *creating* messages. For example, even at the level of conversation, your choices of language and delivery are limited depending on the context (Buttny 1985, 62). Most likely your conversation will be different in content, tone, volume, pace, and delivery depending on whether you are in a cathedral or at a rave. The same holds true when Senator Smith is addressing an audience composed of laborers at a union rally or an audience of academics at a policy conference regarding organized labor. In each case, the context will limit what the senator will talk about and how she'll talk about it.

So, **context** can be understood as *relevant and significant social conditions, needs, or symbols, which serve as guidelines for interpreting messages.* That is, the symbols comprising any messages you are describing trigger recollections of prior experience, which provide hints or guidelines for what meaning you should attribute to that message. We next list three general components of context that you should attend to in your description phase. For any given message, some of these categories might be more relevant or useful than others. Use any or all that may best help you understand the context and, thus, the content of the message.

SPECIFIC CIRCUMSTANCES

Often critics find it useful to understand the specific circumstances in which a message was created. In some cases those circumstances may be very specific: the date and time the message was delivered, as well as the medium by which it was delivered. Knowing, for example, the date Osama bin Laden released his speech to the United States after September 11, 2001, would help in understanding some of its content. A critic would be wise to find out about the American policy and response to bin Laden up to that point. The critic might need to do some background research to learn what, if any, military actions had been taken and what kind of statements U.S. public officials had made about bin Laden. Knowing the medium of delivery would also help the critic understand the message. Perhaps bin Laden's rhetorical strategies would have been different if the speech had been aired live only in the United States immediately following the attacks on the World Trade Center and Pentagon, rather than delivered via a prerecorded videotape nearly a month following the attacks. Knowing this should impact the critic's understanding of the content of the speech.

Sometimes understanding the specific circumstances means understanding the time, place, or venue of delivery of a message. Yet sometimes those immediate physical concerns are less important than the events, issues, and previous messages that gave rise to the one you are describing. A critic cannot understand a televised antismoking ad by the organization *Truth* unless one understands something of the legal and political battles that tobacco companies have fought over the past five years. The specific court cases are clues to understanding the content of the television ads. So, to be fair and precise, the critic needs to research a bit about those cases. The critic might be well informed by reading the court decisions and newspaper reports about the cases and economic conditions of tobacco companies. In sum, the critic cannot fully understand the rhetorical properties of a message that addresses social concerns if the critic knows nothing about those concerns and the events that gave rise to them.

In addition to understanding the immediate circumstances surrounding a rhetorical event, it may be necessary to understand the broader norms, values, beliefs, and expectations of the culture that might influence the way a message is constructed. The values of a group or an individual within a group affect the intended meanings of messages created by those folks, as well as the meanings they attribute to messages directed to them. To understand how the Beatles' music of the 1960s had such impact on popular Western youth culture, for example, one must know something about the changing norms, beliefs, and values of the 1960s among baby boomers. If you are not a member of that generation, you may need to do some reading to fully and fairly understand that culture. By contrast, one cannot understand the lyrics of contemporary rappers like Busta Rhymes, Foxy Brown, or Bone Thugs N Harmony without understanding contemporary black American culture. Failing to understand cultural norms, beliefs, and values is to take a message out of its context and risk making inaccurate inferences or judgments about the rhetorical choices evident in that message. Since we make important decisions based on our cultural patterns, critics are well advised to examine those patterns relevant to the messages they study.

SIMILAR CIRCUMSTANCES OR SIMILAR MESSAGES

Often messages and circumstances can be grouped together around some unifying themes, principles, or rules. For example, themes within discrimination discourse are similar from case to case. The concerns of nineteenth-century women's rights activists were in many ways similar to the concerns of abolitionists. Gay rights activists share similar concerns with black activists, civil liberties activists, and farm labor activists. Similar issues of infringement of rights, mistreatment, abuse, and discrimination concern these groups even though their particular points of concern may differ. Similarly, their rhetorical strategies are often similar. So it is useful for you as a critic not only to understand the events and issues surrounding the particular message you are describing, but also to understand parallel circumstances and/or messages. If you are trying to describe a Weight Watchers website, it would be useful to look at some similar websites like the Jenny Craig website. You may want to describe the patterns of circumstances that these messages share and see if the same or similar circumstances exist for the message you are studying.

Consider, too, that certain types of messages often follow unwritten rules. For example, to joke with your boss at work you must follow a different set of rules than if you joke with your boss on the golf course. If you are examining a single message, like a speech, or proposal, or legal brief, you might want to read similar messages to detect any unwritten rules of content, style, or structure. In a sense, you might also want to find the "norm" for how such messages are constructed. What, for example, is the norm for a legal brief? What is the norm for an inaugural address? What is the norm for a science fiction film? If you are studying an episode of the television show *The West Wing,* you should look at other episodes to be sure you understand the context of the characters and typical structure of the show. If you are studying an advertorial (a combination of an editorial and advertisement) from the *New York Times,* you should look at other advertorials on other topics to get a feel for how they are typically constructed. Or, if you are studying a late-night infomercial, you should look at others to understand the unwritten "rules" or norms of infomercials. In other words, as McGee tells us, part of the context of a message consists of similar messages that help establish expectations and norms for methods of communication (1990, 280).

RHETOR AND AUDIENCE

Another part of the context is the people sending and receiving the messages, so it is essential that you understand as much as you can about the rhetor or message maker(s) and the audience. First, in understanding the rhetor it may be useful to know something of the rhetor's background, reason for speaking, and ethos or credibility on the subject at hand. Knowing how much authority message makers have on the subject will help you understand their construction of the message. It may be important to know the message makers' political leanings or religious leanings. It may be important to know the degree to which the audience perceives the message makers as credible. For example, when studying websites, we often find that the rhetor is masked. The author of the website may not be made evident in the site itself. An "anonymous" rhetor has a different level of credibility than the president of the United States has when addressing the nation on television. Yet even the president may have limited credibility depending on the nation's perceptions of him. President Clinton, for example, had credibility problems after his affair with Monica Lewinsky. President George W. Bush had a credibility boost after 9/11. You as a critic need to know as much as you can about the message makers or rhetors to know how the audience is likely to view their messages.

You also need to understand as much as you can about the audience of a message. Sometimes the audience is plainly evident: a memo to the employees of Microsoft coming from Bill Gates; a commencement speech to the graduates of Stanford University; a speech by a lobbyist to a congressional committee. In each of these cases we can easily determine the sender and receivers of the message; we know to whom the messages are targeted, and we can find out what the attitudes of the audiences are on the topic and rhetor. In some cases, however, the audience may be less easily identifiable. For example, in the case of a message sent to a mass audience via the media, we may not know exactly who the actual audience or "receiver" is. We may not know precisely what the audience's attitudes are toward the subject matter, the rhetor, or the surrounding circumstances. We may not even know for certain to whom the message is actually targeted. In such cases we are required to make inferences based on as much evidence as we can gather. The message itself might give us clues as to who the target audience is. For example, in a late-night infomercial selling the latest exercise equipment, we might infer from the visual and verbal images that the ad targets people of some affluence who are young and single. Or if we are studying a billboard campaign persuading people to consume more dairy products, we might look for clues in the ads themselves about who is being targeted. We might also research the surrounding circumstances in the dairy industry to find out what kind of sales or public relations problems it has recently encountered that motivated this ad campaign. Knowing about the surrounding circumstances might tell us something about the audience's attitudes toward the dairy industry and about dairy consumption.

You also can describe the *relationship* between the rhetor and audience. Relationships involve *agreements* between people as to the definition of their roles. The agreement between a rhetor and the audience can be an important one. Most often the agreements are implicit, but occasionally agreements are formal. For example, in 1978 in a South American jungle compound, cult leader Reverend Jim Jones persuaded nearly nine hundred people to join him in a mass suicide by drinking poison. Knowing he was about to be arrested for murder and that his ministry was at its end, Jones convinced his followers to participate in what he called a "revolutionary suicide" (Ross 2001). The relatively explicit agreement between cult leader Jim Jones and his followers was essentially this: "If you accept what I say to you and act upon it, I will protect you against the uncertainties of life outside the cult." The relationship between the speaker and audience allowed Jones to speak ambiguously, or figuratively, or even falsely as long as he provided the protection promised. However, the relationship between a mainstream newspaper editor and the subscribers is quite different. The more implicit agreement between editor and readers is essentially: "I will provide the sort of relevant and timely information you need, presented as accurately and truthfully as possible, as long as you are willing to consume that information." An editor who permits the reporting of misinformation risks losing her position as editor.

Although difficult to do with any certainty, you may also want to pay attention to the states of mind of the rhetor and audience to help you to understand their relationship to one another. The state of mind of an audience when a message was sent or received may be an important clue in understanding the rhetor's behavior. For example, in the 1930s, what was the nation's state of mind when President Franklin Roosevelt began delivering his "fireside chats" to the nation? What was the effect of the nation's mood on what Roosevelt talked about or how he talked about it? Knowing the nation's state of mind would help you understand how the method of communication in FDR's addresses helped change the nation's self-perception. If we were studying the more recent speeches of President George W. Bush after 9/11 we would want to think about the nation's perception of itself following the terrorist attacks. How did President Bush think of himself after the attacks? By considering these issues of self-perception we can look more fairly and insightfully at President Bush's rhetorical choices in his postattack speeches. As you characterize the rhetor and audience's self-perceptions, you may want to ask yourself: What stated and unstated values are most important to each of the parties? If the values of the speaker and audience are substantially different, you may have a useful clue in understanding the constructions of the message you are studying. In describing these states of mind and values, a critic must be careful not to overgeneralize or project his or her own values into those of the audience, but such description may assist greatly in describing the relationship of rhetor and audience.

As you can see, context is a very complex idea. The three categories just presented are intended to assist you by providing a set of starting points for describing the context of a message, helping you know what you may want to explore. They are *not* intended to be a laundry list that you slavishly step through. You should probably consider all categories initially, but you will find that some are more relevant and helpful to your understanding of the message than others. Creatively focus your description on those most useful to your understanding of the message itself.

CONDUCTING RELEVANT RESEARCH

To complete this description of the context you will likely need to conduct some research to expand your understanding beyond your own knowledge or experience. Sources you might find in your research are likely to fall into one of two categories: scholarly and popular. Scholarly sources are books and journal articles (e.g., *Communication Quarterly, The Journal of American Medicine*) that are written by academic professionals and have gone through a process in which academic peers have reviewed the research/reports to determine their merit for publication. Scholarly sources offer original research and theory and their interests are not for profit. Popular sources (e.g., *Time, Newsweek, The New York Times, Mademoiselle*) are written by journalists or, in the case of the Internet, by anyone, and do not undergo the same sort of rigorous review process. Obviously, journalists must uphold higher standards than the random individual publishing his or her own work on the Internet, but many journalists write for magazines and newspapers with an interest in profit. In any case, it is important to know the credibility and type of source you are reading.

When researching the context of a message, you may find popular sources quite valuable. Some newspapers are important sources of both textual and contextual material. Large, well-respected newspapers such as the *New York Times,* the *Washington Post,* the *Los Angeles Times,* the *Wall Street Journal,* and the *Christian Science Monitor* often print transcripts of significant speeches.

These newspapers also do a good job of presenting the context surrounding significant speeches, and they publish indexes to their papers so you can retrieve specific speech transcripts and related stories. Check with your reference librarian for the newspaper indexes your library possesses. If your library does not have an index for one of the papers listed, ask for the *National Newspaper Index* (this also exists in an electronic form). This is a comprehensive index listing all articles in the preceding newspapers. If the message or speech you are examining was or is only regionally important, and probably was not covered by a national paper like those listed here, we suggest you consult the *Newsbank* index, a selective index to about 400 newspapers and over 180 business journals (Collins, Catlett, and Collins 1990, 95).

Many popular magazines such as *Time, Newsweek,* and *U.S. News and World Report* may help you understand the context of a message. A useful reference is the *Reader's Guide to Periodical Literature.* This resource indexes a wide range of popular magazines from 1900 to the present. When examining messages prior to 1900, we suggest you consult *Poole's Index to Periodical Literature, 1802–1906. Poole's* is a wide-ranging topical index like the *Reader's Guide.* While these kinds of sources may help clarify the context of a message, don't forget about books! Use your library's electronic card catalog to find books that might help you understand a message maker, circumstances surrounding a message, or cultural patterns of a particular group or time period.

Obviously, the World Wide Web offers a wealth of information that may help answer your questions about the context for a message. However, you need to be aware of the two-dimensional nature of the Web. The two dimensions are commonly referred to as the visible Web and the invisible Web. The **visible Web** *consists of billions of webpages and images produced by individuals and organizations of all sorts, and these pages are accessed through search engines such as Google, Yahoo!, Alta Vista, and numerous others.* The visible Web is not controlled in its content nor is it organized or indexed in any way. It is an information free-for-all of unprecedented size and dynamism. Material on the visible Web can range from significant, useful, and accurate to the mundane, obscene, and truly bizarre. Sorting through the material retrieved by a search engine to find reputable and appropriate material for a rigorous academic study requires you to systematically evaluate and sometimes research the site. (Doing research in order to do research can be frustrating and a waste of time.)

Uncritically using material from the visible Web is like answering a research question this way: driving around a large city and, at some random point, stopping to ask a person what he or she knows about your topic. If the person answers, you write the answer and then cite that as a legitimate source of information. You may have accidentally chosen a nationally known expert on the subject, or you may have picked a person willing to take a stab at an answer. The chances of the latter happening are astronomically greater than the former. In sum, the visible Web often can be a poor source of information. Better online sources exist in the invisible Web.

The **invisible Web** *contains information organized within professional and disciplinary databases that is typically reviewed and edited by content experts. Access to these databases is usually controlled by libraries that subscribe to these services.* Your university or college library no doubt has a portal by which you can access these sources of relevant and reviewed information. For example, two of the most widely used databases are InfoTrac: Expanded Academic and EbscoHost Academic Search. Searches from these databases provide you access to a wide range of journals from industry publications to academic journals to news-magazines. Since they index both scholarly and popular journals together, you need to keep your eye on the kind of material you are retrieving for your specific purposes.

Two other databases that may be especially valuable to you are LexisNexis Academic Universe and MarciveWeb DOCS. LexisNexis is a large database that "provides information to legal, corporate, government and academic markets, and publishes legal, tax and regulatory information" (LexisNexis). MarciveWeb DOCS is a catalog of U.S. government publications. This archive provides you with bibliographic information needed to find any particular document. Your librarian can help you determine the accessibility of documents you find in MarciveWeb DOCS.

Use the Web wisely. If you use the visible Web, invest significant time in assessing the quality of the sites you access. The invisible Web, while not infallible, generally will provide you with more reliable sources than you could find elsewhere. However, nothing beats going to the library. Our experience has been that often the best sources we've found were in the same volume of a journal or on a shelf next to the book for which we were searching. The context provided by the material on the library shelves often enriches your study in ways you could not have predicted. Although the Web is convenient, the library provides richness of material that you cannot get elsewhere.

TEXT-CONTEXT INTERACTION

Now, we need to complicate matters a bit since context not only helps us understand messages, but sometimes messages have an impact on how we understand the context. In fact, the contextual components of circumstances, similar messages, rhetor, and audience give rise to expectations among audiences or members about the way communication should occur. For example, if you know that the president is about to address the nation on television, you implicitly have expectations about the way he will speak, what he will wear, what subject(s) he will address, and so forth. And if you are surfing the Web and find a site for Grateful Dead fans, you implicitly have expectations about the layout of the site, its contents, and its style. The medium and the message maker in these two cases differ significantly and shape our expectations of rhetorical events. In essence, texts and contexts interact, as McGee noted, and we need to understand what some of those possible relationships may be in order to describe them (1990, 279).

It seems that texts can be related to contexts in at least four different ways:

1. The text can *conform* to the context.
2. The text can *not participate* in the context.
3. The text can *desecrate* the context.
4. The text can *reconstruct* the context (Branham and Pearce 1985, 28–30).

Let's look at each of these text/context relationships.

CONFORMITY

According to Branham and Pearce, "**conformity** *requires the adaptation of texts to the contexts in which they will operate*" (1985, 28, emphasis added). This is the typical way we talk about messages. In public speaking, for example, you were taught to examine the occasion of the speech and the audience to whom you were speaking in an effort to figure out the context of the speech so you could best adapt your message to that context. When Lloyd Bitzer developed the notion of the rhetorical situation, he essentially was arguing that any rhetorical situation (context) called for messages that were "fitting" or, in other words, conforming to the context (1968, 6). The conclusion that a message is "not a fitting response" is the same as saying that the message failed to conform to the context. Most messages that make sense to us in everyday life, those that we accept, value, and use, tend to conform to their relevant contexts. We expect our legislators to speak in ways that are understandable and predictable; the same goes for our pastors' sermons, our judges' opinions, our managers' memos, or our instructors' lectures. However, a problem with portraying the relationship between text and context by a simple dichotomy of conforming (which is implicitly a good thing in Bitzer's model) or not conforming (which is implicitly bad), is that the relationship of text to context is actually more complex than that. Although most of the time we appreciate messages that are fitting responses which conform to the context, sometimes messages are intended to do something other than respond to the context in an expected and direct fashion.

NON-PARTICIPATION

Another possible relationship between message and context may be one of **non-participation** where *the message is purposely constructed to not "live up to expectations."* This may seem like a strange idea at first. After all, if a message only makes sense within a relevant context, then when that relationship is not properly maintained by a rhetor, confusion seems to be the only outcome. Why would a message maker purposely make the message confusing, difficult to understand, or even incomprehensible? That is a good critical question.

Of course there are many reasons why message creators may "be unwilling to abandon their texts of choice or to place their texts within established contexts" (Branham and Pearce 1985, 28). However, the costs are often so high for making such a choice that something very substantial is at stake in the mind of the rhetor. For example, starting in the 1960s, the great Russian novelist

Alexander Solzhenitsyn refused to write in the state-sanctioned form of literature called "Soviet realism." (At that time, in the Soviet Union, the government controlled all mainstream publishing outlets and demanded that writers serve the propaganda needs of the state.) Rather, Solzhenitsyn wrote about his earlier experiences as a prisoner in Siberian concentration camps in the late 1940s, which exposed the inhumanity of the Soviet system. As a result, he was sent, again, to isolated prison camps in Siberia, "internally exiled" in far-flung parts of the Soviet empire now known as Uzbekistan, and finally deported from what was then the Soviet Union. Had Solzhenitsyn "participated" in the existing literary context, he would have become one more tool of the communist state in promoting its propaganda. He chose "non-participation" to avoid legitimating the authoritarian regime, even though it meant that his work was little known or understood by the general Russian population. Although we may judge his work as a "failure" in terms of success in bookselling, he had little choice to engage in "non-participation" unless he was willing to violate his deepest humanitarian values. Interestingly, once exiled to the West, he found himself deciding to "not participate" in the context of Western culture as well.

Solzhenitsyn was exiled to the United States in the early 1970s and settled in a small community in Connecticut where he continued his work writing about the injustices of the Soviet regime. In June 1978 he was invited to deliver the commencement address at Harvard University. Most people assumed that this would be a traditional epideictic speech praising the students for their hard work and sending them on their way to their careers. However, Solzhenitsyn, again, felt the need to "not participate" in the ceremonial context, and he delivered a scathing prophetlike sermon.[3] Rather than serve the purposes of the capitalist system, represented in his mind by Harvard, a system that he felt was as morally corrupt as the communist system, Solzhenitsyn chose to not participate in the expected benediction on students' completion of Harvard's curriculum that a commencement speech normally enacts. The context of a ceremony designed to validate the investment of the students and their parents in an education designed to support the values of Western capitalism proved to be one he could not accept. Although the "Harvard Address" was not appropriate as a response to the ceremonial context, the choice to not participate in the context afforded Solzhenitsyn a nationwide platform for his critique of Western culture in general, and American culture in particular, as the news media spread word of his address and commented on it for many days following. As it turns out, choosing non-participation may work for a rhetor by causing the audience to revisit its assumptions about the topic of the discourse, or causing it to rethink the arguments it has accepted for the status quo. The trick, for a rhetor, is constructing the message in such a way as to avoid being dismissed by the audience as incompetent.

DESECRATION

A third possible response, according to Branham and Pearce, is desecration of the context. *Desecration* of a context can be described as "the befouling of occasions for public oratory" (Branham and Pearce 1985, 29). *Befoul* is a strong term meaning "to cover with filth," which could be dirt or even animal waste.[4] When we say something was "desecrated," we mean that it was diminished, damaged, or disrespected. For example, spray-painting swastikas on headstones in a Jewish cemetery is an act of desecration—a symbolic befouling of that place. Desecration of a context is different from non-participation in a context. In the examples in the last section, Solzhenitsyn constructed powerful messages that were considered by many observers as extremely artful and rational rhetoric. He took the Soviet government and American culture seriously and attempted serious critiques using all his rhetorical skill. His discourse did not desecrate because it was an attempt to provide an alternative vision of those systems. However, **desecration** is *an attempt to disrupt communication and cause confusion by purposely violating the rules of rational discourse, particularly the rules of interpretation of texts via contexts; desecration is irrational, mocking, and provides no serious alternative vision.* To illustrate such desecration, Branham and Pearce point to the Dada movement in art in the early 1900s. For example, in 1917 Marcel Duchamp's exhibition of a sculpture entitled *Fountain* caused upheaval in the art world because *Fountain* was simply a urinal turned upside down! The notion of "ready-made" art, which was recycled junk, was a mockery of the existing art establishment, including avante-garde. According to Bruce Lincoln, "Such pieces were deliberate provocation, challenging numerous categories fundamental to modern Euro-American society . . . its pretensions of nonconformity notwithstanding" (Lincoln 1989, 145).

Later in the twentieth century, during the trial of the "Chicago Seven," the seven men who were on trial for inciting the riots at the Democratic National Convention in Chicago in 1968, the country was shocked by the defendants' behavior in court. The seven defendants were part of a group of radical activists calling themselves Yippies (YIP stood for Youth International Party and was itself a mockery of "hippy"). Even before the trial, their political activities were designed to desecrate the existing political context. For example, they ran a pig, Pigasus the Immortal, for president; they referred to the Democratic Party as the "National Death Party"; and they planned a mock convention in Chicago at the same time as the Democratic Convention. The convention invitation stated: "Join us in Chicago in August for an international festival of youth, music, and theater. Rise up and abandon the creeping meatball! Come all you rebels, youth spirits, rock minstrels, truth-seekers, peacock-freaks, poets, barricade-jumpers, dancers, lovers and artists!" It ended with the following admonition: "We demand the Politics of Ecstasy! We are the delicate spores of the new fierceness that will change America. We will create our own reality, we are Free America! And we will not accept the false theater of the Death Convention. We will be in Chicago. Begin preparations now! Chicago is yours! Do it!" (Linder 2002).

The trial of the Chicago Seven was a context that the defendants desecrated as well. In contrast to the seriousness of a courtroom, the defendants acted like jesters. Linder describes their behavior:

The defense and prosecution tables stood in dramatic contrast. At the defense table, defendants relaxed in blue jeans and sweatshirts, often with their feet up on chairs or the table itself. [Abbie] Hoffman and [Jerry] Rubin favored attire that included headbands, buttons, beads, and colorful shirts. The defendants passed trial hours munching jelly beans, cracking jokes, offering editorial comments, making faces, reading newspapers, and sleeping. The area around the defense table was littered with clothing, candy wrappers, and even (on one day) a package of marijuana. (Linder 2002)

Clearly, the intent of their behavior was to disrupt and mock the established legal system. The difference between desecration and non-participation lies in the irrational, often incoherent "discourse" of the defendants, which was intended to disrupt and degrade the existing context. There is no alternative articulated by the Yippies; rather, their discourse was an effort simply to fracture the status quo.

CONTEXTUAL RECONSTRUCTION

A fourth response to a context may be to reconstruct or redefine the context itself. **Contextual reconstruction** *occurs when a text violates the expectations but ultimately functions to redefine those expectations, making the violation acceptable to the audience.* Probably the greatest example of contextual reconstruction in our nation's history occurred in Lincoln's Gettysburg Address. In that address, Lincoln certainly violated the expectations of his audience in terms of delivery. His brief oration was much shorter than was traditional in such a ceremonial occasion. Senator Edward Everett's speech, which preceded Lincoln's, lasted about two hours, which was not uncommon in such contexts (Van Doren and Carmer 1946, 39). Everett worked mightily to accomplish the task of dedicating, consecrating, and hallowing the ground. That was, after all, the ostensible reason for the ceremony and the recognized or assumed context of the discourse. Lincoln, however, realized that such an effort was futile. Look at how Lincoln reconstructed the context through his text. After his brief introduction and short history of the republic, Lincoln said:

But in a larger sense, we cannot dedicate—we cannot consecrate—we cannot hallow—this ground. The brave men, living and dead, who struggled here, have consecrated it, far above our poor power to add or detract. The world will little note, nor long remember what we have to say here, but it can never forget what they did here. It is for us, the living, rather, to be dedicated here to the unfinished work which they who fought here have thus far so nobly advanced. It is rather for us to be here dedicated to the great task remaining for us. *(Van Doren and Carmer 1946, 41–42)*

Notice how explicitly Lincoln addresses the context, "this ground," which was the battlefield, and the associated symbols of ceremony: flags, a podium populated by veterans of Gettysburg (themselves standing for their comrades), dignitaries, and a waiting audience. Each element of the context provided cues to those present as to how to interpret the experience. We emphasized the place where Lincoln reconstructs the context, literally turning the situation inside out, essentially reversing the rules of interpretation of the parts of the context itself. Through his choice of focus of attention and his words, Lincoln makes the audience the recipient of blessing and the attendant responsibilities of blessing, and he retires the audience's perceived role as dispenser of authentication or validation of soldiers' courage. Imagine yourself in that place at that time; imagine the effect on you when you fully absorb the profound insight and power of Lincoln's short address. His ability to completely change the reality of his audience in a moment, using only words, must have seemed like the conjuring of a magician, leaving the observer only to wonder how the deed was done!

A more recent rhetorical effort at contextual reconstruction can be found in Martin Luther King Jr.'s "I Have a Dream" speech. King's effort was substantially different from Lincoln's due to the nature of the exigence each confronted. According to Branham and Pearce, "Styles of contextual reconstruction vary in accordance with the breadth of context assaulted and the possibility of meaningful discourse within the revised context. Motives range from the purification or subversion of particular images to fundamental challenges to the intellectual or social orders in which such images function" (1985, 30). That means different situations allow for different sorts of approaches for using messages to change how people understand the context in which they exist. For example, the job can range from something as limited as changing the image of a corporation to something as sweeping as changing the social relations of groups within a society. If you are familiar with King's address, you know that King's intent was to subvert particular images of race relations existing in America at that time. His speech was primarily a challenge to the social order and his "dream" served to provide a new context for our racial discourse. His vision provided a new set of interpretive rules (a reconstructed context) that featured collaboration rather than competition between races. He asked his audience to project themselves into a different future that he was describing and asked listeners to re-view their experience through a new context. King's speech, as Lincoln's, using a kind of "word magic," was able to help audiences more effectively give meaning to their own experiences (Branham and Pearce 1985, 30).

APPLICATIONS OF TEXT-CONTEXT INTERACTIONS

Now, how can you, as a critic, make use of the text/context relationships presented in the preceding section? Knowing potential relationships between text and context, you now have some vocabulary to describe them more precisely. Such description serves to reconnect text and context, which helps to frame the text/fragment in a way that avoids the mistakes of treating a text in isolation. Think how often answers to communication questions begin with, "It depends." If you ask, for example, how one should use nonverbal communication effectively, the answer must be connected to the context—"It depends" (on context).

You will also find these ideas useful as analytical tools. Try using the preceding ideas informally and see how they work in everyday conversation. For example, think of yourself as a manager in an office or factory where you ask one of your subordinates why he missed the last three days of work. That person's behavior exists in some context, and, in order to make sense of the story you are given, you may ask: Is this story an effort to conform to or affirm the context? ("I understand that my absences cause problems for everyone on the project. I'm sorry about the trouble and will try not to miss anymore.") Is the story an effort to "not participate" in or avoid attending to the situation? ("I didn't realize missing was a problem. Say, did you see the Oscars the other night . . . ?") Is the story designed to desecrate the context? ("Where I am and where I go is my business. You have no right bugging me about where I've been—you don't own me!") Is the subordinate's response an attempt to re-create the situation? ("I know missing is not good for the group. However, I had a larger concern on my mind because I was counseling my little brother to get him away from a cult. His life was literally at stake and I had to consider the relative importance of the demands upon me—I chose to save my brother's life.") The seemingly innocuous context of missing a few days of work is not an uncommon "exigence" or situation needing an explanation. The preceding responses are true to life—you could find yourself dealing with something like each of them. Examining the interaction between the text and context can help you figure out the most appropriate response on your part.

More significant analyses of the text-context interaction are made all the time. Judges have to examine defendants' explanations in light of their relationships to the context of the law; negotiators have to assess their opponents' cases in light of how those cases or "stories" stack up against the context as understood within the parameters of a contract; staffers for politicians or government bureaucrats have to assess their bosses' messages to the public to ensure that those messages most effectively respond to the context. As you confront a variety of significant messages in your life, ask yourself what relationship exists between message and context. We think it will give you a new and useful perspective on messages. This simple model is one you can easily carry around in your head and use as a starting place for making sense of messages.

SUMMARY

Good critics must monitor their thinking and consciously focus their attention toward significant messages. At this point, description is part of the exploratory process of message analysis as it helps you to transform initial reactions into thoughtful critiques, by consciously slowing down and taking a long, hard look at a message and its context. One significant effect of describing a message and its context is that it helps you move into the "balcony," thus sharpening your perspective on the message. As you attempt to see and then articulate the essential characteristics of a message, your relationship to the message evolves from reactor to critic.

Describing a message is enhanced by having a plan that serves to control thinking and better ensure that you will look at the message completely. If you construct your plan with the intent of causing yourself to think in new ways about a message, you will have a more distanced perspective, and you will see more than you would without such a guide. What you see in the descriptive phase lays the groundwork for analysis, interpretation, and evaluation. As you practice the skills of description, pay close attention to how your perceptual skills develop; note what you begin to see that you would not have seen without controlling your thinking.

EXERCISES

1. Review the description of the National Smokers Alliance ad modeled in Chapter 3. Highlight in one color the description of the text; use a different color to highlight the description of the context.

2. Review the Arnold Schwarzenegger website, *Join Arnold,* at the end of Chapter 2. Create *two* plans for exploring the message, using the two strategies we suggested: planned survey and list of questions. Apply both plans and describe the webpage. What differences are there in what you see in the message when using each plan?

3. Experiment with different means of taking notes as you describe the *Join Arnold* webpage. Which do you like the best? Why?

NOTES

1 You probably can see that inherent in precise description is a kind of analysis. As we explained in Chapter 3, description and analysis *are* related and you will often find that some preliminary analysis happens as you work on description. That's good, and you should be prepared to note ideas and message characteristics that merit further investigation when you intentionally begin the analysis of the message. However, it is important that you don't lose control when describing the message and give in to the temptation to skip the important step of description. You can control your thinking and facilitate your success by creating a plan for description.

2 For further instruction on how to use graphic organizers as thinking tools, consult the following sources: Tony Buzan, *The Mind Map Book: How to Use Radiant Thinking to Maximize Your Brain's Untapped Potential* (New York: Plume, 1996); Joyce Wycoff, *Mindmapping: Your Personal Guide to Exploring Creativity and Problem-Solving* (Berkeley: Berkeley Publishing, 1991); and Gabriele Lusser Rico, *Writing the Natural Way: Using Right-Brain Techniques to Release Your Expressive Powers* (Los Angeles: Tarcher, 1983).

3 Scholars refer to this type of speech as a "jeremiad," a kind of sermon that condemns the congregation's or audience's moral conduct. In this speech, Solzhenitsyn played a role like that of Jeremiah, the Old Testament prophet, prophesying the demise of Western civilization due to its weakness of character brought about by too much freedom and prosperity, and too little responsibility and hardship. For a detailed analysis, see Mark Stoda, "Jeremiad at Harvard: Solzhenitsyn and 'The World Split Apart.'" *Western Journal of Communication* 64 (2000): 28–53.

4 *The Oxford English Dictionary,* 2nd ed. (Oxford: Oxford University Press, 1992), *s.v.* "Befouled."

WORKS CITED

Bitzer, Lloyd F. "The Rhetorical Situation." *Philosophy and Rhetoric* 1 (1968): 1–14.

Branham, Robert, and Barnett W. Pearce. "Between Text and Context: Toward a Rhetoric of Contextual Reconstruction." *Quarterly Journal of Speech* 71 (1985): 19–36.

Buttny, Richard. "Accounts as Reconstruction of an Event's Context." *Communication Monographs* 52 (1985): 57–77.

Buzan, Tony, and Barry Buzan (Contributor). *The Mind Map Book: How to Use Radiant Thinking to Maximize Your Brain's Untapped Potential.* New York: Plume, 1996.

Collins, Donald E., Dianne B. Catlett, and Bobbie L. Collins. *Libraries and Research: A Practical Approach.* 2nd ed. Dubuque: Kendall/Hunt, 1990.

Langer, Susanne K. *Philosophy in a New Key: A Study in the Symbolism of Reason, Rite, and Art.* New York: Mentor, 1959.

LexisNexis, "Company Information." http://www.lexisnexis.com/about (accessed March 29, 2004).

Lincoln, Bruce. *Discourse and the Construction of Society: Comparative Studies of Myth, Ritual, and Classification.* New York: Oxford University Press, 1989.

Linder, Douglas O. "The Chicago Seven Conspiracy Trial." *Famous Trials.* August 16, 2002. http://www.law.umkc.edu/faculty/projects/ftrials/Chicago7/Account.html.

McGee, Michael. "Text, Context and the Fragmentation of Contemporary Culture." *Western Journal of Speech Communication* 54 (1990): 274–89.

Rico, Gabriele Lusser. *Writing the Natural Way: Using Right-Brain Techniques to Release Your Expressive Powers.* Los Angeles: Tarcher, 1983.

Ross, Rick. "The Jonestown Massacre." *Cult and Education Recovery.* February 2001. http://www.culteducation.com/jonestown.html (accessed September 5, 2003).

Scudder, Samuel H. "How Agassiz Taught Professor Scudder." In *Louis Agassiz as a Teacher: Illustrative Extracts on His Method of Instruction,* compiled and edited by Lane Cooper, 55–61. Ithaca, NY: Comstock, 1917.

Stoda, Mark. "Jeremiad at Harvard: Solzhenitsyn and 'The World Split Apart.'" *Western Journal of Communication* 64 (2000): 28–53.

Van Doren, Carl, and Carl Carmer. *American Scriptures.* New York: Boni and Baer, 1946.

Vatz, Richard E. "The Myth of the Rhetorical Situation." *Philosophy and Rhetoric* 6 (1973): 154–61.

Wycoff, Joyce. *Mindmapping: Your Personal Guide to Exploring Creativity and Problem-Solving.* Berkeley: Berkeley Publishing, 1991.

THE PROCESS
OF ANALYSIS

5

If you injured your foot, you would go to a physician, and you likely would begin your office visit by describing your symptoms to the doctor. You might say, "My foot is black and blue; it hurts internally when I put any pressure on the sole. I can hardly walk." The doctor might ask you questions that prompt you to describe the context for your injury. "When did it begin hurting?" "Do you recall any event that triggered the pain?" To those questions you answer, "Yes, yesterday I ran a marathon." All of this description of your injury is necessary information for the doctor, but this information alone is not a sufficient analysis of your condition. You have not yet learned what really is going on with your foot just by describing it. Furthermore, your description is based on your untrained observations, and though it may be thorough (including a description of the context), it isn't all that systematic. As a matter of a fact, your description probably could be given by most anyone. But you would expect a physician to be able to say more about your condition. Indeed, that is why you sought the physician's help and expertise.

What you expect from the doctor is, first, an analysis of your condition. Later, from that analysis the doctor will draw inferences (interpretations) about what the analysis means in terms of the healing process, the future of your running career, and proper treatment. Without the doctor's analysis and interpretation, you do not learn anything new about your condition. So, too, in critiquing a message it is necessary for the critic to move beyond description. As we saw in Chapter 4, description is necessary for a critic to move from "reacting" to a message to "critiquing" a message, but stopping with description is insufficient: description initiates the process of criticism, but it does not provide any way to conduct a fully systematic critique.

To teach an audience something new and useful about a message, you need a second type of thinking, which we call "analysis." In the context of message criticism, **analysis** *refers to the process of systematically discovering, identifying, and articulating the various parts of the message and the relationship of those parts to one another.* Critics must use their knowledge of rhetoric to examine the components of any message and to see how one component relates to (impacts and is affected by) the next. Let's return to the doctor's examination of your foot. You expect the doctor to surpass your rough, naïve, and uninformed description of your foot. Indeed, you expect your doctor to use knowledge of anatomy and podiatry to consider all the components of your foot and how they relate to one another before making a diagnosis of your problem. Whereas you can only say, "My foot is black and blue, and it hurts," the doctor can say, "You have damaged and swollen tissues in your foot. A tear in your plantar fascia causes this inflammation. All the running you did yesterday probably caused your fascia lining to tear away from the muscles in your foot." Notice two things the physician did with your description: he or she (1) named precisely the relevant parts of your foot (plantar fascia, muscles, tissue) and (2) noted patterns in the way the parts of the foot relate to one another and to your activities (damaged and swollen tissues are caused by a tear, caused by your running). Although your description was a necessary starting point, the analysis was necessary for moving you toward helpful, healthy healing. So too, analysis of messages is necessary if the critic is to move others toward thoughtful consumption of messages.

In this chapter we help you learn how to do analysis by showing you two parts to this thinking process: (1) naming the parts of a message and (2) looking for rhetorical patterns within and among messages. We recommend that after you read this chapter, you read some of the chapters that explain rhetorical theory and vocabulary that will aid you in the analysis process.

NAMING THE PARTS OF THE MESSAGE

How does a critic know what "elements" to look for in a rhetorical message and how to name them? The critic, like a physician, must draw upon existing research and theory that is relevant to the problem at hand. To examine your foot, the doctor relies on knowledge of anatomy, chemistry, and more. The doctor chooses which pieces of knowledge to draw upon, which, in turn, determines the point of view from which the doctor will offer a diagnosis. For example, one physician might rely on a chiropractic point of view, in which case the focus is on the relationship between the foot and the rest of the body's skeletal system. Another doctor specializing in exercise physiology, however, might focus on the muscles, tendons, and ligaments within the foot that are only directly related to the injury. Each doctor's analysis, consequently, will look somewhat different, and certainly the interpretations each doctor derives from his or her analysis will differ, as will the recommended treatments.

USING SEARCH MODELS

Likewise, critics rely on expert knowledge of rhetoric to conduct their analyses. Often, this knowledge comes from rhetorical theories that give the critic knowledge and vocabulary to use in examining messages. Recall that in Chapter 3 we defined *search models* as organized sets of related concepts that provide a critic with a ready-made set of topics to examine or questions to ask about a message. Search models are derived from theories about rhetorical communication that identify different rhetorical properties or components of messages (e.g., visual style, type of argument, language style, or parts of a story). Each search model causes you to take a particular **point of view** when analyzing a message, leading you to *focus on particular rhetorical properties and not others*. So, different search models will enable you to see different rhetorical properties in a given message, somewhat like sunglasses with different colored lenses. A pair with blue lenses might bring out the blue in everything you see, whereas a pair with yellow lenses would bring out the yellow tints in everything you see. Some search models lead you to focus more deeply on the evidence and reasoning in a message, whereas other search models might lead you to focus on the metaphors in a message. Some search models lead you to see the message as a drama, whereas other search models cause you to focus on how the message portrays gender. You will find that the more points of view you can take with a message, the more you are able to see beyond what the average person can see, thus making you more of an expert.

Part III of this book explains nine different search models that you might use to get started in your analysis. Most of those models fall within one of three broad schools of thought about rhetoric: *classical approaches,* which focus on persuasive appeals and argumentation; *dramatic approaches,* which focus on the storylike qualities of messages; and *sociopolitical approaches,* which focus on the way messages critique and create social power relationships. We've also included a chapter on visual communication, which gives you some vocabulary for analyzing visual images while drawing from any of the other three theoretical schools of thought. You will need to study these different types of approaches to give yourself a sufficient working vocabulary to help you see and name the rhetorical properties of any message. The more comfortable you become with a variety of different approaches, the more useful your criticism will be. Just as the doctor reads about medical knowledge to learn anatomy and relationships between various body parts, so too the critic must read rhetorical theory to learn about rhetorical strategies, devices, and components. In fact, you likely have some initial knowledge to work from, knowledge gained in public speaking courses, persuasion courses, literature courses, or other relevant studies and experiences.

Sometimes new critics are bothered by the technical jargon derived from rhetorical theories. Words you will encounter like *hegemony, warrant,* or *pentad* are sometimes difficult to understand. You yourself might ask why the "technical" language that comes from theory is necessary for conducting analysis. For us, technical language is important because it adds precision to the analysis. Experts in any field use technical jargon because it allows them to speak precisely and efficiently to one another. Just think of how many words would be required to refer to "plantar fascia" if you were a podiatrist. While the layperson would need the technical vocabulary to be translated, the expert knows that the technical vocabulary is what enables him or her to see what the layperson cannot and is what permits the expert (in this case a doctor) to be extremely precise in research and treatment. Would we want anything less from our doctor? The more you understand rhetorical theory, the more you will use its vocabulary because that vocabulary articulates what you see in messages more precisely than your everyday language.

USING GENERAL KNOWLEDGE

In addition to using existing rhetorical knowledge, critics may also rely on their knowledge from other fields of study or seemingly unrelated contexts that help the critic see and name certain elements in the message. For example, in the 1970s, Professor Wil A. Linkugel and his student B. L. Ware studied speeches in which famous politicians attempted to restore their credibility to the public (Ware and Linkugel 1973, 279). They drew from Robert Abelson's theory in the field of psychology, which outlines four different strategies individuals typically use when defending themselves to one another after some sort of personal attack on their character: (1) *denial* (claiming innocence); (2) *differentiation* (making distinctions between what one did and other circumstances in order to justify the behavior); (3) *bolstering* (associating oneself with people, ideas, or things that are appealing to others); and (4) *transcendence* (admitting guilt but suggesting that the reason for the behavior was justified by a more important cause) (275). Ware and Linkugel took what they knew from this psychological theory and applied it to rhetorical messages to name precisely the rhetorical devices they saw in speeches of self-defense by politicians such as President Richard Nixon.

Ware and Linkugel used critical thinking to systematically analyze their particular messages, but at the same time, by drawing on their knowledge of a seemingly distant or unrelated field, they used the kinds of creative thinking skills you read about in Chapter 3. So you see, the process of analysis is critical and systematic, but also creative. We encourage you to draw from not only what you read in this text but also what you have learned in other contexts, whether from different communication courses, courses in other disciplines, or contexts seemingly unrelated to communication.

RECORDING YOUR THINKING

Finally, we encourage you to take careful notes during the process of naming the parts of a message. Although an expert, experienced physician may be able to make an insightful diagnosis without taking a single note about what was observed, a new doctor just learning to diagnose patients will likely take copious notes while conducting the examination. She might write her observations, or she might note them aloud on a tape recorder. So too, in the process of analysis, novice critics carefully note their observations, either in writing or by recording them on tape.

A model of analysis in action follows this paragraph. First, you will read the speech President Clinton delivered to the annual National Prayer Breakfast on September 11, 1998, the morning after attorney Kenneth Starr's report of the Lewinsky affair was released to the public. Then you will read some brief notes indicating our description of the message. Next you will read (in the left-hand column) our notes from the beginning of an analysis of the speech in which we name the various elements we see. In the right-hand column you will read our comments on how we generated these ideas. Read each part carefully to get a sense of how the process of doing analysis works.

For Immediate Release   *September 11, 1998*

REMARKS BY THE PRESIDENT
AT RELIGIOUS LEADERS BREAKFAST

The East Room[1]

9:40 A.M. EDT

THE PRESIDENT: *Thank you very much, ladies and gentlemen. Welcome to the White House and to this day to which Hillary and the Vice President and I look forward so much every year.*

This is always an important day for our country, for the reasons that the Vice President said. It is an unusual and, I think, unusually important day today. I may not be quite as easy with my words today as I have been in years past, and I was up rather late last night thinking about and praying about what I ought to say today. And rather unusual for me, I actually tried to write it down. So if you will forgive me, I will do my best to say what it is I want to say to you—and I may have to take my glasses out to read my own writing.

First, I want to say to all of you that, as you might imagine, I have been on quite a journey these last few weeks to get to the end of this, to the rock bottom truth of where I am and where we all are. I agree with those who have said that in my first statement after I testified I was not contrite enough. I don't think there is a fancy way to say that I have sinned.

It is important to me that everybody who has been hurt know that the sorrow I feel is genuine: first and most important, my family; also my friends, my staff, my Cabinet, Monica Lewinsky and her family, and the American people. I have asked all for their forgiveness.

But I believe that to be forgiven, more than sorrow is required—at least two more things. First, genuine repentance—a determination to change and to repair breaches of my own making. I have repented. Second, what my bible calls a "broken spirit"; an understanding that I must have God's help to be the person that I want to be; a willingness to give the very forgiveness I seek; a renunciation of the pride and the anger which cloud judgment, lead people to excuse and compare and to blame and complain.

Now, what does all this mean for me and for us? First, I will instruct my lawyers to mount a vigorous defense, using all available appropriate arguments. But legal language must not obscure the fact that I have done wrong. Second, I will continue on the path of repentance, seeking pastoral support and that of other caring people so that they can hold me accountable for my own commitment.

Third, I will intensify my efforts to lead our country and the world toward peace and freedom, prosperity and harmony, in the hope that with a broken spirit and a still strong heart I can be used for greater good, for we have many blessings and many challenges and so much work to do.

In this, I ask for your prayers and for your help in healing our nation. And though I cannot move beyond or forget this—indeed, I must always keep it as a caution light in my life—it is very important that our nation move forward.

I am very grateful for the many, many people—clergy and ordinary citizens alike—who have written me with wise counsel. I am profoundly grateful for the support of so many Americans who somehow through it all seem to still know that I care about them a great deal, that I care about their problems and their dreams. I am grateful for those who have stood by me and who say that in this case and many others, the bounds of presidency have been excessively and unwisely invaded. That may be. Nevertheless, in this case, it may be a blessing, because I still sinned. And if my repentance is genuine and sustained, and if I can maintain both a broken spirit and a strong heart, then good can come of this for our country as well as for me and my family. (Applause.)

The children of this country can learn in a profound way that integrity is important and selfishness is wrong, but God can change us and make us strong at the broken places. I want to embody those lessons for the children of this country—for that little boy in Florida who came up to me and said that he wanted to grow up and be President and to be just like me. I want the parents of all the children in America to be able to say that to their children.

A couple of days ago when I was in Florida a Jewish friend of mine gave me this liturgy book called, "Gates of Repentance." And there was this incredible passage from the Yom Kippur liturgy. I would like to read it to you: "Now is the time for turning. The leaves are beginning to turn from green to red to orange. The birds are beginning to turn and are heading once more toward the south. The animals are beginning to turn to storing their food for the winter. For leaves, birds and animals, turning comes instinctively. But for us, turning does not come so easily. It takes an act of will for us to make a turn. It means breaking old habits. It means admitting that we have been wrong, and this is never easy. It means losing face. It means starting all over again. And this is always painful. It means saying I am sorry. It means recognizing that we have the ability to change. These things are terribly hard to do.

"But unless we turn, we will be trapped forever in yesterday's ways. Lord help us to turn, from callousness to sensitivity, from hostility to love, from pettiness to purpose, from envy to contentment, from carelessness to discipline, from fear to faith. Turn us around, O Lord, and bring us back toward you. Revive our lives as at the beginning, and turn us toward each other, Lord, for in isolation there is no life."

I thank my friend for that. I thank you for being here. I ask you to share my prayer that God will search me and know my heart, try me and know my anxious thoughts, see if there is any hurtfulness in me, and lead me toward the life everlasting. I ask that God give me a clean heart, let me walk by faith and not sight.

I ask once again to be able to love my neighbor—all my neighbors—as myself, to be an instrument of God's peace; to let the words of my mouth and the meditations of my heart and, in the end, the work of my hands, be pleasing. This is what I wanted to say to you today.

Thank you. God bless you. (Applause.)

DESCRIPTION NOTES	COMMENTARY ON DESCRIPTIVE PROCESS
Description of Context ■ Place of speech—Annual National Prayer Breakfast ■ Audience—Clergy (find out who) and the nation, since it was known that the speech would be broadcast, reproduced on the Internet, etc. ■ As noted in Chapter 1, in President Clinton's August 17 speech to the nation on the Lewinsky issue, he asked for people to forget more than he asked them to forgive. Yet the press, Democrats, and others continued to insist after the August speech that he needed to ask for forgiveness. ■ President Clinton's "rhetorical bind" seems to be that if he plans to stay in office he must confess and seek forgiveness, but he must also maintain a "presidential persona" of strength. **Description of President's Text** ■ Speech focuses largely on forgiveness and repentance this time—contrast to previous speech in which he blamed others for invading his private life and defended his attempt to keep the affair silent. This speech was hardly defensive at all—much more humble, even "sheepish." ■ Contains efforts to show President Clinton's humility and sincerity (by explaining that he was up late working on this speech himself, that he struggled to know what to say, and that he may have to use his eyeglasses to read his handwriting). ■ He explicitly asks for forgiveness (unlike previous speech) and makes religious references about repentance and forgiveness (paragraph 3).	We read several articles in the <u>Sacramento Bee</u>, which reported this ongoing request that the president more explicitly ask for forgiveness. We're keeping copies of the articles so we can reference them when we're ready to write a final report (Pine 1998). We're reminded of some research on inaugurals that tells us that in inaugural addresses, presidents must show a certain humility (by asking for the help of a higher power) and at the same time show their personal strength of character to lead the country, as commander in chief among other things (Campbell and Jamieson 1986, 213–14). Our descriptive process involved outlining the primary "tasks" of the speech to get a sense of what President Clinton's main ideas were and how he ordered them. The outlining process brought to our attention several strategies President Clinton used and it led us to compare this speech to his first speech, as well as to a speech of self-defense by Reverend Jimmy Swaggart (Church of God leader) in 1988 after he was caught in the act of adultery.

DESCRIPTION NOTES (cont.)	COMMENTARY ON DESCRIPTIVE PROCESS (cont.)
<ul><li>He establishes his own criteria for receiving forgiveness (paragraph 5): genuine repentance and a "broken spirit" and shows how he is meeting those criteria. Criteria come from President Clinton, not from some other source (like the Bible, the Koran, etc., even though he makes references to those religions). This is curious—he establishes his own criteria and applies them himself? Interesting strategy—something to keep in mind.</li><li>Speech has a strong religious tone to it—makes sense given his audience.</li><li>Draws from the external authority of the Jewish tradition, reading a passage from the Yom Kippur liturgy in the *Gates of Repentance*.</li></ul>**Description of Swaggart's Speech**<ul><li>The Swaggart speech was very emotional. He cried throughout. He began with expressions of appreciation to members of the media who broke the story about his behavior.</li><li>Swaggart begged forgiveness from (in this order) his wife, family, Assemblies of God church and Bible college, professional associates, fellow televangelists, general public and followers, and to God.</li><li>Swaggart claimed God's forgiveness and assured the audience that the ministry of his church and college will continue.</li></ul>	

ANALYSIS NOTES	COMMENTARY ABOUT ANALYSIS PROCESS
■ First Strategy: Kenneth Burke writes that there are two ways to restore order in situations like President Clinton's: (1) through scapegoating—which is blaming someone or something else for an error, and (2) through mortification—which is self-blame (1962, 406). President Clinton primarily used mortification in this speech: e.g., his self-blame is apparent in his requests for forgiveness; he establishes two criteria that are about self-blame (he, not Lewinsky, Starr, or his opponents, must have genuine repentance and a broken spirit, he says).	After outlining the speech, we began thinking about what strategies we saw. We thought that Kenneth Burke's theory of guilt and redemption in rhetoric would be an appropriate way to look at and name some of the strategies, but we also looked back at the first President Clinton speech and noted some differences in President Clinton's self-defense strategies. This led us to look, also, at the apologia theory we mentioned in Chapter 2 as a way to name some of the president's strategies.
■ President Clinton also uses scapegoating (though as a rhetorical device, it is less developed than his use of mortification) when he says, "the bounds of presidency have been excessively and unwisely invaded."	
■ Second Strategy: Ware and Linkugel note that another common strategy in apologias (speeches of self-defense) is "transcendence." Ware and Linkugel say, "transcendental strategies . . . psychologically move the audience away from the particulars of the charge at hand in a direction toward some more abstract, general view of [a speaker's] character" (Ware and Linkugel 1973, 280).	Three strategies stuck out to us more than anything else did: the use of mortification more than victimage; the use of transcendence; and the use of identification.
■ President Clinton uses transcendence when he says, "And if my repentance is genuine and sustained, and if I can maintain both a broken spirit and a strong heart, then good can come of this for our country as well as for me and my family." (Applause.) "The children of this country can learn in a profound way that integrity is important and selfishness is wrong, but God can change us and make us strong at the broken places."	Notice that at this point we are merely naming the strategies. We haven't yet looked at their relationship to one another, nor have we considered real patterns of usage of these strategies.

ANALYSIS NOTES (cont.)	COMMENTARY ABOUT ANALYSIS PROCESS (cont.)
Good can come and children can learn from his failures. He focuses on a more "abstract, general view of his character" by featuring his humility, his willingness to learn from his mistakes, his having a "broken spirit." ■ Third Strategy: what Burke calls "identification" (1969, 19–27), i.e., making himself out to be like his audience in at least two ways: 1. Showing his humanity in the introduction ("I stayed up late struggling with this speech," "I need my glasses to read it to you" and saying he may not be easy with his words). 2. Identifying with both Christian and Jewish belief systems. Referring to repentance (an Old Testament concept), which requires good works to receive forgiveness, rather than grace (a New Testament concept), which requires faith to receive forgiveness.	

In the foregoing analysis, we applied our knowledge of Burke's theory of guilt and identification and our knowledge of Ware and Linkugel's theory of apologia. How did we know to use those theories? This is a tough question to answer because this was a *creative* move in the analytic process. There are no rules telling critics which theories are appropriate for which messages. Instead, critics must look for clues in the text they are analyzing—clues that inspire creative thinking about which search models to use, not clues that lead to absolute answers. For example, a text that is full of logical evidence and reasoning might be appropriately analyzed from a classical approach, but a text that has lots of storylike qualities might be better analyzed with a dramatistic or narrative approach. A text that bothers the critic because of its unexpected sexism or racism might inspire the critic to use one of the sociopolitical approaches. These cues become evident in the descriptive phase, which is why that first step is so important. Critics must decide what search model or models seem to make sense with a particular message, asking themselves which theories will reveal the most about how that message is working. Critics may even try out different theories to determine which would help them see the most; they may then decide that a creative combination of search models would be most useful. Actually, in our case we considered using an argument-oriented theory like Stephen Toulmin's (see Chapter 10), but it was not a good fit because President Clinton does not make assertions that he must back up with factual evidence. Such an approach might be more fitting for an analysis of Kenneth Starr's report than it would be for Clinton's second apology. Like physicians, we as critics consider different theoretical lenses that might help us more clearly understand the message we're studying. Two critics might choose two different lenses and have equally interesting, though different, insights about the message. Nothing is wrong with that if both insights are useful in teaching others to become more critical consumers of messages.

Let's look now at what critics do with analysis in addition to naming what they see.

LOOKING FOR RHETORICAL PATTERNS

In order for your physician to determine anything meaningful from the things observed in your foot, the physician may ask questions about patterns of pain or symptoms. For example, the physician may ask if you have run other marathons and, if so, whether you had similar symptoms. She may ask about how you run to determine patterns of pressure placed on the foot. She may think back to other runners she has had as patients and ask herself whether she notices similar symptoms. She may also look at how the symptoms in your case are unique. She might find, for example, that most runners experience the type of pain you describe, but none have the bruising you have. This deviation from the pattern may be an important clue in helping her diagnose your problem.

Similarly, in addition to naming the relevant elements of a message, critics look for **rhetorical patterns** within those rhetorical elements. In other words, critics look for *patterns of rhetorical devices used within messages: repetition of particular devices; patterns in the sequencing of particular devices; patterns of omitting particular devices or pieces of information.* A tailor cannot simply be given a pile of "parts" for a jacket (i.e., the sleeves, buttons, lapel, bodice, and lining). The tailor must also be given a pattern to make sense of those parts. The pattern shows how the parts are connected to one another and reveals recurring themes in parts (e.g., stitching style). So too, a critic cannot simply compile a list of rhetorical elements. To make sense of those elements, the critic must observe patterns in the way the parts are connected to one another. Some suggestions follow for ways you might look for patterns.

PATTERNS OF REPETITION

In looking for rhetorical patterns a critic might ask, what sorts of rhetorical devices are used repeatedly in a message or among messages? What sorts of strategies, wording, symbols, evidence, or reasoning techniques are used repeatedly in or among messages? Here a critic is looking for patterns of similarity either within a single message or among two or more messages. One critic, Stephen Perry, raised this question when he studied the speeches of

Adolf Hitler. He began to notice a pattern of repetition in Hitler's use of certain metaphors to refer to Jews. Perry's analysis revealed that Hitler repeatedly used words like *cancer, incurable tumors, inner decay,* and *deadly cancerous ulcers* rather than *people, race,* or *nation* to refer to the Jewish population (1983, 233). Seeing this pattern helped Perry explain how Hitler was so subtly powerful in shaping Aryan German attitudes toward Jews.

PATTERNS OF SEQUENCING

A critic might also look for a pattern in the placement, ordering, or sequence of certain devices in a message. What you hear first and last in a speech, what your eye sees first in a picture, or the order of events that you read in a story can affect the way you respond emotionally or intellectually to a message. So critics need to examine the patterns by which rhetorical properties are arranged in a message. In studying eulogies, for example, critic Kathleen Hall Jamieson observed patterns in the content of eulogies and in the sequencing of that content. She discovered that, first, the eulogist must acknowledge the death; second, the eulogist must help transform the mourners' relationship with the deceased from present to past tense; third, the eulogist must console the mourners by arguing that the deceased lives on; and finally the eulogist must help the mourners find a way to reknit their community (Jamieson 1978, 40–41). The ordering of these rhetorical tasks is important because it coincides with the typical order by which mourners work through the grieving process.

PATTERNS OF OMISSION

Additionally, a critic might look for patterns in what has been omitted from a message. Sometimes a recurring missing element from a message can reveal something important to the critic. The fact that President Clinton did not explicitly say he was sorry for his affair with Monica Lewinsky was a problem for many in his audience. The omission of character witnesses in the defense of someone convicted of murder might pose concern for critically thinking jurors. The elimination of any mention of women and African Americans in old American history books was an important discovery among critical readers of history in the latter half of the twentieth century. Sometimes a rhetor's omission of information is intentional and strategic. For example, a rhetor speaking against gun control may choose not to mention a counterargument that favors gun control if that rhetor is confident his or her audience is unlikely to accept the competing point of view. A good message analyst notices what is *not* in a message as well as what *is* in a message.

ANOMALIES TO PATTERNS

A critic might look for anomalies in a message: things that break the pattern or diverge from the expectations of pattern. The unexpected rhetorical device, argument, image, or phrase may be just the thing that makes a message powerful. For example, most memorials and monuments in Washington, D.C., fit a common pattern: they are white and elevated; they valorize their subjects and Americans generally; they evoke feelings of patriotism; observers are made to feel small in the presence of the larger-than-life statues. An insightful analysis of the Vietnam Memorial requires the critic to consider how this memorial differs from those around it: it is black, it is lowered into the ground rather than elevated; it evokes strong feelings of various sorts from visitors and "it provokes engagement; it is not easily consumed or immediately intelligible. Its rhetoric does not sanction a touristic, consumptive response; it invites an engaged and thoughtful reading" (Blair, Jeppeson, and Pucci 1991, 278).

A critic also might notice a deviation from a pattern within a single message. For example, in Appendix 1 you will find a sample essay about the Beatles' hit song "She's Leaving Home." When preparing that sample, Mark discovered that one of the final lines of the song, "Fun is the one thing money can't buy," defies the audience's expectation to hear "*Love* is the one thing money can't buy" (emphasis added). This deviation from the expectation, Mark argues, is how the authors mock traditional values about human relationships. Mark's observation of the subtle deviation from expectation was significant in his ability to hear beyond what the average listener would hear in that song. Observing a shift or change in a pattern may be an important discovery for a critic.

PATTERNS OF RELATIONSHIPS

Finally, a critic may also look for how the rhetorical elements of a message connect with one another. Recently Mark took his car into the shop for some work. He first described the problem to the mechanic. The mechanic then proceeded to conduct his analysis, using his knowledge of automobiles to identify and name the various "parts" underneath the hood of Mark's car. Mark would have been rather disappointed, however, if the mechanic came to him with just a list of all the elements present in Mark's car. Had the mechanic simply named the parts, Mark would not have learned anything about how his car worked. Moreover, the mechanic would not have been able to make an inference about what was wrong with the car and how it might be fixed. Instead, Mark needed his mechanic to analyze how the various parts of his car were working (or not working) together. That is to say, it is one thing for Mark to know that his car has a broken shock absorber and worn ball joints and tie rod ends, but it is another thing for him to know that those parts *are causing* severe vibration that ultimately *will lead to* failure of the steering mechanism. Notice the language shift in this last sentence. Phrases like "are causing" and "will lead to" indicate some sort of relationship or connection between the parts being named. This relationship constitutes an important pattern.

Similarly, in the brief analysis of President Clinton's and the Reverend Jimmy Swaggart's speeches presented in Chapter 2, we noticed a pattern in the relationship between the specific, target audiences and the tone selected by each speaker. We also noted the relationship between the type of audience for each speech and the type of evidence the audiences demanded of their speakers. We concluded, for example, that one part of Swaggart's speech, his tone, was well suited to his audience. Swaggart faced a multifaceted audience with varying needs: his wife and family, his immediate congregation, the Assemblies of God denomination, the Bible College and its leaders, other televangelists, and members of the media. The most important audiences he needed forgiveness from were his wife, family, and church. Members of the Assemblies of God denomination are accustomed to charismatic, highly emotive preaching. The spiritual experience is often one filled with tears, hand-raising displays of ecstatic emotions and music. So, though he may have risked losing credibility among news reporters and the general public because of his emotional tone, he was more likely to gain credibility in the eyes of those he most needed to persuade. Had Swaggart adopted a tone like President Clinton's he would have sounded fraudulent and unconvincing to his primary target audience. In sum, then, we see a relationship between the tone of the address and the audience, two important elements of this rhetorical event. Only in seeing this relationship are we able to learn something significant about Swaggart and his perception of his audience.

The critic, then, gains insight into how a message works not only by naming the various parts that may be present in a message, but also by studying patterns among those parts. This process also requires both critical and creative thinking: critical insofar as the critic pulls apart and questions the message, and creative insofar as the critic attempts to look at the message in new ways, putting the parts together in a manner that reveals relationships not apparent to the naked eye.

SAMPLE ANALYSIS

Next refer to our continued analysis of President Clinton's apologia at the White House prayer breakfast on pages 83–85. In the left-hand column you will see our notes about patterns we observe in the rhetorical elements of the speech. In the right-hand column you will see commentary about our thinking in this part of the process.

Notice that our analysis is becoming more interesting and useful as we move from merely "naming the rhetorical elements" to seeing how elements relate to one another and then seeing patterns in the usage of those elements. We saw our patterns only after we began comparing the message with other messages (President Clinton's first speech and the Swaggart speech). This is not always necessary as a way to see patterns, but in our case it was one possible creative move that helped us get insight into how this presidential speech functions. Just as there is no formula or recipe for seeing the relationships between parts, there is no formula for seeing patterns. However, the questions to keep in mind include: What patterns of repetition do I see? What patterns of sequencing or ordering do I see? What patterns of deviation do I see? What patterns of omission do I see? What elements seem connected to one another? You may not always find interesting patterns in every message. Just as every message is different, every analysis is different. Critics must be prepared for adventures into the unknown as they begin cracking open a rhetorical text.

ANALYSIS NOTES	COMMENTARY ABOUT ANALYSIS PROCESS
■ *Pattern of deviation and frequency of use/repetition:* President Clinton switches strategies from his August 17 apology to this apology. In the first apology, he relied on scapegoating more than mortification. He spent the second half of the first speech blaming his opponents for invading his privacy inappropriately, etc. He spent little time (*pattern of omission*) in the first speech blaming himself. The proportions of those two strategies in this speech are quite different. He features mortification far more than scapegoating in the second apology. ■ President Clinton also switches from the strategy of *differentiation* in the first speech to the strategy of *transcendence* in the second. Ware and Linkugel define "differentiation" as a division of the issue at hand into two or more "constructions of reality" to change an audience's meanings. The strategy places "whatever it is about [the President, in this case] into a new perspective" (Ware and Linkugel 1973, 278). In the first speech, the president divided the issue into his "wrongdoing" and the inappropriate invasion of privacy by his accusers. In the second speech he focuses on the transcendent characteristics of "learning from mistakes" and "good coming from evil," so to speak. ■ *Pattern of omission:* We also notice something President Clinton omits in order to achieve identification. He refers to his need for "repentance," an Old Testament concept (the OT being appropriate for both Christian and Jewish religious leaders) rather than the New Testament emphasis on "grace" (i.e., the reliance on faith rather than good works for forgiveness). He also quoted from the Jewish text. Reverend Swaggart, by contrast, featured the fact that by grace (through Christ's death) he is forgiven	Notice that in this particular case we found it useful to compare the message to another message. Only in the comparison did we really notice any significant patterns. That, however, isn't always the case with all messages. Notice that to accomplish this part of the analysis we had to rely on our knowledge not of rhetorical theory but of the Bible, which is a relevant source of knowledge for this particular speech. We also found it useful to look at Swaggart's apology as a point of contrast to understand what Clinton was doing.

ANALYSIS NOTES (cont.)	COMMENTARY ABOUT ANALYSIS PROCESS (cont.)
and saved, which required the audience to do the same (*pattern of similarity and difference between President Clinton and Reverend Swaggart*). ■ *Pattern of sequencing:* (We noticed that Clinton starts by establishing common ground, preparing his clergy audience to forgive him.) Identification (1)—Makes Clinton human and forgivable ↓ Mortification—Self-identified criteria for forgiveness ↓ Scapegoating—Minimal but present *after* Mortification ↓ Transcendence—Comes *after* confession ↓ Identification (2)—Connects with both major religious traditions in U.S. (Gates of Repentance) ↙ ↘ Transcendence and Identification—From being human to being God's instrument Relationships between devices: Note that identification strategies are placed at beginning and end of speech (primacy-recency effect?). Also, the mortification strategy comes right before the scapegoating strategy, so President Clinton accepts blame before placing it, which is consistent with Christian theology. In the New Testament there is a statement from Christ that one must not judge another unless one	We decided that the relationship between these four strategies of identification, mortification, scapegoating, and transcendence would best be represented visually because it was the *order* in which Clinton used the strategies that was most interesting. His choice to arrange the strategies as he did seemed particularly interesting. These relationships became apparent once we outlined the order in which the rhetorical devices appeared in the speech. We noticed how mortification is related to the use of scapegoating, because of the way they are ordered. So too, the "blame" is sandwiched between the identification.

ANALYSIS NOTES (cont.)	COMMENTARY ABOUT ANALYSIS PROCESS (cont.)
has judged oneself first by the same measure. "And why do you look at the speck in your brother's eye, but do not consider the plank in your own eye? . . . First remove the plank from your own eye, and then you will see clearly to remove the speck out of your brother's eye" (Matthew 7:3–5). Only after he sought to remove the "plank" from his own eye (confessing his sexual indiscretion) did he accuse others of their sin (invading his privacy). Then, we noticed how *quickly* the president moved from scapegoating to transcendence, trying to get past the sin ASAP. We noticed the president ended with both identification (making connections, being "like" his religious audience), but moving from being human (as in the introduction) to being godly, "God's instrument." So, blame is sandwiched between efforts at identification. It's much easier to forgive another whom we see as like ourselves. Why didn't President Clinton use the same strategy as Swaggart? Maybe because his audience was made up of both Jewish and Christian religious leaders and because the two dominant religious traditions in the U.S. are Judaism and Christianity. Taking this route prevents him from alienating anyone in his audience and helps build identification.	The process of analysis is quickly leading us to ask questions that are moving us toward the act of interpretation. Notice here our urge to explain why Clinton made the choices we're observing. The statements directly to the left border on interpretation.

DERIVING QUESTIONS FROM THE ANALYSIS

The analytical process of naming parts, looking at their relation to one another, and discovering rhetorical patterns in a message typically raises questions in the critics' minds that ultimately lead to interpretation. Once you notice patterns, you will begin to ask why those patterns exist, what purpose they may serve, whether or not those patterns were appropriate, what consequences those patterns might have, and more. If a pattern is disrupted, you might ask, Why? To what end? With what consequence? If you notice that a rhetor chose to arrange the rhetorical devices in a particular way, you might ask what difference that choice might have made or what other possible choices might have been made. The answers to these questions are typically uncertain, which means that these questions lead the critic to make inferences or tentative conclusions, which we call interpretations. We say more about interpretations in Chapter 6, but for now it is important for you to understand that the process of analysis, done properly and thoroughly, opens the door for you to begin the most interesting and worthwhile part of the critical process.

In the case of the president's speech, our analysis automatically led us to raise interpretive questions. Recall that we asked why President Clinton did not use the same strategies Swaggart used. Now that we have a good start on the analysis, we might also ask whether a secular nation is likely to consider the president's apology convincing, given that it relies on religious dogma and imagery. We might ask whether the president's choice to rely on mortification allows him to sustain a presidential persona of strength. We might ask whether the president's effort to identify with the broader Judeo-Christian community gives him as much rhetorical power as Swaggart's strategy of boldly claiming God's grace and forgiveness. Although we cannot be absolutely certain about the answers to these questions, we know that these questions move us beyond analysis into the third type of critical thinking, interpretation, which we take up in the next chapter.

SUMMARY

In Chapter 2 you learned that a critical response differs from a glandular response in two ways: critics study messages systematically, and they teach others how to respond to messages more critically. The ability to see more than the average person sees and to see patterns comes from the systematic approach a critic takes, which begins with analysis. The act of analyzing a rhetorical message requires careful use of rhetorical theory and procedures as well as knowledge from other disciplines that can help you observe what the untrained eye would likely miss. That knowledge and those procedures will help you (1) name precisely the rhetorical properties of a message, (2) identify patterns in the use of those properties, and (3) ask yourself questions about those patterns. This step in the process prevents the critic from making unsubstantiated assertions about a message and from jumping to conclusions prematurely. Ultimately, then, when the critic does draw a conclusion or make a judgment, the critic has a strong foundation upon which to stand.

EXERCISES

1. Read the speech President George W. Bush delivered the night of September 11, 2001, after the terrorist attacks (we've reprinted it at the end of the exercises). Make a plan for describing the speech and context and then complete the plan. Use the two-column chart to record notes from your description (on the left) and thoughts, concerns, or questions you have about the process of describing (on the right).

DESCRIPTION PLAN AND NOTES	PERSONAL COMMENTS ABOUT DESCRIPTION

2. Now read Chapter 9 on the classical approach to analysis. Use that approach to analyze the speech. Again, use the two columns to record your observations from analysis (on the left) and your personal comments, concerns, or questions about the process of analysis (on the right).

ANALYSIS NOTES	PERSONAL COMMENTS ABOUT ANALYSIS
Rhetorical Properties of the Speech	

ANALYSIS NOTES (cont.)	PERSONAL COMMENTS ABOUT ANALYSIS (cont.)
Patterns in the Rhetorical Properties	

3. Write a paragraph explaining how the classical approach affected your analysis and your observation of the speech.

4. List questions you have about the rhetorical properties and patterns you observed in your description and analysis.

8:30 P.M. EDT

THE PRESIDENT: Good evening. Today, our fellow citizens, our way of life, our very freedom came under attack in a series of deliberate and deadly terrorist acts. The victims were in airplanes, or in their offices; secretaries, businessmen and women, military and federal workers; moms and dads, friends and neighbors. Thousands of lives were suddenly ended by evil, despicable acts of terror.

The pictures of airplanes flying into buildings, fires burning, huge structures collapsing, have filled us with disbelief, terrible sadness, and a quiet, unyielding anger. These acts of mass murder were intended to frighten our nation into chaos and retreat. But they have failed; our country is strong.

A great people has been moved to defend a great nation. Terrorist attacks can shake the foundations of our biggest buildings, but they cannot touch the foundation of America. These acts shattered steel, but they cannot dent the steel of American resolve.

America was targeted for attack because we're the brightest beacon for freedom and opportunity in the world. And no one will keep that light from shining.

Today, our nation saw evil, the very worst of human nature. And we responded with the best of America—with the daring of our rescue workers, with the caring for strangers and neighbors who came to give blood and help in any way they could.

Immediately following the first attack, I implemented our government's emergency response plans. Our military is powerful, and it's prepared. Our emergency teams are working in New York City and Washington, D.C. to help with local rescue efforts.

Our first priority is to get help to those who have been injured, and to take every precaution to protect our citizens at home and around the world from further attacks.

The functions of our government continue without interruption. Federal agencies in Washington which had to be evacuated today are reopening for essential personnel tonight, and will be open for business tomorrow. Our financial institutions remain strong, and the American economy will be open for business, as well.

The search is underway for those who are behind these evil acts. I've directed the full resources of our intelligence and law enforcement communities to find those responsible and to bring them to justice. We will make no distinction between the terrorists who committed these acts and those who harbor them.

I appreciate so very much the members of Congress who have joined me in strongly condemning these attacks. And on behalf of the American people, I thank the many world leaders who have called to offer their condolences and assistance.

America and our friends and allies join with all those who want peace and security in the world, and we stand together to win the war against terrorism. Tonight, I ask for your prayers for all those who grieve, for the children whose worlds have been shattered, for all whose sense of safety and security has been threatened. And I pray they will be comforted by a power greater than any of us, spoken through the ages in Psalm 23: "Even though I walk through the valley of the shadow of death, I fear no evil, for You are with me."

This is a day when all Americans from every walk of life unite in our resolve for justice and peace. America has stood down enemies before, and we will do so this time. None of us will ever forget this day. Yet, we go forward to defend freedom and all that is good and just in our world.

Thank you. Good night, and God bless America.

END 8:35 P.M. EDT

NOTES

1 This is the first speech delivered by the president after Kenneth Starr's investigation report into the Lewinsky affair was released to the public.

WORKS CITED

Blair, Carole, Marsha S. Jeppeson, and Enrico Pucci Jr. "Public Memorializing in Postmodernity: The Vietnam Veterans Memorial as Prototype." *Quarterly Journal of Speech* 77 (1991): 263–88.

Burke, Kenneth. *A Grammar of Motives.* Berkeley: University of California Press, 1962.

———. *A Rhetoric of Motives.* Berkeley: University of California Press, 1969.

Bush, George W. Address to the Nation. September, 11, 2001. http://www.whitehouse. gov/news/releases/2001/09/20010911-16.html (accessed September 15, 2003).

Campbell, Karlyn Kohrs, and Kathleen Hall Jamieson. "Inaugurating the Presidency." In *Form, Genre, and the Study of Political Discourse,* edited by Herbert W. Simons and Aram A. Aghazarian, 203–225. Columbia: University of South Carolina Press, 1986.

Clinton, William G. Address to the Religious Leaders' Annual Prayer Breakfast. September 11, 1998. http://www.whitehouse.gov/WH/New?html?19980911-3640.html (accessed September 13, 1998).

Jamieson, Kathleen H. *Critical Anthology of Public Speeches. Modules in Speech Communication.* Chicago: Science Research Associates, 1978.

Matthew 7:2–5. *The Holy Bible.* The New King James Version. New York: Thomas Nelson Publishers, 1983.

Perry, Steven. "Rhetorical Functions of the Infestation Metaphor in Hitler's Rhetoric." *Central States Speech Journal* 34 (1983): 229–35.

Pine, Art. "Clinton Hints at Apology in Speech." *The Sacramento Bee,* 29 August 1998, A1+.

Ware, B. L., and Wil A. Linkugel. "They Spoke in Defense of Themselves: On the General Criticism of Apologia." *Quarterly Journal of Speech* 59 (1973): 273–83.

THE PROCESS
OF INTERPRETATION

6

Vocabulary
➤ interpretation
➤ inferences
➤ evaluation

You read in Chapter 5 that analysis is the process of systematically uncovering what rhetorical elements are in a message and how those elements work together. But if we stop at analysis, we're left with the question, so what? So what does it matter that President Clinton used the rhetorical devices of mortification, transcendence, and identification in his speech, and that he used the mortification strategy proportionately more than scapegoating? Who cares? Although we may learn something interesting by naming the devices, showing how they relate to one another, and identifying patterns among those devices, the analytical process is merely an intellectual exercise unless we can reach some useful conclusion from that analysis.

Let's say, by way of comparison, that the doctor who examines your sore foot says, "You have damaged and swollen tissues in your foot. This inflammation is caused by a tear in your plantar fascia. All the running you did yesterday probably caused your fascia to tear away from the muscles in your foot." Your response, of course, is, "So what does that mean?" You want to know both what the doctor means in laypersons' terms and what the diagnosis means for your life: your running habits, your potential to run future marathons, the healing process you will need to initiate. You want to know what the doctor's *conclusion* is about the analysis of your foot. If you had only the doctor's analysis but no conclusion, you would be left saying, "So what?" You need the interpretation. In fact, the interpretation is what you were looking for by going to the doctor in the first place.

So what is meant by interpretation in the critical process? Interpretation is the necessary step of drawing conclusions about the rhetorical patterns you discover in the analysis so that something significant is learned from the analysis. **Interpretation** is *the process of deciding what it means that the rhetor used the particular devices you discovered in the analysis phase.* Interpretation is *not* simply saying what the message itself means; any reasonable person can probably figure out what the message itself means. Rather, the critic interprets what it means that the rhetor made particular rhetorical choices. Interpretations are what individual critics "construe" based on the evidence they observe in the analysis. Thus, interpretations are **inferences**, *reasonable conclusions based on evidence from one's analysis of how a message is constructed.* Interpretations are not, however, absolute truths or fully certain conclusions. Whereas statements of analysis are more or less factual and can be proven with

FIGURE 6.1

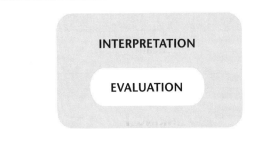

sufficient evidence from the message being studied, statements of interpretation are arguable. Two critics may look at the same analysis and reach different interpretations of what it means that the rhetor chose particular rhetorical strategies. Consequently, both critics must make a convincing case for their conclusions.

You will notice in Figure 6.1 that evaluation is a subcategory of interpretation, specifically **evaluation** is *an interpretation that makes a judgment about the discoveries from the analysis.* Although we say more about evaluation in Chapter 7, we want you to be aware of the fact that some of your interpretations may have an evaluative component to them. That is acceptable since evaluation is a particular type of interpretation, one with a judgment of quality, but we urge you to be conscious of whether you are making an evaluative move or a more neutral interpretive move. Figure 6.1 demonstrates the fact that although all evaluative conclusions about a message are inherently interpretive, not all interpretive conclusions are necessarily evaluative. For the moment, let's look more specifically at the characteristics of interpretation and some examples.

CHARACTERISTICS OF INTERPRETATION

Interpretation may be characterized at least three ways.

CREATIVE THINKING PROCESS

First, interpretation is a creative thinking process. Recall the discussion in Chapter 3 about the two ways critics attack critical problems: critically and creatively. The process of interpretation relies heavily on the creative act. No formula exists for determining what it means that a rhetor chose particular rhetorical strategies. No "right answer" exists that you should be looking for. The doctor examining your foot relies on years of medical study and training, technical knowledge, and prescribed methods of analysis to look at your condition, but if the analysis presents inconclusive results, the doctor must us creative thinking to consider possible explanations for what is going on and what treatment might be best. The doctor must consider many possibilities and determine which is most soundly arguable. There may be no one "right" answer. The absence of a single right answer is more likely the case in criticism because we are dealing with symbols rather than empirical reality. So, critics, perhaps more than doctors, must use their creativity in drawing conclusions about their observations from analysis.

SUBJECTIVE THINKING PROCESS

Second, not only is the interpretive process creative, it is also somewhat subjective and allows the critic's own voice to be heard. This does not mean, however, that the critic suddenly sides with or opposes the ideas in a message. Instead, a critic reasons carefully in order to draw conclusions about the observations from the analysis. This means that two critics may reach different conclusions about what they observe in their analyses, even though they are looking at the same data. For example, several years ago critic Bonnie Dow wrote a critique of the television series *Murphy Brown,* popular in the 1980s. The show was about a female star reporter, Murphy Brown, who worked for a television newsmagazine. Murphy was a strong, confident, intelligent woman and yet a comedic character who was often laughed at because she was so rough around the edges. Dow used a dramatistic search model and a feminist search model (see Chapters 13 and 15) to analyze particular episodes of the show, explaining that Murphy herself was a scapegoat (always the one blamed) who was often humiliated, embarrassed, and ridiculed by her colleagues; her aggressive competitiveness was portrayed as inappropriate and undesirable (Dow 1992, 149). After analyzing how the drama portrays Murphy Brown as a woman, Dow draws the following interpretive conclusions:

> *For those who search for emancipatory images of women on television, Murphy Brown is exemplary. . . . Her struggles make her sympathetic to an audience that empathizes with the contradictions that she faces.*
>
> *However, for an audience uncomfortable with the challenge that feminism presents . . . Murphy's function as a comedic character, whose extreme personality traits are often the source of humor, provides the [comic] relief necessary to keep her [feminist] character appealing. The fact that Murphy "suffers" for her success makes it easier to accept her rejection of traditional womanhood.*
>
> *. . . As a feminist critic, however, I find it difficult to celebrate Murphy Brown's qualified feminist vision. . . . Murphy Brown illustrates a variation on television's general rhetorical strategy of coopting feminist content to serve patriarchal interests. (1992, 152)*

In this interpretation, Dow makes the arguable claim that viewers might have different responses to Murphy depending on their attitudes toward feminism, and that by making Murphy a "comedic scapegoat" the show may appeal both to feminists and to those uncomfortable with feminism. At the same time, we hear Dow's own voice as she argues that while the show may be pleasing to some feminists, for other feminists like herself, its strategies appear to perpetuate patriarchal interests. In a sense, Dow (1992) offers three possible interpretations of the strategies she sees in *Murphy Brown*, one from her own personal perspective ("I find it difficult to celebrate Murphy Brown's qualified feminist vision" [153]), and two potential perspectives of others ("For those who search for emancipatory images of women on television, Murphy Brown is exemplary" and "for an audience uncomfortable with the challenge that feminism presents . . . Murphy's function . . . keeps her character appealing" [152]). All three interpretations are "arguable," which Dow acknowledges by offering all three possibilities. Yet she is willing to make clear her own conclusion.

MAKING INFERENCES

Third, interpreting any message requires us to make inferences—to extend our knowledge beyond what we can observe. For example, astronomers developed a great deal of knowledge about the structure of our solar system, our galaxy, other solar systems, and galaxies outside of ours by drawing inferences based on the evidence (patterns and relationships among celestial elements) they observed in their scientific analyses. The distant planets of Neptune and Pluto were known to exist well before they were ever seen by astronomers. Observations of light passing through the solar system as well as wobbles in planets' orbits suggested that something was making those events happen. The evidence was used to make an inference, to extend knowledge beyond just what could be seen, allowing astronomers to say, "We have strong reason to believe that there is a planet beyond Jupiter," or "We know there is a planet or similarly large body beyond Jupiter. It is probably a planet because the evidence suggests a mass much larger than any asteroid or comet, and a regular orbit around our sun." Astronomers make inferences about phenomena they don't directly observe by drawing upon evidence they have collected from their analyses. Those arguments may be more or less plausible and compelling to other astronomers. Message analysts work in a similar fashion when they make inferences about the audiences of a message, about the potential impact of a message on an audience, or about the ideology being reinforced by the particular strategies of a message. These conclusions must be based on the critic's observations from the analysis, but they are likely to be arguable conclusions that are more or less conclusive, more or less convincing, more or less believable, depending on the strength of the critic's evidence.

In Dow's interpretation of *Murphy Brown*, she makes claims about that which is *not* observable, based on her analysis of that which *is* observable. That is, watching many episodes of the show allowed Dow to observe the scapegoating strategies in *Murphy Brown*, yet her conclusions about how audiences might perceive the feminist nature of *Murphy Brown* were unobservable. She did not have empirical proof that people do or will interpret the show in one of the three ways she has named. Rather, those conclusions were based on careful reasoning from the analysis of the rhetorical devices in the show itself.

HOW DOES A CRITIC DEVELOP AN INTERPRETATION?

At this point you may be asking, how do I know what to interpret and how do I decide what conclusions to draw about my observations from the analysis? Think about what a homicide detective does in trying to draw conclusions about who the murderer was in a particular case. A detective studies the evidence and plays with it—looks for patterns, imagines what might have happened, imagines missing pieces of evidence, looks for what's most plausible, looks for the interesting, curious, important, absent patterns or discoveries from her analysis. The detective pursues answers to things she found most puzzling, unexpected, or curious in her analysis. If the detective cannot know *for certain* who the murderer was, she puts together the pieces from her analysis and draws the most plausible conclusion.

ASKING QUESTIONS FROM ANALYSIS

As we mentioned at the end of Chapter 5, your analysis results in the development of some questions about your message. The analysis should pose for you something that is interesting about the construction of the message, something that leads you to ask, for example, "Why did the rhetor construct the message that way?" "Why might that device have been used and what might be its impact?" These questions should be the starting place for your interpretation. For example, in the analysis of President Clinton's address in Chapter 5, we were left with several questions about the president's rhetorical choices: Is a secular nation likely to consider the president's apology convincing, given that it relies on religious dogma and imagery? Was the president's rhetorical strategy sufficient to ward off potential impeachment? What does President Clinton's shift in rhetorical strategy say about him or his audience? Does the president's choice to rely on mortification allow him to sustain a presidential persona of strength? Will his effort to identify with the broader Judeo-Christian community give him as much rhetorical power as Swaggart's strategy of boldly claiming God's grace and forgiveness?

In the process of interpretation you must begin asking questions about what you see in your analysis. Notice that the questions raised in the preceding paragraph vary widely. Some ask about the potential impact of President Clinton's rhetorical choices; some ask about what the rhetorical choices indicate about the president himself; some ask about the various audiences for the president's speech and how his rhetorical choices might be received by those audiences. In other words, a critic might ask a variety of different questions before determining which line of questioning will produce the most insight. Next we have listed a few lines of thinking you might use to help prompt your interpretation. Remember, though, that because interpretation is a creative process, there is no recipe of questions to be asked. This list is not exhaustive and may not contain the kind of question that will initiate your interpretation. You may generate different questions about the rhetorical strategies identified in your message. Here are some general categories of questions that you may want to ask.

1. **Why were particular rhetorical choices made by the rhetor(s) or creator(s) of the message?** The obvious answer to that question is that a rhetor employs particular rhetorical tools to persuade an audience to think or do as the rhetor desires, but a careful analysis of the construction of a message may reveal goals or interests from the rhetor that may differ from the stated or apparent goals and interests. If, for example, you are looking at Nelson Mandela's speech opposing the United States' proposal to go to war with Iraq in 2003, you would discover that in the speech he harshly criticized President George W. Bush and the United States. He referred to President Bush as "a president who has no foresight, who cannot think properly" and who wants "to plunge the world into a holocaust." He said the United States is a country that "has committed unspeakable atrocities in the world." He even accused the United States of racism against UN Secretary-General Kofi Annan, saying, "They do not care. Is it because the secretary-general of the United Nations is now a black man?" ("Mandela" 2002). Many found Mandela's comments offensive and shocking. To many Americans, Mandela had always seemed a reasonable man and appeared to have good rapport with the United States. So a critic would be interested in asking why Mandela would choose such a bold, accusatory, and relationally risky strategy. Since we cannot know Mandela's motivations for certain, any conclusion we draw necessarily would be an inference that would require careful reasoning and research.

2. **What impact might the rhetorical choices have on different audiences? Would the impact be the same for different people?** Let's say you work for a trial attorney who is preparing her closing argument for a murder case. Since you are a communication expert, you've been asked to study the closing argument and offer an interpretation of how you think the jury will respond. Before drawing any conclusions from your analysis of the rhetorical choices the attorney has made, you would think about the different members of the jury and what you know about them—their ages, occupations, marital status, political leanings, and so on. This might tell you a great deal about the potential effect the rhetorical strategies could have and how the strategies could impact each jury member differently.

3. **How do the rhetorical choices made compare to other possible choices the rhetor(s) could have made?** Imagining alternative rhetorical strategies can be a useful tool in interpreting what choices were made. Assume for a moment that you work for a state senator who is running a reelection campaign. He gives a speech to the local labor union and feels that the speech did not go over well. Since you are a communication expert, he assigns you the task of figuring out where he went wrong. After

analyzing the rhetorical properties and patterns in his speech, you would need to consider what he *could* have said, if you want to teach him anything. For example, you might suggest that his stories lacked certain important narrative qualities or that his arguments needed different types of evidence or that he should have used a different organizational pattern or metaphors. Your knowledge of rhetorical theory would be useful here in helping you identify alternatives.

4. **What do the rhetorical choices indicate about the rhetor(s)?** Sometimes the rhetorical choices and patterns can reveal a lot about a person that is never said explicitly, especially if one message is compared to another. A rhetor's choice of language, drama, imagery, structure, and so on, may implicitly indicate things about the rhetor's views of his or her audience, the rhetor's views of humanity, the rhetor's ideology, the rhetor's philosophical perspective. For example, a careful analysis of the portrayal of alcoholics in Alcoholics Anonymous material would reveal a philosophical perspective on alcoholism that might differ significantly from the perspective apparent in the literature from the Betty Ford Rehabilitation Center or from Mothers Against Drunk Drivers (MADD). Differences in their portrayal of the dramas of alcoholism might reveal important differences in the two organizations' views of humanity that could have an important bearing on a couple's choice to send a child to one place over another for help. Interpreting something about the rhetor from a message requires careful analysis but can have great ethical and moral rewards.

5. **What do the rhetorical choices and patterns indicate about the audience, society, or culture in which the message sits?** Not only do rhetorical patterns indicate a rhetor's perspective, they also offer clues about a culture's or an audience's perspective. For example, a thoughtful analysis of the music, symbols, and architecture of a church or synagogue tells you not so much about the architect who designed the building or the musicians who wrote the songs as it tells you about the theology of the congregants. Whether the lyrics are *about* God or directed *to* God reveals something important about the way the members of a church or synagogue conceptualize God and interpret Scripture. Whether the architecture is casual, simple, and intimate between leader and congregants or formal, complex, and distant between leader and congregants indicates a great deal about the way the members of those religious groups conceive of God and their relationship to God. In other words, we can interpret and learn a lot about ourselves as a culture by studying the rhetorical properties of public messages.

Questions like these keep you focused on rhetorical patterns and can help you move past the "so what?" of analysis. After identifying interesting questions, you may then pursue which questions are most interesting and consider how you might answer those questions. You may be able to create an answer with careful, creative thinking on your own, or you may find that you need additional theory or research on the historical context to answer your questions.

COMPARING OBSERVATIONS FROM ANALYSIS

In addition to asking questions to get to an interpretation, as a critical "detective," you may also find it useful to compare the patterns you see in a message to something else that would help you make sense of your analysis. Critic Bonnie Dow says, "criticism relies on some kind of implicit or explicit comparison at every level" (1994, 99). Gregory Bateson argues in *Mind and Nature* that thinking itself centers around information that is "news of difference." In other words, at its most basic level, thinking about the world stems from some difference in sensation—a change of condition—that is noticeable. For us to think, and consequently generate new insight or knowledge, we must compare conditions or ideas in some fashion (Bateson 1979, 249). The means of comparison are manyfold. For example, we know we burned our hand by comparing its condition at T_1 with its condition at T_2 (after touching the burner on the stove). The "news of difference" we use is the information discovered in the feelings, as well as the condition and even the smell of our hand. Another example, of a different sort, would be the presentation of one person's perspective on a topic of argument against another's. The two perspectives provide information that we use to understand the world. What is important to understand is that insight can only be generated from a comparative view of the world. Without some change, or news of difference, we are unable to detect our environment. We become habituated or desensitized just as we lose a sense of motion in a jet plane until it speeds up or slows down—that is news of difference, or information, that we can use to understand our movement through space.

So, for a critic to make meaning of the rhetorical patterns in a message, the critic must at some level compare the observations to something similar we've already seen, to some information we have, or to some standard we know or create. Listed next are a few ways one might compare the observations from analysis.

1. **Communication research or theory.** You may find it useful to look at the rhetorical properties of a message against some communication research or theory. Let's say a friend of yours has been asked to deliver the eulogy at her favorite aunt's funeral. Knowing that you have studied communication, the friend asks you to read a draft of the eulogy and offer any comments. You may find it valuable to read the speech against rhetorical theory about the genre of eulogies (Jamieson 1978, 40–42). Comparing the speech to the theory may give you important insights to offer your friend about the structure or content of her eulogy.

   In the case of the presidential address to the annual White House prayer breakfast, we might read more of Burke's theory of mortification, scapegoating, and identification (Foss, Foss, and Trapp 2002, 192, 209–12). Burke (1969) argues that identification is necessary to persuade another person, so we might conclude that the president's use of identification at the beginning and end of his speech was rhetorically appropriate. However, we might note that in building identification with the Judeo-Christian audience broadly, he was unable to create the specific theological identification that Swaggart was able to create with his audience. In essence, the president's speech actually lacked a certain depth of identification or what Burke calls "consubstantiality" (the joining of two or more substances), thus limiting its persuasive power. One might also conclude that although he builds some degree of identification with his religious audience, the president did not attempt to create identification with his political audience (Democrats and Republicans). In either case, our understanding of Burke's theory helps us draw the inferences about the potential appeal of the president's strategies.

2. **Information you have about the context.** Sometimes valuable interpretations can be made by putting the message back into its context after having analyzed the rhetorical patterns. If you are a public relations manager for a large drug company and the company CEO has just been accused of embezzling money, you and your staff would need to craft a press release that would ease consumer confidence and restore the credibility of the company apart from the CEO. If one of your staff members came to you with a draft of a press release, you would need to analyze the rhetorical choices made in the press release, but in order to draw any inferences about what impact you think the press release might have, you would need to know a great deal about the context: who the target audience is, what concerns they have about the company, what the media has reported about the situation, what the audience believes about the company and its CEO, what actually happened with the CEO, and so forth. In a sense, you would look at the rhetorical strategies in the press release against the context in order to make your best guess as to how the audience will most likely respond.

In the Clinton case it might be important for us to know more precisely who was in his audience at the prayer breakfast. We should also examine when this speech occurred in relationship to the preceding events surrounding the Lewinsky fiasco and what the media had been reporting most recently (his approval ratings, editorials, statements from the Clinton family, etc.). Reviewing Clinton's first public apology (which was an important part of our description and analysis) would also help us understand the context and interpret the rhetorical choices made in this speech. Additionally, it might be important to know that many members of Congress, both Democrat and Republican, wanted Clinton to make a stronger apology in his speech. All this information about the context might lead us to draw the inference that Clinton was saying exactly what he knew his audience wanted to hear and, thus, his challenge was to make his apology genuine. We might then wish to evaluate the sincerity of the speech, which would require us to look closely at his rhetorical choices again to see if there are any clues as to his sincerity or lack thereof. We might even want to look for an audio- or videotape of the speech so that we might listen to his voice for cues of sincerity.

3. **Similar messages.** You may also find that comparing the message to other messages you are familiar with helps your interpretation. For exam-

ple, scholar Barry Brummett (1979) studied gay rights rhetorical messages and anti-gay-rights messages. In analyzing both sets of messages, he was able to draw inferences about the underlying ideologies of each group. He concluded that the gay rights rhetoric featured the gay *person* ("agent") in its discourse, whereas the anti-gay-rights rhetoric featured homosexual behavior ("act") (252). From this discovery, Brummett inferred that anyone who generally takes on a person focus has a different sort of political ideology than a person who focuses on behavior. So the rhetoric of both groups, he concluded, tells us something about the kind of people creating it. Brummett's interpretation would not have been possible had he not compared the two types of messages.

A similar need to compare similar messages would arise if a critic were examining the website www.whitehouse.org, a political parody of the regular White House website www.whitehouse.gov. The parody contains, among other things, political posters and mock speeches. The posters resemble 1940s World War II posters distributed by the government to rally support for the war effort. Only when a critic studies the posters on the website against some actual World War II posters can she reliably interpret the strategies being used in the mock posters. So too, only when a critic examines other portions of the ".org" website against the legitimate ".gov" website can he draw reasonable conclusions about what the parody is attempting to say and how.

In the case of President Clinton's speech, we might extend our comparison to Swaggart's speech. We observed that although both President Clinton and Swaggart used "mortification" in their speeches, the president focused on attaining purification through repentance (an Old Testament, Jewish orientation), whereas Swaggart focused on attaining purification by accepting the grace of God and the forgiveness offered through the death of Christ (a New Testament, Christian orientation). Knowing that difference between the two messages, we might infer that the president's use of mortification is problematic because it means he must work to earn forgiveness, so his audience cannot grant him immediate forgiveness and his "sins" cannot be easily forgotten. The president also has to rely on and create his own future credibility to be forgiven, and he must leave his audience with the choice of forgiving him or not, based on how he will live in the future. Swaggart, in contrast, relies on the credibility and authority of God because he claims that through Christ, God has already forgiven him and so the audience must also forgive him; they have no choice. Furthermore, Swaggart does not have to make promises about his future behavior and he can claim that his forgiveness is already present, whereas the president's forgiveness must be attained over time as he proves himself worthy. Swaggart's rhetorical strategy allows him to put his transgression in the past, whereas President Clinton's did not.

In this case, the comparison of the president's speech to Swaggart's proved useful in helping us draw inferences about the limitations of the president's appeals.

4. Something from another context altogether. Sometimes an interpretation might be drawn by comparing the rhetorical patterns in a message to something categorically different from rhetoric. Assume, again, that you are a communication consultant to a defense attorney. In this instance the attorney just lost a medical malpractice case and is trying to figure out what went wrong. Apparently, in a posttrial debriefing with the jury, he learned that they were especially dissuaded by his closing argument. He asks you to analyze his closing argument and offer an explanation as to what went wrong. Although you might compare the patterns you see in his speech to theory, to similar closing arguments, or to the context of the jury, you might decide that the best way for you to understand and explain the problem with the speech is to compare it to something altogether different from a closing argument. In fact, you might use some of Aristotle's theory on forensic (legal) rhetoric to examine the speech and decide that the speech actually resembles a website full of hyperlinks that lead to lots of tangents more than it resembles a kind of tightly woven logical argument suggested by Aristotle. The more you show the attorney how the speech resembles a website, the more the attorney begins to see the structural problems that led to the jury's confusion. The analogy might be especially useful in explaining why the older members of the jury were so much more confused than the younger members of the jury. By interpreting the patterns in terms of something categorically different from a speech, you might offer a real insight to yourself and another person.

For the Clinton speech we might try comparing the president's speech to a familiar prayer to see if that helps us understand his intentions or his perception of his audience. If, for example, the structure of the speech resembled the structure of a rosary, the Lord's Prayer, or the Prayer of St. Francis, we might be able to explain why it appealed to certain clergy at the breakfast.

Once you have asked and answered questions about what you have observed, and once you have compared your observations to something, how do you decide which interpretation is worth sharing? You may find that more than one interpretation is interesting, but your most worthwhile interpretations are those that give you the most insight about how the message works; those that cause you to say, "Ahaaaaa! *Now* I get what's happening in that message. That really teaches and persuades me to see the message in a particular way."

In the presidential speech examples, we played with a number of possible interpretations using different types of comparisons and asking different types of questions about what we observed in the analysis. In other words, we traveled down a number of paths, some of which led us to greater insights than others. The interpretive paths we found most helpful were in comparing the president's speech to Swaggart's, comparing the president's speech to Burke's theory, and looking at the context of the audience. For us (notice the subjectivity of this decision), these comparisons yielded more interesting ideas than

INTERPRETATION NOTES	**COMMENTARY ABOUT INTERPRETATION PROCESS**
The president's frequent reference to *repentance* rather than *grace* puts him in a weaker position rhetorically.	Notice that the first sentence is not a statement of certainty, but an inference about the strength of the president's rhetorical position.
At the same time, because he had to identify with a broader audience than what Swaggart had to identify with and with an audience that did not share a single theological orientation, he could not refer specifically to the forgiveness of God through the death of Christ, even though President Clinton claims to be a Christian. He was rhetorically limited by having to create identification with an audience full of differing theological positions. Consequently, he was not able to develop deep theological identification and he was unable to claim the authoritative forgiveness of God that Swaggart could claim.	Here we use the *comparison to Swaggart* to extend the idea that he was in a rhetorically weak position. In a sense, here we begin to say yes, he seemed weaker but . . . in comparison to the context, he had no choice. We're combining the insights from our comparison to Swaggart and our *comparison to the context*. Note the use of Burke's theory of identification to help explain what Clinton was unable to do.
Furthermore, the audience who has the most power over his future (members of Congress) was not his immediate audience, so he was unable to develop identification with the people he most needed to establish it with: Republican congressional representatives.	Again we look at the speech against the context, in this case the nonimmediate audience of congressional representatives, not present at the prayer breakfast, but people he must appease nonetheless. This examination of the context and the theory of identification help explain the limitations of the president's rhetorical choices.
It appears, then, that the president was rhetorically trapped, having limited options in what he could say because of his audiences.	This statement is our primary interpretive conclusion.

the comparison to the prayer. We felt the comparisons to Swaggart's speech and to Burke's theory gave us the most interesting and useful insights about the president's speech because they help us answer several of the questions raised by the analysis. A rough draft of our interpretation about the president's message follows.

These conclusions came from a number of different creative processes: comparing the president's speech to the Reverend Jimmy Swaggart's apology, comparing the president's speech to Kenneth Burke's rhetorical theory, and asking questions about other devices that might have been used given the context of who his audiences were. We asked whether the president's rhetorical devices were sufficient to ward off impeachment efforts and whether his identification with the broad Judeo-Christian community gave him sufficient rhetorical power.

Once you have developed your interpretations of what it means that particular rhetorical choices were made by a rhetor, you are nearly ready to move from the *process* of critiquing a message to creating a *product* in which you teach others about what you have discovered, trying to persuade them to see the message as you see it. To do this you will need to focus your argument into a thesis statement or a major claim. That statement should be interpretive in its focus and should advance a claim that is arguable rather than factual or obvious. The more arguable your thesis, the more you are likely to teach your own audience something new. To decide on a thesis you must study your own interpretation and ask, "What am I arguing about the rhetorical properties in this message?" In this case we decided to focus our product around the following argument (thesis statement):

> *The success of a public figure's apology that is based in religious thought may depend upon two conditions: the theology implied in the rhetorical strategies and the degree to which the audience agrees with that theology.*

Notice that this claim broadens our thinking beyond President Clinton's speech alone; it is a claim about apologies by public figures generally. We could have chosen to make an argument about President Clinton's speech only. For example, we might have made the thesis something like this: "Due to the variety of religions represented at the National Prayer Breakfast and the absence of his primary target audience (Republican congressional representatives), President Clinton was constrained in his ability to use theology to identify with his audience and convince them to forgive and forget his extramarital affair." This statement makes a legitimate, arguable claim about President Clinton's rhetorical choices. We thought, however, that the first statement would teach our audience more and stretch us to think beyond the Clinton case. In part, this choice comes from the fact that our analysis and interpretation became dependent on our comparison to the Swaggart case. The comparison of the two situations allows us to make a broader claim about public figures, though we know that claim is not one of certainty. Rather, it is an interpretation of what we *think* might be the case, given the evidence we have seen.

SUMMARY

Interpretation is a creative process, much like writing poetry. If poets were told by a teacher what to say and how to say it, their work would no longer be creative. The teacher might give the poet the syllabic parameters and rhyme scheme of a sonnet, but the teacher could not give the poet the words to use or ideas to explore. So too, we have tried to provide you with questions and possible avenues of comparison to help you progress through your interpretation, but ultimately personal creativity is needed from you to develop an interesting and useful interpretation of a rhetorical message. Use the suggestions listed in this chapter but also use anything else that helps you make sense of a rhetor's rhetorical choices.

EXERCISES

1. Review your description notes, analysis notes, and questions you raised from your analysis of President Bush's post-9/11 speech. Or, if you are working on some other text, use this exercise to begin your analysis of that piece. Review the list of questions in this chapter and decide which questions most interest you in getting to a meaningful interpretation of what you see in the speech. In the left-hand column that follows list the question or questions you want to pursue and come up with as many possible answers as you can. In the right-hand column make notes about what additional research you need to do to help yourself answer the questions.

INTERPRETATION NOTES	QUESTIONS, COMMENTS, ADDITIONAL RESEARCH

2. Review four ways you might compare the rhetorical patterns in the speech to develop an interpretation. In the left-hand column note the types of comparison(s) you think might help you interpret the patterns you see. Then attempt to make those comparisons. If you are using theory or research, do the necessary reading and make notes about how the rhetorical patterns compare to what the theory or research suggests. If you are looking at the rhetorical patterns against the context of the message, similar messages, or something different, explain what the comparison indicates to you about the 9/11 speech. In the right-hand column note any additional research you need to do and any questions, comments, or observations you have about your thinking in the interpretation process.

INTERPRETATION NOTES	QUESTIONS, COMMENTS, RESEARCH NEEDED

3. Now, review your interpretation notes and identify what kind of arguments you are making about the rhetorical patterns in Bush's speech. Remember that in order to be instructive to others, your inferences should make claims that are not certain. Try writing a thesis statement from your interpretation. Be sure that your thesis statement makes an inferential claim that would teach other people something valuable about the rhetorical patterns in Bush's speech.

WORKS CITED

Bateson, Gregory. *Mind and Nature: A Necessary Unity.* Toronto: Bantam Books, 1979.

Black, Edwin. *Rhetorical Criticism: A Study in Method.* New York: Macmillan, 1965.

Brummett, Barry. "A Pentadic Analysis of Ideologies in Two Gay Rights Controversies." *Central States Speech Journal* 30 (1979): 250–61.

Burke, Kenneth. *A Rhetoric of Motives.* Berkeley: University of California Press, 1969.

Dow, Bonnie J. "Femininity and Feminism in *Murphy Brown*." *The Southern Communication Journal* 57 (1992): 143–55.

———. Commentary and "Feminist Criticism and *The Mary Tyler Moore Show*." In *Critical Questions: Invention, Creativity, and the Criticism of Discourse and Media,* edited by William L. Nothstine, Carole Blair, and Gary. A. Copeland, 97–117. New York: St. Martin's Press, 1994.

Foss, Sonja, Karen A. Foss, and Robert Trapp. *Contemporary Perspectives on Rhetoric.* 3rd ed. Prospect Heights, IL: Waveland Press, 2002.

Jamieson, Kathleen H. *Critical Anthology of Public Speeches.* Modules in Speech Communication. Chicago: Science Research Associates, 1978.

"Mandela: U.S. Wants Holocaust." CNN.com./world. January 30, 2002. Cable News Network. http://www.cnn.com/2003/WORLD/meast/01/30/sprj.irq.mandela/ (accessed September 17, 2003).

The White House. September 15, 2003. Chickenhead Productions, Inc. http://www.whitehouse.org/initiatives/posters/index.asp (accessed September 18, 2003).

THE PROCESS
OF EVALUATION

7

Assume for the moment that a communication professor wrote the following comments in response to a student's persuasive speech:

> *In your presentation you mentioned the specific needs expressed by Jerome, Bob, and Sasha in your audience. This indicates that you listened to their discussion of financial planning. The modifications you made to the graphs found in your research materials and your use of visualization tells me that you understand the motivated sequence and the need to adapt to the different learning styles of your audience members. In sum, your presentation suggests that you understand the concept of audience analysis, message adaptation, and the motivated sequence. In comparison to the grading criteria and in comparison to other student presentations, your speech merits a grade of B+.*

This statement by the professor has all the characteristics of interpretation: it is an arguable inference based on observable evidence, and yet, it is somewhat subjective. The claim that the speech is worth a B+ is more than an interpretation; it also passes judgment on the *quality* of the speech.

As you read in Chapter 6, interpretation has several characteristics. First, interpretative claims make inferences about the rhetorical patterns observed in the analysis. Second, the interpretation process requires the critic's subjectivity, although that subjectivity is based on evidence rather than sheer bias. Finally, an interpretation answers the "so what?" question about what was observed in the analysis. For example, in the case of the student's speech, a teacher's critical observation from analysis might sound something like this:

> *The student's introduction had a preview statement; the speech had lots of evidence from accepted sources; the conclusion lacked an "exit" statement.*

The professor is naming the various components of the speech, recognizing patterns of commission and omission. If this was all the professor wrote as feedback, the student inevitably would say, "So what? What does that mean?" In other words, the student wants to know what those observations mean in terms of a grade. Interpretations offer a "so what does it mean" answer to the questions raised in the analysis.

As we noted at the beginning of the previous chapter, evaluation is a form of interpretation. Recall that the evaluation field was embedded in

Vocabulary
- ➤ evaluation
- ➤ criteria
- ➤ external evidence
- ➤ ideology

the interpretation field. Hence, all evaluations are a form of interpretation, though not all interpretations are evaluations. Evaluations have an additional quality not present in every interpretation: a judgment about the rhetorical properties of a message. An **evaluation,** then, is *a critic's use of stated criteria to determine the merit, worth, significance, or effectiveness of the rhetorical strategies in a message.* **Criteria** are *the standards by which the rhetorical choices are measured to determine their quality.* Criteria may come from communication theory, society, or critics themselves, but they must be made explicit and valid to be acceptable. The grade B+ is a judgment or evaluative interpretation based on whatever criteria the professor uses. The professor is judging the merit or worth, the "goodness" or "badness" of the speech. Presumably the professor is using the standards of his discipline or standards he has derived from viewing hundreds of speeches over the years. Recall that interpretation often requires a critic to look at the rhetorical patterns in a message against something else (e.g., the context, similar messages, rhetorical theory). Evaluation relies on this same process insofar as it requires the critic to look at the rhetorical properties and compare them to some stated criteria, as we see the professor doing in his evaluation of the student's presentation.

Look at the following statements. Decide which are purely interpretive and which have an evaluative quality.

1. Because it relies primarily on a legal and ceremonial style and provides evidence for an argument about the past rather than the future, the Ronald Reagan Tribute video shown at the 1996 Republican Convention suggests that the Republican Party sees itself as having completed its major contribution to the twentieth century and offers no real vision for leadership in this final decade.

2. The defense attorney effectively used the narratives of malpractice victims to raise the jury members' sympathy and, thus, their support for a conviction.

3. Andrew Dice Clay's use of humor in his response to the death of the governor was an inappropriate strategy.

4. Hitler's use of infestation metaphors to refer to the Jews was a deceptive rhetorical strategy.

5. The Beatles' song "She's Leaving Home" presents a set of characters in a struggle for self-satisfaction in order to mock the traditional moral purposes of significant relationships.

Statement 1 and statement 5 are interpretive claims with no explicit evaluation. In the first statement no judgment is made whether the video was good or bad. As is, the statement merely makes an inference about how the Republican Party perceives itself. One certainly might conclude that the rhetorical choices were not good for the Republican Party, but that may not be the only evaluation to draw. Statement 5 makes a claim about what the rhetorical strategies of narrative indicate regarding the goal of the song "She's Leaving Home." No judgment is made as to whether these choices were appropriate or whether the goal was good or bad.

By contrast, statements 2, 3, and 4 are evaluative. Statement 2 evaluates the narrative strategies in a malpractice trial as being effective, hence, those strategies are good. Statement 3 evaluates the rhetorical strategies of humor as being inappropriate and, thus, bad. Statement 4 judges Hitler's use of metaphors as deceptive and, thus, bad. Key terms that signal evaluation might include *(in)effective, (in)appropriate, deceptive, truthful, (un)helpful, (un)ethical, fitting,* or *not fitting.* What others come to your mind?

Evaluations can be useful in the critical process. At times, your analyses and interpretations may lead to judgments about the effectiveness of a message, the appropriateness of a rhetor's rhetorical choices, or the ethics of a rhetor's rhetorical choices. These kinds of judgments may be extremely worthwhile to the people you are trying to teach. By making evaluations you may prevent others from accepting a message at face value. You may prevent others from swallowing deceptive strategies or passively assuming a message is appropriate for a particular situation when, indeed, it is not. Your evaluations may help others become more critical consumers. Your evaluations might also persuade others to change their rhetorical strategies. That said, however, we should note that you do not always have to evaluate a message in order for your work to be useful. Often a critic's nonevaluative interpretation is worth a great deal to others because the interpretation taught them how the rhetorical devices of a message worked, which in turn tells them how those devices may or may not work in parallel circumstances.

For example, in our interpretation of President Clinton's apology at the White House prayer breakfast, we concluded that the effectiveness of apologies using religious ideals may depend on two things: the theological perspective implied in the rhetorical devices and the extent to which the audience shares that theological perspective. This interpretation teaches us something important about how the rhetorical devices in apologies work, yet it currently contains no evaluation. This interpretation contains no judgment of the president's speech, and yet it is a worthwhile inference that teaches others. We could forge ahead to make an evaluation of the speech, but if we stopped at this point, we would still have done a valuable study. Thus, we reiterate our point that you are not necessarily required to provide an evaluation of the message in order to develop a useful critique; a nonevaluative interpretation may be sufficient.

TYPES OF JUDGMENTS

You may be wondering what types of judgments critics make about messages. What do they evaluate and how do they establish their criteria for evaluation? In the paragraphs that follow we describe four different qualities that you may choose to evaluate in a message: (1) the truthfulness of the message; (2) the reasonableness of the argumentation in a message; (3) the ethics of a rhetor's rhetorical choices; and (4) the desirability of the ideology in a message. Which one of these four avenues you select depends on what you discovered in your analysis. If, for example, you see the rhetor relying heavily on a particular form of reasoning and/or evidence, you may select to evaluate the quality of the argumentation. If you found the rhetor relying on metaphors that may falsely portray the subject, you may evaluate the truthfulness or the ethics of that choice of metaphors. Before selecting an avenue of evaluation, however, it is important that you understand at least these four types of judgments.

TRUTHFULNESS

When judging the truthfulness of the message, a critic asks whether the information presented in the message is accurate or true. You may examine the rhetor's evidence, for example, to determine whether the evidence is true. Or you might examine the rhetor's use of metaphors to determine whether they are an appropriate and fair representation of the subject. Or you might examine the rhetor's use of narrative to determine whether the story rings true or is like reality (what Walter Fisher calls "narrative fidelity" as explained in Chapter 11). In essence, you must study the content of the rhetor's message to determine whether it is truthful.

How do you know whether the evidence or the metaphor or the story is truthful? At this point, you may need to rely on **external evidence**, meaning *evidence outside of or beyond the message itself*. That is, you may need to conduct research to develop a standard of truthfulness against which you can measure the truthfulness of the message. For example, in her analysis of President Nixon's 1969 "Vietnamization" address to the nation, Karlyn Kohrs Campbell (1972) discovered that one of Nixon's most significant rhetorical strategies was to portray the dissenters as a radical, homogeneous minority who sought "immediate, precipitate withdrawal from Vietnam" (51). She also noted his strategy of providing a chronology of how and why the United States became involved in Vietnam (52). Campbell then conducted research about the Vietnam situation and Americans' attitudes toward it. After reading reports about Americans' responses to the United States' policy on Vietnam, she concluded that Nixon's rhetorical choice to portray the dissenters as the minority was an inaccurate representation. She provided evidence to suggest that only a small minority of people supported immediate, total withdrawal from Vietnam, not the large, raucous group Nixon characterizes. Campbell also concluded that Nixon misrepresented the fundamental issues he described in his chronology. She wrote the following in her evaluation of Nixon's speech:

> *Two major contradictions damage the President's status as a truthteller. Early in the speech he tells the audience that immediate withdrawal [of troops from Vietnam] would be the popular and easy course, enhancing the prestige of the Administration and increasing its chances of reelection. Yet at the end of the speech it is clear that the President believes his opposition is a "vocal minority" and that his policy represents the will of the "great, silent majority." If so, isn't his policy the popular and easy one with the best chance of returning him to the White House? (Campbell 1972, 52)*

Campbell identifies a contradiction of logic in Nixon's speech, which she interprets as a failure of Nixon to tell the truth. Here she uses the commonsense understanding of logical consistency as her criterion for judgment.

In other cases, critics might use the narrative paradigm notions of "probability" (whether a story is coherent and hangs together) and "fidelity" (whether a story rings true to life) to determine the truthfulness of a story. Let's say that you observe that a rhetor speaking on behalf of MADD (Mother's Against Drunk Drivers) tells the story of a group of teenagers killed in an automobile accident. As the story goes, the driver who hit the teens' car was drunk. In her story, the rhetor portrays the drunk driver as the antagonist who tragically took the lives of the protagonist teens, all of whom had promising futures ahead of them. However, upon reading more about the legal case that followed the accident, you discover that the "drunk driver's" blood alcohol level was .05, within the legal limit, though there was a hint of alcohol detected. Also, you discover that although the teens had not been drinking, the accident occurred at 4 A.M., after the teens had been to a cast party for a theater performance they had been in together. They had been on the road, headed home, for nearly an hour. Apparently, the teens' insurance companies were all convinced by the evidence (how the cars were hit, etc.) that the teen driver *could* have fallen asleep at the wheel, thus possibly contributing to the cause of the accident. You learn, then, that the legal evidence of the cause of the accident is inconclusive, though the rhetor speaking on behalf of MADD portrays the story as if the teens were entirely without fault and the driver was fully drunk. You, having conducted this research, must evaluate the rhetor's rhetorical strategy of telling a dramatic story as untruthful.

Sometimes you may not rely on external evidence to determine the truthfulness of a story so much as you may rely on your commonsense knowledge. For example, in Mark's sample analysis of the Beatles' song "She's Leaving Home" (see Appendix 1), he concludes that the song's conclusion that "Fun is the one thing money can't buy" does not ring true. Mark says, "society has never said that, and the testimonies of individuals who have tried hedonism attest to the fact that fun is not the path to personal meaning and value." He goes on to point out, however, that the use of this untruthful statement, "Fun is the one thing money can't buy," is an appropriate rhetorical strategy given the revolutionary goals of the Beatles and this song. In this case, Mark relied on his common social knowledge to determine the absence of fidelity (failure to ring true to life) in this song's narrative and the rhetorical purpose of its absence.

QUALITY OF EVIDENCE AND REASONING

In addition to examining the truthfulness of the rhetorical strategies, a critic might be interested in the quality of evidence and reasoning posed by the rhetor. This type of evaluation may be particularly important when you analyze the "logos" of the message or when you use Toulmin's model (discussed in Chapter 10) to focus on the claims made by the rhetor and data (evidence) and warrants (reasoning) used to support the claims. When making this type of judgment, you ask whether the claims are sufficiently supported by the evidence and reasoning, whether the evidence is sound, and whether the reasoning is logical. What standards do you use to determine whether the claims are sufficiently supported and the evidence and reasoning sound? You must rely on what are known as informal rules of logic.

Just as there are many different types of evidence and reasoning, there are many different informal rules of logic, too many to be named here. We explain a few tests of evidence and reasoning that you might use, but you may wish to consult additional resources for more complete ideas about tests of evidence and reasoning. If the logos of a message you are studying seems particularly significant, we urge you to find some of these additional sources in the library so you can develop more specific criteria for your evaluation.

Following this paragraph are some sample tests we've adapted from Robert Vancil's work (see Tables 7.1 and 7.2). You might run these on the evidence and reasoning you see in a message. The tests consist of questions critics ask of the evidence or reasoning they see in order to determine the extent to which it is logically sound. Asking these and other questions about specific forms of evidence and reasoning can help you determine the quality of the argumentation used by a rhetor.

In addition to suggesting these specific questions, Vancil names three general tests that can be used for the evaluation of *any* argument. The general tests entail the following three questions (Vancil 1993, 102):

- Are the reasons for accepting a rhetor's claim true or acceptable?
- Are the reasons for accepting a claim properly related to the claim? Are they relevant?

TABLE 7.1

Type of Evidence	Questions to Ask of the Evidence
Examples	1. Is the example representative or could it be an isolated instance? 2. Is the number of examples provided sufficient to support the generalization in the claim? 3. Are there any contradictory examples not mentioned? (137–38)
Statistics	1. Was the sample from which the statistics were drawn representative of the larger population? 2. How many subjects were sampled? (195–96)
Testimony	1. Is the source of the testimonial credible? 2. Is the source of the testimonial biased? 3. Is the source reliable? (184–91)

Source: Vancil (1993).

TABLE 7.2

Type of Reasoning	Questions to Ask of the Reasoning
Analogy	1. Are the two things being compared really similar? 2. In what ways are the two things different? 3. Do the differences mean that the comparison is meaningless? 4. Is evidence provided to prove that the two things are similar? (141–42)
Cause-Effect	1. Is the first phenomenon the necessary cause of the second? 2. Are there other possible causes? 3. Did the phenomenon believed to be the cause happen before the effect occurred? 4. Does the alleged cause have the power to pro duce the effect? (147–48)
Sign	1. Is the sign invariable or infallible? 2. Are there a sufficient number of signs? 3. Are there contradictory signs not mentioned? (152–54)
Definition	1. Are there other possible definitions for this concept or word? (82–83) 2. Is the definition true, or accepted as true, or appropriate? (118–19) 3. Are there any exceptions to the definition? (265)

Source: Vancil (1993).

■ Are the reasons for accepting a rhetor's claim sufficient to establish the claim?

In 1995 President Clinton gave a radio address to the nation opposing cigarette advertising targeted to youth. In analyzing that speech, we found that the president relied on cause-effect reasoning and applied generalizations (a form of reasoning by definition). He used data in the form of examples, statistics, and testimony, yet none of these sufficiently supported his causal reasoning. The analysis also revealed that the examples he used were weak because they were contradictory and thus easily refuted. The statistics were weak because they did not necessarily prove a cause-effect relationship between tobacco ads and teen smoker habits. Thus, the president's data failed to pass the test of relevance, and they failed to pass the specific tests for testimonies, examples, and statistics. The analysis also revealed that no data were used at all to support the logic of applied generalization. We concluded our evaluation and interpretation this way:

> *The lack of proof in Clinton's speech gives us reason to wonder whether a personal story might not be more effective than rational evidence and logic. While President Clinton's use of personal testimony might be effective in the short term by capturing the listeners' attention and involving them emotionally, it will not likely be effective in the long term. That is, to be passed as policy, the President's arguments will be confronted through debate on the House and Senate floor, and in that process the insufficient causal logic and the assumptions in the generalizations will likely be caught and argued.*

Our evaluation judged President Clinton's rhetorical effort as insufficient, and we predicted at the time that his choices would likely fail him. Note, too, that our conclusion used the strategy mentioned in Chapter 6 of identifying other possible strategies the president might have used.

EFFECTIVENESS

A third type of evaluation a critic might make is about the effectiveness of a rhetor's rhetorical choices. Here you ask whether the rhetor's rhetorical choices were, or were likely to be, effective. Typically, this question is difficult to answer. In some cases (e.g., for a presidential speech), there may be polls indicating peoples' responses to a message that give you some clue as to whether the rhetor's choices were effective, but even that data may not necessarily indicate that particular rhetorical strategies were effective. For example, polls following a president's State of the Union address may indicate that the nation liked the speech or particular policies and agenda items outlined in the speech, but this does not necessarily mean that the president's rhetorical choice to arrange the speech in a problem solution format was effective. The poll may simply mean that Americans agree with the president's concerns, or that they like the president. In a different context, if you are studying a persuasive memo written by the CEO of a corporation, you may find that data indicating the employees' response to the memo may not exist.

If you just want to determine whether a message was effective, it may be more appropriate to conduct a research study in which audience members are surveyed. However, a critic is more interested in how the message was constructed in such a way as to make (or not make) an impact on the audience. Since you may not have (or be interested in) the data from a survey or poll, you are more likely to examine the rhetorical strategies with this question in mind, Given what I know about the context for this message—to whom it was delivered, when, why, and with what purpose—how appropriate were the rhetor's choices and how effective are those choices likely to be in helping the rhetor achieve his or her purpose? In this case, you seek to explain why particular strategies are more or less likely to be effective. You may need to draw upon persuasion or rhetorical theory to make this judgment, or you may need to rely on good reasoning and common sense. For example, in our interpretation of President Clinton's speech at the annual White House prayer breakfast, we decided that in his effort to build identification with his audience, he ended up using an Old Testament, Hebraic theological position on forgiveness, which trapped him rhetorically. We argued that his choice required him to earn the forgiveness of his audience, putting him in their control. Our judgment of the effectiveness of that choice is based, partially, on Kenneth Burke's theory of rhetoric in which he argues that to persuade someone, identification between the rhetor and audience must exist. We might then judge the president this way: "Although his general choice to use the strategy of identification with a wider audience than just Christians was appropriate, his specific theological choice had the negative consequence of not featuring the existing forgiveness of God. President Clinton could have strengthened his strategy not by focusing on the New Testament sacrifice of Christ (an appeal he could not use with Jews), but on God's common mercy to all people as seen in both the Old and New Testaments. This way he could have built stronger identification with all segments of his audience." Here we are judging the lack of effectiveness of the president's rhetorical strategies, offering a suggestion of how the rhetorical choices might have been stronger. This is an arguable judgment, certainly not a factual, conclusive one, but it is based on both theory and commonsense reasoning.

Proving effectiveness or ineffectiveness is difficult for a critic to do. For this reason we urge you to keep your focus on the rhetor's rhetorical choices and whether those seem fitting or likely to be effective, given what you know about the situation. Such an approach places a burden of responsibility on you to know as much as possible about the context for the message. No good judgment can be made without putting the message in its appropriate context. If you make a claim about the appropriateness of the rhetorical patterns in a message, remember that you bear the responsibility of explaining how you know that particular rhetorical choices were or were not likely to be effective. You must identify the criteria upon which you are making such a judgment, and you must explain how you know that the devices you see do or do not meet those criteria.

ETHICS AND VALUES

A fourth evaluative focus a critic might take is on the ethics or values embedded in a rhetor's rhetorical choices. Here you ask, did the rhetorical devices in a message uphold desirable values? Or, you ask, were the rhetorical devices used ethically? To answer these questions you must lay out the ethical standards you are using to judge the message. Obviously, the standards themselves cannot be absolutely neutral, but they can be applied fairly and rigorously if you are honest and explicit about what those standards are.

A variety of types of standards may be applied. For example, you may ask whether the message is good or bad for society as a whole or whether the message has social value. Here you may set a standard of what is good for a majority of people in a culture. The standard might be based on economic values, religious principles, liberal or conservative politics, or democratic principles. You might also ask whether the message and the rhetorical choices made by the rhetor have moral value. Are the rhetorical choices honest? Hateful? Lawful? For example, one might argue that Hitler's choice to use infestation metaphors to refer to the Jews in his speeches (Perry 1983, 233) was hateful and deceptive, hence, unethical.

Critics sometimes assert a particular political ideology as the basis for an ethical judgment of a rhetor's rhetorical choices. Ideologies are prevailing systems of ideas about how the world is and ought to be. Felix Gross (1985) defines **ideology** as a *"dominant way of perceiving and interpreting phenomena, explaining human existence and the surrounding world and setting the limits of such understanding"* (27). For example, in the nineteenth century, the dominant way of perceiving gender was to assume that men, by nature, belonged in the public sphere of politics, economics, and industry, whereas women belonged, by nature, in the private sphere of the home. A critic might have ethical disagreements with the ideology perpetuated or advanced by a particular text, or a critic might be concerned with the ways in which rhetorical strategies implicitly or explicitly sustain a particular ideology. In a sense, you would ask whether the ideology implied in a message and its rhetorical strategies is an appropriate and/or desirable ideology. While it may be useful and appropriate to expose the problematic ideology in a text from the nineteenth century, recognizing the impact of history on contemporary thought, it is equally important that your judgment of that text fairly take into account the historical context and presumptions of thought at that time. Judging a text as unethical may be grossly unfair if the social knowledge and customs of that day differ from those of your time. Assuming, however, that your judgment gives fair consideration to the historical context, you might build your conclusions around a feminist ideology, a conservative ideology, or a Marxist ideology, among others. For example, in her analysis of the television show *Murphy Brown,* Bonnie Dow (1992) concludes that although the show's strategies are acceptable from the liberal feminist perspective (which argues that women are entitled to equal access, pay, and opportunities), the strategies are unacceptable from a radical feminist perspective (which argues, first, that sexual relations are political and, thus, patriarchy—including sex roles and sex status—must be effaced and, second, that sexism underlies class structure and, thus, a noncapitalist system must accompany the elimination of sexism). Dow proves that various comedic devices in the show undermine the feminist nature of the main characters.

No matter what ideology guides your judgment, it is necessary that you be explicit in stating your ideological criteria. Dow, for instance, explicitly stated in her report that she was judging the *Murphy Brown* show from a radical feminist perspective (1992, 153). Naming your ideology and its standards of evaluation makes your subjective judgment more acceptable to others because you are being honest and, thus, ethical in your own work as a message analyst. You must also keep in mind the importance of fairly deriving an evaluation from your analysis. In other words, even if you choose to make an ethical or value-oriented judgment, you must not suddenly fall from the balcony and begin arguing with the author. The judgment must be an evaluative inference about the discoveries made in the process of analysis.

SELECTING A TYPE OF JUDGMENT

How does a critic select which type of judgment to make? You, the critic, should pay attention to two things. First, you should review your analysis to see what sorts of questions you had upon discovering the rhetorical patterns in the text. If you wondered about the ethics of any rhetorical choices, you should pursue that path of judgment. If you wondered about the effectiveness of the rhetorical choices, you should pursue that path, and so on. Second, and perhaps more important, you should listen to the "aha's" you got in your analysis and interpretation phases; listen to what bothers you or impresses you about what you found in your analysis. Be careful not to simply return to your initial reaction to the message, but look carefully at the patterns you discovered and what the person inside of you thinks about those patterns. Listen for your own responses to the patterns like, "Wow!" or "How smart of that rhetor," or "If only she had . . ." or "That's awful."

Once you have decided whether to evaluate and how to evaluate the rhetorical patterns in a text, and once you have established your criteria and conducted the evaluation, you are ready to report your critique in the form of a product to an audience. Your thesis statement may incorporate your evaluation or you may choose to add your evaluation to the end of your report. In either case, if you choose to draw any evaluative conclusions in your report, you need to include your criteria for judgment in order to make your case as credible and convincing as possible.

SAMPLE EVALUATION

In sum, any of these four types of evaluations are legitimate and useful. Obviously, some evaluative schemes are more subjective than others, and those that are more subjective call for more developed argumentation on your behalf to convince others of your evaluation. No matter what type of judgment you make, however, it is important that you make your standards as explicit as possible. This will make the evaluation itself easier and will make your conclusions more convincing to others.

Refer to pages 118 and 119 for a sample of a critic working through the evaluation process. Note that our evaluation ideas are recorded on the left and commentary about that process is noted on the right.

In this particular sample, we worked only with the effectiveness criterion. We could have evaluated the ethics of President Clinton's choices, the truthfulness of his apology (though that may have been difficult to prove), or the quality of his argumentation. The choice to evaluate effectiveness rather than ethics, truthfulness, or quality of argumentation came from the inferences drawn in the interpretation phase. Note that we started the evaluation by picking up where the interpretation left off. We reread our interpretation and

PROCESS OF EVALUATION (NOTES)	CRITICS' COMMENTARY
In our interpretation of the president's speech, we concluded that his use of the Old Testament repentance version of mortification probably was less powerful than Swaggart's use of the New Testament claim that he is already forgiven by the scapegoat of Christ.	Here we refer to what we concluded in our interpretation phase.
One type of evaluation we might draw is that of effectiveness. It seems that the president's strategy was probably less effective for two reasons:	Here we decide on the effectiveness evaluation, largely because the interpretation automatically raised questions about the limitations (hence, the degree of effectiveness) of President Clinton's strategies.
1. By trying to identify with a broader audience he couldn't rely explicitly on New Testament theology and, thus, couldn't say, "My sins have been paid for by Christ."	
2. Whereas Swaggart used Christ as the ultimate scapegoat (a scapegoat his audience *agreed* was the perfect sacrifice for his sin), President Clinton chose to use his accusers as his scapegoat, saying that they didn't honor his right to privacy. This scapegoat was probably *not* a perfect sacrifice in his audience's minds because it wasn't universally agreed that the president's privacy had been invaded or that he should not have been investigated so thoroughly. Many people agreed that the investigation was needed and that the president is not above investigation into his private affairs.	We considered using quality of reasoning, but we didn't discuss forms of argument in the analysis. It didn't make sense to change focus in the evaluation. We also considered using truthfulness as a standard, but since President Clinton was talking about what was going on internally, we could do nothing to test these statements; we must either accept them and assume he was telling the truth—that is, Grice's Cooperative Principle (Grice 1989, 28–31), or cynically reject his statements. Truthfulness was not a workable standard.
Additionally, we can imagine other possible rhetorical choices President Clinton could have made that might have given him more rhetorical power. Rather than focus on repentance and his need to prove himself in upcoming days, he could have maintained his identification with Jews and Christians by focusing on God's mercy. He did not need to focus on God's mercy through Christ, per se (since that is Christian theology), but could have focused generally on the mercy of God, as evident in both Old and New Testament	Finally, we considered ethics and values. We decided that although this could be used, because of the context of the situation and purpose of the speech, ethics and values standards didn't fit as well as the effectiveness standard. However, we may develop our evaluation further using ethics as a second, complementary standard to effectiveness.

To determine effectiveness, we also used other possible rhetorical choices as a standard against which to measure President Clinton's choices. This is another way to establish a rationale for an argument about effectiveness. |

PROCESS OF EVALUATION (NOTES) (cont.)	CRITICS' COMMENTARY (cont.)
scriptures. Since both Jews and Christians rely on Old Testament theology and stories, he could have drawn solely from the Old Testament but still talked about God's mercy.	

noted it again here. The evaluative questions of effectiveness naturally flowed from the interpretation drawn previously.

As you may recall, in the interpretation, we decided to focus our report on the following thesis:

> *The success of a public figure's apology that is based in religious thought may depend upon two conditions: the theology implied in the rhetorical strategies and the degree to which the audience agrees with that theology.*

Although it makes an inference, this claim is not evaluative. We have decided that we would focus on the necessary conditions for the rhetorical strategy of using theology as a way to direct the audience's thinking about one's apology, but out of that process we will make the judgment that President Clinton made some poor choices in how he represented his religious thinking and that he may have been more effective with an alternative approach (focusing on God's mercy as evident in both Jewish and Christian theologies).

We urge you to start your evaluation (if you select to make one) by revisiting your analysis and interpretation. Ask yourself if your evaluation could have been made without you ever having done the work of the analysis. If the answer is yes, then you may be falling from the balcony and arguing with the rhetor rather than judging the rhetorical choices you observed in the process of analysis. Ideally, you may find that your interpretive claim naturally leads you to make an ethical evaluation of the rhetor's rhetorical choices or that it naturally leads you to consider whether the logic of the message is valid.

SUMMARY

As stated earlier, evaluation is not a necessary component of your process, but in some cases it could be the most important component. You as a critic will have to decide whether your own audience would benefit from your making a judgment or whether there is sufficient learning to be gained from your analysis and interpretation alone. If your evaluation feels arbitrary, it is probably best left unsaid, but if it flows naturally from your interpretation, pursue it. Remember, however, that like your interpretation, your evaluation is an arguable claim about a rhetor's choices and, thus, requires good evidence and reasoning on your behalf. You must be prepared to be able to defend your case well.

EXERCISES

1. Choose two of the four types of judgment (truthfulness, effectiveness, quality of argumentation, ethics/values) to evaluate the rhetorical patterns you discovered in the Bush speech after 9/11 (see Chapter 5).

2. List criteria for each type of judgment. Explain the source of your criteria (e.g., values of democracy, values of feminism, informal tests of argument, etc.).

3. Apply the criteria to evaluate the rhetorical patterns in the speech. What judgments do you make? How would you support them?

WORKS CITED

Campbell, Karlyn Kohrs. "An Exercise in the Rhetoric of Mythical America." In *Critiques of Contemporary Rhetoric,* edited by Karlyn Kohrs Campbell, 50–58. Belmont, CA: Wadsworth, 1972.

Dow, Bonnie J. "Femininity and Feminism in *Murphy Brown." Southern Communication Journal* 57 (1992): 143–55.

Grice, Paul. *Studies in the Way of Words.* Cambridge, MA: Harvard University Press, 1989.

Gross, Felix. *Ideologies, Goals and Values.* Westport, CT: Greenwood Press, 1985.

Perry, Steven. "Rhetorical Functions of the Infestation Metaphor in Hitler's Rhetoric." *Central States Speech Journal* 34 (1983): 229–35.

Vancil, David L. *Rhetoric and Argumentation.* Boston: Allyn and Bacon, 1993.

Writing Your Ideas

Most of you who read this book will not make your living writing formal rhetorical criticism for academic journals. In fact, the folks who do write such critical essays don't make their living doing critical studies. They generally work in universities as teachers or administrators, where, as part of their jobs, they practice the skills of and develop the theory for rhetorical analysis. However, if you do work in any occupation in which communication is a central function of your job or any part of your life as a citizen, you will need to do message analysis in some form or another. As we argued in Chapter 2, there are many reasons to engage in the *process* of message analysis. In some instances the critical process alone will help you accomplish whatever task you are given. But in other instances, whether in an academic class, a job, or a volunteer position, you may need to report your findings in writing to others in an effort to explain to them how a message or set of messages work as a communication effort. You may be asked to produce some kind of *product,* or written document, reporting your analysis of a court decision, a politician's position paper or speech, a competitor's advertisements, a proposal, an editorial, a sermon, or a community activist's impromptu speech. Consider in the next few paragraphs how those products might differ for different audiences and purposes.

The product of criticism may be a rigorous academic essay intended for a wide audience of colleagues. In that case, you would have to review all relevant literature and research that may have already been done on your topic of study; you would have to explain your methods as precisely as possible, argue your case carefully, provide lots of support for your conclusions, and precisely document your uses of other people's ideas. The main thrust of an academic analysis is developing rhetorical theory by testing established concepts or new ones you've created. These are very important activities, but they are practiced by only a few thousand faculty and graduate students, in any given year, in the fashion just described.

Perhaps you'll write movie, theater, book, or music reviews for an alternative press publication, or an organization's newsletter, or a school paper. If you write movie reviews for your college paper, the students read them because you know your audience's interests and tastes, and you provide the students with a needed opinion and some guidance on how to spend a rare evening free of responsibilities or studying.

Others of you may report your analyses of all sorts of messages to a narrow professional audience. You may work for a philanthropic foundation or state agency that must analyze proposals requesting grant monies. You may go on to clerk for a law firm or judge, and much of your job would be analysis of opinions and briefs that are substantial attempts to persuade an audience. You may work for a television network reviewing treatments for new programs or reviewing internal reports on operations. In these cases, your audience may be only one person—your boss—nevertheless, you would have to teach your reader about the significant dynamics of the message so that person can make an informed and effective decision about the truth, validity, or value of the material you examined.

The level of rigor you apply to the analysis will depend on the purpose of your criticism and your audience. So too, the way you write up your findings will depend on your purpose and audience. But no matter what the purpose or audience, certain issues must be considered when writing your report. So as you move from the process of studying a message to the construction of a product reporting the results of the study, you will discover that in every case, the presentation of insights from the analysis must be cogent, well organized, well proven, precise in language use, and thoughtfully shaped for the intended audience. In this chapter, we present five basic guidelines on how to argue your conclusions effectively.

EFFECTIVELY ARGUING YOUR CLAIMS ABOUT MESSAGES

As you engaged in the process of message analysis, you developed insights about the message or messages you were examining; that is, you discovered something about the dynamics of the message. Your discoveries provide some knowledge about how communication works in specific contexts and you need to share your ideas with others with like interests in or needs for such knowledge. Interestingly, when you move from the process of analysis to the creation of a product reporting what you discovered in your study, you must engage in rhetoric yourself. That is, as a message maker you must make decisions about the construction of your message for identifiable audiences. You need to understand the rhetorical situation you face and attempt to respond to it fittingly.

Understanding your rhetorical situation means you must know who composes your audience. As we mentioned at the beginning of the chapter, critical analysis of messages may be done for many reasons and many different sorts of audiences. As you well know, you must adapt your message to the audience you are addressing. Are you writing for other critics? Professional colleagues? General readers? Beyond identifying your audience, it is important that you identify the purpose for your critical writing. Are you intending to help someone appreciate a message (Rosenfield 1974, 492)? Teach them how a message works? Develop rhetorical theory? Critique or debunk a message? Of course each purpose requires a different approach, but an underlying requirement of all good criticism is that *it makes an argument* (Brockriede 1974, 165). Prior to writing you have attempted to take a distant or impartial stance—you observed the message from a balcony, and as a result you have gained some insight about communication. To preserve that work and convey your insights powerfully to your audience, you must argue your case so that you avoid slipping into a glandular presentation of your findings. Wayne Brockriede posits the following five conditions must be met if criticism is to be useful. He writes:

> By "argument" I mean the process whereby a person reasons his way from one idea to the choice of another idea. This concept of argument implies five generic characteristics: (1) an inferential leap from existing beliefs to the adoption of a new belief or the reinforcement of an old one; (2) a perceived rationale to justify that leap; (3) a choice among two or more competing claims; (4) a regulation of uncertainty in relation to the selected claim—since someone has made an inferential leap, certainty can be neither zero nor total; and (5) a willingness to risk a confrontation of that claim with one's peers. (1974, 166)

What do these conditions mean for you, as you report your critical findings?

PRESENT NEW IDEAS

First, for your criticism to be useful, you must present a new idea for your reader. Because you have carefully stepped out of the position of the audience member and into the balcony; because you have slowed your thinking down to describe the message carefully; because you have used your theoretical knowledge via search models to discover rhetorical patterns in the message; and because you have thoughtfully consulted additional resources to interpret or evaluate the patterns you see, you ought to have some insights about the rhetorical properties of the message that your readers don't have. As you look back on the notes you have taken during the phases of description, analysis, interpretation, and evaluation, you must ask yourself, "What have I discovered here that likely is not already evident to my audience but would enhance their understanding of the nature of communication in this message?" Telling your readers the obvious is a waste of their time. If it is obvious that a message relies on fear appeals, your readers will not learn anything new if that's what you report. If it is obvious that your message tells a story, your readers will not learn anything new if that's what you report. But if, for example, you discovered that the fear appeals of the message will only work if the audience agrees to a particular set of assumptions and if those fear appeals are presented to the audience in a particular order, then you might have a useful insight to teach your readers about how the fear appeals work. This insight would help them understand either their personal responses to fear appeals as consumers or effective construction of fear appeals as rhetors. In essence, by explaining the dynamic between two or more rhetorical properties (in this case, the fear appeals, the organization of those appeals, and the assumptions of the audience) you can offer your readers a new idea and deeper understanding about something they saw on a superficial level or not at all.

When preparing to write your critical product, reflect on your description, analysis, interpretation, and evaluation. What have you figured out about the dynamics of the message that most reasonable people wouldn't see without your instruction? Your answer to this question will be key in helping you decide how to shape your report to your readers.

MAKE AN ARGUMENT

Second, your critical product should make an argument. It will be most useful and interesting to your readers if you make an argument about the rhetorical dynamics of the message at hand. To simply identify rhetorical components (e.g., act, agent, agency;[1] data, claim, warrant;[2] or visual metaphors, parody, and subjective points of view[3]) without showing the relationship between those properties and their intended audience or without making an argument about what it means that those components are used as they are in a message offers little of interest to your readers. This is why interpretation is a necessary part of the critical process. During the interpretation phase you draw conclusions about what it means that the rhetor made certain rhetorical choices. The interpretation answers the question, so what? For example, what does it mean that the graphics on the NAACP website represent time from present (left side, modern color images) to past (right side, old sepia images)? What does it mean that the Reebok homepage is dominated by presentation of a fictional character, Terry Tate, Office Linebacker, who terrorizes Reebok employees? Or what does it mean that Martha Stewart's webpage relies heavily on ethical appeals? Your answer to the "so what?" question should have come out in your interpretation (as you worked through it in the critical process), and from that you can develop a central claim or thesis that will guide your critical product. That central claim will serve as a compass to keep your report focused on what is most important, useful, and interesting to your readers.

By way of example, let's consider Martha Stewart's webpage, www. marthatalks.com before she was found guilty in court. During the analytical process, having applied dramatistic search models,[4] you may have concluded that the narratives or stories embedded in her webpages served as the means or "agency" by which she reconstructed the situation or "scene" such that she appeared to be an average person who was the target of a misguided prosecution rather than a superrich elite who was caught attempting to pad her wealth at the expense of others. Also, you may have found by applying the classical rhetorical tools that Stewart appealed to credibility via her original open letter, continuing open letters and photos, "selected comments" from fans, and the link to "Other voices." Finally, you may have observed in the construction of the page a distinct feminine style.[5]

Although these observations may have been interesting and may have helped you along the way, your readers are more likely to learn from your critique if you keep your report focused on the discoveries that led to your primary conclusion about the message. Let's say your central claim is that Martha

Stewart's webpage, www.marthatalks.com, drew on both liberal and cultural feminist approaches in an attempt to reach the widest possible audience. To argue this claim, you will need to stay focused on applying rhetorical concepts drawn from or relevant to feminist criticism. You may have to let go of the dramatistic and classical elements you found in order to create a coherent and insightful study. In essence, then, framing the argument helps you sort out what discoveries from your description and analysis you need to report to your audience and which discoveries you can discard. The central claim should help you avoid extraneous details about the message, unless those details are central to what you want to argue about the message.

When crafting your central argument, keep the following guidelines in mind:

- Your argument should be about particular rhetorical properties of a message.
- Your claim about those rhetorical properties should be debatable, uncertain, requiring evidence.
- Your claim should not be obvious without the work of careful description and analysis.
- Your claim should teach another person about how a message communicates.

Consider the difference between these two claims:

1. To persuade his audience, Jesse Jackson establishes his credibility throughout his speech.
2. Throughout her campaign speeches, Elizabeth Dole's use of domestic metaphors reveals an unexpected sexist perspective that seems to contradict her stated support of women.

The first statement about Jackson's speech does not identify any particular rhetorical properties of the message. It asserts that Jackson establishes his credibility, but it never identifies any particular rhetorical dynamic that accounts for how that credibility is established. The statement also offers little that is debatable. Most speechmakers attempt (successfully or unsuccessfully) to establish credibility to help enhance their persuasiveness. No real argument is being made here about how Jackson attempts to establish credibility, what that implies about him, or whether his choices are reasonable given whatever his persuasive goals might be. To be sure, the claim teaches the reader little about how Jackson's speech communicates to his audience.

By contrast, the claim about Dole's speech takes us someplace interesting. The thesis statement focuses on the rhetorical properties of domestic metaphors and the dynamic relationship between those metaphors and Dole's statements about women's issues. Certainly, the statement is debatable. The critic making this statement must prove that there is some pattern in Dole's use of domestic metaphors, and the critic must show how those metaphors contradict more explicit statements Dole made about women and women's issues.

The relationship between the metaphors and other statements might not be apparent to more casual readers. The critic would have to do some convincing. Also, the statement obviously is drawn from the critic's description and analysis where he or she observed both the patterns of metaphor use and the patterns in explicit statements about women's issues. This kind of observation came from careful study, not haphazard observation. Finally, although a reader ultimately might not agree with the critic about the contradictory nature of the metaphors, the reader is likely to learn something new about two important dimensions of Dole's speech and/or something about the significance of metaphors in campaign rhetoric. The claim attempts to teach a reader something important about communication, which is a central function of criticism.

SUPPORT YOUR THESIS

Third, you must rigorously support your central claim (thesis) by providing the best evidence and theoretical rationale you can to diminish your reader's uncertainty about that claim. In developing new knowledge, you are building beyond the established, agreed-to notions about any message or theory related to it. Recall the example of astronomers knowing Pluto existed before it was actually observed. From the available data, from what astronomers did see, they were able to make an inferential leap. They knew something was out there and posited a planet. Their knowledge was a result of a logical inference. During the period between the claim being made and the actual observation, they continued to collect data, building a stronger case. By doing that, they were becoming more and more certain that Pluto was out there—they were regulating uncertainty. Finally, they risked publishing their still somewhat uncertain claim that an as-yet-unobserved planet existed. They were willing to take that risk because they knew they had good evidence to report. When you read here that evidence is needed, you shouldn't panic. Rather, think of yourself like those astronomers. If you've carefully gone through the processes of describing, analyzing, and interpreting/evaluating your message, you have already gathered the evidence. You simply need to pull it together in a logical and convincing manner for your reader.

The evidence you use to support your central claim will come from three general sources: (1) the text you have analyzed; (2) the research you conducted on the context; and (3) theoretical information that helped you understand/explain the rhetorical dynamics of the message. Take, for example, the claim about Elizabeth Dole's campaign speeches. First, to support that claim you would need to offer your readers examples from the text of her speeches to prove that there is a pattern in her use of metaphors and to show your reader what she says explicitly about women's issues. Keep in mind that a single short quotation from a text is rarely convincing that a pattern exists. To prove that this is a significant rhetorical pattern, you would need to offer numerous quotes so your readers "see" what you see in the message even though your readers may not have the text in front of them. As you provide evidence of patterns, make it easy for your readers to read and understand the examples you give. Clearly articulate or name a rhetorical dynamic, explaining technical terms whenever necessary, and give sufficient quotes to prove the pattern, providing your reader context from the texts themselves as necessary. Then be sure to explain what the patterns mean. Offer statements that connect your evidence to your central argument. In other words, don't force your readers to make the connections for you, and don't assume the readers will make the connection. The more explicit and clear you are in connecting your evidence to your claim, the more convincing your argument will be.

Additionally, it is often important to give your readers some information about the context for the texts by explaining, in this case, which campaign speeches you are looking at, where they were delivered, and to whom they were delivered. For example, if you discovered in your study of the context that women's issues were an important concern among Republican and undecided voters and that women's issues were an important theme of the campaign, you should report that to your reader, citing your sources appropriately.

Finally, if you are drawing upon some research about metaphors and their rhetorical function, you may need to cite that theoretical information to help support your argument that the contradiction between Dole's use of metaphors and her explicit statements about women's issues is problematic. A reader might not value your isolation of Dole's contradictions until you are able to use theory to show their rhetorical importance.

The conclusions you can draw about message dynamics will always be of things unseen. Unlike the astronomers who can eventually provide concrete evidence of certain celestial phenomena, you will never be able to observe physically the abstract dynamics of messages. Consequently, you must rigorously support your claim by providing the best evidence and theoretical rationale you can to reduce your readers' uncertainty regarding your claim.

LOGICALLY ORGANIZE IDEAS

Fourth, organize your report according to your readers' needs. In our Western culture, a fairly rigid, linear kind of logic is valued and expected in formal writing. Generally, as we talk, we often make claims that are not well articulated; we move from topic to topic without transitions, and we offer only the barest of support for assertions we make. In conversation, we often seem to make sense to each other and persuade each other using such fragmented arguments. Listen closely to people you perceive as very intelligent. Their speech is full of fragmented sentences, some started and abandoned partway through; some are run-on; some have problems of reference, agreement, or tense. We expect things to sound a certain way, and we rely on the rich vein of information provided by nonverbal communication to help clarify our meanings. If speakers are too precise grammatically, we think they sound stuffy and overblown. But writing is a different form of communication that has a different set of expectations and rules for presentation. While in your first draft you can get away with the messiness of speech, you can't get away with it when you write your final written draft. Although ideas presented orally may be more or less logically organized, when you write, ideas are expected to exhibit a clearly defined logic that moves sensibly from one point to the next by those who read your written message. Readers in Western societies have learned to expect certain patterns of logic and by meeting those expectations you help readers understand the case you are trying to argue. Some writers organize their ideas in an outline before they write while others prefer a concept map (see Figure 4.2) or simply jot notes to get something on paper. Whichever method you prefer, remember that you need to modify your first draft considerably to meet the organizational and grammatical needs of your readers so your ideas are easy for them to read and understand in your final draft.

To ensure that your ideas are understandable to your readers, first you need to assess their knowledge of rhetorical and communication theory. If it is minimal, consider using alternative language or defining terms for your readers so you can use the precise terminology of theory. Also, assess your readers' knowledge of the message and its context. If your audience has never encountered your message before, you may need to provide a descriptive summary of the message before advancing your argument. If, however, your readers are very familiar with the message, you might offend or bore them by rehashing the message or making statements about the context (e.g., the rhetor's background, the surrounding circumstances) that they already know.

Once you have assessed your readers' knowledge of rhetorical theory and the message and its context, you will need to think through the best way to organize your evidence to convince them of your argument. There are endless possibilities for arrangement, and you must create the pattern most fitting for your reader and purposes. For the sake of illustration, however, here is a sample outline.

I. Introduction
   A. Purpose of analysis
   B. Identify the message(s) under examination
   C. Provide basic information you found when researching the context to help the reader understand the circumstances, rhetor, etc.
II. Describe the message (assuming an unfamiliar reader)
   A. Briefly summarize the message
   B. Briefly characterize rhetorical characteristics to give a flavor for the message
III. State central thesis (claim)
IV. Offer evidence to prove and explain central argument
   A. Define any technical terminology necessary to understand analysis
   B. Name rhetorical dynamics and patterns
   C. Offer proof of patterns within the text
   D. Explain your argument about those patterns. Use external evidence (theory, other information, etc.) to support your inferences about those patterns
V. Draw conclusions telling your reader what your insights mean for them, the lessons learned, etc.

Again, this outline is simply a sample, not a formula. As you have learned by now, no two rhetorical messages are alike because the circumstances, rhetors, audiences, and motivations all differ. So too, no two reports will be alike because the critics, their circumstances, their audiences, and their motivations all differ. Assess your own rhetorical situation carefully as you prepare the product of your critique.

WRITE WELL

Fifth, write well. The strongest arguments are written clearly. Good ideas can be masked by poor message construction, so it is important that you pay close attention to your writing. For example, in expository writing of this sort, transitions between paragraphs and main ideas are essential in clarifying the direction of an argument to readers, yet we find that many student writers forget to provide those transitions. Arguments articulate complex relationships between ideas whereby ideas are presented linearly—one after another. To help your reader follow your thinking as you attempt to explain complex relationships, you must give your reader cues about changes in topic. Think of yourself as a tour guide for your reader as you point out those parts of the rhetorical event that you think are important. Transitions occur within paragraphs and between paragraphs and larger sections of some works. Help your reader know when topics are changing and explain to your reader how the ideas relate to each other before moving on.

Transitions are just one of many technical components of good writing. Grammatical accuracy is also highly important. When you converse with someone face-to-face you rely on many channels for clarifying your meaning to your conversational partner. You use the nonverbal mechanisms of your voice (e.g., pitch, pace, tone) and your body (e.g., gestures, movement, facial expression) to clarify your meanings, and you may repeat yourself as necessary. In written communication, however, those mechanisms are absent, which is why grammar is so important. Grammatical rules and punctuation are socially agreed upon codes that essentially replace the mechanisms of nonverbal communication. A comma, for example, indicates change of pace or subordination of ideas; an exclamation point indicates tone of voice! These graphic "replacement" mechanisms only work, however, if you generally abide by the rules of punctuation. When you break the rules unintentionally (due to carelessness or ignorance), your meanings become unclear and difficult for readers to understand. We strongly urge you to use resources available via the Internet and libraries to help yourself ensure clarity of your written ideas.

DOCUMENTING YOUR SOURCES

Historically, it has been a basic value of academic work to cite sources; that is, to give credit to those whose ideas you have used to develop your own. If you use a direct quotation, diagram, picture, or idea of another person, you must give that person credit for what you use. In recent years, due to technologies that allow easy reproduction of others' work, holders of copyrights are becoming increasingly aggressive in protecting what is called "intellectual property." As a result, you now have two good reasons to give credit when you use others' material: it's the ethical thing to do, and you protect yourself from getting sued. Better to err on the side of giving too much credit than not giving enough. At any rate, a number of systems are available for citing sources. Some of these have been devised by the Modern Language Association (MLA style), the American Psychological Association (APA style), Kate Turabian (Turabian style), and the University of Chicago (Chicago style). These systems differ and you need to familiarize yourself with the style manual that your instructor, university department, or profession prefers. Scholars in communication and rhetoric seem to prefer the MLA, APA, or Chicago style because they best fit the critical and social science research we do. Each system standardizes the form of citation and ensures that appropriate and sufficient information is included in each citation to assist other scholars in finding the same sources should they wish to do so.

Each system provides some kind of information for the reader in the text that indicates what material is being cited or "documented" by the writer; it may be a number or a parenthetical reference. If a number is used, it will correspond to the numbered information either at the bottom of the page in a footnote or at the end of the essay or chapter. If a parenthetical reference is given, the bibliographic information will be at the end of the text in alphabetical order. Both the MLA and APA styles do this. We suggest that you use a parenthetical style because it is easy and efficient. It avoids page formatting and renumbering problems you may face when revising your essays. It also avoids the duplicate work of creating both footnotes or endnotes and a bibliography since all necessary information is in a single section titled "Works Cited" (MLA) or "References" (APA).

MLA STYLE

Look at this example of MLA documentation in action:

> *Rhetorical criticism is more than describing precisely and analyzing completely. Those actions are necessary, but "useful rhetorical criticism, whatever else is may be, must function as an argument" (Brockriede 165). Good criticism, then moves beyond mechanical or technical dismantling of messages to creative interpretation of the analysis that requires you to make a case for what you've discovered about how communication works between human beings.*

You see the quotation that we borrowed and in the parentheses at the end, the last name of the author, Brockriede, and the page number from the text he wrote, page 165. The interruption is minimal, and you easily continue reading with the added knowledge of the author responsible for the key idea. To know the author's full name or what document this is from, you would turn to the end of the chapter or essay and find "Works Cited." Here's what you would see:

Works Cited

Brockriede, Wayne. "Rhetorical Criticism as Argument." *Quarterly Journal of Speech* 60 (1974): 165–74.

The author's name is placed last name, then first name. The title is in quotation marks; the journal title (as are all titles of complete works) is italicized; the volume number is placed after the title, the year is in parentheses, and the page numbers of the essay follow a colon. Note that the page numbers, as written, refer to the pages 165 to 174. The second numeral "1" is dropped in the citation because it is redundant. If the article spanned the pages 165 to 214, then the "2" would be included because it is necessary to indicate that the citation spans the next hundred pages. When you go to the library to find this article you know the journal to search for, and when you find it in the stacks, you know to find volume 60, page 165.

APA STYLE

The APA form is similar. Here's what it would look like:

> *Rhetorical criticism is more than describing precisely and analyzing completely. Those actions are necessary, but* "useful *rhetorical criticism, whatever else is may be, must function as an argument*" *(Brockriede, 1974, p. 165).* (In APA, the name and year separated by a comma are included; you *may* also include the page number to be more precise. In MLA style, the name and page number are used without a comma.)

Here is what you would then find at the end of the essay:

References

Brockriede, W. (1974). Rhetorical criticism as argument. *Quarterly Journal of Speech, 60,* 165–174.

Notice the differences between the MLA and APA format: in the APA example, the name is indented and only the first initial of the first name is used, not the whole name. The date comes immediately after the name (month and day are included if available). Only the first word of the title is capitalized and the title has no quotation marks. The journal title and the volume number are italicized and all digits are used in designating the inclusive pages.

In either system, the goal is to document as closely as possible the ideas or words borrowed and to provide a simple, clear means for recording bibliographic information for interested readers. Each kind of source you use has its own unique rules for citation within any system. That is, within the MLA style, citation in text and bibliographic forms differs for journals, books, newspapers, CD-ROM, websites, and so on. We strongly recommend that you purchase your own copy of the MLA or APA stylebook or whatever stylebook your department, professor, or profession requires. An outstanding, free resource can be found on the Web at http://www.docstyles.com/apacrib.htm (Dewey 2003). Here you will find a handy, easy-to-use APA manual with links to MLA documentation help. You can also find copies of the MLA and APA stylebooks available in your library reference section.

Remember, documentation is essential to your work as a professional. Do not avoid or fail to give credit to others from whom you have borrowed information, pictures, or ideas. At first, it is difficult and time-consuming, but as you learn the appropriate system, the job becomes easier. Good writing is marked not only by appropriate documentation, it is marked by precision in idea construction and presentation. Don't damage a good idea or argument by sloppy presentation of it.

SUMMARY

Once you have developed your ideas through your thinking and research, you will need to convey your findings to others, most often in the form of a written document. Presentations of findings are not uncommon, and most of what we have discussed here is directly applicable to the creation of an oral report as well. Creating a valued and useful product from your analytical work is a difficult task that requires organizing your ideas to communicate your findings clearly and effectively. No matter what your specific purpose, be it appreciating a message, teaching, or developing theory, you must skillfully shape the presentation to accomplish your purpose.

Precision and clarity are two important tools for making your logical case compelling to your reader or listener. You must know what you want to argue about the message at hand. You must decide what evidence from the text and the context as well as what theory is necessary to reduce your readers' uncertainty about your argument. You must consider how much or little your audience knows about communication and the context of this particular message. Then you must decide how to arrange the evidence and explanations your readers need in a manner that is sensible. It is essential that you write and proofread your material mindfully and critically. Serious or pervasive flaws in writing tend to mask the good ideas that may be embedded in it. Finally, you should not be afraid to use the good ideas of others, but be sure that you properly credit others whose work assists you in developing your own insights. It is important to become familiar with and use the stylebooks preferred or demanded by your audience or profession.

Good thinking deserves to be presented through good writing. The hard work it takes to become an effective writer will pay off in the success it brings you personally and professionally.

EXERCISES

1. Explain how a written report of an analysis of www.marthatalks.com would differ if you were writing it for (a) your boss, a prosecuting attorney preparing the case against Stewart; (b) a citizen action committee promoting legislation to increase regulation of stock trading; or (c) Martha Stewart, who is considering webpage designs of which this is one possible choice.

   What would be featured in each analysis? What would be masked in each analysis?
   What sorts of documentation would be expected for each?
   What kind of evidence from outside research would be needed?

2. Rewrite each of the following excerpts from student papers so they are correct grammatically and clearer to a reader.

> Emotional appeals involve the reader in the message emotion acts as sort of a motivator.

> If the rhetor can involve the readers in your message then they'll probably finish reading it and it will stay in your mind longer.

> It moves on to its point that when politics get involved they loose.

> The first section is a general description the second section was as story.

> Finally, the story of Jesse Owens rising above the racist Nazi beliefs.

3. Read Appendix 2, a student paper entitled "Barbara Jordan's Keynote Address at the 1992 Democratic National Convention: A Neutral Approach to a Partisan Task" or Appendix 3, a student paper entitled "A Response to the Death of a Princess: The Form and Function of a Eulogy" at the end of this book. From either essay, select a section of about twenty-five lines that contain one or more writing errors that diminish the power of the writer's ideas. Explain the error(s) found and the negative effect they had on your understanding of the argument. Then write an appropriate revision.

4. Read the student essay in Appendix 2 or 3 at the end of this book and identify each of the following:

- The student critic's claim
- Evidence provided to support the claim about Barbara Jordan's speech or the Queen's speech
- Other evidence used to support the claim

NOTES

1 These concepts are drawn from the Burkeian model we discuss in Chapter 13.

2 Data, claim, and warrant are explained in Chapter 10, "The New Rhetoric."

3 Chapter 17 discusses these visual concepts as rhetorical elements.

4 Chapters 11, 12, and 13 present three related approaches in that they treat human symbolic interaction as "dramatic." Due to the relatedness of the models, you will often see specific concepts from each particular model used in conjunction with concepts from others.

5 Chapter 15 provides a summary of feminist approaches that you may find useful for analyzing a wide variety of messages.

WORKS CITED

Brockriede, Wayne. "Rhetorical Criticism as Argument." *Quarterly Journal of Speech* 60 (1974): 165–74.

Dewey, Russ. "APA Research Style Crib Sheet." January 2003. http://docstyles.com/apacrib.htm (accessed September 5, 2003).

Martha Stewart. July 24, 2003. http://www.marthatalks.com.

NAACP.ORG. NAACP. August 20, 2003. http://www.naacp.org.

Reebok. July 29, 2003. http://www.reebok.com/us/index.htm.

Rosenfield, Lawrence. "The Experience of Criticism." *Quarterly Journal of Speech* 60 (1974): 489–96.

CLASSICAL APPROACHES

The following two chapters are a unit because the approaches are complementary. Chapter 9, "Classical Approaches: Ancient Rhetoric," explains the relationships of rhetorical concepts drawn primarily from Aristotle and Cicero. Chapter 10, "Classical Approaches: New Rhetoric," draws from the work of Stephen Toulmin as well as Chaim Perelman and Lucie Olbrechts-Tyteca. Although these three began their work in the mid-twentieth century, the groundwork for their approaches was laid by Aristotle. Consequently, both approaches are essentially classical in nature.

Just as this is a textbook for contemporary students of rhetoric, about twenty-five hundred years ago, Aristotle put together a series of lectures that have come to us as *The Rhetoric*—Aristotle's "textbook" (1984, sec. 1354a–1355b). Interestingly, Aristotle's initial training was in botany. When you read his *Rhetoric,* you will quickly see how his skill in observing and categorizing the plant world spilled over into how he approached the communication process. Aristotle's categorical approach has proven to be useful to both new and experienced critics in "seeing" better what persuasive tools have been selected by any message maker. Three particular foci emerge from his study of rhetoric: logic, emotions, and credibility. We'll be digging into these three quite a bit in Chapter 9, where we'll pay close attention to the relationships between these phenomena—the emotions or states of mind of the audience, the logic of the speaker and the audience's ability to follow it, and the importance of how an audience perceives the speaker. This model helps you see how these and other rhetorical elements we discuss work together to create a dynamic within a message that affects audiences.

Although classical concepts have been important in understanding rhetoric from ancient times to the present, those ideas have been developed, modified, clarified, and augmented by other scholars. Stephen Toulmin is a philosopher who has played an important role in determining how rhetorical critics analyze argumentative discourse. Just like Aristotle, Toulmin was seeking to understand how people argue in real life and set about observing closely the patterns of argument to be found there. His model of argumentation helps us better see elements of argument at work in messages. Toulmin's focus on everyday use of logic was, in part, intended to fix a wrong turn he felt many scholars had taken in their understanding of Aristotle's approach to argument (Toulmin 1969, 95–96). You will find his model quite a flexible tool for analyzing arguments. However, you will also find that flexibility challenging when you apply the model to messages. We try to assist you in making the most of Toulmin's model while avoiding the temptation to use his model as a template for neatly packaging every sentence in a message.

Chaim Perelman and Lucie Olbrechts-Tyteca also offer a contemporary view of rhetoric that is rooted in classical theories. Whereas Toulmin was a philosopher, Perelman was a lawyer interested in understanding how arguments about values (i.e., the issues with which judges struggle) were not completely arbitrary (Perelman 1979, 8). Since values are extremely important to us in our political, religious, civic, and economic lives, Perelman's work provides a way of analyzing value-laden arguments. Just as Toulmin started with Aristotle's study of logic, so do Perelman and Olbrechts-Tyteca. Consequently, the new rhetoric is connected to the old in that it extends, develops, and elaborates the ancient theories.

This unit will help you form a foundation of critical concepts that have proven themselves useful as critical tools. Together, the ancient and contemporary approaches to rhetoric provide useful theories for understanding how people attempt to persuade each other on issues important to them. Keep in mind though that this is an introduction. Each of the concepts discussed herein is complex and merits further exploration by you. As you apply the models in these two chapters, you will see the value of elaborating your understanding of them.

WORKS CITED

Aristotle. *The Rhetoric and Poetics of Aristotle.* Translated by W. Rhys Roberts. New York: The Modern Library, 1984.

Perelman, Chaim. *The New Rhetoric and the Humanities: Essays on Rhetoric and Its Applications.* Dordrecht, Holland: D. Reidel, 1979.

Toulmin, Stephen. *The Uses of Argument.* Cambridge: Cambridge University Press, 1969.

CLASSICAL APPROACHES: ANCIENT RHETORIC

9

Although there were many important ancient scholars of rhetoric, Aristotle towers over them all. Born in 384 B.C., he was a student of Plato and later a teacher in Plato's academy; he also served as tutor to Alexander the Great. Aristotle was initially trained by his father as a biological scientist, which may explain his penchant for classification that plays a large part in his presentation of ideas in *The Rhetoric*. Even though Aristotle worked hard at systematically presenting his discussion of rhetoric, the "messy" nature of persuasive discourse often requires even Aristotle to backtrack and skip around in his discussions to deal with the complexity of the questions raised by inquiry into human communication.

Another important rhetorical scholar whose work has much influenced modern thinking about rhetoric is the Roman teacher Cicero (106 B.C.–43 B.C.). For the Romans, who were building on the Greek tradition, training in rhetoric was central to a liberal education. Cicero's work, by his own admission, was a synthesis of ideas he'd collected from other scholars, but the manner and presentation of those ideas set him apart from his contemporaries. Just as Aristotle assisted his students by classifying and organizing rhetorical elements, so did Cicero. Consequently, when we bring their works together, we have a way of seeing rhetoric that is not just Aristotelian or Ciceronian but classical. Take a look at Figure 9.1; then, in the following sections, we'll discuss each of its elements.

SOME CLASSICAL RHETORICAL CONCEPTS

Recall our discussion of search models in Chapter 3. The real values of such models are that they assist you in systematically searching your text for significant uses of particular rhetorical tools, and they suggest a constellation of useful critical questions to be asked about any particular message. We'll show you some examples of how the classical model in Figure 9.1 suggests critical questions as we work through it.

Central to Aristotle's initial discussion of rhetoric are the kinds, or genres, of rhetoric that he identified: (1) deliberative, or political; (2) forensic, or legal; and (3) epideictic, or ceremonial. Aristotle perceived

Vocabulary

➤ political speaking
➤ forensic speaking
➤ ceremonial speaking
➤ canons of rhetoric
➤ invention
➤ arrangement
➤ elocution (style)
➤ memory
➤ delivery
➤ simile
➤ metaphor
➤ irony
➤ personification
➤ visual images
➤ parallelism
➤ antithesis
➤ alliteration
➤ credibility
➤ emotions
➤ enthymeme
➤ syllogism
➤ maxim
➤ enthymematic
➤ induction
➤ apology

FIGURE 9.1

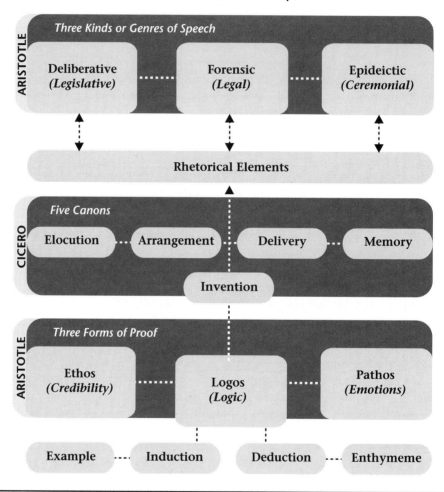

Classical Rhetorical Concepts

particular patterns of rhetoric associated with each of these classifications. That is, those who made or listened to speeches in the legislature had learned to expect certain kinds of arguments or kinds of evidence and proof as well as certain kinds of organization and delivery in that context. Those who made or listened to speeches in a court had certain expectations and so on. These patterns developed over time through the experiences of those who spoke in those contexts. Aristotle made assumed and expected patterns explicit to his students so that they could better see what made one person more persuasive than another. By making this initial division of kinds of speech, he began to show his students how to systematically analyze discourse, which is exactly the same concern we have today. In the first paragraph of Book I of *The Rhetoric*, Aristotle states:

> *Ordinary people do this [speech making] either at random or through practice and from acquainted habit. Both ways being possible, the subject can plainly be handled systematically, for it is possible to inquire the reason why some speakers succeed through practice and others spontaneously; and every one will at once agree that such an inquiry is the function of an art [or methodical treatment of a subject]. (1984, sec. 1354a)*

The three genres of discourse identified by Aristotle are important because they are "determined by the three classes of listeners to speeches. For the three elements in speech-making—speaker, subject, and person addressed—it is the last one, the hearer, that determines the speaker's end and object" (sec. 1358a). Notice how Aristotle is already building a set of categories and explaining their relationships—three kinds of speeches, three parts of the rhetorical situation. Aristotle characterizes the genres as follows:

- **Deliberative** "Political speaking *urges us either to do or not do something. . . . it is concerned with the future: it is about things to be done hereafter that [one]* advises, for or against."
- **Forensic** "Forensic speaking *either attacks or defends somebody. . . . The party in a case at law is concerned with the past; one [person] accuses the other, and the other defends [oneself], with reference to things already done.*"
- **Epideictic** Ceremonial speaking "*is, properly speaking, concerned with the present, since all [people] praise or blame in view of the state of things existing at the time, though they often find it useful to recall the past and to make guesses at the future.*" (sec. 1358b, emphasis added)

Political speech was primarily the province of the legislature. Today, that is still very much the case, but due to the size of present democratic states, and the use of the mass media, political speech is found on our televisions and radios, in our newspapers, magazines, and websites. When we listen to politicians argue about proposed laws, policies, or regulations, they do exactly what Aristotle observed—they argue the expediency or harmfulness of proposals; they also argue whether a proposal is good or bad, just or unjust, honorable or dishonorable. Legal speech is similar but the focus is on what is just or unjust while sometimes praising or attacking defendants or witnesses (sec. 1358b). On the other hand, ceremonial speeches such as eulogies, speeches of introduction, acceptance speeches, and so on feature praise of others, but sometimes also attempt to persuade audiences to adhere to ideas or values dear to the person or people who were the subject of the speech. An excellent example of this is Lyndon Johnson's eulogy for President Kennedy in which Johnson praised Kennedy and advocated continuing the programs Kennedy had initiated in order to honor his work.

Aristotle laid out the general patterns of speech associated with specific contexts of discourse. His three categories are clear, but notice how Aristotle acknowledges the messiness of rhetoric as he reminds his students that legal discourse is often wedded to ceremonial speech (which features praising or blaming) to reach the ends of the defense or prosecution. Attorneys often make a case by praising or blaming a defendant or witness.

Nevertheless, the idea of genre or kind of speech is essential for you to start with because it invites you to look for the patterns that are central to the genre, while being flexible in recognizing variations needed to accommodate the unique circumstances of fluid, evolving, and complicated public discourse. It requires a balance of rigor of definition and flexibility of application that we mentioned earlier. As a result of continued research and development of rhetorical concepts, the number of known genres of discourse is much greater than the three identified by Aristotle. You will find the concept quite useful in many practical applications of criticism. For example, if you are working for a congressional representative analyzing an opponent's campaign literature, an initial question you may ask is, in what genre of discourse do these messages operate? Each genre of message has different purposes, structures, and styles that guide your analysis. Your analysis of the assigned material would be affected by whether the answer to the genre question is, for example, a position paper or a floor speech. Once you know the kind of message you are working with, the concepts and questions you ask about it may be somewhat different.

If the text is a position paper, you may ask:	**If the text is a floor speech, you may ask:**
What are the common, expected attributes of political position papers?	What are the common, expected attributes of floor speeches?
How similar is the paper I'm studying to the expected patterns?	Was the speech intended for a live audience or was it merely intended to be "read into the record"?
If it differs, do the differences matter?	Was there anything extraordinary about the context surrounding this speech to set it apart from speeches delivered regularly in the legislature?
What kinds of arguments are common to position papers?	
What documentation is required of an effective position paper?	

You need to bring the concept of genre to bear on anything you examine. If the only starting point you have is the tripartite list of Aristotle's, at least that focuses your description and analysis and leads you to ask appropriate questions about the text. But generic categories alone usually are not sufficient to see how messages work as persuasion.

According to Cicero, the messages created within any of the three genres identified by Aristotle are created through the use of certain rhetorical elements. Those elements were identified nicely by Cicero in his book *De Inventione*. Commonly, these elements are called the **canons of rhetoric**. Think of canons as *primary rules or principles of rhetoric*. These five categories are important tools for message analysis because they provide a handy list of potential choices made by a rhetor when constructing a message. According to Cicero, rhetoric can be divided into five components: invention, arrangement, elocution, memory, and delivery (1988, Bk I, ch. vii, emphasis added). **Invention** is *the process of selecting such things as arguments, illustrations, examples, facts, testimony, documents, images, and so on that will be persuasive to an audience.* **Arrangement** is *putting the pieces gathered in invention into an order of presentation that makes the most sense to, and will have the most impact on, the audience.* **Elocution** (or **style**) involves *selecting the most appropriate vocabulary and turns of phrase that will make sense to a particular audience.* Today, **memory** is *the creation of a lasting impression and understanding of the message in the minds of the audience.* Finally, **delivery** has to do with *the presentation of voice and gesture that is appropriate to the speaking situation as well as the design of mediated messages, selection of media, and their presentation in the media.* Each canon describes basic operating elements of rhetoric, and you can use each canon as a starting point for framing questions that will deepen and focus your study of any text. We'll look at each of the canons in an order slightly different from the preceding, ending with invention—the most significant of the canons.

STYLE

Aristotle taught his students that each kind of oratory (as well as poetry and prose), has its own style (sec. 1413b). For Quintilian, "style is revealed both in individual words and in groups of words" (1920, Bk VIII). The pattern of word choice is what makes a "style" of discourse. There can be no one style that is always effective since rhetors, audiences, and the audiences' needs change with their nature or circumstances. Consequently, Aristotle doesn't describe specific styles, but instead, lays out ideal qualities of any style as they relate to the kind of discourse being created. A good style, then, is clear, impressive, appropriate, and lively. A bad style is frigid. Bad style is marked by misuse of compound words, strange words, epithets, and weak metaphors (sec. 1406). Not much has changed in our response to bad speaking or writing over twenty-three hundred years.

In describing style, Aristotle referred primarily to language since he observed only oratory. Today, however, because many of our rhetorical messages come in forms other than oratory (e.g., newspapers, magazines, billboards, television), style is developed through nonverbal devices as well as through language. A number of stylistic devices are named in the following sections, though some of these terms are derived from other sources and are not found in Aristotle's treatise, *The Rhetoric.* Again we urge you to remember that rhetors do not use formulas when they construct their messages; rather, they act creatively. So, as you systematically apply the classical concepts you are learning, keep your mind open to seeing and naming stylistic devices other than those listed here. Ask yourself: What patterns of word choice exist in this message? Are those choices appropriate for the audience? Are there any unexpected choices here that make a difference in how the message works?

■ Simile

Figures of speech (or what Aristotle called "tropes") are language devices commonly used to influence how an audience imagines something. One such figure of speech is called a simile. A **simile** *compares two or more things, using the words* like *or* as, such as "He rushed on like a lion." In his "I have a dream" speech, Martin Luther King Jr. used the following similes: "No, no, we are not satisfied, and we will not be satisfied until justice rolls down *like* waters and righteousness *like* a mighty stream" (1998, 782). Where he could have simply said, "We will not be satisfied until we have justice and righteousness," King chose to compare justice to waters and righteousness to a mighty stream. If we apply the qualities of good style already mentioned, we are able to judge his use of simile as effective because it is correct, impressive, appropriate, and lively.

■ Metaphor

Metaphor is *a more subtle comparison in which a rhetor refers to one thing in terms of something it is not, never using the words* like *or* as. For example, one may say of an angry man, "A lion, he rushed on." Aristotle felt metaphor was extremely important for clarity of message as well as for shaping audience responses. Again in "I have a dream," Martin Luther King Jr. relied on metaphor to convey the notion that because black Americans are Americans they, by definition, are owed certain rights by the government. King could have said just that, but instead, he used the metaphor of a checking account. Take a look at this extended metaphor:

> *So we've come here today to dramatize a shameful condition. In a sense we've come to our nation's capital to cash a check. When the architects of our Republic wrote the magnificent words of the Constitution and the Declaration of Independence, they were signing a promissory note to which every American was to fall heir. This note was a promise that all men—yes, black men as well as white men—would be guaranteed the unalienable rights of life, liberty, and the pursuit of happiness.*
>
> *It is obvious today that America has defaulted on this promissory note insofar as her citizens of color are concerned. Instead of honoring the sacred obligation, America has given the Negro people a bad check, a check which has come back marked "insufficient funds." (1998, 781)*

Metaphor, for Aristotle, constituted one of only two ways language can be used. Since it often requires audiences to involve themselves in making sense of the trope, and since the metaphor may also stir audience memories and emotions, this was for him, central to good style. Look carefully at the metaphors constructed in any message you are examining, for they will tell you much about the capability of the rhetor in handling language. In short, Aristotle asks speakers and listeners to pay close attention to specific language choices when composing a message. So, when examining the style of a message, you need to pay attention to the kind of message and the expectations raised by it, and then the specific use of language. However, metaphor and simile are not the only tropes you may find working in any message you examine. Let's look at a few more possibilities.

▪ Irony

Irony is *the intentional use of a word in such a way as to convey a meaning opposite the literal meaning of the word; the use of a word or phrase unexpected in that particular context.* For example, if you were describing a party you really enjoyed and didn't want to leave, it would be ironic or unexpected for you to say, "I was overjoyed to leave the party and go to the library to do my chemistry homework."

▪ Personification

Personification is *used when a rhetor gives an abstract concept (e.g., freedom) or inanimate object (e.g., land) human qualities or abilities.* For example, in the song, "God bless America," we personify America as we sing the phrase "Stand beside her, and guide her . . ." as if America is a female person to be guided and stood by.

▪ Visual Imagery

Visual images consist of *words intended to convey the tone or feeling of a message.* For example, Tom Hanks's film *That Thing You Do* is light, peppy, cheerful, and fun—certainly not dramatic, academic, heavy, or sad. In part, the tone we just described is conveyed through the use of bright colors in the film. The title sequence is made up of thick block lettering with alternating colors of bright yellow, fuchsia, kelly green, and aqua blue. In contrast, a cursive font and earth tones would have conveyed a significantly different feeling.

Often, visual images are created through a rhetor's descriptive language. Martin Luther King Jr. creates a vivid image of the plight of black Americans in the following passage:

> But one hundred years later, the Negro still is not free. One hundred years later, the life of the Negro is still sadly crippled by the manacles of segregation and the chains of discrimination. One hundred years later, the Negro lives on a lonely island of poverty in the midst of a vast ocean of material prosperity. One hundred years later, the Negro still languishes in the corners of American society and finds himself in exile in his own land. (1998, 780)

When studying the tropes of a message to get a sense of the style, you should not merely list all the tropes used in a given message. Instead, you are looking for significant patterns in the use of tropes. If particular metaphors, similes, or visual images, for example, continuously recur in a message, or if they recur in conjunction with a recurring line of reasoning, you might note the pattern and begin asking yourself questions about why that pattern exists and what its potential impact might be. In addition to studying the patterns of tropes, you might also examine how words are arranged to convey a particular feeling. These rhetorical devices are called "schemes."

■ Parallelism

Parallelism is *the schematic repetition of a phrase in a series of phrases or sentences.* Think of this in terms of the parallel bars in men's gymnastics. The two bars run side by side and are alike in height and length. The same is true of parallel phrases or sentences. For example, the National Smokers Alliance ad in Chapter 3 uses parallel phrases in the stacked blocks: "The right to eat bacon and eggs!" "The right to enjoy coffee!" "The right to make your own choices!" "The right to speak your mind!" "The right to smoke!" "The right to think for yourself!" Notice that each title is phrased exactly like the one before it, "The right to . . ." and notice that the blocks on the bottom contain more abstract, commonly valued rights than those on top.

■ Antithesis

Antithesis is *the schematic juxtaposition of contrasting ideas, often in parallel structure.* A rhetor uses antithesis when he or she sets side by side two opposing ideas to make a point. For example, you may have heard a speaker say, "If you're not for us, you're against us." John F. Kennedy's famous antithesis is still remembered today: "Ask not what your country can do for you, ask what you can do for your country."

■ Alliteration

Alliteration is *the repetition of beginning consonant sounds in a series of words.* We often associate alliteration with nursery rhymes like "She sells seashells down by the seashore" or "Peter Piper picked a peck of pickled peppers." Yet rhetors may also use alliteration to draw attention to their message. Southwest Airlines uses alliteration, for example, in their advertising campaign slogan, "Friends fly free."

Use these concepts to assist you in searching any text for functional stylistic elements—those that seem to make a difference in the quality or effectiveness of any message. Remember that this is not an exhaustive list. It will be necessary for you to expand your knowledge of this canon through further research. Now, to quote Aristotle, "This concludes our discussion of style. . . . We have now to deal with arrangement" (sec. 1413b).

ARRANGEMENT

The process of arrangement or organization of a message is Cicero's second canon of rhetoric. Remember, earlier we defined arrangement as putting the pieces gathered in invention into an order of presentation that makes the most sense to and will have the most impact on the audience. Another way of thinking about arrangement is as the "management of ideas." Rhetoric is about the presentation of ideas, and it seems to matter which ideas are chosen by a rhetor and in what order those ideas are presented. Over the years, some stock patterns of arrangement have been identified. Teachers of composition (and later teachers of speech), from the late 1800s to the present, have often described the arrangement of essays and paragraphs as problem-solution, chronological, comparison-contrast, and so on—you may have been given the impression that these ways of arranging an essay or speech are fixed. These are, in fact, common forms of arrangement because we often write about problems and their solutions, or tell a story by presenting a report of events as they happened (chronology). However, message makers are seldom required to use a particular pattern. Instead, they exercise their creativity in arranging ideas (Mendelson 1988, 68). Actually, arrangement is fluid because, like a fluid, it can shift to fit the specific rhetorical situation. As a critic, you must be open to perceiving any pattern devised by a message maker who is responding to the specific context of the rhetorical situation. So, although you may start your analysis with a list of common patterns in mind, be sure to keep your eyes open for creative applications of those patterns, modifications of them, or creation of completely new ones. Asking questions about arrangement will help you. For example, if you ask yourself how the same message could have been reorganized, the existing pattern will take on new significance. If you can think of no other arrangement, perhaps the message maker had little choice given the context. If so, then you may want to minimize discussion of the arrangement itself in favor of one that looks at the powerful contextual dynamics that constrained the message maker. If you can think of one or more alternative arrangements, you know that arrangement is a creative choice made by the message maker. In that case, the choices about arrangement may merit more discussion than context.

Described next are four common patterns that may or may not be apparent in any given message. Knowing these four patterns, however, may help you begin to identify the particular pattern in the messages you are studying.

■ Comparison and Contrast

This structure might involve an explanation of one idea in the first part of the message and a comparison to a second idea in the latter part of the message, or it might involve the constant comparing and contrasting of two or more entities throughout the message. This type of organizational pattern is often used in commercials where one product is being compared with another. First Product A is shown to work better than Product B, then Product A is shown as costing less than Product B.

■ Problem-Solution

Problem-solution is a commonly used structure in which a problem is named and explained and then followed by the offering of a solution. Kenda Creasy, a student at Miami University (Ohio), spoke on the topic of hospice in a speech entitled, "A time for peace." In the following excerpt, note the structure of the argument as a paragraph outlining the problem followed immediately by a paragraph presenting a solution.

> *The traditional American approach to terminal illness ignores three basic facts of life: the limits of curative medicine, the isolation of institutions, and the psy-*

chological impact death has on both the patient and his family. The first problem is the inherent limits of a medical system designed to cure. Hospitals maintain life: everything from visiting hours to progress reports are designed for the temporary stay. But the terminal patient's stay is not temporary; he will not get well. Time magazine pointed out in June, 1978, "Imbued as the medical establishment is with the idea of fighting at all costs to prolong life, it is naturally geared to the hope of success rather than to the fact of failure." But as Changing Times explained in April, 1979, "When care designed to cure and rehabilitate is applied to a person who knows he has a terminal illness, it creates a feeling of isolation and despair, especially if he senses the staff is just going through the motions."

Hospices make no such false promises. Dr. James Cimino explains, "For the hospice patient, it is too late for cures. The operations, radiation, and chemotherapy have been tried elsewhere. They've been declared incurable and inoperable. The patient is entirely aware of his situation." Hospices provide two choices: either the person can go the hospice or, more likely, the hospice will come to him, 24 hours a day, if necessary, with a team of doctors, psychologists, clergy, good neighbors, and volunteers. Treatment is palliative—that is, designed to ease pain and manage symptoms, such as nausea, but no heroic effort is made to cure the disease. The results? The person is comfortable, and his mind is clear. (Linkugel, Allen, and Johannesen 1982, 309)

Notice how each paragraph is structured. The problem paragraph lays out three problems that, taken together, constitute the problem that hospital care is misapplied to terminally ill patients. In paragraph two, Creasy presents a solution, but she does not attempt to deal with each of the three specific problems noted in paragraph one. Rather, she presents a general solution to the overall problem and focuses on alternatives within the solution.

■ Chronology

The ideas in some messages are organized chronologically. This means that the main topics in the message are organized according to a time sequence. A speech might address how things were in the past, how things are today, and how things need to be in the future. Martin Luther King Jr.'s famous "I have a dream" speech is organized this way. He begins by briefly describing the condition of slavery experienced by African Americans. He then describes where the African American community is "today" (1968) in standing before the government to demand their full rights as Americans. In the last third of the speech he describes his vision for the future in the well-remembered "I have a dream" section. A chronological message might also be arranged according to specific time periods. A eulogy, for example, might begin by describing the deceased's childhood, then early adulthood, middle age, and, finally, retirement.

■ Topical

Some messages are arranged topically. That is, the rhetor simply moves from one topic to the next in an order the rhetor feels makes most sense. State of the

Union speeches are often arranged this way as the president speaks to a wide variety of issues. He might first address the current economic situation, then he might address his plan for cutting or increasing taxes, then he might address the issue of health care, then education, and then crime. Often there may be some significance to the order in which the president chooses to arrange the various topics: perhaps from most to least important or from least convincing to most convincing. A wise attorney presenting the closing argument to a criminal case might present the strongest evidence at the beginning and end of the speech, leaving the weakest evidence to rest in the middle, the part of the speech the jury is least likely to remember.

These four organizational patterns indeed are commonly used, but keep in mind that rhetors creatively invent and organize their messages often without considering these or any other categories. Thus, you may find that none of these four categories accurately describes the structure you see in the message you are studying. If that is the case, try creating your own label to accurately and precisely represent the way ideas are organized in the message. Keep in mind that the rhetor could have chosen a different way to arrange his or her ideas. By asking yourself how the message might have been arranged differently, you are more able to understand the choices the rhetor *did* make. Having considered arrangement, we are now going to briefly examine the canons of delivery and memory.

DELIVERY

In ancient times, delivery referred to the physical delivery of the speech: the use of the voice and body. Today, the canon of delivery might be broadened to include the medium by which a message is delivered (e.g., television, magazines, newspaper, billboard, radio, etc.). To use the concept today, it has to be expanded from the limited nonverbal description provided by Aristotle, Cicero, and others. While speech still requires attention to the use of vocal volume, rate, tone, and pitch as well as gestures, emblems, and illustrators, the media suggest other dimensions of delivery, such as image placement, size, focus, cuts, camera angles, and so on. For example, where a political ad is placed in a newspaper may be an important part of its strategy; also, how a candidate is lighted, the angle of the camera, and the size of the picture along with the specific facial expression or gestures that are chosen all constitute elements of delivery. Likewise, the delivery of a television advertisement of a hair cream may be analyzed using many of the same dimensions just listed, as well as voice-overs, music, and visual effects. A critic, then, should make note of how a message was delivered and how that physical medium might impact the other rhetorical strategies employed by a message maker.

MEMORY

In the preliterate ancient world, memory served as the "resource library" for any orator. To speak on the broad range of subjects that citizens encountered in the courts and legislature, a large mental storehouse of information, anecdotes, illustrations, and quotations was necessary to quickly provide the ideas needed to create compelling arguments. The focus of most classical instruction regarding memory was about how to memorize and retrieve needed material for speaking. In literate society, the canon of memory has a different focus. We tend now to store specific bits of information in writing and remember where or how to find the information as needed. Cicero actually seems to have anticipated this modern condition in his definition of the canon of memory as "the lasting sense in the mind of the matters and words corresponding to the reception of these topics." Today, rhetors don't rely so much on memory in the creation of a message as they use the memory ("the lasting sense in the mind") of the audience to provide context and meaning for the message. For example, we see this use of audience memory in daily political cartoons. (See Medhurst and DeSousa [1981] for an interesting discussion of all five classical canons applied to political cartoons.) Given the limited ability of the cartoonist to include *all* relevant information in a single panel, the cartoonist includes cues to pique the memory of the reader, who then supplies information needed to make sense of the cartoon and interpret the argument it is making. That's why old political cartoons often don't make any sense to a reader who lacks the necessary memory to appropriately or sufficiently add to the message. How a rhetor both creates memorable messages for audiences or taps the memory of audiences to assist in making a message is an important area of critical consideration. We discuss in the next chapter how this general principle is used regularly in making arguments. Both the old and new versions of memory are important as search tools for you as a contemporary message analyst.

INVENTION

Finally, we need to examine the concept of invention, which is probably the most important of the canons. It is treated at great length by Aristotle and Cicero, both of whom focused on the invention or creation of arguments. Aristotle offered "three means of effecting persuasion . . . (1) to reason logically, (2) to understand human character . . . and (3) to understand the emotions . . ." (sec. 1356a). These three means are also known as logic, credibility, and emotional appeals or as the traditional terms: logos, ethos, and pathos. Due to the complexity of the topic of logic (logos), we are going to treat that in some length in the next chapter. Here we focus attention on the concepts of credibility (ethos) and emotions (pathos).

■ Credibility as a Means of Persuasion

Credibility or *believability* by an audience stems from *the audience's perception of the speaker's intelligence, honesty, and goodwill.* Aristotle's observation makes sense—if you are going to make an important decision based on the opinion of another person, you look for an opinion leader who you perceive to be smart, honest, and well intentioned. According to Aristotle, those are the qualities that constitute character and create a perception of believability (sec. 1378a). He observed, too, that the construction of a perception of credibility was important, so important that sometimes character "may almost be called the most effective means of persuasion" (sec. 1356a). Roman rhetorician

Quintilian also recognized the centrality of a speaker's character to effective persuasion. However, for Quintilian, the character of the speaker was even more important than it was for Aristotle. Quintilian defined rhetoric as a good person speaking well whereby a speaker's character is the central element of oratory (speaking well). For him, rhetoric had a decidedly moral purpose, for it was through the discourse of honorable citizens that difficult decisions could be made that would preserve the life and lifestyles of the population. Corrupting the rhetorical process through deceit or self-interest makes it difficult for citizens to trust what their leaders say and make well-informed decisions that will promote their safety and prosperity. Much of the discussion about George W. Bush's reference to alleged Iraqi efforts to purchase uranium from Niger in Bush's 2003 State of the Union address was rooted in this concern. We see the consequences of "bad" people speaking, be it well or poorly, in today's politics. People are less inclined to vote because they often don't trust the candidates' promises or proposals. Quintilian deeply understood how lack of character in political leaders will negatively affect a society.

Interestingly, Aristotle took a seemingly contemporary position on credibility as a persuasive tool by recognizing that character is a perceived quality that is essentially constructed by the audience. Credible speakers appear to an audience to be intelligent, honest, and of goodwill, and they will be more effective than those lacking one or more of these perceived qualities. Aristotle was not advocating deception, but he recognized the role of the audience in creating meaning in any communication event, and he clearly laid out the three building blocks of credibility to assist his students in appropriately using this powerful persuasive tool.

Aristotle recognized not only that credibility (ethos) is a powerful persuasive tool in its own right but also that it is related to emotional appeals. In appearing to be capable and interested in what is good for the audience, a speaker puts the audience in a proper frame of mind such that the audience feels compelled to give the speaker's ideas substantial weight.

■ Emotion as a Means of Persuasion

At the beginning of *The Rhetoric,* Aristotle complains that other writers on the topic have misplaced their efforts by giving too little attention to logic as a persuasive tool and too much attention to emotions. This focus perverts justice just like if you "warp a carpenter's rule before using it" (sec. 1353a). It would seem, at first glance, that Aristotle discounts the use of emotional appeals; however, such a conclusion is absolutely wrong. Aristotle understands human passions to be powerful motivators and understands that our emotions are directly tied to our logical abilities and performance. To persuade, that is, not just prove an argument but actually get people to respond as we want them to respond, message makers and analysts need to understand human emotions.

Although Aristotle's psychology was primitive, it had much greater sophistication and complexity than the contemporary stimulus-response model of human emotions. Such a model reduces people to machines wherein we believe (and we actually use this language) if we "push someone's buttons" we can elicit an automatic emotional response. This model is too simple to really explain how emotions do become stirred by messages or explain how the emotions affect our judgments.

Aristotle talked of **emotions** as *"states of mind"* that are the result of the interaction of three elements: (1) the frame of mind, (2) who is related to certain frames of mind, and (3) on what grounds an audience may adopt a frame of mind (sec. 1378a). He makes clear from his discussions of specific emotions later that passions are aroused using a complex set of rhetorical devices and strategies and are not simple, mindless responses to single words. Rather, audiences are brought into certain frames of mind over time by carefully considered actions on the part of the rhetor that builds grounds for emotional responses. As critics, then, we need to look at the cluster of rhetorical devices or strategies rhetors use to bring an audience to some frame of mind.

Often, novice critics will write something like this: "In his first inaugural address, Lincoln mentioned God, so everyone felt a religious connection with him and supported him." This simplistic notion misunderstands the complexity of human thinking and judgment and diminishes all communication to a formula of "mentioning" a series of "correct" words that "make" audiences respond exactly as a rhetor wishes. In Lincoln's first inaugural, his focus was on developing a complex argument for why the Union had to be preserved. His single mention of "the Almighty Ruler of Nations" was consistent with his apparent religious belief and that of many, but certainly not all, in his audience. However, that single mention of God has little or no persuasive weight given Lincoln's clear rhetorical purposes and the structure of the speech. What merits attention is not his mention of the Almighty, but the ways in which he attempts to create an emotion or frame of mind in his audience (which still included Southerners) wherein all felt compelled to work hard to find ways to deal with the country's problems without tearing it apart, and possibly destroying for all time the greatest experiment in democracy ever attempted. When you figure out how Lincoln created this frame of mind or passion in his audience, you learn something substantial about rhetoric. Pointing to a single word, phrase, or image and declaring that all audience members immediately responded emotionally in the same way misunderstands the nature of persuasion and fails to uncover anything new about the communication process.

Aristotle actually took the study of human emotions seriously. When he condemned those writing competing texts as focusing on emotions and dealing with nonessentials, his grievance was essentially what we have already outlined. Emotions are important, complex, and connected to other rhetorical elements of character and logic, he argued. To treat emotions alone or superficially is to deal in nonessentials. In other words, Aristotle felt that treating the emotions apart from their dynamic relationship with other rhetorical elements was pointless. How seriously he took emotions is evidenced in Book II of *The Rhetoric* wherein he outlined sixteen specific emotional states and explained all that is involved in getting someone into such frames of mind.

For example, he began with one of the most powerful of emotions: anger. Always conscious of the three elements of emotions, he explored at length the sources of anger and how anger can be controlled. He identified three specific means of creating an angry state of mind called "slights." These slights are ways of communicating with another to elicit anger. The first is treating another with contempt, the second is spite, and the third is insolence. Each of these operates most effectively given certain conditions related to the frame of mind sought (in this case anger), who makes audiences angry, and the grounds for such a response to those people. Contempt does not work exactly like spite, and spite works differently from insolence. To get a better picture of the carefulness of Aristotle's analysis, we recommend you read section 1378a of *The Rhetoric*.

Following anger, Aristotle explored at some length the other emotions: calm, friendship (liking and love), and enmity; hatred, fear, confidence, shame, and shamelessness; kindness and unkindness; pity, indignation, satisfaction, envy, and emulation (sec. 1380a–1388b). This is quite a list, but certainly not exhaustive. With a moment's reflection we notice that such frames of mind as guilt, redemption, altruism, optimism, pride, and patriotism are missing. The goal is not to create the magic list, but to realize that we can identify specific emotional states, and as Aristotle taught us, we can figure out what rhetorical devices and strategies can bring audiences into specific emotional states that complement (or fail to complement) appeals to credibility and logic in order to persuade an audience to believe or act as a rhetor may desire. When we can figure those things out, then we are dealing with important and essential questions of message analysis.

As a critic, be sure to take emotional appeals seriously, as did Aristotle. That is, treat emotional appeals as complex rhetorical tools. Typically, there is more to putting an audience into a particular frame of mind than just "mentioning" something. For example, each Christmas season, Hallmark runs a series of ads that are based on emotional appeals so powerful that people often cry during a thirty-second spot. What elicits such responses? When we look at such messages, we discover that the ads use a narrative form (we discuss this at length in Chapter 11) wherein images are arranged so that they tell a story that is common to our experience—the desire for and achievement of an important human relationship. All of us have suffered the loss of a close friend or relative, and the stories in the Hallmark ads evoke our memories of those events. The characters in the stories are designed to be like our perception of ourselves (although they may not necessarily look exactly like us): caring, intelligent, successful, altogether normal people who mourn the loss of a relationship with a relative or close friend. The implicit solution to the problem is in sending and receiving Hallmark cards. The themes, images, narratives, characterizations, and plots all work together to create an emotional response that, for many, is very persuasive. These sophisticated emotional appeals are effective because they employ a cluster of related tools that are designed to create targeted frames of mind or emotional responses in audiences. Nevertheless, as Aristotle noted, emotions alone are not enough. Reason complements emotion.

■ Reason as Means of Persuasion

The third means by which rhetors invent persuasive messages is through reasoned argument. Aristotle taught that there were essentially two forms of reasoning available: enthymemes (i.e., deduction) and induction (sec. 1356b). Both forms of reasoning deal with those areas of life that are contingent or probable. For example, the establishment of guilt or innocence in a court is based on a judgment made from evidence pieced together by lawyers that is presented to and interpreted by a jury. A jury has to decide if in fact some act was committed by a defendant at some point in the past. Proof is not absolute; rather, a jury is persuaded to make a particular judgment that is probably correct. The same goes for legislative debate. Is a tax cut the best action for the government to take in the future? No one knows absolutely, but we must decide what is probably the best course of action and implement it. Aristotle valued deductive enthymemes over inductive arguments because enthymemes are constructed from premises that have already been argued and established, bringing a greater degree of certainty to the reasoning process. An **enthymeme** is *a kind of syllogism in which part of the syllogism is left unstated,* inviting the audience to add in the missing component. A **syllogism** is *an argument that follows a particular form: the first statement is a general premise; the second is a specific premise that leads directly to a specific conclusion.* Given the form of the argument, no other conclusion can be drawn. For example, a syllogism might go like this: "All humans are mortal. Jason is human. So Jason is mortal." The formal structure of the syllogism prevents errors of reasoning. But few issues in everyday life admit to such certainty. So, enthymemes are a kind of syllogism that leads to probable rather than certain conclusions and they are more suited to the kind of topics argued in the court or legislature.

As mentioned, an enthymeme has a structure similar to a syllogism but is missing some part. For example, a speaker may say, "All humans are mortal and Jason is human." The audience moves in their own minds to the conclusion that Jason is mortal. This sounds more like how we talk to each other, doesn't it?

You may have used a very similar enthymeme at some point, perhaps after denting your parent's car: You may have said to your angry parent, "Everybody makes mistakes. I should be forgiven for my mistake." "Mistakes are forgiven," the assumed premise, was left unstated by you. Or, when the dent was discovered, you may have only said, "Everybody makes mistakes!" and walked away. In this second case, "Mistakes are forgiven" was the assumed premise and "I should be forgiven for my mistake" was the assumed conclusion and both were left unstated because everyone knows the specific premise and conclusion when you say, "Everybody makes mistakes." Aristotle called this second kind of enthymeme a **maxim**, which is *a common saying, truism, or indisputable proposition.* The rhetorical dynamic of either an enthymeme or a maxim is similar to playing a familiar tonic phrase on a piano, but not finishing it. You've heard the beginning of Beethoven's Fifth Symphony that begins, Da- Da- Da- Dah! When you hear only Da- Da- Da-, you want to finish the phrase with an emphatic Dah! The same is understood of the enthymeme—the audience finishes the argument because the structure invites the audience to fill in the missing piece or pieces.

Another use of the concept of the enthymeme is hinted at by Aristotle as he describes some arguments as "enthymematic." That is, we often structure arguments using not only logical appeals, but also appeals to credibility and emotions. *When the parts of an argument are arranged such that, taking all the material presented, the audience is able to fill in missing elements, and thus help construct the argument,* that argument is **enthymematic** in nature. For example, you may see an advertisement in your local newspaper taken out by an animal shelter that has the headline "We are all God's creatures." Under the statement are pictures of kittens and puppies that need to be adopted in order to survive. The maxim, coupled with the images, serves to create an informal argument that invites the reader to finish the argument ("I should adopt one of those poor creatures"). Although the structure is less defined in this case than in a deductive enthymeme, the nature of the argument overall works the same way, so it is enthymematic.

Finally, the basic nature of arguments by induction or example must be discussed. (We discuss the nature of inductive arguments in detail in the next chapter.) **Induction** is *argument from a number of similar cases; it is reasoning from a sample to draw a probable conclusion about an entire class or universe.* This is essentially the nature of scientific argument. For example, a scientist may run a number of experiments testing the safety of a drug on a sample of people. When the results show a consistent pattern, the scientist then draws a conclusion about the safety of the drug. The conclusion is probably correct, but since it was based on a sample that equals a number of examples, it cannot be certain. There is always the possibility that one or more people not tested as part of the sample will have a fatal response to the drug. That's why sample size is important in scientific research; it is also why arguments supported by numerous examples are more compelling than those with few examples or none at all.

When doing message analysis, keep in mind that ethical, emotional, and logical appeals work together. We've seen that in the preceding examples, but the need to look for the dynamic relationship between these appeals is important enough to bear repeating. Credibility is assigned by an audience that feels and thinks the speaker is trustworthy. Emotions are elicited by believable sources or speakers who give reason for feeling a certain way. Sometimes even bad reasons can be persuasive when presented by credible speakers who are able to put the audience into the appropriate state of mind. When you find one sort of appeal, spend some effort in figuring out its complex nature. Then look for how it is supported by other appeals. The process of the search is the source of insight about how the message works (or doesn't work) as persuasion.

Before concluding the chapter, we think it is useful to for you to see how the classical model may be applied. The previous discussion may have suggested to you that all elements of the model must be used as they were described; it also may have suggested that the boundaries of the model presented in Figure 9.1 were fixed. Neither conclusion is correct. The example provided is intended to help you see how to use the classical model to analyze a message.

The Classical Model Applied

The classical model continues to be useful, even when applied to new media such as the World Wide Web. The Web, as a medium, has the flexibility to be interactive and diverse in content and presentation while serving a single purpose. For a rhetorical critic, the Web provides unique critical problems that can be very interesting. A particularly interesting webpage is www.marthatalks.com as seen prior to her guilty conviction. The site was created by Martha Stewart as a response to her indictment on charges of securities fraud, obstructing justice, and making false statements. Application of the classical model to this new medium and message structure, we think, will help you see more clearly how a critic makes use of a search model and avoids being too constrained by it. Keep in mind that we are analyzing the webpage that was posted online before the trial in which she was found guilty.

As suggested by the classical model, one of the first questions we must ask about the message is, what is the nature of the message or what genre does it occupy? Marthatalks.com is a webpage with five parts that, taken together, we will consider as the text.[1] The parts consist of an "open letter" that immediately addresses the issue of her indictment and presents a brief defense. The content of this particular piece remains constant. A second and related letter changes from time to time in content. For example, one version displays a picture of Stewart hosting a baby shower for two of her employees. She is standing between them, all are smiling brightly, and on a table in front of the trio appears to be a cake uniquely decorated with daisies and an array of beautifully wrapped gifts. At a later date, Stewart is pictured beside Eliot Coleman, who is characterized as expert in organic gardening. She is turned slightly away from the camera, but looking directly at it, with her arms folded; and Coleman, standing close, has his arm around her back with his right hand resting on her shoulder. These photos serve to represent Stewart in ways the audience has come to know her. Such images serve as a kind of visual rebuttal to pictures and descriptions of Stewart doing the "perp walk" at her arraignment and looking haggard and pressed.

The content of the pages changes somewhat from week to week, but the topics are similar each time: expression of gratitude to the reader for visiting; an update on how much the page is used and notations of new material in it; a description of her work schedule and progress of the legal proceedings; her promise to keep working for the reader. The conclusion is a second acknowledgment of gratitude for support. The other parts of the marthatalks.com page consist of an e-mail link, "Notes to Martha," "Other Voices," and "Setting the Record Straight." "Notes to Martha" is a regularly updated posting of selected letters of support to Stewart. "Other Voices" is a listing of links to articles in a variety of publications as diverse as the *Wall Street Journal, New York Times, Indianapolis Star, New York Sun,* and Canada's *Globe and Mail.* An interesting quality of the entire page is the color scheme of pale green and blue—the signature colors of the Martha Stewart product line.

Although all parts of the page are significant, those that are authored by Stewart are found in the original "Open Letter" and the current letter of greeting. "Notes to Martha" are selected by Stewart, but the content is created by others; "Setting the Record Straight" is authored by her attorneys, Robert G. Morvillo and John J. Tigue. Taken together, the webpage presents Martha Stewart as a focused, competent person who remains true to the values of civility and gracious living in the face of inappropriate legal charges. Marthatalks.com also makes clear that many people, both common customers and fans, as well as informed news analysts and commentators believe Stewart has been improperly charged.

So, given the description, what kind of message is marthatalks.com? Stewart's material, which we consider the controlling part of the message, seeks to prove her innocence, which, in Aristotle's array, would make it forensic. To establish the kind of message we are examining is important because it then suggests certain patterns of speech that can be anticipated by the critic, and it sharpens the critic's senses to anomalies that may be important to note. The nature of the "Open Letter" is that of a forensic argument. However, the concept of forensic discourse is a broad one, and over the years more generic categories have been named. The more precise we can be, the better. In this case, we know that forensic discourse specifically created as a defense of one's moral character is called apologia, or apology (Ware and Linkugel 1973, 224). Kruse provides a relevant definition of **apology** as *"public discourse produced whenever a prominent person attempts to repair his [or her] [perceived] character if it has been directly or indirectly damaged by . . . charges . . .which negatively value his [or her] behavior and/or . . . judgment"* (1981, 279). Stewart's page is certainly public discourse presented by a prominent person with the purpose of repairing perception of her character. Before we move along too much further, recall that Figure 9.1 also points out that the three genres of discourse noted by Aristotle are distinct but related. We know that although discourse of apology is primarily forensic, we need to keep our eyes open for places where either deliberative or epideictic forms may be appropriated for the purposes of self-defense. Also, since the Stewart case is being pursued heavily in the media, we can anticipate that the constant barrage of questions and reports about her necessitate constant responses and explanations—an apology campaign (Gold 1978, 311). A webpage that is dynamic, allowing interactivity with the audience, provides a medium that suits the rhetorical demands Stewart faces. Since apologia is a response to a problem of ethos, the next logical questions we may ask are, What rhetorical tools does Stewart choose to use in her defense and how does she use them to repair perceptions of her character?

The first question leads us to the canon of invention. Given that her rhetorical problem is ethical, we should see how she uses pathos and logos to repair it. As the description of the webpage indicated, substantial parts of the content are drawn from her fans in "Notes to Martha," commentators in "Others Voices," and her lawyers in "Setting the Record Straight." This makes sense in that the statements of the accused claiming innocence only go so far in making a case for innocence. If such pleas were sufficient in and of themselves, we wouldn't need to have trials to establish innocence or guilt. So,

Stewart draws upon other sources: fans who provide important emotional or sympathetic appeals and commentators and lawyers who provide more substantial, reasoned arguments on her behalf.

"Notes to Martha" are selections from the vast number of e-mails the site has received. On the first day the site was up, June 5, 2003, Stewart had received 13,522 individual e-mail messages, with the bulk of them being supportive (Horowitz 2003). The volume of e-mail provides Stewart with a tremendous amount of material from which to select those she posts on her page.

Over the two months of June and July 2003, the "Notes to Martha" section presented four distinct themes: expressions of gratitude; expressions of relationship and support; expressions of material well-being; and expressions of female solidarity.

In one of the first letters posted from June 6, a woman writes, "You are a remarkable person who has been given many gifts, abilities and talents. . . . There are and have been many positive role models for women, but few have your strength and resolve. You really can do anything you have set your mind to. . . . Be assured of my thoughts and prayers and if there is anything that I can do for you, please do not hesitate to contact me." Here we see the first statements of female solidarity as well as one of the most personal relationship statements in the sample.

In another example, a Canadian woman recounts an experience in which she and a sister were trapped in their house during an ice storm. She writes, "In the midst of the 1998 ice storm . . . when we were camping out in our living room, in front of the fireplace, no heat, no electricity, Sheila doing all our cooking over the fire, she sat up and asked, 'What would Martha do?' The result was a place neatly set by the fire, every candle we could find lit, and we ate our meager meal in peace and quiet. It was special, thanks to you." Within a single e-mail, the themes of gratitude, relationship, and material well-being are exercised in the narrative recounted by the writer.

In postings from late July, the themes remain the same. A female correspondent writes, "I feel deeply saddened by the charges against you. I do feel if you were a man the circumstances would be different. . . . If the government wants to make these accusations they should spend some time in the men's locker room of the fortune [sic] 500." The complaint that Stewart's gender is a factor in her situation continues but is not elaborated as an argument. A male writer has different foci when he writes, "I have just gotten to see the furniture that will be offered next spring and I want to tell you that it is WONDERFUL! . . . THANK YOU so very much for not giving up, and continuing to offer such great products for us to enjoy. My thoughts and prayers continue to be with you." Clearly, the themes of material well-being and relationship are central to this contribution. The contributors, in each case, speak as individuals to other individuals reinforcing a perception of personal relationship with and belief in Stewart. The notes are all emotional celebrations of Stewart's accomplishments, giving the content an epideictic quality. The effect is reconstruction of a persona of Stewart that is consistent with her persona prior to her indictment. Nothing about her has changed, we infer; she's the same trustworthy person she's always been.

The "Notes to Martha" section continues to grow each week. The themes continue to be developed, and the number of contributions, coupled with the diversity of the writers in gender, employment, and residence communicate the message that most people believe Stewart to be a person of courage and character, whose mission is to enhance the lives of all people. The personal notes comprise a complex set of emotional appeals that serve to put the reader of the webpage into a frame of mind that is sympathetic to Stewart. The diverse contributors primarily report their feelings about Stewart both explicitly and implicitly. Professional, affluent women and men as well as middle-income folks from across the globe repeatedly voice their feelings of admiration for and identification with Stewart while expressing disgust and frustration with the prosecution. The emotional appeals are powerful, but the forensic nature of the legal charges invites presentation of more-considered arguments on Stewart's behalf. Repair of ethos (the goal of apology) is inextricably tied to rational argument (Willard 1989, 131). "Other Voices" provides a rational link between these sorts of appeals.

"Other Voices," as noted earlier, consists of links to commentaries about Stewart that appeared in a variety of news outlets between June 5, 2003, and May 25, 2004. As of this writing, this portion of marthatalks.com consists of 24 such articles, seventeen of which were authored by men. It is important to note, too, the nature of the sources, which are decidedly conservative in ideology.[2] The articles are much different in nature, tone, and themes compared with "Notes to Martha." Each of the articles presents an argument in defense of Stewart personally or Stewart's legal position. Consequently, we can see a complementary rhetorical relationship between the logical nature of "Other Voices" and the emotional nature of "Notes to Martha" as tools used to repair the ethical problem Stewart faces. For example, one of the earliest essays in "Other Voices" is by Alan Reynolds writing in (Canada's) *National Post,* June 6, 2003. The core of Reynolds's inductive argument is revealed in the title: "The Sleazy Political Persecution of Martha Stewart." Reynolds uses a series of examples of the government shifting its charges against Stewart as each charge loses its relevance or appropriateness given new facts. She is the victim of "prosecutorial bullies":

> *Believe it or not, the government now charges Martha Stewart with "securities fraud" . . . because she supposedly tried in vain to prop up her own stock by denying that she was guilty of the crime then charged—insider trading. Yet the government now admits she was never guilty of that crime. Instead, she supposedly "obstructed justice" . . . and made "false and misleading statements" about her reasons for making a perfectly legal sale of ImClone shares. Any jury of passably sane people would laugh this out of court.*

About three weeks later, June 25, 2003, in a second defense of Stewart, Reynolds complained, "The name of the alleged criminal is the same as it was a year ago—Martha Stewart—but the alleged crimes are now entirely different.

It used to be about insider trading. Now it's about felonious fibbing." What follows is a rebuttal of the assertion that Stewart was an inside trader based on a series of fact statements, which can presumably be checked in the public record. The argument resembles the opening statements of a court trial.

Shortly after Stewart's indictment, Brad Skolnick, an attorney commenting in the *Indianapolis Star,* offered a legal analysis of Stewart's case that concluded the charges were out of proportion to her behavior. The next day, Jack Kemp, former pro football player, U.S. representative, vice-presidential candidate, and currently a columnist and consultant, wrote a similar essay outlining the legal weakness in the case against Stewart, grounding his argument in references to federal statutes. Others followed a similar line of reasoning, but with less-detailed attention to legal details.

A second line of argument emerges among the commentaries that is complementary to "Notes to Martha." These essays extol Stewart's character, arguing that she has been targeted due to her celebrity status (Donlon 2003; Safire 2003). Others more directly recount personal interactions with Stewart and make the case that she is a really nice person and hasn't harmed anyone (Heaster 2003; Robinson 2003; Steyn 2003). The arguments typically compare Stewart's behavior and the consequences of it with others involved in her case or with other notable defendants such as Enron's Ken Lay and WorldCom's Bernard Ebbers (Skolnick 2003); Stewart is at best a victim and at worst naïve, but not a criminal, the commentators agree.

Taken together, the arguments provide a consistent case that Stewart is not a criminal. What we need to keep in mind is that these essays have a very uniform ideological agenda, and all were selected by Stewart for inclusion here. Certainly, the perspectives in these essays are not the only reasonable perspectives on Stewart, but both the growing number of supportive arguments, coupled with the predisposition of those who read or watch Stewart, give the arguments collective power. All the arguments, taken together, shift attention from Stewart's alleged negative actions to the actions of others and to Stewart's character and underlying likability. The grounds for judgment of Stewart are shifted by these arguments. Instead of trying at length to defend herself, which can backfire ("The lady doth protest too much, methinks," *Hamlet,* Act iii, Scene 2), Stewart chooses to enlist the arguments of others who are themselves perceived as credible by her audience.

So what rhetorical tools does Stewart use? How does she attempt to repair her character? Stewart's webpage, <u>marthatalks.com,</u> provides a medium that allows her to make her case in opposition to the state and some media reports by drawing upon both forensic and epideictic forms of argument. Her apology makes use of substantial emotional and logical appeals in efforts to repair her ethos or credibility. Since statements of denial of guilt are weak defenses in the public arena (in spite of the formal presumption of innocence operative in court), Stewart's apology is a three-pronged approach consisting of Stewart's personal rebuttal, notes of support from a broad range of common people, and links to essays supporting her position written by news commentators or lawyers. The emotional appeals of "Notes to Martha" serve to create sympathetic states of mind to Stewart, predisposing readers to accept or confirm the logics of the "Other Voices." Much is at stake for Stewart since her "trade good" is, in fact, her ethos, which is the "value added" to the products she sells. Without her personal identification with those products, they become just so much stuff on Kmart's shelves. At this point, it is too soon to know for sure if her mediated apologia has been successful. However, from a theoretical perspective, it appears she is making appropriate choices in service of her purpose of repairing her reputation.

SUMMARY

The classical model is a good starting point for message analysis because it provides a handy list of related concepts to search for in any message. It helps us remember that context (e.g., legislature, court, ceremonies) affects the choices rhetors typically make in constructing messages. Figuring out to what degree the rhetor followed expected patterns or not is important in understanding how rhetoric works.

The model then outlines the basic dimensions of message construction we call the canons of rhetoric: style, arrangement, delivery, memory, and invention. These basic principles of operation are complex and interrelated. It is important that, as a message analyst, you do not limit your analysis to the few concepts we were able to present here but that you use the model as a starting place in analyzing the message as well as raising new questions that you solve by researching the concepts further to expand your skill as an analyst.

Messages most worthy of examination are persuasive, and persuasion is accomplished by creating or inventing arguments. Persuasion is grounded in the credibility of the speaker, the emotions of the audience, and the reasoning about the problem that prompted the message. These "forms of proof" are interrelated, as Aristotle has pointed out numerous times. As a message analyst, you must keep that insight in mind; never treat these elements as isolated "stimuli" that produce a singular "response," but as tools by which rhetors are able to construct complex messages that persuade intelligent human audiences. That is, avoid simplistic arguments that attribute the effects of a message to an isolated rhetorical element. Keep in mind that messages are structures that have internal dynamics whereby all the message parts work together more or less to affect some judgment or action by audiences in a variety of situations.

The application of the classical approach to www.marthatalks.com was not a complete analysis but a model of how a search model provides a set of concepts, some of which are selected and used. The discussion was intended to show you how a model facilitates apprehension of the interaction of rhetorical elements and how a model can be elaborated theoretically as needed.

The nature of everyday discourse, be it in courts, legislatures, conference rooms, congregations, or kitchens, is decidedly informal yet it merits critical attention. Stephen Toulmin and Chaim Perelman have added substantially to the classical model we have discussed in this chapter. In the next chapter, we focus specifically on logic as a part of invention, and we examine in detail the nature of inductive arguments using contemporary developments of classical understandings of rhetoric.

EXERCISES

1. Choose a rhetorical text that you think merits some critical analysis. If you don't have a text in mind, we suggest two that are freely available in the public domain:

   ■ "The Mayflower Compact" (1620) is short but poses interesting critical challenges in understanding the context and purpose of the document. To get to it, type "The Mayflower Compact" (in quotation marks) in the Google search bar.
   ■ Patrick Henry's speech "Give me liberty or give me death." Henry's speech is longer and provides more internal critical challenges in the nature of the arguments he poses. You can easily find it by typing "Give Me Liberty or Give Me Death" (in quotation marks) in the Google search bar.

2. Describe and characterize the text you have chosen.

3. Using the classical model, systematically search through the text to discover specific rhetorical tools used by the message maker. List those rhetorical elements you think are operating and provide some evidence to support your conclusion.

4. Generate at least three significant critical questions about the text that you believe would help you organize your analysis.

NOTES

1 The procedure we use here is drawn from Harrell and Linkugel's (1978) work. A generic study, they say, has three main sections: generic description, generic participation, and generic application. Generic description lays out for the reader those contextual and textual elements that mark a pattern of discourse that is similar to other messages. Generic participation explores how the specific message being studied participates in the genre, looking for those points of participation and those elements of the message that suggest specific adaptations to the demands of the context and audience as well as the needs of the speaker. Finally, generic application assesses, given the findings of the analysis, what new insights we have about how a particular kind of speech actually works. It is here that we can probe the boundaries of the genre or make adjustments to what we may say fits the genre. New theory may result from this effort.

   Notice how this procedure is complementary to our four-part model of description, analysis, interpretation, and evaluation.

2 The sources of articles are The Cato Institute, *Wall Street Journal, New York Sun, Globe and Mail* (Canadian), *Kansas City Star, Indianapolis Star, National Post* (Canadian), and Copley News Service. Although some are certainly more conservative than others, all have a decidedly sympathetic stance toward business coupled with antigovernment sentiments. It is interesting that Paul Craig Roberts, a columnist for the conservative *Washington Times* writes, "Conservatives feel no sympathy for Martha. She is one of those rich people who support the Democratic Party, the raison d'etre of which is to dispossess rich people like Martha." Although the logic of Roberts's comment is unclear, his point appears to be that Stewart, in spite of her political imperfection, merits conservative support given the government's behavior toward her.

WORKS CITED

Aristotle. *The Rhetoric and Poetics of Aristotle.* Translated by W. Rhys Roberts. New York: The Modern Library, 1984.

Cicero. "De Inventione." *The Orations of Marcus Tullius Cicero.* Translated by C. D. Yonge. London: George Bell and Sons, 1988. *Peithô's Web: Classical Rhetoric and Persuasion.* http://www.classicpersuasion.org/pw/cicero/dnv1-1.htm#6 (accessed July 18, 2003).

Donlan, Thomas G. "Hamming It Up." June 16, 2003. http://www.marthatalks.com/voices/index.html (accessed August 4, 2003).

Gold, Ellen Reid. "Political Apologia: The Ritual of Self-Defense." *Communication Monographs* 45 (1978): 306–16.

Harrell, Jackson, and Wil A. Linkugel. "On Rhetorical Genre: An Organizing Perspective." *Philosophy and Rhetoric* 11 (1978): 262–81.

Heaster, Jerry. "Stewart Case Is a Specious Undertaking." June 11, 2003. http://www.marthatalks.com/voices/index.html (accessed August 4, 2003).

Horowitz, Bruce. "Stewart Uploads Her Cause to Web Site." *USA Today,* June 6, 2003, B1.

King Jr., Martin Luther. "I Have a Dream." In *American Rhetorical Discourse,* 2nd ed., edited by Ronald F. Reid, 780–83. Prospect Heights, IL: Waveland, 1998.

Kruse, Noreen Wales. "The Scope of Apologetic Discourse: Establishing Generic Parameters." *Southern Speech Communication Journal* 46 (1981): 278–91.

Linkugel, Wil A., R. R. Allen, and Richard L. Johannesen, comp. and eds., *Contemporary American Speeches: A Sourcebook of Speech Forms and Principles.* 5th ed. Dubuque: Kendall/Hunt, 1982, p. 309.

Medhurst, Martin J., and Michael DeSousa. "Political Cartoons as Rhetorical Form: A Taxonomy of Graphic Discourse." *Communication Monographs* 48 (1981): 196–236.

Mendelson, Michael. "Teaching Arrangement Inductively." *Journal of Business Communication* (1988): 67-83.

Quintilian. "Quintilian Institutes of Oratory." Vol. 4. In *Institutes of Oratory,* translated by H. E. Butler. 4 vols. London: William Heinemann, 1920. *Sophia Project.* Department of Philosophy, Molloy College. http://www.molloy.edu/academic/philosophy/sophia/Quintilian/style.htm (accessed September 5, 2003).

Reynolds, Alan. "The Sleazy Political Persecution of Martha Stewart." June 6, 2003. http://www.marthatalks.com/voices/index.html (accessed August 4, 2003).

Roberts, Paul Craig. "A Comedy of Injustice." July 17, 2003. http://www.marthatalks.com/voices/index.html (accessed August 4, 2003).

Robinson, Spider. "Lay Off the Lady." June 11, 2003. http://www.marthatalks.com/voices/index.html (accessed August 4, 2003).

Safire, William. "Fight It, Martha." June 12, 2003. http://www.marthatalks.com/voices/index.html (accessed August 4, 2003).

Skolnick, Bradley W. "Is Justice Served by Martha Stewart Circus?" June 8, 2003. http://www.marthatalks.com/voices/index.html (accessed August 4, 2003).

Steyn, Mark. "Martha Stewart Surviving." June 6, 2003. http://www.marthatalks.com/voices/index.html (accessed August 4, 2003).

Willard, Charles Arthur. *A Theory of Argumentation.* Tuscaloosa: University of Alabama Press, 1989.

Ware, B. L., and Wil A. Linkugel. "They Spoke in Defense of Themselves: On the Generic Criticism of Apologia." *Quarterly Journal of Speech* 59 (1973): 273–83.

SUGGESTED READINGS

Aden, Roger C. "The Enthymeme as Postmodern Argument Form: Condensed, Mediated Argument Then and Now." *Argumentation and Advocacy* (1994): 54–63.

Brockriede, Wayne. "Toward a Contemporary Aristotelian Theory of Rhetoric." *Quarterly Journal of Speech* (1966): 33–40.

Enos, Richard Leo. *Greek Rhetoric Before Aristotle.* Prospect Heights, IL: Waveland Press, 1993.

Gross, Alan G. "Reviewing Aristotelian Theory: The Cold Fusion Controversy as a Test Case." *Quarterly Journal of Speech* (1995): 48–62.

Hill, Forbes. "Conventional Wisdom-Traditional Form: The President's Message of November 3, 1969." *Quarterly Journal of Speech* 58 (1972): 373–86.

Leff, Michael, and G. P. Mohrmann. "Lincoln at Cooper Union: A Rhetorical Analysis of the Text." *Quarterly Journal of Speech* (1974): 346–58.

Mohrmann, G. P., and Michael C. Leff. "Lincoln at Cooper Union: A Rationale for Neo-Classical Criticism." *Quarterly Journal of Speech* (1974): 459–67.

Ziff, Howard. "The Use of Rhetoric: On Re-Reading Aristotle." *Critical Studies in Mass Communication* (1986): 111–14.

CLASSICAL APPROACHES: NEW RHETORIC

10

This chapter focuses on the invention of logical appeals—the making of arguments. We use the work of Stephen Toulmin and Chaim Perelman to elaborate and expand the classical model of rhetoric. Their work spanned the 1970s and 1980s, respectively. Toulmin, an English philosopher, and Perelman, a Belgian philosopher and legal scholar, interestingly enough, came to similar but independently developed critiques of the existing philosophical study of argument. Toulmin was led to his break with the formal/mathematical approach to argumentation due to its lack of connection to how people actually argue.[1] Toulmin found in Aristotle's work a starting point for an applied theory of argumentation. Perelman, as a legal scholar, was concerned with the question of justice and how it is enacted. Starting with the assumptions of the formal, mathematical approach that had been developed in philosophy, he examined how people argued in court. At first, he concluded that "if justice consists in the systematic implementation of certain value judgments, it does not rest on any rational foundation" (1979, 8). Justice must be either completely subjective or absolute. Each of these possible conclusions, though, does a poor job of describing how people actually deliberate. As he and his colleague Lucie Olbrechts-Tyteca continued to study this problem, Perelman notes, "Without either knowing or wishing it, we had rediscovered a part of Aristotelian logic that had been long forgotten or, at any rate, ignored and despised. It was the part dealing with dialectical reasoning as distinguished from demonstrative reasoning" (9). That is, they found Aristotle's descriptions of inductive arguments more useful in explaining everyday human reasoning and persuasion than descriptions of syllogisms or formal arguments.

In this chapter, we first look at Toulmin's examination of the elements of arguments and their relationships. In the second part of the chapter, we look at Perelman and Olbrechts-Tyteca's description of argument in everyday contexts. Then we examine how these two theories might change our analysis of the Martha Stewart webpage.

TOULMIN AND EVERYDAY ARGUMENT

Most likely, from time to time in your classes, you've found discussions to be irrelevant to your everyday life. Sometimes the ideas

Vocabulary
- argument field
- field invariant
- field dependent
- modal terms
- force
- criteria
- claim
- data
- reason/warrant
- qualifiers
- rebuttals
- backing
- universal audience
- creating presence
- quasi-logical arguments
- appeal to the real
- dissociation

seem so idealized, so removed from your experience, that you get frustrated with the material. (You may even think that occasionally while reading this book!) There are many reasons why theory may sometimes appear to be irrelevant. Our Western commitment to the scientific method as a way of knowing and the scientific values of "certainty" and "elegance" feed the problem. In the study of argument, the desire for certainty of conclusions led scholars to focus on formal (syllogistic) arguments as the preferred model. Although elegance was a goal, too, the need to constantly elaborate the mathematical models of argument so that they could be useful led instead to increasingly complex and abstract formuli (Toulmin 1969, 147).

When Toulmin started studying the arguments people actually make, he became convinced that a whole new approach was needed. The nature of rhetoric is too messy for formuli. What makes common arguments so difficult to analyze is their fluid structure and the nature of the language used. Informal arguments, Toulmin concluded, in comparison to formal ones, are "less trustworthy and more tentative, involved substantial leaps . . . were expressed in terms of vague, unlogical words and in some cases, appealed to no established or even recognizable warrant" (149). In other words, the arguments we use in everyday life are pretty messy, vague, and ill-formed—but we use them and they work. Consequently, a new way of describing and explaining argument had to be developed (167). Let's look at some of the ideas Toulmin offers for making sense of the messy business of arguing and persuading.

ARGUMENT FIELDS

Toulmin begins almost where Aristotle began: examining kinds of discourse. Aristotle named three kinds of rhetoric: legal, political, and ceremonial. As we saw in the previous chapter, this was based on patterns of speech and common lines of argument that were demanded by the historical context. Toulmin changed the approach slightly, expanding the concept of genre to identify many more kinds of discourse. Toulmin found that arguments were constrained by the field in which they occurred. By analogy, baseball and football are different, in part, due to the fields on which they are played—the fields imply certain constitutive rules and limit what procedural rules can be made. More abstractly, we use the metaphor of a field to name related topics of study like medicine, physics, history, law, philosophy, or rhetoric. For Toulmin an **argument field** *exists when two or more different arguments possess elements of the same logical type* (1969, 14). For example, the kinds of claims a theologian may make about the nature of human beings will be of a different logical type than the claims of a biologist. If a theologian claimed, "The purpose of humanity is to love God and serve God only," the theologian will have to give reasons to support that claim. If she is committed to having a theological discussion, she must accept the rules and rationality of that field of argument. A reason given in support of the claim may be, "God is the source of life for all human beings." Backing for such the reason may be, "The existence of a transcendent, omniscient God best explains the complexity of life on Earth." Within the field of theology, all these terms make sense, and all the elements of the arguments are of the same logical type.

In contrast, a biologist, whose field has different rules for what counts as rational, will offer very different arguments about the nature of humanity. A biologist may claim, "The purpose of all human beings is to reproduce." A reason from that field may be, "The drive for reproduction is basic to the preservation of the species." Backing may be, "Preservation of a species appears to be a universal preoccupation of all living organisms." Notice how completely different these arguments are. Those who argue within the rules of each field may not always agree, but they will make sense to each other. But if you try to argue in one field using the rules of another, you may be seen as irrational. If a theologian asks, "What is the purpose of humanity?" and the biologist responds, "To reproduce," the theologian would not treat the response as legitimate given the intent of the question. The argument field in which an argument is placed makes a difference in how the argument can be appropriately invented.

As a critic, you must consider the *kind* of argument being put forward and the *field* in which it exists. Asking questions about these two topics will provide you with important insights about the intent, structure, function, and quality of arguments you examine.

FIELD INVARIANT AND FIELD DEPENDENT ELEMENTS OF ARGUMENTS

If you reread the comparative examples in the preceding section, you'll see that two qualities of arguments exist: invariant and dependent. Notice that in both "nature of humanity" arguments there were claims, reasons, and backing; these are **field invariant.** That is, *these elements exist in any argument no matter what the field.* These are structural elements of arguments. On the other hand, *elements of argument that vary due to the argument field* are called **field dependent.** Some of the field dependent elements were vocabulary, meaning, and assumptions. These terms are important for our understanding of and analysis of arguments. Knowing what field invariant structural elements to look for and knowing that their content is field dependent is important to insightful message analysis. These terms can help you explain why some persuasive efforts seem at first glance to be very sophisticated, but fail miserably as persuasion.

MODAL TERMS

The kinds of things argued in courts, legislatures, most academic arenas, and in everyday life rarely have absolute or exact answers. Rather, the answers we can give each other are more or less likely the best available. For example, no one knows absolutely what new changes in our national security policies will eliminate terrorism. All we can do is put together the best arguments available for what we think will be the best procedures. Undoubtedly, whatever final policies are accepted will be imperfect, but they should be the best we can figure out as a result of carefully arguing our positions—we can't come to certain conclusions given future actions. The uncertain nature of our most important arguments is why Aristotle spent so much time describing inductive arguments and why he preferred enthymemes over syllogisms. It is also what launched both Toulmin and Perelman on their analyses of contingent or probable arguments.

One of the elements of informal, inductive arguments is **modal terms:** *words that describe the possibility of conclusions.* So, instead of saying, "Giving broad powers to the FBI to tap the phones of suspected terrorists will eliminate domestic terrorism," we say, "Giving broad powers to the FBI to tap the phones of suspected terrorists will *probably* eliminate domestic terrorism." Words such as *probably, possibly, may, might, must,* and *necessarily* are examples of modal terms. Such terms are important for making claims more reasonable. The second claim will be accepted by many more people than the first because its recognition of uncertainty and contingency in human action is reasonable. Whether or not such a policy or law is the best course of action will be known only over time, if ever.

Now, it is also important to recognize that modal terms work differently in different argument fields. Consider these two example claims:

1. You cannot pick up a Ford Suburban single-handedly.
2. You cannot ignore your adult child's request for money.

In claim one, we are roughly in the field of physics, and the modal term *cannot* means "impossible." The laws of physics, in that case, absolutely prevent the action. One person picking up a Suburban is impossible. In claim two, which is roughly in the field of ethics, the term means "improper," which is obviously quite different. Cultural rules and ethical standards generally disapprove of parents ignoring requests for help by their offspring. But circumstances in families vary considerably and there is actually nothing to prevent parents from ignoring requests for money. In fact, we can imagine cases in which withholding money is the best course of action for all involved. To say parents *cannot* do so is to use the term in a way that means, "It is not generally the favored course of action." Looking for modal terms in persuasive messages is a useful analytical move that will pay dividends in analyzing the appropriateness and reasonableness of arguments you examine. When analyzing arguments, ask yourself, what modal terms are being used in the argument? What do the terms mean within the argument field in which they are offered?

FORCE AND CRITERIA

To really understand the nature of the language we are analyzing in significant messages, we need to add two more dimensions to the concept of modal terms. The first is a field invariant element called *force.* **Force** *indicates the strength of your judgment.* Consider these two examples: (1) Microsoft XP is a good operating system; and (2) The Airbus is a good airliner. In both cases, *good* performs the same function, which is to positively describe the strength of our judgment about the object of discussion, be it software or an airliner. In two different fields, *good* praises the object of the claim. So, the force of a claim is field invariant.

The second dimension of modal terms is **criteria**, which are *the explicit or implicit reasons for your judgment.* Criteria are field dependent, of course. When we say that XP is good, the criteria for goodness may be that the software is stable and highly compatible with other applications. When we say the Airbus is a good airliner, the criteria are not the same as for software but that the plane is safe, easy to fly, and cheap to maintain. Criteria of a claim are field dependent.

The value of these concepts of force and criteria lies in the fact that they prompt you to ask important questions about words that can easily miss serious consideration because such evaluative terms as *good, bad, right, wrong, best, worst,* and so on are so commonly used. We usually interpret them within our own mental schemes without asking how powerful they are intended to be or what criteria led to their use. Keep in mind that informal or inductive arguments are by nature probable, but often packaged rhetorically to appear to be certain, or at least more certain in conclusion than is truly warranted. Since force is field invariant, use of modal terms between fields can sometimes mask the lack of certainty inherent in a claim. Look carefully at the language used to invent an argument, and keep in mind that modal terms have two important dimensions that need to be explored if you are going to uncover the patterns of argument that make a persuasive message effective or not.

THE PARTS OF ARGUMENTS

Toulmin's goal was to discover the general nature of informal arguments, so he looked for field invariant elements within the process of arguing. Take a look at this example:

1. Let's say we make the claim, "The Sacramento Kings are losers."
2. A friend asks, "What makes you say that?"
3. We reply, "The Kings lost the division playoffs." (Now, the discussion may or may not go on depending on our friend's interest or desire for a more developed argument.)
4. Our friend decides to persist, "How do you come to the conclusion the Kings are losers? How do you get there?"
5. We reply, "Since teams that lose playoffs are necessarily losers, we conclude that given the Kings' loss of the division playoffs, they're losers!" (Of course, this sounds a bit stuffy but please bear with us for purposes of the example.)

What are the parts of this argument that Toulmin would point out? Statement #1 is a claim or conclusion that we came to after watching the team, listening to and reading commentary, and talking about it among ourselves. A **claim** is *a statement of conclusion.* No argument can exist without such a declarative statement because without a claim, there is no possible controversy or need for two people to talk to resolve their differences. The question our friend posed

(#2) is a natural one that asks for us to make clear what we used to draw the conclusion. Our reply (#3) Toulmin would call *data*. **Data** are *the observations, bits of information, and opinions that we collected and put together in some way to draw our conclusion.* If the discussion had stopped at that point, there would not yet be any argument but simply an assertion about the team. Had our friend not continued, there would be no evidence of reasoning exposed. There would be no more discussion, just the acceptance or apparent acceptance of our conclusion by all involved. Now, our friend was a reasonable person and wanted us to provide a rationale. When he asked, "How did you get there?"(#4) he asked us for a reason or warrant for our conclusion. In essence, a **reason,** or **warrant,** is *a statement that connects the data to the claim in a way that provides a logical bridge that legitimates or explains a conclusion.* We provided a warrant in the form of a definition: teams that lose playoffs are losers (#5). Granted, this is a lame reason. But not all reasons are good reasons. Even though the argument may not be a good one, it does have the essential components needed to make an argument: a claim, data, and reason. These three must be present for an argument to be said to exist.

As Toulmin continued to examine how people argue, he found that in informal or inductive arguments (which we know are fraught with uncertainty), some other elements are used by people to be or appear to be more reasonable. We often realize that our claims hold only under certain circumstances or conditions, so we add qualifiers to our claims. **Qualifiers** *serve to qualify or limit the applicability of a claim so the claim is reasonable* (Toulmin 1969, 101). These are the modal terms discussed earlier that allow a statement to be more reasonable. For example, imagine you are playing Twenty-One at Harrah's Casino. You turn to your friend and say, "The next card will be the ace of spades." Given the context of a game of chance, this statement is too certain. It is merely a guess. However, if you whisper, "The next card will probably be an ace," the statement has the ring of a reasoned claim. If your friend asks, "Why do you think so?" you may say, "I've been keeping track; there are only fifteen cards left, and all the aces are still in the deck, so the next card will probably be an ace." It is reasonable to say that with a ratio of four aces to fifteen cards, a draw will more than likely be an ace. Qualifiers make for more reasonable claims.

Another way to make claims more reasonable is by limiting the circumstances under which your claim may hold. Toulmin calls this element of an argument a *rebuttal*. **Rebuttals** are *statements that confirm or limit the applicability of a warrant* (102). Another commonly used word for rebuttal is *reservation*, which well describes its function in an argument. What these statements do is say, "My claim holds except under X circumstances." Using the preceding examples, you might say, "The next card will probably (qualifier) be an ace (claim), unless I miscounted the cards" (rebuttal or reservation).

Finally, Toulmin found that in the interaction between rhetor and audience, questions arise concerning the applicability of some reasons or warrants. Some people are really skeptical and not only ask for reasons, but even challenge the reasons; they ask for backing for the warrants. **Backing** amounts to *statements that justify or explain the acceptability, relevance, or authority of reasons.*

Backing is more information that supports the reason in the form of related examples, appeals to the credibility of the sources of the warrant if there are outside sources, definitions, principles, rules, laws, and so on. For example, when playing Twenty-One, if the argument presented was not sufficient, you may add backing by saying, "As a rule of thumb, odds of slightly more than one to four are generally seen by gamblers as excellent odds." This added information serves to affirm or legitimate the reason you gave for predicting an ace on the next draw.

In sum, we have explored some of Stephen Toulmin's contributions to our understanding of invention in general and informal logic in particular. Toulmin's concepts provide a useful search model. Keep in mind that the structure of arguments he outlines is field invariant, but the content of them is field dependent. As you use these concepts, first use them to see what in any message is devoted to logical appeals; then look at the use of each within the argument field from which the argument comes. Use the concepts to help you see as best you can. Toulmin himself had to deal with the problem of "correctness" when laying out an argument for analysis. In considering the use of these concepts Toulmin himself asked:

> *Will it always be clear where a man who challenges an assertion is calling for the production of his adversary's* data, *or for the* warrants *authorizing his steps? . . . By grammatical tests alone, the distinction may appear far from absolute. . . . For the moment, the important thing is not to be too cut-and-dried in our treatment of the subject, nor to commit ourselves in advance to a rigid terminology. (1969, 99, emphasis added)*

In other words, use the concepts to facilitate your analysis, but don't get hung up on whether or not a specific sentence is absolutely classified. The process of informal argument is too messy to permit such decisions. There is no single "correct" application of this model to any given argument. Most likely, any message maker is not consciously using any or all of these elements when constructing arguments. However, you can use the model to help you make sense of any argument; use it to help you see what essential argumentative parts are present (or apparently missing), and how they are used (or apparently misused). What is important is that you use Toulmin's ideas to search through a message. For example, here's a portion of the text on a recent poster for the Boy Scouts of America titled "Scouting Believes in Us":

> *The Boy Scouts of America believes in young people and their ability to change lives and entire communities. Thanks to the people of Ft. Washington, Maryland, and Ebenezer A. M. E. Church, these 19 young men achieved Scouting's highest rank, Eagle Scout.*

> *Every day millions of young people across America reach new heights by participating in the values-driven programs of Scouting. With the support and encouragement of countless volunteer leaders, Scouting prepares young people to make better choices over their lifetimes.*

> *By mentoring young people, we teach them the timeless tradition of giving back.*

Certainly, this poster is intended to persuade its target audience by making an argument about the value of scouting. It is exactly the sort of argumentation we use in everyday life. As critics, if we want to get past our own gut reactions (some of you may have a fond relationship with scouting; others of you may despise the organization), we need to see what's going on in this message. Toulmin's model prompts us to look for the claim or conclusions that the rest of the message supports; we also ask if the claims exhibit any qualifiers, or reservations. What seems to be the data from which the claim springs? Where are the reasons supporting the claim? Is there any backing offered to support the reasons? To put the whole thing in context, we need to figure out the argument field that this message occupies because that will affect our judgments regarding the quality and appropriateness of the argument. Take a minute and see if you can figure out which parts of an argument actually were used by the message maker; which are missing, if any? Given what is used in inventing the argument, how well does it work? Keep in mind Toulmin's advice "not to be too cut and dried in our treatment of the subject, nor commit ourselves in advance to a rigid terminology."

Now look at Figure 10.1 to see what we found when applying the model. Our decisions for where to place each element were guided by what function each seemed to be playing in the argument rather than the order in which they

FIGURE 10.1

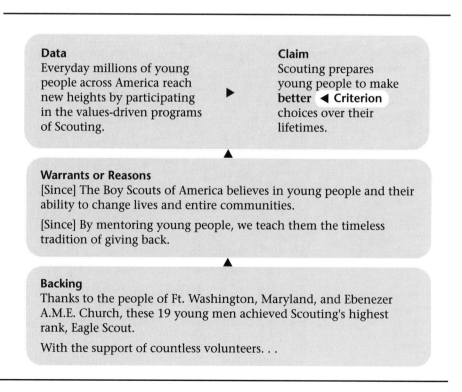

Data
Everyday millions of young people across America reach new heights by participating in the values-driven programs of Scouting.

Claim
Scouting prepares young people to make **better** ◄ Criterion choices over their lifetimes.

Warrants or Reasons
[Since] The Boy Scouts of America believes in young people and their ability to change lives and entire communities.

[Since] By mentoring young people, we teach them the timeless tradition of giving back.

Backing
Thanks to the people of Ft. Washington, Maryland, and Ebenezer A.M.E. Church, these 19 young men achieved Scouting's highest rank, Eagle Scout.

With the support of countless volunteers. . .

came. People process arguments as a web of ideas wherein the relationships of ideas make sense. We are not computers that require certain kinds of data to be inserted before other data can make sense. Toulmin's model is not an organizational one, but rather a functional one. How does our layout compare to your reading of the argument?

You may be wondering how we distinguished between data and claim. It was not an easy decision, but we felt the claim was a significant assertion about scouting. Also, as we mentioned, criteria are associated with claims as a means of increasing their power or reasonableness. For us, the presence of *better* marked the claim. Reasons connect data and claim by providing a rationale. Notice we added *since* to make clearer how the reasons do that. That's a good trick to use as you try to distinguish the function of similar statements within an argument. Backing provides more concrete statements that support the reasons. In the case of the first backing statement, the specific reference to a particular group of people functioned less as logical justification and more like an example. You may be wondering, too, if this is the correct layout. The better question is, does the layout help you see the relationships of the ideas in the argument more clearly? Use the model as a tool to assist you in sorting through arguments. When using it, the goal is clearer understanding of the rhetorical effort you are studying, not production of a Toulmin-style model.

PERELMAN AND THE NEW RHETORIC

Toulmin focuses on the technical elements of argument. Now, we turn our attention to Chaim Perelman's work, which provides a larger rhetorical context for the process of argumentation.

REASONABLENESS AND AUDIENCES

Toulmin features the structure of argument while Perelman features the uses of argument and focuses on people as decision makers. His work helps us keep in mind and explain how people behave reasonably as people in a context rather than as machines existing in a vacuum.

Perelman named his model of rhetoric the New Rhetoric, even though it is founded primarily on the works of Aristotle and Cicero. What is new is Perelman's reconnecting of the reasoning processes that Aristotle had separated due to his categorical approach (which we discussed in the previous chapter). Consequently, Perelman's is a broader approach to rhetoric than Aristotle's or even Toulmin's because he reintroduces the roles of *audience* and rhetorical *context* into the reasoning process. Perelman focuses on the meanings people give to the language used in everyday argument. Like Aristotle, Perelman factors in the role of emotion in how people make judgments and draw conclusions. Consequently, reasoning is not objective, nor is it arbitrary, but somewhere in between. As Harold Zyskind observes, "For the new rhetoric, not logic but the quality of the audience is prior" (Perelman 1979, x).

Given Aristotle's enthusiasm for the enthymeme, reasoning has long been described as linear: line up the premises, be they explicit or implicit, and arrive at the conclusion. However, for Perelman, argumentation and persuasion are not grounded in a linear chain of reason, but a back-and-forth confrontation of ideas. For Perelman, "The form of inference is neither deductive nor inductive, but comparative" (1979, xvi). That is, we make our decisions about difficult issues by comparing the proposals (claims) to some facts, principles, policies, traditions, laws, or values and making a preferential decision rather than making a syllogism. Perelman concludes that people are persuaded to take a side, rather than discover and act on the truth. Consequently, "the quality of the discourse is judged not only by its efficacy, but especially by the quality of the audience it has succeeded in persuading" (57).

The Universal Audience

The universal audience is central to Perelman's analysis of argumentation and serves to completely change how we understand argumentation and persuasion. Notice in the preceding quote that Perelman judges an argument on the quality of the audience it persuades. It follows that an argument that persuades the best audience is the best argument. The **universal audience** is "thought of as including *all [people] who are rational and competent with respect to the issues being debated*" (Perelman 1979, 48). Now, this notion exists both as reality and abstraction. Notice the qualifier Perelman includes in the definition. The universal audience is not all possible people, but those who are "competent with respect to the issues being debated." Probably a better term for universal audience would be *qualified audience* or *expert audience*. Real applications of this idea of a qualified (universal) audience occur every day in all professions. For example, medical foundations convene expert panels to review research or grant applications. Editorial boards for academic journals serve to determine what knowledge claims should be published. The Supreme Court is an exemplar of the expert panel convened, literally, to decide which arguments are best. The notion of relevant competence is important. Although we, the authors of this book, have served on editorial boards for communication journals in our areas of expertise, we never would review medical or legal issues because we are not competent to do so. In fact, within our discipline, neither of us would review an essay in media production because we are not sufficiently expert to judge the knowledge claims in this specific area of communication studies. Since we are not the most expert readers, we would not be as likely to detect significant flaws in the arguments presented as would those who are qualified readers. The more expert the audience, the better the argument needed to persuade those in it.

Aristotle and others unwittingly created contempt for rhetoric over the years because the techniques they described were to persuade essentially ignorant audiences. Aristotle notes, "The duty of rhetoric is to deal with such matters as we deliberate upon . . . in the hearing of persons who cannot take in at a glance a complicated argument, or follow a long chain of reasoning" (1984, sec. 1357a). When this is the case, the rhetorical goal is less about putting forward the best argument than putting forward one that the audience will accept. The effort needed to construct arguments that are persuasive to a universal audience creates a useful standard by which to judge rhetorical arguments you may encounter and criticize.

Perelman is nevertheless realistic about the use of the concept of universal audience, which can be an abstraction of the highest order. He notes that for real people who may qualify as members of a universal audience, each "is a member of a plurality of particular audiences, to whose theses he [*sic*] adheres with variable intensity, as well as being a member of the universal audience. It is always important to know with which of these particular audiences any concrete individual is going to identify himself [*sic*] in case of conflict" (1979, 49). This recognizes that reasonable people are biased and their judgments have context and history. It can be no other way because people reason; they are not machines. Consequently, we must realize that rhetoric is about making decisions regarding things that are not self-evident; its goal is the formation of good opinions rather than discovery of absolute truth. The concept of the universal audience gives us some means by which to assess the quality of arguments under those circumstances. The value of this concept lies in the fact that it causes you as a critic to factor in the nature of the audiences addressed by a rhetor when evaluating the quality of the message. Remember that rhetors are often addressing more than one audience at a time—some expert, some not. For example, when President George W. Bush argued for his policy of limiting stem cell lines, experts in genetic research were listening as well as the general public. For political reasons, his interest was in the public's reaction to the speech more than a very small group of researchers. From a political, rhetorical perspective, his message seemed to succeed. From the perspective of an expert in genetic engineering, the speech was wanting. This slightly more sophisticated analysis of audience (as opposed to thinking of audience as just a monolithic entity) results in a better understanding of how political speech operates in society and why. The audience can get lost as a factor when doing a critical study because our critical procedures and concepts feature rhetorical tools and their arrangement; we experience the truism, "Out of sight, out of mind." It is essential that you ask yourself who comprises the audience for any message. Who represents the universal audience for the message? When you are analyzing a message, and you pay attention to the intended audience, you may begin to see the text in a whole new light.

MEANS OF FORMING GOOD OPINIONS

For Perelman, invention of persuasive arguments is based on ideas, not techniques per se. Certainly, the common rhetorical tools we discussed in the previous chapter (and others that we have yet to discuss in upcoming chapters) are used to articulate and present ideas in ways that audiences will prefer. Rhetoric is grounded in human thought, not mere applications of rhetorical techniques. The use of specific rhetorical techniques must be understood as means, not end. The purpose of rhetoric is to get audience agreement by providing compelling justifications for the audience's judgments or decisions. It is important to understand that Perelman's model of argument is neither subjective on the one hand, nor absolute on the other. Rather, it accounts for the existence of reasoned opinions that reflect efforts of people to get as near to the truth as possible. The question is, how does one go about creating particular opinions in the mind of the audience?

CREATING PRESENCE

Perelman observed the following about how people come to conclusions: "What an audience accepts forms a body of opinion, convictions, and commitments that is both vast and indeterminate. From this body the orator must select certain elements on which he [sic] focuses attention by endowing them, as it were, with a 'presence' " (1979, 17). Think of what Perelman said like this: imagine the facts you know and the beliefs you have are all on index cards. The index cards are in a large pile on a table. If I wanted to form a particular opinion in you, I would need to pick through the pile, choose those facts and opinions relevant to the argument, pull them out, and put just those cards in front of you. I would try to keep your attention on just those ideas and my way of organizing and interpreting them. That is essentially what a message maker does when creating presence. **Creating presence** is *bringing something to the audience's mind*. Such is the nature of rhetoric: inventing or selecting appropriate content, arranging it, and delivering it to an audience in such a way as to gain the adherence of the audience to the rhetor's perspective. The task is to draw audience attention to things in the environment or to get the audience to recall relevant things from memory or to imagine a future in a way that is compelling.

Even though Perelman's idea is contemporary, classical figures of speech[2] can be employed to make relevant ideas present to the audience. Along with classical devices special attention should be given to language choices used in how events, facts, statistics, and so on are interpreted; today we call it "spin." For example, some politicians describe the future of the Social Security fund as *stable* while others describe it as being in crisis. Depending on the speaker's political agenda for the fund, an audience can be led to perceive Social Security as a national financial asset or liability. When considering how presence is working as a rhetorical tool you may ask such questions as: What exactly is the rhetor asking me to pay attention to? What other relevant facts, illustrations, examples, and interpretations are missing? In what other ways could the subject of discussion be named or described? What differences in meaning or effect do I detect among the possible choices made by the rhetor? Asking such questions is not easy but pays off in maintaining a critical perspective on the text.

USING ARGUMENT STRUCTURES

Creating presence using such devices can be effective. Also, structuring arguments in particular ways can be effective. Perelman outlines three general structures: quasi-logical, appeals to the real, and dissociation. **Quasi-logical**

arguments are *those arranged in a way that mimics formal arguments.* For example, as a union representative, you may argue something like this in a negotiation session: Equal pay for equal work is a basic value in our country (major premise). The men and women in this company do essentially the same jobs (minor premise). We are only asking for what is right when we say that the pay scales for men and women must be exactly alike here (conclusion). This argument mimics the formal structure of a syllogism, and it leads the audience to the desired conclusion by keeping attention on the thread of reasoning that holds it together.

A second general persuasive strategy identified by Perelman is **appeal to the real.** These are *strategies commonly used in science that are causal or correlational in nature* (Perelman 1979, 21). Scientists regularly use inductive arguments that use examples, illustrations, metaphors, and analogies to make a case. Scientists who are attempting to describe and explain the physical or social world they investigate build theory by example. Replicated experiments or studies provide a series of examples that, taken together, expose a pattern we can take to be "the way things are" in our experience. Explanations of the patterns and principles exposed by the studies make use of illustrations; metaphors and analogies make complicated or new concepts understandable by comparisons to things we already know or experience. Using these devices, it is possible to create for an audience a way of seeing the world that compels them to revise their knowledge and accept new facts or principles. Scientists appeal to the real.

Finally, and directly related to appeal to the real, is the process of dissociation of ideas. According to Perelman, "Dissociation is the classical solution for incompatibilities that call for alteration of conventional ways of thinking" (1979, 23). In other words, **dissociation** is *the process of creating sufficient cognitive dissonance in an audience that they reduce their uncertainty by recognizing and accepting a new way of describing or interpreting the real.* For example, we often see this in use in arguments that present "myths" and "reality." The form is to set out a commonly accepted understanding of a topic as myth, which creates dissonance, followed by the reality, which is a new interpretation of reality.[3] Another example can be drawn from our legal system. It is the task of the defense attorney to create uncertainty about the prosecution's case and offer a new way of interpreting the real. When analyzing arguments, ask if the appeals to the real are grounded in appropriate data or if examples are sufficient and relevant. Are the assertions about "how things are" supported by the best possible evidence? Are alternative interpretations of accepted knowledge or beliefs compelling? If so, what about the alternative interpretation presented leads the audience to accept it?

It is important to understand that in spite of the classification and description needed to help you see how arguments are invented, the reality is that they usually consist of a wide assortment of rhetorical devices that have been selected for the particular audience that must make a decision or judgment about a particular topic at a particular time. Arguments, as Toulmin pointed out, are really messy affairs that are intended not as proof but as a compelling justification. As Perelman says, "Nonformal argument consists, not of a chain of ideas of which some are derived from others according to accepted rules of inference, but rather of a web formed from all the arguments and all the reasons that combine to achieve the desired result" (1979, 18). That is, the kinds of arguments we encounter in everyday life are not rigorously organized with one premise following another, but rather as a collection of various kinds of appeals, evidence, and reasons clustered together to create an impression, promote a particular interpretation, or encourage certain behaviors in the audience.

THE NEW RHETORIC APPLIED

Before ending our discussion, let's see how some of the concepts we've discussed work in real life. Since in the previous chapter we promised to reexamine Martha Stewart's page, that's exactly what we'll do. As you read this, keep in mind that the webpages under analysis were online prior to the trial in which Stewart was found guilty.

Our description in Chapter 9 treated the five major sections of marthatalks.com. One of the most relevant parts that invites an analysis of argument is Stewart's open letter ("Read My Letter"). This letter of just over two hundred words presents a very brief argument for her innocence and an acknowledgment of fan support and concludes with an invitation to visit the rest of marthatalks.com. As an apology, it has a two-pronged approach relying on specific and general logical appeals as well as emotional appeals designed to create a perception of a continuing relationship with the audience.

The logical structure of the Open Letter is interesting. The very first sentence provides a context and data to ground the argument. "After more than a year" (context), she writes, "the government has decided to bring charges against me for matters that are personal and entirely unrelated to the business of Martha Stewart Living Omnimedia" (data). It is that context/data that invites her clear claim of innocence: "I want you to know that I am innocent." As a claim, its force is grounded in the presumption of innocence that is basic to our justice system. It also is, as you can see, an unqualified declaration. The argument directly related to that declaration is minimal. It is warranted by her statement that, "I simply returned a call from my stockbroker." Backing for that warrant is immediately provided as she continues, "Based in large part on prior discussions with my broker about price, I authorized a sale of my remaining shares in a biotech company called ImClone." This informal argument serves as the kernel of a larger argumentative strategy that is grounded in dissociation. (Recall that dissociation is intended to loosen the audience's adherence to an existing interpretation and provide an alternative interpretation of a situation.) This is accomplished through Stewart's statements of explanation coupled with her expressions of thanks to readers. Her invitation to explore further the contents of the website link both logical and emotional appeals to repair perception of her character. By explaining how she has been caught in a web spun by prosecutors wherein her denials of wrongdoing brought criminal charges, by rising above the situation, and by providing more information to readers, Stewart's letter serves to reconfigure "incompatibilities that call for alteration of conventional ways of thinking." That is, Stewart's apology provides information about and interpretations of events that are designed as alternative ways of thinking about her behaviors.

The strategies of informal argument supplemented by emotional appeals featuring Stewart's civility, grace, and care for others are replicated within the rest of the webpage. The "Letter from Martha" that changes from time to time rehearses her characteristic public civility. A series of photos of Martha hosting friends at her home or in her gardens enacts her graciousness and sociability. The "Letter" always includes an expression of her concern for the reader as she states, "I'll continue to do my best to keep this site up to date with items I think you might enjoy." Only the most allocentric person is concerned about the needs of strangers while that person struggles with personal pain and crisis. It is the ultimate expression of civil behavior.

"Setting the Record Straight" (June 10, 2003), written by her lawyers, provides a much more developed argument for her innocence to dissociate her from a potentially criminal persona. The shift in attention is attempted in the first paragraph when Morvillo and Tigue (2003) write, "The government is making her the subject of a criminal test case designed to further expand the already unrecognizable boundaries of the federal securities laws." The rest of the text goes on to support that claim. As they elaborate their case, Stewart is moved to the background and others take her place in the foreground. Morvillo and Tigue then ask, rhetorically, why the government is belatedly filing charges against Stewart, then ask another question that serves the dissociative function, ". . . is it because the Department of Justice is attempting to divert the public's attention from its failure to charge the politically connected managers of Enron and WorldCom who may have fleeced the public out of billions of dollars?" When that question is posed, more are raised in the mind of the receiver, creating some dissonance about Justice Department priorities. Stewart becomes not only unimportant as a target of investigation but, in fact, an innocent victim of a justice system run amok. The "Open Letter," "Letter from Martha," and "Setting the Record Straight" reflect a general rhetorical strategy of dissociation. In each, Stewart attempts to reinforce perceptions of her character as both honest and civil to rebut media accounts of her as dishonest and uncivil.

This example analysis was intended to show you how you may apply the concepts we've discussed. Notice that our goal was understanding the rhetorical nature of Stewart's discourse, and we appropriated the concepts necessary to do so. We encourage you to do the same. Don't feel compelled to use every concept in a kind of shotgun approach. Also, when using Toulmin's ideas, don't get stuck trying to force every statement of a text into one of the categories of the model. You can account for the function of many statements using other conceptual frameworks just as we did using Perelman's ideas.

SUMMARY

Toulmin's work provides us with concepts to help determine the structure of informal arguments. His concept of argument field coupled with Aristotle's notions of genre keep us mindful of the context in which any argument is presented. Understanding that there are field dependent and field invariant parts of arguments helps us determine how fully and appropriately an argument has been developed. Toulmin's discussion of modal terms provides us with a tool for assessing the reasonableness of arguments.

Perelman's ideas help us to see better that rhetoric is focused on audiences—the judges or decision makers to whom arguments are addressed. We are reminded by him that argumentation is not mechanical, but humane and therefore much more than the mere sum of an argument's parts. The goal of argument is the formation of opinions in others. Although we are able to identify specific argumentative tools a rhetor may select, Perelman makes clear that arguments are webs of connections between ideas that are interpreted by human beings, making the outcome of rhetoric always tentative and uncertain.

Taken together, this chapter and the one before it try to lay out for you some basic concepts of rhetoric that, over thousands of years, have helped message makers and message analysts use communication to create the social world in which we live today. Volumes could be written about the ancient and contemporary classical models, so these chapters must be understood to be incomplete. They do provide starting points for analysis that, with further research, should give you a strong beginning for analyzing any significant message in your professional or private life.

EXERCISES

1. Read the argument here and then apply to it the critical questions that follow:

   "Michael Moore's movie *Bowling for Columbine* is a weaker documentary than his earlier one, *Roger and Me.*"

   "I don't know about that. I liked *Bowling for Columbine.* What makes you think that *Roger and Me* was so good?"

   "I didn't say *Roger and Me* was good. I said Bowling was weaker. Look, there were two big problems with *Bowling.* First, it got off the point too often. We didn't need all that stuff back in Flint, Michigan. Second, his treatment of Charlton Heston was unfair—the guy is suffering from Alzheimer's disease. It's one thing to go after Roger Smith who could defend himself, but it's unfair to make fun of a guy who is suffering a brain-damaging disease."

   "How do you know Heston has Alzheimer's?"

   "I saw a report on CNN last summer."

   - In what field of argument does this argument operate?
   - What is the claim or conclusion that the rest of the message supports?
   - Does the claim exhibit any qualifiers, or reservations? If so, identify them.

- What seems to be the data from which the claim springs?
- Where are the reasons supporting the claim?
- Is there any backing offered to support the reasons?
- Are any parts of the argument missing? If so, how is the argument affected?
- Given what is used in inventing the argument, how well does it work?

2. Construct a hypothetical argument using the following elements of an argument: data, claim, warrants, backing, and rebuttal. Lay the argument out in the same fashion as Figure 10.1.

3. Go to the "Trial Update" section of the marthatalks.com website and read the press statements from January 4, 2003 and April 8, 2004. The URLs for those sites are http://www.marthatalks.com/trial_update/010403.html and http://www.marthatalks.com/trial_update/040804.html. After reading the press statements, apply the following questions drawn from Perelman and Olbrechts-Tyteca's work to uncover some of the rhetorical strategies in the site:

- What are the identifiable (potential) audiences for the "Trial Update"?
- Who exactly constitutes the universal audience for this part of marthtalks.com? What evidence from the press statements leads you to your conclusion?
- What is "presenced" for the audience in these press statements? What else could the authors have focused on?
- What kinds of appeals dominate in the press statements—quasi-logical arguments, appeals to the real, or dissociation? Provide the specific evidence from the press statements that led you to your conclusion.

NOTES

1 The term *formal/mathematical approach* refers to an approach to logic that had developed in philosophy and attempted to reduce arguments to rule-governed formulas. To give you a sense for what this kind of theoretical work looks like, here is an abstract of a recent article from the *Notre Dame Journal of Formal Logic*:

Sacchetti, Lorenzo. "The Fixed Point Property in Modal Logic." *Notre Dame Journal of Formal Logic* 42 (2001): 65–86.

Abstract
This paper deals with the modal logics associated with (possibly nonstandard) provability predicates of Peano Arithmetic. One of our goals is to present some modal systems having the fixed point property and not extending the Gödel-Löb system **GL**. We prove that, for every $n \geq 2, K + \Box \ (\Box^{n-1}p \rightarrow p) \rightarrow \Box p$ has the explicit fixed point property. Our main result states that every complete modal logic L having the Craig's interpolation property and such that $L \vdash \Delta \ (\nabla(p) \rightarrow p) \rightarrow \Delta(p)$, where $\nabla(p)$ and $\Delta(p)$ are suitable modal formulas, has the explicit fixed point property.

Clearly, this does not resemble anything we discussed in Chapter 9. Toulmin found such an approach to be not very useful in analyzing how people argue in everyday situations. As a result, he changed his approach from a formal mathematical one like this to a descriptive approach to which you will be introduced.

2 Some examples of such classical terms are chronographia, past fact and future fact, witnesses, anamnesis, and ampliatio. Here are the definitions of these terms taken from *Silva Rhetoricae* (2003): *Chronographia*—vivid representation of a certain historical or recurring time (such as a season) to create an illusion of reality; *past fact and future fact*—a topic of invention in which one refers back to general events in the past or to what we can safely suppose will occur in the future based on the record of the past; *witnesses*—calling upon a person or persons who have personally seen or experienced something to lend credibility to one's argument; *anamnesis*—calling to memory past matters, more specifically, citing a past author from memory; *ampliatio*—using the name of something or someone before it has obtained that name or after the reason for that name has ceased.

3 Examples are easily found on the Internet. Here are a few widely varied topics treated using one version of dissociation as an argument tool:

American culture: http://www.intstudy.com/articles/usamyth.htm

Cigarette smuggling in Canada: http://www.nsra-adnf.ca/DOCUMENTS/PDFs/part4.pdf

Industrial hemp: http://www.votehemp.com/mythfact.html

WORKS CITED

"American Culture Myths and Realities." *The International Education Site.* http://www.intstudy.com/articles/usamyth.htm (accessed September 16, 2003).

Aristotle. *The Rhetoric and Poetics of Aristotle.* Translated by W. Rhys Roberts. New York: The Modern Library, 1984.

"Hemp and Marijuana Myths and Realities." *Vote Hemp.* http://www.votehemp.com/mythfact.html (accessed September 16, 2003).

Morvillo, Robert G., and John J. Tigue. "Setting the Record Straight." *Martha Stewart.* http://www.marthatalks.com/legal/060403.html (accessed June 10, 2003).

Perelman, Chaim. *The New Rhetoric and the Humanities: Essays on Rhetoric and Its Applications.* Dordrecht, Holland: D. Reidel, 1979.

Toulmin, Stephen. *The Uses of Argument.* Cambridge: Cambridge University Press, 1969.

"Scouting Believes in Us." Boy Scouts of America. Advertisement. *Black Enterprise* (December 2001): 88.

Silva Rhetoricae, edited by Gideon Burton. http://humanities.byu.edu/rhetoric/default.htm (accessed July 14, 2003).

SUGGESTED READINGS

Brockriede, Wayne, and Douglas Ehninger. "Toulmin on Argument: An Interpretation and Application." *Quarterly Journal of Speech* 46 (1960): 44–53.

Dearin, Ray D. "The Philosophical Basis of Chaim Perelman's Theory of Rhetoric." *Quarterly Journal of Speech* 55 (1969): 213–24.

Perelman, Chaim. "The New Rhetoric and the Rhetoricians: Remembrances and Comments." *Quarterly Journal of Speech* 70 (1984): 188–96.

Trent, Jimmie D. "Toulmin Model of Argument: An Examination and Extension." *Quarterly Journal of Speech* 54 (1968): 252–59.

Warnick, Barbara, and Susan L. Kline. "The 'New Rhetoric's' Argument Schemes: A Rhetorical View of Practical Reasoning." *Argumentation and Advocacy* 29 (1992): 1–15.

DRAMATISTIC APPROACHES

PREFACE
TO
CHAPTERS
11–13

The search models introduced in the next three chapters are all related by their basic dramatistic approach to rhetoric and criticism. In a nutshell, dramatism describes how people use rhetoric to make sense of their life experiences. It is probably easier to understand dramatism in contrast to scientism. We have all been taught that if you want to know or understand something, you must control identifiable variables, collect unbiased data, and then draw very specific and limited conclusions from the experiment. The process pits the intellect of the individual scientist against nature, which seems loath to give up its secrets. In contrast to scientism, dramatism describes the process of knowing and understanding as a creative and communal effort. People talk to each other and act (in this sense, acting is not "portraying" but rather "doing by acting upon"), which is "dramatic." From a dramatistic perspective, what is important is understanding the process by which people create their understanding of the world through all sorts of communication. Rather than understanding people as isolated investigators of experience as a rational scientistic model would, dramatism sees people creating their reality by influencing each other through rhetoric.

In Chapter 11 we look at Walter Fisher's idea of the narrative paradigm. Fisher helps us see how stories are central to how we reason about things, how we use stories to argue. You'll see how people make claims about experience and provide justifications for them by telling stories of all sorts. The interaction of people talking together is how we know what is going on in our experience, much like what happens on a stage and what happens when we witness what happens on a stage.

Next, in Chapter 12, we examine fantasy theme analysis developed by Ernest Bormann. Fantasy theme analysis uses some of the same language or terms that narrative criticism does, but its roots are in the "psychology of small groups." Bormann has creatively taken findings of research in how small groups cope with, argue about, and make sense of their situation as a kind of community. The ideas we draw from fantasy theme analysis will be added to our knowledge about how we use stories as rhetorical tools in everyday life.

Finally, we introduce Kenneth Burke's dramatistic theory in Chapter 13. Burke began his work as a literary critic. As he looked closely at how people use language in literature, he began to recognize how language, even in literature, is purposefully used by people to accomplish certain ends, which makes the "poetic" discourse as rhetorical as traditional forms of argumentation. What makes Burke's work so powerful is that he asked the next logical question of such human activity—what are the authors' motives? This question drives all he has to say about how and why human beings communicate with one another. The question is basic to any dramatistic perspective on human action.

Our discussion of his rich and expansive theory will serve to get you oriented with Burke so you can develop more of your own understanding of what he has to say. In fact, the discussions of all three approaches necessarily will be for the purpose of getting you started with them. Your task will be to apply what we present here, with an eye to expanding your understanding of each so that your analyses are insightful and useful.

THE NARRATIVE PARADIGM

11

The next time a friend is late to meet you, nicely ask her for an explanation, and listen closely to how she explains things. We're confident that what you'll hear is a story. Look at the "Zits" comic in Figure 11.1 and notice that Jeremy's explanation is a story. That's why we can relate so well to the comic—we've all been there, as it were. We've all used stories to persuade people to our point of view, and we are constantly hearing stories that ask us to see situations as the storyteller sees them. Thus, narratives are important rhetorical phenomena worthy of analysis.

This chapter introduces an analytical approach based on the narrative paradigm developed by Walter Fisher. First, we introduce you to some of the vocabulary of Fisher's model, then we show you how the concepts work in some extended and very different examples. The first example is a classic speech, Abraham Lincoln's Gettysburg Address, and the second is an episode of the World Wrestling Federation's *WWF Smackdown!* (since the time of our analysis the World Wrestling Federation has been renamed World Wrestling Entertainment). Our intention is to bracket the range of messages you'll encounter as a critic—these two messages are about as different as narratives get. Nevertheless, we think you'll see in them similar elements that yield insight about how stories work as rhetoric. First, we need to know something about the basic starting points and vocabulary that Fisher uses.

Vocabulary

➤ narrative paradigm
➤ narrator
➤ characters
➤ plot
➤ setting (context)
➤ narrative probability
➤ narrative fidelity

FIGURE 11.1

ZITS — BY JERRY SCOTT AND JIM BORGMAN

SOME VOCABULARY OF THE NARRATIVE PARADIGM

The **narrative paradigm** is anchored in Walter Fisher's contention that *the most basic human symbolic response to rhetorical exigencies is storytelling* (1984, 6–8). Fisher argues that the earliest propensities of human beings were to merge logic and poetic in narratives or stories (1985a, 76). In other words, since the beginning of human history, when we have needed to make sense of the world to each other, we have told stories. Ancient myths are narratives to explain the purpose and meaning of life. Even such documents as the Declaration of Independence are grounded in a story about the injustices of the British government's treatment of the colonies. The pervasiveness of storytelling among us is actually quite astounding. As we noted in the cartoon in Figure 11.1, Jeremy's argument was framed as a story; it is the default strategy for self-defense.

Why is this worth noting? Due to our place in history, we generally operate under the belief that reasoning, or logic, is a no-nonsense, relatively formal set of mental operations that is used in contexts clearly marked "argument"; contexts such as legal briefs, academic essays, and business memoranda seem to be the province of argument. This view of arguing, according to Fisher, is a result of Plato's effort to make logic the province of the philosophers, not just everyday folks (1985a, 77). Once that separation was accomplished, argument became the territory of experts such as lawyers and scientists. Fisher wants to reconnect logic and poetic because, as he has noted, that's how we still actually persuade in everyday life. Notice that this paragraph is itself a story offered to make sense of the use of stories in modern society. Although the paragraph may not strike you as a narrative, it nevertheless is presented as a rationale for the narrative paradigm; it recounts a history of narrative with Fisher and Plato as characters in a plot that depicts a causal relationship between Plato's efforts to privilege logic over poetic and Fisher's efforts to restore a normative connection between them. It is a story of a sort, and the concepts of the narrative paradigm help us account for what was said and why.

NARRATIVE ELEMENTS

Test Fisher's idea, again. Ask someone—a parent, roommate, friend, or coworker—to explain or justify something he or she has done. Most likely, what you'll get in return is a "story" told to provide reasons for what the person has done. Of course, the story may not have all the trappings of a full-fledged play or a novel, but most likely you will hear in the explanation the use of such interconnected elements as narrator, character, plot, and setting (context), to name a few. No doubt you are already somewhat familiar with these concepts from courses in literature or theater, or even other communication courses. But it's important that we grab hold of these ideas and see what complexity they have to offer as analytical tools. Take note here: although we are going to discuss these concepts individually to get started, they are actually interrelated such that, in any narrative, changes in one of the elements affect all the others, more or less.

All stories must be told, so they are narrated in some fashion—the "how" of the narrative can make a big difference. At a minimum, we can distinguish the **narrator** as *a character in the story or an observer of events*. Think of it as the difference between "telling" the story and "showing" or "recounting" the story (Chatman 1990, 109). For example, consider the difference between your friend saying, "I was in the Sports Pub last night, when in walked a priest and a rabbi . . ." or "There was this bar, and in walks a priest and a rabbi. . . . " In the first case, your friend seems to be recounting his actual experience (first person)—that is, he's part of it; but in the second he's "showing" or "recounting" it (third person). The difference in your friend's mode of narrating the story will signal a different purpose on his part and may increase or diminish your interest in it. You get a clue from the narrative position taken whether the story is intended as a recounting of actual events or as a joke.

Character is a related concept, obviously. **Characters** are *the people in the story or things that function like people in the story* (e.g., R2D2 or C3PO in the *Star Wars* series). Characters act; they are motivated to act by others or by the context, and critics try to understand what those actions mean.

To follow the characters through the story is to follow the plot. The **plot** is *the underlying structure or pattern of actions and causality in the narrative* (Martin 1986, 81). In a good story, causality connects actions to reveal a rationale for them. For example, consider the difference between these mininarratives: "The king died, and the queen died" and "The king died, and the queen died of grief" (Martin 1986, 81). In the first case, two events merely occurred, whereas in the second case, the actions are connected and there is a rationale for the queen's death. The second example has the quality of a plot because there is a recognizable pattern of causality that connects the deaths of the king and queen.

Finally, all these elements exist within a setting or context. As we've noted in Chapter 4, context is a complex thing. In a narrative, setting is more than decor or time and place. **Setting (context)** is *a fusion of all the details of the story external to the characters* (Martin 1986, 122). The setting serves as indicator of prior events, circumstances, and conditions surrounding the characters. Setting may even present themes of the story that help us interpret characters' actions. For example, in the cartoon in Figure 11.1, the late-night setting is indicated by the dark background and the disheveled appearance of the mother in what seems to be a bathrobe. The fact that the meeting occurred at the door suggests that Jeremy has been late before or previously given the parents a reason to anticipate violation of curfew; the setting hints at some relevant prior events that contextualize the present story and provides some guidance as to how to interpret it.

These concepts of character, plot, and setting are somewhat familiar to us from our experiences with literature, no doubt, and they serve us well in providing a vocabulary to talk about the specific elements, devices, or structures within any story we examine. Together they serve as an initial search model for analyzing texts of all sorts. But the narrative paradigm is more than a sorter of story elements.

Walter Fisher has a bigger purpose in mind for the narrative paradigm—one that gets us past a mere description of story parts. The paradigm is not a "specific method of analysis" (1985b, 357). Rather, he argues:

> *the narrative paradigm is a paradigm in the sense of a philosophical view of human communication; it is not a model of discourse as such.* The primary function of the paradigm is to offer a way of interpreting and assessing human communication *that leads to critique, a determination of whether or not a given instance of discourse provides a reliable, trustworthy, and desirable guide to thought and action in the world. (1985b, 351, emphasis added)*

Notice the significant goals of narrative criticism: "interpreting and assessing [or evaluating] human communication." Fisher's concern as a critic is not just to say, "Here's a character, in this scene, which is part of the plot." (Stopping at that would be to offer only a description.) As we examine the narratives we encounter in everyday life, our real interest is "determination of whether or not a given instance of discourse provides a reliable, trustworthy, and desirable guide to thought and action in the world." Fisher features the most significant of the four kinds of critical thinking we have been developing throughout this textbook: interpretation and evaluation of the rhetoric. Such an approach makes the critical task important, valuable, and purposeful. You may be wondering, if the narrative paradigm is not a specific method, how can we use it? Good question. In the next sections, we show you some examples.

NARRATIVE PARADIGM APPLIED

It's often easier to understand abstract ideas when they are applied to a case. Let's take a look at two very different rhetorical texts, the Gettysburg Address, and an episode of *WWF Smackdown!*, to see how narrative criticism may be used in making sense of them. First, take a look at one of the great rhetorical texts in U.S. history, the Gettysburg Address.

The Gettysburg Address
Abraham Lincoln
Thursday, November 19, 1863

> *Four score and seven years ago our fathers brought forth on this continent, a new nation, conceived in Liberty, and dedicated to the proposition that all men are created equal.*
>
> *Now we are engaged in a great civil war, testing whether that nation, or any nation so conceived and so dedicated, can long endure. We are met on a great battle-field of that war. We have come to dedicate a portion of that field, as a final resting place for those who here gave their lives that that nation might live. It is altogether fitting and proper that we should do this.*

But, in a larger sense, we can not dedicate—we can not consecrate—we can not hallow—this ground. The brave men, living and dead, who struggled here, have consecrated it, far above our poor power to add or detract. The world will little note, nor long remember what we say here, but it can never forget what they did here. It is for us the living, rather, to be dedicated here to the unfinished work which they who fought here have thus far so nobly advanced. It is rather for us to be here dedicated to the great task remaining for us—that from these honored dead we take increased devotion to that cause for which they gave the last full measure of devotion—that we here highly resolve that these dead shall not have died in vain—that this nation, under God, shall have a new birth of freedom—and that government of the people, by the people, for the people, shall not perish from the earth.

Remember, our critical goal, using a narrative approach, is to determine whether or not a given instance of discourse provides a reliable, trustworthy, and desirable guide to thought and action in the world. We are seeking to understand how the story provides a rationale for some course of action (the goal of rhetoric).

In characterizing the Gettysburg Address, we can say it is a brief and pointed epideictic speech that is marked by its simplicity of language and powerful emotions. The emotional dimension of the speech quickly reaches its zenith in the first sentence of the third paragraph wherein Lincoln "turns the tables" emotionally from grief to zeal—from a focus on loss to a focus on constructive action. Lincoln presents a concise history of the United States in the first and second paragraphs, then a statement of America's potential future in the third and final paragraph. As a ceremonial speech, it brackets the present with past and future.

So, from our effort in characterizing the text, it is apparent that Lincoln was trying to do something by way of the speech. In featuring time and people (or characters) within that time line, we get a sense of the storylike quality of the speech. Let's look at some of those qualities that immediately surface. Recall the first sentence of the speech: "Four score and seven years ago, our fathers brought forth on this continent, a new nation, conceived in Liberty, and dedicated to the proposition that all men are created equal." In these few words, we have some basic elements of a good story. Although the story elements in the left column in Table 11.1 are rudimentary at this point, Lincoln goes on to develop each, more or less, over the course of the short speech.

To create a plot, he takes his audience on a historical journey from the founding of the nation eighty-seven years earlier, to their present time, and then to an undefined point in the future. Characters are named who are related to each other in the moral struggle—people who "gave their lives that that nation might live." Certainly, these are heroic individuals, "these honored dead," who gave of themselves individually for the larger, common good.

The plot is brief and chronological: eighty-seven years prior, a nation was founded on the pillars of liberty and equality; a test of those principles has engulfed the country, and presently has yet to be concluded; a potential future can be drawn from the courage of those who have died for the original vision.

TABLE 11.1	
Characters	The founding fathers of the country; "we"; "these honored dead"
Plot	Founding of a new nation; crisis of war; dedication to a better future
Setting	This continent, generally; Gettysburg battlefield, in particular
Narrator	Lincoln

The question we want to keep in mind is the degree to which the plot exhibits causality—are the plot elements related? If so, how?

The setting is used to give meaning to the events of the plot. Lincoln shifts the setting from "this continent, a new nation" to "a great battle-field." What he does verbally is similar to "rack focus" in a movie or television program, where the focus starts with the background clear and the objects in the foreground blurred, then switches to the foreground objects, leaving the background blurred. Our attention is moved with the focus. The shift makes us ask, What conditions, circumstances or theme does Lincoln now feature, given the shift? Why does he make the shift?

There is no doubt that the Gettysburg Address is a narrative, a brief history of our nation as well as a "fantasy" of the nation's future. Treating it as a narrative opens possibilities for understanding it that escape us if we mechanically identify some classical elements of speech such as introduction, body, and conclusion or ethos, logos, and pathos. These concepts can still be used (Fisher 1985b, 350), but if they are used to complement a creative dramatistic/narrative approach, we are more likely to discover dynamics of the communication event we might have overlooked otherwise.

TWO CONCEPTS—FOUR CONCERNS

So far, we have been able to describe and initiate analysis of the text using concepts from narrative theory to serve as the search model. However, according to Fisher, we have further to go—we need to examine the text as a rationale for action. At this point we must understand two significant (although, at times, problematic) concepts: narrative probability and narrative fidelity. According to Fisher, **narrative probability** *"refers to formal features of a story conceived as a discrete sequence of thought and/or action in life or literature (any recorded or written form of discourse); i.e., it concerns the question of whether or not a story coheres or 'hangs together,' whether or not the story is free of contradictions"* (1985b, 349). **Narrative fidelity** *"concerns the 'truth qualities' of the story, the degree to which it accords with the logic of good reasons: the soundness of its reasoning and the value of its values"* (349–50).

These two concepts require our careful attention and thought when we are conducting critical analysis using the narrative paradigm. Unfortunately, they are the most ambiguous and problematic concepts of the approach. Barbara Warnick (1987, 173) gives us a little help in understanding these concepts by laying them out as shown in Figure 11.2. As you can see, in order to interpret and judge the argument of the narrative, we must look at four different dimensions. Regarding narrative probability, to determine whether the story hangs together and is free of contradictions, the critic must think hard about the nature of the message as a whole. At its most basic level, one can understand narrative probability as the degree to which events of the story follow one because of another (causality). That is, when there is a certain compelling logic to the story, we would describe it as *probable*. When you read a good story, you can't put it down because one event leads to the next—"one thing *because* of another." Recall the example of our mininarrative, "The king died, and the queen died of grief." There is a rationale of events—a reason why the queen died. Poor stories are often episodic, which means that events just seem to happen "one event after another" rather than "one event because of another." Such is the case in the narrative, "The king died, and the queen died." The more logical the relationship between plot events, the more powerful the story. However, if a narrative does not follow a strict chronological order, that doesn't mean necessarily the story automatically fails the test of probability (e.g., the queen dies grieving, and the story flashes back to the events that led to the king's demise). A very powerful device for engaging an audience is to break up the events of the plot in ways that make the audience work at holding them in memory and rearranging them so they have logical coherence. For example, in the film *Memento* (2000), the story is told in reverse. Rather than just "going with the flow" of a traditional chronological story, the audience has to hold

FIGURE 11.2

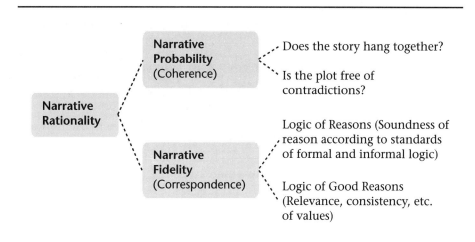

more and more information in memory to make sense of the main character's actions and motives. As a result, the audience experiences many of the same frustrations as the main character, Leonard Shelby, who suffers short-term memory loss. The plot form requires effort by the audience to understand what is going on, which invites more engagement with the film. One lesson we learn from this case is that effective narratives must not always present the events of the plot in chronological order.

To properly evaluate a narrative plot, you must assess it on its own merits within the context of the message and the audience to which it is addressed. You can't assume any particular structure does or does not cohere. In each case you must take the elements of probability (Do things hang together? Are events contradictory?) and apply them to the message you are studying.

GETTYSBURG ADDRESS AND PROBABILITY

Although the plot in Lincoln's speech is extremely brief, it does capture the essence of what everyone in the audience understood as the story of our nation's past. Notice the logical connection between the first two sentences: "Four score and seven years ago, our fathers brought forth on this continent, a new nation, conceived in Liberty, and dedicated to the proposition that all men are created equal. Now we are engaged in a great civil war, testing whether that nation, or any nation so conceived and so dedicated, can long endure." A paraphrase of Lincoln's ideas could read, "A nation was created on the premise of all people being equal; now we are testing that premise." One event, the construction of a new social order, a social experiment called the United States, has caused people to test the strength and limits of that new order: one thing because of another. In absolute historical terms, the narrative is distorted because it treats so few historical details with little concern for nuances of fact. Nevertheless, Lincoln "told it like it was" as far as the audience was concerned. The history of the United States, although highly edited by Lincoln, made logical connections from one segment to another—one thing because of another. The Address passes on the criterion of probability, we think.

GETTYSBURG ADDRESS AND FIDELITY

The criterion of fidelity is more complicated. This criterion zeroes in on the nature of the argument made within the narrative. If we assume that narratives may possess a logical dimension, we have to ask how a critic can discover the argument in a text that may have an overwhelmingly attractive delivery.

First, you have to figure out what is being argued—the claim and its reasons and backing—then assess the quality of the argument. At this point, you may find it useful to review traditional concepts used in argument analysis such as fallacies or forms of refutation. (Chapters 9 and 10 provide resources to do this.) However, just as it is insufficient for you as a critic simply to identify the narrative elements (characters, plot, setting, etc.), it is insufficient for you to just list specific argument forms you discovered in the analysis. An analysis of the logic of good reasons will lead you to significant, useful, and interesting insights about any text. What we mean is that as a critic, once you figure out what arguments exist in the message, you must determine if the arguments reflect good values or bad ones. (That's the difference between a *logic of reasons* and a *logic of good reasons*.) Lincoln's speech argues that it is appropriate to honor the soldiers who died at Gettysburg. It is an argument grounded in the value of universal human worth and the value of sacrificing one's life for another's. These seem to be better reasons than, say, honoring the dead because their victory will make a stronger economy. We conclude that Lincoln's reasons were good reasons because they appeal to the highest possible values.

So, to get at what Fisher deems important, the interpretation and evaluation of a message, we need to use two specific criteria: narrative probability and narrative fidelity. Our concern regarding probability is the degree to which the plot moves from one event to another for cause or reason rather than just happening. As we examine fidelity, we should concern ourselves with the nature of the argument put forward within the story and then judge the values that drive the argument itself. This is difficult stuff to absorb. Let's try applying these concepts to a more contemporary and complex message in a very different medium.

NARRATIVE APPLIED TO <u>WWF SMACKDOWN!</u>

So far, we've looked at a classic speech, but many of the texts we may wish to examine these days are of a very different nature. Let's look at a radically different form of discourse—televised World Wrestling Federation (WWF) wrestling. WWF wrestling is an interesting phenomenon. Its tremendous growth in popularity and accessibility via broadcast and cable television, coupled with the elements of spectacle, violence, and sexuality make it worthy of critical attention. Using the narrative paradigm, we are going to examine a randomly chosen episode of *WWF Smackdown!* broadcast on March 8, 2001. The intent of the following discussion is to illustrate our ideas about applying the narrative paradigm; this is not a model of a complete and thorough analysis.

Recall that the focus of narrative criticism is to uncover the logic of the narrative. We'll begin by describing various dimensions of a narrative as the first step of any analysis.

The literal setting for this particular episode is the MCI Center in Washington, D.C. However, since the literal setting of the arena doesn't tell us much, we need to place the setting within a larger social context. The episode actually sets itself not in the arena per se—the actual location of the ring or stage is not that important—but the show begins with the narrators recounting the battles a week earlier between the main characters: The Rock, Stone Cold Steve Austin, Kurt Angle, The Undertaker, Triple H, and others. The narrators, voicing over an MTV-style montage of action, interpret for viewers the spectacular and violent maneuvers these men use on each other in order to create a context for the conflicts to follow. The production fits well within the social context of "extreme experience" marked by a variety of more or less violent or risky television programs such as *Survivor, Fear Factor, Real TV,* and *Lost,* not to mention the increasingly legitimate *X Games* and the completely legitimate broadcasts of the National Football League and NASCAR Racing. The WWF operates at the periphery of both sport and social interaction.

The characters of the narrative are a series of stock heroes and villains; friends and enemies; provocateurs, victims, and saviors; cheats and clowns. A central character within the episode's main narrative is Vince McMahon, the owner of the WWF. Interestingly, McMahon's character is that of a smarmy, ingratiating, ingenuous, manipulative, mean-spirited misogynist. Nevertheless, everyone involved, from other characters to the narrators, refer to him unceasingly as Mr. McMahon. Other significant characters in the narrative are Debra, who is Stone Cold Steve Austin's wife; Trish Stratus, who is McMahon's mistress; Linda McMahon, who is Vince McMahon's wife; Steve Austin; and The Rock. Other minor characters who are necessary to punctuate the perverse soap opera of the main narrative also appear in matches. These stock characters play out the common plots in which, typically, a crowd favorite finds himself or herself cheated or disadvantaged by a villainous character. The favorite then usually stages an incredible comeback or is rescued by a team member or some other similarly heroic character. Good is not always "good" in the sense of playing fair, but evil is always very evil and that can be "good." For example, The Undertaker is a crowd favorite; he's so evil he's bigger than life and therefore admirable—the consummate antihero for whom the crowd cheers.

The plot of this episode is grounded in Vince McMahon's plan to embarrass and dishonor his wife publicly because he had asked for a divorce in front of the crowd at an event months earlier; she denied him the divorce and has since had a nervous breakdown. Even though she is unable to walk or talk, apparently in a near catatonic condition, McMahon hatches a scheme to humiliate her in front of the crowd by groping his mistress onstage with his wife placed beside them in her wheelchair.

A secondary plot is related to McMahon attempting to disrupt the marriage of Steve Austin and Debra by assigning Debra as The Rock's manager even though he is an enemy of Austin. Thus, in response to McMahon's seemingly irresistible directive, Debra must manage the enemy of her husband while The Rock, wanting no manager at all, must endure the arrangement. These two plots are gradually developed through the device of the audience "overhearing" backstage conversations (with a camera obviously present to capture the conversations); these conversations provide the audience with the information needed to understand what is going on when the same characters enter the arena. The plots are punctuated by the ongoing card of matches for the evening. As described earlier, these follow a predictable formula and create a polarized atmosphere wherein the single most common emotion is anger or rage.

The narrators in this production play an important role. Throughout the entire broadcast, the narration is itself extreme in volume, pace, and content. The narration adds a layer of auditory stimulation complementary to the visual display of mayhem on the screen, as well as the social mayhem being played out in the McMahon plots. The narrators often serve to voice the anticipation or reaction of the audience. For example, they shout the question, "Why is Mr. McMahon doing this to his own wife?" Then they provide the requisite counterpoint by shouting "This is just disgusting!" as the camera zooms in on McMahon groping Trish directly in front of Linda McMahon. The voyeuristic experience is heightened by the "forbidden" nature of the event keyed by the narrators' response.

Beyond describing and interpreting the action, the narrators, Michael Cole and Tazz, constantly advertise upcoming events by grounding them in the present conflict. For example, they ask how The Rock will be able to defend his championship the following week given the damage he is sustaining in the present match. This sort of promotion of events is thoroughly woven into the commentary.

Finally, the audience plays a significant role in the televised event as they are the focus of attention for the main characters. Although the characters interact with each other, their interactions always have a self-conscious element. For example, as Triple H takes the ring for his match, a character by the name of The Undertaker unexpectedly arrives, takes the ring, and begins posturing to the audience. He confronts Triple H and declares the ring "my private property" and pauses to allow the audience to respond. He gazes out at the audience, then slowly walks around the ring and back to Triple H, who has turned to the audience with a stunned look. The camera sweeps the audience, which is on its feet, clapping or jeering for each character, waving signs of support or derision, and often wearing T-shirts or costumes announcing their preference for one or the other wrestlers.

The audience's greater participation occurs during the backstage moments (which are broadcast in the arena on large screens) and during McMahon's humiliation of his wife. The audience is set up via contrived dialogues, providing information that would have been known only to those in the conversation but is necessary for the audience to understand the motive and meaning of the onstage activity. The audience is exploited while simultaneously given what it wants—titillation and the sense of amazement to be felt as one safely observes the suffering of others.

The plots are central to this episode. Narrative probability, you recall, was defined as the degree to which events of the story follow one because of another. The description of the plots suggests that there is little probability to the events. In regard to the matches themselves, they typically have a pattern, but the pattern does not necessarily make for logical connections between actions. The participants hate each other because they are supposed to, given their characterizations, rather than for reasons. Changes in behavior designed to surprise the audience, which is familiar with the plot patterns, seem to happen randomly rather than for reasons. For example, a wrestler may jump into the ring to assist another who, until that moment, has been a sworn enemy of

his savior. No rationale is provided, but a new alliance is created that antici-
pates a future set of conflicts for all involved. These subplots lack probability.

However, the lack of probability is most obvious in the main plots involving McMahon. These plot developments present one thing after another and
fail to create a compelling logic for the narrative. In spite of this tentative finding, it is important that we examine the nature of narrative fidelity before
drawing final conclusions about the narrative.

Narrative fidelity is concerned with the truth quality of the narrative, the
soundness of the reasons, and the value of its values. Given that this episode
of *WWF Smackdown!* mocks the notion of logical progression (probability), it
seems safe to suspect that it also mocks mainstream cultural values. This
episode presents a value scale in which the essential value to be enacted is
domination. The exercise of power is a taken-for-granted value both in physical and psychological terms. Power is exercised for personal aggrandizement
and personal pleasure rather than for any constructive communal purpose.
Reasons for behavior are grounded in vendetta, desire for retribution, and personal success and reward. Alliances are formed and broken only for the more
clever characters to promote their own agendas. Exercise of personal power is
the driving motive; each character operates in the same frame, consequently
blocking one another and building frustration and anger, expressed in a constant rage. Especially frustrating is that the characters are in what appears to be
a Darwinian system of survival of the fittest, but the logic of evolution is constantly thwarted by arbitrary actions of characters within the narrative. The
arena is a world of constant frustration and surprise. As the narrators state
regarding the seemingly insane behavior of Kurt Angle, "Kurt Angle has
snapped, and he *should* snap because it brings out the mean streak in him!"
The world presented here is one of treachery and chaos, and those who succeed are the most aggressive—usually.

The case made here is ultimately antihuman and existential. That is, it
argues that the individual is pitted against all others in a kind of prehuman
free-for-all in which civil rules are ineffective and all that matters is survival at
any cost. Given the alternative ways of thinking and talking about the world
that are available to us, we conclude that the arguments of this set of narratives
are destructive in their conclusions. They discourage patience, self-control,
honesty, forthrightness, and concern for others in favor of personal power
exercised for personal gain.

In sum, the logic of the narratives played out in *WWF Smackdown!* is found
to be wanting in both probability and fidelity. As logical efforts, these stories
are seriously flawed. Beyond that, we have found that the characters are motivated by seemingly arbitrary events in their environment, or by uncontrol-
lable, almost animalistic, urges. From the perspective of the narrative
paradigm, the stories in this episode of *WWF Smackdown!* appear to be complete failures. However, this finding leads us to some larger and quite interesting questions for future research: Given the technical inferiority of the
narratives, how can we explain their popularity with the audience? And we
may also ask, what are the effects of such discourse on the audience?

SUMMARY

The narrative paradigm has provided a way of looking at two very different forms of discourse in different social contexts and delivered via different media. In both cases, the narrative paradigm has provided useful tools for describing, analyzing, and interpreting rhetoric. These tools consist of concepts for searching through the text in a systematic fashion—narrator, character, plot, and setting give us places to look and things to look for in the text. Beyond that, the concepts of narrative probability and fidelity extend the analysis and also provide the means to determine if a text is a "reliable, trustworthy and desirable guide to thought and action."

The findings of the narrative analysis, we think, are interesting and useful. However, we recognize that not all that can be known regarding the Gettysburg Address or WWF wrestling spectacles as rhetoric has been uncovered. The next chapter introduces another method, fantasy theme analysis, which offers ways of gaining insights about dramatic messages.

EXERCISES

1. Review the "Zits" cartoon (Figure 11.1) at the beginning of the chapter. Analyze the cartoon from two different perspectives. First, consider Scott and Borgman as the rhetors. Given that starting point, answer the following questions:

   ■ Who is the narrator?
   ■ What characters exist within the text? Which ones are most important to the narrative?
   ■ What is the plot?
   ■ What is the setting?
   ■ What is the context?

   Now, consider Jeremy the narrator. Given that starting point, answer the following questions:

   ■ What characters exist within the text? Which ones are most important to the narrative?
   ■ What is the plot?
   ■ What is the setting?
   ■ What is the context?

   What difference did the starting point make in how you answered the questions? What does the exercise tell you about the stance you adopt as a critic?

2. Jeremy's story is judged by his parents as "not holding water." In other words, Jeremy's argument fails to persuade his audience. Use the narrative probability and narrative fidelity concepts to explain why the parents did not accept the story as a compelling argument for his tardiness.

WORKS CITED

Chatman, Seymour. *Coming to Terms: The Rhetoric of Narrative in Fiction and Film.* Ithaca, NY: Cornell University Press, 1990.

Fisher, Walter R. "Narration as a Human Communication Paradigm: The Case of Public Moral Argument." *Communication Monographs* 51 (1984): 1–22.

———. "The Narrative Paradigm: In the Beginning." *Journal of Communication* 35 (1985a): 74–89.

———. "The Narrative Paradigm: An Elaboration." *Communication Monographs* 52 (1985b): 347–67.

Martin, Wallace. *Recent Theories of Narrative.* Ithaca, NY: Cornell University Press, 1986.

Warnick, Barbara. "The Narrative Paradigm: Another Story." *Quarterly Journal of Speech* 73 (1987): 172–82.

SUGGESTED READINGS

Bishop, Ronald. "The Pursuit of Perfection: A Narrative Analysis of How Women's Magazines Cover Eating Disorders." *Howard Journal of Communication* 12 (2001): 221–40.

Fisher, Walter R. "The Narrative Paradigm and the Assessment of Historical Texts." *Argumentation and Advocacy* 25 (1988): 49–53.

———. "The Narrative Paradigm: In the Beginning." *Journal of Communication* 35 (1985): 74–89.

Griffin, Charles J. G. "The 'Washington Revival': Narrative and the Moral Transformation of Temperance Reform in Antebellum America." *Southern Communication Journal* 66 (2000): 67–78.

Kuypers, Jim A., Marilyn J. Young, and Michael K. Launer. "Composite Narrative, Authoritarian Discourse, and the Soviet Response to the Destruction of Iran Air Flight 655." *Quarterly Journal of Speech* 87 (2001): 305–20.

Lewis, William F. "Telling America's Story: Narrative Form and the Reagan Presidency." *Quarterly Journal of Speech* 73 (1987): 280–302.

Opt, Susan K. "Continuity and Change in Storytelling About Artificial Intelligence: Extending the Narrative Paradigm." *Communication Quarterly* 36 (1988): 298–310.

FANTASY THEME ANALYSIS

You have probably noticed that people tend to repeat things that are important to them. Perhaps you have an aging uncle who, every time you visit, tells the story of how he broke his hip falling over his two-pound puppy just two days after he bought her. Although it may be annoying at times, he's just trying to make sense of his situation. Individuals retell events that they find interesting, shocking, funny, frustrating, or confusing. Sometimes those stories strike others in the same way, are remembered, and are retold creating a chain of stories (and meanings) among them. Groups share "lore," and even nations create chains of stories that serve as a tool for the population to make sense of important events. The United States is experiencing this phenomenon post-9/11.

On September 15, 2001, four days after the Twin Towers and the Pentagon were attacked, President Bush, accompanied by Secretary of State Colin Powell and Attorney General John Ashcroft, held a press conference at Camp David. Bush declared, "I've asked the highest levels of our government to come to discuss the current tragedy that has so deeply affected our nation." In order to begin making sense of the terrorist attack, they had to talk about it. The public also needed to make sense of events; folks talked to one another and listened to President Bush and his staff closely in order to reorient themselves. A crisis such as 9/11 provides a deep soil from which fantasy themes sprout and grow. Look at this initial segment of the Camp David press conference:

> Q: Sir, what do you say to Americans who are worried that the longer it takes to retaliate, the more chance the perpetrators have to escape and hide and just escape justice?
>
> THE PRESIDENT: They will try to hide, they will try to avoid the United States and our allies—but we're not going to let them. They run to the hills; they find holes to get in. And we will do whatever it takes to smoke them out and get them running, and we'll get them.
>
> Listen, this is a great nation; we're a kind people. None of us could have envisioned the barbaric acts of these terrorists. But they have stirred up the might of the American people, and we're going to get them, no matter what it takes.
>
> In my radio address today I explained to the American people that this effort may require patience. But we're going to—
>
> Q: How long—

Vocabulary
➤ fantasy theme analysis
➤ fantasies
➤ manifest content
➤ here and now
➤ rhetorical vision

THE PRESIDENT: As long as it takes. And it's not just one person. We're talking about those who fed them, those who house them, those who harbor terrorists will be held accountable for this action.

Q: Sir, are you satisfied that Osama bin Laden is at least a kingpin of this operation?

THE PRESIDENT: There is no question he is what we would call a prime suspect. And if he thinks he can hide and run from the United States and our allies, he will be sorely mistaken.

Q: Mr. President, do you have a message for the Reservists that you called up yesterday? Can you tell us whether you think more may have to be called up?

THE PRESIDENT: The message is for everybody who wears the uniform: get ready. The United States will do what it takes to win this war. And I ask patience of the American people. There is no question in my mind we'll have the resolve—I witnessed it yesterday on the construction site. Behind the sadness and the exhaustion, there is a desire by the American people to not seek only revenge, but to win a war against barbaric behavior, people that hate freedom and hate what we stand for.

And this is an administration that is going to dedicate ourselves to winning that war. (Bush, Powell, and Ashcroft 2001)

The story at this point was fragmentary and not yet developed, but within four days of the attack, we could see nascent characterizations, evolving descriptions of setting, and previews of plots. The press was as involved as the administration in the creation of fantasy themes. Notice that the first reporter's question assumed and articulated a moral setting marked by the need for hasty "retaliation" against "perpetrators" who were trying to "escape justice." Bush extended and elaborated the characterization of the attackers as cowardly and primitive (hiding in holes). In contrast, Americans were characterized as mighty, relentless, and patient. However, the most important theme initiated and constantly elaborated here was the president's description of the setting as a state of war.

One year later, the themes had *chained out* through the population via the media and were established as taken-for-granted truths. In remarks at the Pentagon "in observance of September 11th," President Bush began, "One year ago, men and women and children were killed here because they were Americans. And because this place is a symbol to the world of our country's might and resolve. Today, we remember each life. We rededicate this proud symbol and we renew our commitment to win the war that began here" (Bush 2002). The theme of American might and resolve is present as is the theme of war.

In the years since September 11, 2001, we have as individuals, organizations, communities, and a nation persistently rehearsed the themes we saw in the President's initial press conference. The result has been a reshaping of our perceptions of ourselves as a nation, perceptions that are reinforced by our talk. We talk about the war on terrorism as a taken-for-granted condition, attributing the same meanings to the term *war* in the context of terrorism as we do in the context of our preemptive attack on Iraq. As critics, our task is to

> *take the social reality contained in a rhetorical vision which [we have] con-structed from the concrete dramas developed in a body of discourse and exam-ine social relationships, the motives, the qualitative impact of that symbolic world as though it were the substance of social reality for those people who [participate] in the vision. (Bormann 1972, 401)*

How such convergence is achieved, and how it affects our understanding of our reality, is what we study using fantasy theme analysis.

FANTASY THEME ANALYSIS CONTRASTED WITH NARRATIVE

Ernest Bormann, the rhetorical scholar who developed the fantasy theme approach, conceives of human communication in ways similar to Walter Fisher. Both are interested in understanding how people explain their experi-ences and persuade one another using common dramatic tools. Bormann notes, as did Fisher, that drama is related to rationality (1972, 405). In spite of the basic similarities, Bormann's approach is significantly different from Fisher's narrative paradigm. Here are the foundational differences in a nutshell:

1. When we use the narrative paradigm, we focus on the stories as a whole. Fisher's focus is the total argument stories make. On the other hand, Bormann's approach focuses on how narratives evolve; that is, how they develop and how they eventually wane or disappear. Fantasy theme analy-sis helps us see how stories sweep through a group of people, how people latch on to them, repeat them, and elaborate and use them (Bormann 1972, 399). As a result, when you are using a fantasy theme approach, you will often find it necessary to examine numerous related texts in order to establish the existence of a significant theme.

2. The narrative paradigm focuses on the values elaborated in a story. Fisher made a point of saying his approach was a "philosophical view," not a method (Fisher 1985, 351). Bormann, on the other hand, lays out specific methodological steps for doing a critical analysis of a text using fantasy theme concepts.

SOME BASIC CONCEPTS OF FANTASY THEME ANALYSIS

Fantasy theme analysis was developed by Bormann as *a means of account-ing for how groups of people use stories (in a broad sense) to see the world in* *similar ways.* Bormann actually borrowed the idea from the work of Robert Bales (1970), a psychologist specializing in the study of small group communication. According to Bormann, "Bales provided the key part to the puzzle when he discovered the dynamic process of group fantasizing. Group fantasizing correlates with individual fantasizing and extrapolates to speaker-audience fantasizing and to the dream merchants of the mass media" (1972, 396). In other words, Bormann could use Bales's small-group concept of fantasy to explain rhetorically how a collection of folks becomes a group, community, organization, or congregation that believes and acts in substantially similar ways.

The central concept in Bormann's method is that of fantasy. **Fantasies** are *stories, recollections of events involving the group, or discussions of (usually recurring) topics that may seem, at first, to be irrelevant to the group's task.* That is, the **manifest content** *(the actual topics, ideas, images, etc. of the group's talk)* of the discussion is not explicitly related to the **here and now** *(present conditions, concerns, or tasks)* of the group. It is important that you understand that *fantasy* is a technical term here that is actually quite different from the common meaning of "caprice, whim, fanciful invention."[1] Group fantasies are not entertaining flights of imagination, but a useful form of group talk that serves specific rhetorical purposes.

Here's a hypothetical example: if a product-design group in an electronics company is having trouble working with an overbearing leader, the "manifest content" of the group's talk may often shift to discussions of the president's lack of consultation with Congress before making significant policy decisions. The here and now problems of the group's leadership are vented and analyzed via the fantasy. By talking about how the president's approach disrupts congressional progress on important legislation, the group may indirectly persuade the leader to be more consultative; or the fantasy may serve to help the group figure out how to adapt to an authoritative leader; or it may simply provide catharsis. The fantasy provides a kind of code, a way to gripe about the problem without getting into trouble. In such a group, if the fantasy (with its characters, setting, plot, etc.) serves the needs of the group for explaining, figuring out, or complaining about what's going on, the fantasy will chain out among the group members, and may even spread to other groups, if leadership problems exist in the other groups as well. If it doesn't help, it will be dropped and replaced by another fantasy.

Once the fantasy reaches a critical mass of those involved in the group, a rhetorical vision may develop. That is, the way people talk about leadership would be so common that it would, in a sense, impose itself on everyone; it would be *the* way folks envision leadership in action. In other words, the **rhetorical vision** becomes *the taken-for-granted description of how things should be.* As a result, rhetorical visions affect how people perceive and interpret their reality. In the preceding example, the group's fantasy, if sufficiently repeated and elaborated, constructs the group members' understanding of what makes effective leadership. People in the work group may come to demand a democratic, consultative leader because within their rhetorical vision "that's what good leaders do." Whether or not that is absolutely true is immaterial because the widely shared and often repeated rhetorical vision becomes reality for the participants.

In sum, Bormann explains common understandings of the world among people by tracing a series of communication links from (1) individuals using language to construct narratives, dramas, or fantasies that (2) serve a group of people in making sense of their experience, so that (3) when groups share their fantasies with other groups many people use the same dramatic construction to explain their experience, thus creating a rhetorical vision (Bormann 1972, 402). In other words, at the point when you and those around you talk in similar ways to explain or account for your experiences, you exist within a symbolic construction called a rhetorical vision. A rhetorical vision then becomes a taken-for-granted explanation of experience and controls how those who share it interpret experience and act on it; essentially, it is how you attribute meaning to your experience.

THE PROCESS OF FANTASY THEME ANALYSIS

Bormann (1972) lays out four major steps for conducting a fantasy theme analysis. First, you must become very familiar with the text or texts under analysis (401). As is always the case, you, as a critic, begin by describing the text(s) carefully.

Second, look for patterns among the dramatic elements of characters, plots, and settings (401). The search for patterns is essential in any critical approach, and Bormann notes its importance here for discovering the nature of the relationships among fantasies. For example, you may ask, Are characters or actions or settings related by repetition, or by comparison, or by contrast? Discovering which narrative elements are featured (e.g., character, plot, setting) will help guide you in interpreting and evaluating the fantasy themes.

Third, you "must then creatively reconstruct the rhetorical vision from the representative fantasy chains" (401). Notice that the task here, to "creatively reconstruct the rhetorical vision," is very similar to narrative criticism when you reconstruct the argument being presented in the narrative. This is not an easy job, and it is not one that can be thoughtlessly accomplished by simply repeating a gut reaction to messages. Just as a detective carefully reconstructs the events and actions of a crime, the critic must carefully look at the fantasy themes in the discourse, coupled with how they are dramatically presented, and make a case for the rhetorical vision the critic believes is operating.

Finally, you must ask probing questions about the patterns of the fantasy themes you discover (401). After carefully describing the text, if you recognize a number of brief narratives or themes that seem to be related, you may want to examine them more closely to see how they are functioning rhetorically. That is, do the ministries you see appear to be intended as occasional illustrations as support for an argument, or are they clustering to create a rhetorical vision? If the latter, you'll want to query them further.

Starting with patterns of characterization, you can ask critical questions such as the following from Bormann (1972):[2] Who are the dramatis personae? More specifically:

- Does some abstraction personified as a character provide the ultimate legitimization of the drama? God? The People? The Young? . . .
- Who are the heroes and the villains?
- How concrete and detailed are the characterizations?
- How are motives attributed?
- How are the members of the rhetorical community characterized?
- For what are the insiders praised, or the outsiders or enemies castigated?
- What values are inherent in the praiseworthy characters? (401)

The context or setting of each story helps you better interpret the meaning and purpose of it as fantasy theme. You may ask:

- Where are the dramas set?
- In the wilderness? In the countryside? In the urban ghetto?
- Is the setting given supernatural sanction? (401)

Inasmuch as characters and contexts are identifiable, those characters must be doing something within the scene; the actions of the characters are significant within particular contexts. To better understand the nature and function of action with a fantasy theme, ask:

- What are the typical scenarios?
- What acts are performed by the ultimate legitimizer? The neutral people? The enemy?
- Which are sanctioned and praised; which censored?
- What life styles are exemplified as praiseworthy?
- What meanings are inherent in the dramas? (401–2)

Since emotional appeals are important to persuasion, within a fantasy theme approach, we may ask:

- What emotional evocations dominate the dramas?
- Does hate dominate? Pity? Love? Indignation? Resignation? (402)

Audiences are central to any rhetorical effort. To determine the relationship between the text and the audience, you may want to ask:

- How does the fantasy theme work to attract the unconverted?
- How does it generate a sense of community and cohesion from the insider? (402)

Finally, the delivery of rhetoric matters. Questions concerning the quality of the construction and delivery of any message marked by fantasy themes include:

- How artistic is the development of the fantasy theme?
- How skillful [is] the characterization?
- How artistic [is] the use of language?
- How rich [is] the total panorama of the vision?
- How capable is the drama to arouse and interpret emotions? (402)

Bormann provided an example of fantasy theme criticism in action at this point in his description of method. Taking a lead from him, we'll do the same. Let's see how fantasy theme criticism works first on Lincoln's Gettysburg Address. Then we'll apply it to *WWF Smackdown!*

FANTASY THEME APPLIED: GETTYSBURG ADDRESS

Since the Gettysburg Address (see the speech reprinted in Chapter 11) was so much a product of its times, it is important that we begin our analysis by describing the context of the message, especially the discursive context, which has to do with other relevant messages of the time.

CONTEXT DESCRIBED

Even though the Gettysburg Address was a single, epideictic text delivered on a ceremonial occasion to memorialize the battle fought there, it also had a political dimension. Since the speech was delivered by the sitting president, and since the exigence for the speech could be traced back to a political disagreement over slavery, we must consider the existing political climate and associated rhetorical vision of the ruling Republican Party at that time. This suggests that we need to learn something about the political and social conditions at the time of the speech (context).

Slavery was a divisive issue early in U.S. history. In 1840 the Liberty Party was formed around the issue of slavery, as was the Free Soil Party (1848), both of which were responses to attempted extensions of slavery's reach. The Republican Party was formed officially in 1854 for purposes of opposing the extension of slavery into the Kansas and Nebraska territories. In 1856 Republican presidential candidate John Fremont's campaign slogan was "Free Soil, Free Labor, Free Speech, Free Men, Fremont" (Mayer 2002). Obviously, freedom was a central theme of the campaign.

THEORY APPLIED

Most likely, then, the scene surrounding Lincoln's address was constructed from the themes of the antislavery movement as well as the necessary propaganda generated by any nation at war. We learn from William Taylor's early study of pre–Civil War literature that even before the political rift between North and South, a clear social divide separated the Northern and Southern regions. Taylor's study explains the literary construction of the "Yankee" versus the "Cavalier," which started as a series of fantasy themes in popular literature, later to become rhetorical visions describing the character of the populace in the North and South. Each character (Yankee and Cavalier) represented a different set of social values. According to Taylor, "the North had developed a leveling, go-getting utilitarian society and the South had developed a society based on the values of the English gentry" (Taylor 1961, 15). The Northern themes of thrift, industry, and the value of labor powerfully contrasted with the Southern themes of honor, independence, and civility. The Yankee character was consistently presented as energetic and ready to work. "The idea of leisure was unacceptable to a great many Americans in the nineteenth century. . . . The gentleman of leisure has little place in the fiction of this time, except as a warning" (Taylor 1961, 136).

Even the popular music of the age served to reinforce the social structures of North and South. According to Catherine Moseley, "The popular songs sung by North and South during the war reflected and reinforced those perceptions, strengthening each side's identity and firming its resolve against the other" (1995, 45). Music provided a powerful means for the sharing of group fantasies. Moseley notes that, "Popular music was an integral part of many people's lives more than it is today . . . more people, regardless of sex and social station, sang out loud in front of other people than is customary today, and more in wartime than in time of peace. . . . Soldiers sang, young women sang, generals sang" (48).

Two examples of very popular songs give a glimpse of the sorts of fantasy themes that chained out among the Northern and Southern populations (Lupher 2001). The Northern song "The Battle Cry of Freedom" was extremely significant in the Northern repertoire with lyrics that featured the concept of freedom. For example, the chorus says, in part, "Yes, we'll rally 'round the flag, boys, we'll rally once again, / Shouting the battle cry of Freedom." On the other hand, the lyrics of the Southern anthem "The Bonnie Blue Flag" feature a much more concrete set of concerns. The soil and property, in the context of rights, dominate the first verse: "We are a band of brothers, and native to the soil, / Fighting for the property we gained by honest toil; / And when our rights were threatened, the cry rose near and far." This is a very different set of values from those rehearsed in "The Battle Cry of Freedom." For the North, the scene constructed is much more abstract, more like a bare stage from which the actors *announce* their intentions to protect freedom. On the other hand, the scene constructed by the Southern song is like a realistic stage setting with the actors *acting out* (dramatizing) their struggle with their adversary. The fantasy created by the South is more personal, immediate, and earthy than that created by the North. "The Bonnie Blue Flag" features the characters of bold men of the soil, courageously fighting against a lesser foe, one that is duplicitous rather than forthright. This is a song of the chivalrous duelist who courageously faces his opponent directly. The North is portrayed as a treacherous character operating by political intrigue, stealing rights first, then the land.

So far, we have explored the context of Lincoln's speech by looking at some discourse surrounding it. We discovered patterns of communication and behavior that we can name as themes of the discourse. Fantasy theme analysis features the notion of "theme," and themes are generated via a series of interactions. Looking for themes in the context was especially important in this case since the Gettysburg Address is a single text. And since it is also extremely brief, it needs to be placed in the context of other communications that can provide points of comparison so we can actually see and assess it as a part of a rhetorical vision. Discovering these facts about the literary and musical context of Lincoln's speech invites us to look directly at his speech to see if he had responded to the themes other media were constantly feeding his audience. Now that we better understand the thematic context of Lincoln's speech, let's take an analytic look at the speech itself.

SPEECH ANALYSIS

First, the Gettysburg Address clearly fits the existing Northern rhetorical vision that features the notions of freedom and equality. Lincoln presents the characters of the fantasy in an extremely abstract fashion: *we, our,* and *us* are words used to name those who have standing to participate in the ceremony. The pronouns are ambiguous and inclusive. The ambiguity of his references to "those who gave their lives" may allow inclusion of those from the South who died for their cause as well. (Lincoln was highly conflicted about where to lay blame for the war as his second inaugural and "Meditation on the Divine Will" indicate.) Commitment to the Puritan vision of freedom and equality requires tolerance of many points of view, and if the Union was to be reestablished, Lincoln seemed to believe that tolerance of those who did not agree would be essential.

Also, the rhetorical vision of the North was marked by a commitment to industry and work. What does Lincoln say the audience is to do? "It is for us the living," he argues, "rather, to be dedicated here to the unfinished work which they who fought here have thus far so nobly advanced." They are to "be dedicated to the great task" of bringing forward a "new birth of freedom." His words are consistent with the Northern rhetorical vision, and he gives powerful voice to the specific themes of freedom, equality, and industry explicitly; to forgiveness, tolerance, and humility implicitly. Lincoln's speech, then, celebrates the themes of the North, but he modifies them somewhat to create opportunity to include the sister states of the South. Lincoln's own theme of rebuilding the original union of states becomes a central theme of American political talk.

In sum, the analysis of the Gettysburg Address using a fantasy theme approach has yielded a different, but complementary understanding of the speech than the one resulting from application of the narrative paradigm. Both analyses featured such dramatic elements as character, setting, and plot. However, each approach started from different places (narrative starts with the idea that storytelling is a form of argument, whereas fantasy theme begins with the idea that storytelling is a form of interpreting or coping with a group's real-life conditions), leading to different insights about how the Gettysburg Address worked as rhetoric.

As we did in the previous chapter, let's now try applying the fantasy theme approach to the case of professional wrestling. Seeing how one analyzes a speech and how one analyzes a mediated text should help you envision how you, as a novice critic, may use the fantasy theme approach.

The Fantasy Themes of <u>WWF Smackdown!</u>

Obviously, the context of this text is much different from the context of Lincoln's speech or that of the small groups from which Bormann first drew his insights. When we examine something like a two-hour video, as opposed to a brief speech, we are working with a complex, multipart text. Given Bormann's description of the method, our first task is to discover basic fantasies, and then we can "creatively reconstruct the rhetorical vision from the representative fantasy chains" (1972, 401).

The two hours of *WWF Smackdown!* that comprise our text can be divided into two general segments: the bouts themselves in the arena and the social dramas that occur mostly backstage. The first group features material, physical portrayal of fantasies, whereas the second group features the more abstract fantasies of social and political power.

There are a series of announced bouts: The Dudley Boys v. The Hardy Boys; Chris Jericho v. Val Venis for the "Intercontinental Championship"; and Chris Benoit v. The Radicalz, a three-man team, in what is called a handicap bout. In the midst of the planned card, Kurt Angle challenged Test to a match that appeared to take place spontaneously. Then William Regal wrestled Al Snow for the position of WWF commissionership. Triple H was to have a scheduled bout, but The Undertaker suddenly appeared, taunted Triple H into fighting, and quickly disposed of Triple H. The final bout was a second handicap match with The Rock v. Rishiki and Haku.

We observed that in spite of the organization of the evening's events, things can get out of control. The planned card can shift with the mercurial emotions of the wrestlers; within the bouts themselves, both planned and spontaneous, people get out of control. We soon learn from the WWF to "expect the unexpected." A theme we can describe from the events is that the world is a random place, and one just needs to be ready to confront unexpected enemies and difficulties.

As recently as 1989, Bruce Lincoln argued, "At its most fundamental level . . . wrestling offers an extravagantly staged combat between good and evil" (154). Twelve years later, the wrestling scene is not so easily summarized. With the exception of The Rock, it appears that all participants have the potential to go wrong. Just as Kurt Angle, a former U.S. Olympic champion who wears red, white, and blue, can "snap" emotionally and allegedly break the ankle of another combatant in a fit of rage, anyone can go wrong. A fantasy theme that accrues from watching these bouts is that *good* and *evil* are relative terms. The fantasy suggests that there are few people, if any, without the potential to do harm. The line between good and evil is murky; what makes a person good or bad will be determined by his behavior depending on the circumstances.

The themes developed in the second thread of events, those featuring social interactions, are even darker. McMahon's goals of humiliating people are fulfilled and unchecked. He apparently had publicly humiliated Trish Stratus, his mistress, twice in the two weeks prior to the event we're analyzing; he humiliated his wife using Stratus on this evening. Later in the episode, as Linda McMahon is being wheeled from the arena, she is met in a hallway by her daughter, Stephanie, and Stephanie's husband, Triple H. They both mock her with feigned joy at the apparently chance meeting, putting their faces close to hers, shouting as if she was hearing impaired, and waving and grinning at her in an exaggerated fashion. The theme that runs through this is that personal pleasure can be had at the expense of others. It is an uncivil notion that is typical of junior high schoolyards rather than healthy homes.

A closely related theme is that manipulation and deceit are the province of the more clever person. McMahon celebrates his manipulation of women. The wrestlers conspire with each other to humiliate their opponents. In this case, the most troubling discussion is played out backstage between Rishiki and Haku. There they plan to humiliate Debra, who has become The Rock's manager, by sticking Rishiki's ample, and mostly bare, rear end in Debra's face. Although they don't succeed, they come close. Their actions of capturing her and holding her in position to be so humiliated is disturbing, and their partial success is sufficient to reinforce the idea that they were clever enough to pull off the demeaning prank.

Taken together, the themes suggest that no clear moral lines exist. The fantasies constructed here run counter to traditional values in almost every case. The fantasy themes when clustered as they are in this event create a rhetorical vision in which there are few rules to govern behavior; consequently, the individuals decide what is acceptable to them. It is similar to a passage in the Old Testament book of Judges that describes that period of Jewish history as desperate and chaotic, one in which "every man did what was right in his own eyes" (Judg. 21:25, New American Standard Version).

INTERPRETING THEMES

WWF Smackdown! seems to be quintessentially postmodern in its themes. According to Kenneth Gergen, the postmodern rhetorical vision is marked by skepticism, relativism, and irony. In the postmodern world, no one is confined to specific rules of communal expectations but all are free to be and behave as they wish. Sudden shifts in appearance or behavior are celebrated rather than condemned. All dress is costume, all behavior is an act, and all motives are ironic, so nothing is to be taken seriously. Gergen characterizes the postmodern condition as a kind of carnival (1991, 187). The carnival atmosphere created by *WWF Smackdown!* and its related productions, the constantly shifting relationships among characters, the lack of clear moral codes, the focus on individual expression, and the easy remaking of the presented self are all markers of a postmodern rhetorical vision. Given our findings from our fantasy theme analysis, *WWF Smackdown!*, as discourse, serves to enact and elaborate social themes that celebrate the freedom and potential power of individuals over themes of civility and social organization. Whether *WWF Smackdown!* is a mirror held up to our society or a rhetorical engine driving its evolution to an increasingly individualistic one, we cannot know for sure. However, it seems clear that *WWF Smackdown!*, apart from distracting its audience for some hours each week, rehearses and develops fantasy themes that run counter to the kind of themes that mark a civil society.

SUMMARY

Our fantasy theme analysis of these two extremely different texts yielded useful findings. In each case, we had to employ the method somewhat differently. For example, since the Gettysburg Address is such a brief text we needed to pay more attention to the context of the message in order to discover the themes to which it seemed to be a response. On the other hand, the *WWF Smackdown!* episode was sufficiently complex as to allow us to look for patterns of themes within the text itself, with minimal attention to the context. These are examples of the kinds of decisions regarding actual application of the method you will have to make as a critic. You will need to decide whether your text is sufficiently complex in itself to present fantasy themes, or whether you will need to look at additional, related texts (e.g., we looked at antebellum literature and songs in relation to the Gettysburg Address) to determine how your text exhibits significant fantasy themes.

EXERCISES

The address following the exercises, delivered on September 12, 2003, begins with a rehearsal of themes that were initiated in the days immediately following the terrorist attack on New York and Washington and have chained out into our national discourse.

1. Using a highlighter, identify themes that have chained out in our national discourse such that they are now used to describe the "way things are." In other words, identify themes that are still in use.

2. Using a different color, identify what you believe to be emerging themes; what new ideas are being increasingly rehearsed by the administration, the media, and the public?

3. Apply the questions posed in the "The Process of Fantasy Theme Analysis" section to the president's radio address. As a result of your analysis, what patterns of characterization, dramatic situations (context), actions, emotional appeals, and delivery emerge? What rhetorical vision is being constructed from the fantasy themes you were able to discover?

4. As a result of what you have learned, what advice would you give a friend for listening more critically to political, religious, or scientific discourse?

President's Radio Address

THE PRESIDENT: Good morning. Two years ago this week, America suffered a brutal attack. We will never forget the burning towers and the smoke over Arlington Cemetery, and the passengers who rushed the hijackers. Yet history asks for more than memory. On September the 11th, 2001, we began a war on global terror that continues to this hour.

In the decades before that terrible day, the terrorists conducted a series of bolder and bolder attacks in the Middle East and beyond. They became convinced that free nations were decadent and weak, and would never offer a sustained and serious response. They now know otherwise.

Together with a coalition of nations, we have struck back against terror worldwide, capturing and killing terrorists, and breaking cells and freezing assets. In Afghanistan we removed the Taliban regime that harbored al Qaeda. In Iraq, we defeated a regime that sponsored terror, possessed and used weapons of mass destruction, and defied the United Nations Security Council for 12 years. We have helped to liberate people from oppression and fear.

Today, with our help, the people of Iraq are working to create a free, functioning and prosperous society. The terrorists know that if these efforts are successful, their ideology of hate will suffer a grave defeat. So they are attacking our forces, international aid workers, and innocent civilians. Their goal is to drive us out of Iraq before our work is done. They are mistaken, and they will fail. We will do what is necessary to win this victory in the war on terror.

We are following a clear strategy with three objectives: Destroy the terrorists, enlist international support for a free Iraq, and quickly transfer authority to the Iraqi people. Through a series of ongoing operations, our military is taking direct action against Saddam loyalists and foreign terrorists. One major effort underway right now, called Operation Longstreet, is seeking and finding our enemies wherever they hide and plot. Already, this operation has yielded hundreds of detainees and seized hundreds of weapons, and we will remain on the offensive against the terrorists.

We are expanding international cooperation in rebuilding Iraq. Today in Geneva, Secretary of State Powell is meeting with Secretary General of the United Nations and representatives of the five permanent members of the Security Council. They are discussing ideas for a new resolution to encourage wider participation in this vital task.

And we're moving forward on a specific plan to return sovereignty and authority to the Iraqi people. We have created a governing council made up of Iraqi citizens. The council has selected a committee that is developing a process through which Iraqis will draft a new constitution for their country. Day to day operations of many government tasks have been turned over to ministers appointed by the Governing Council. And when a constitution has been drafted and ratified by the Iraqi people, Iraq will enjoy free and fair elections, and the coalition will yield its remaining authority to a free and sovereign Iraqi government.

We have a strategy in Iraq and a mission. We will fight and defeat the terrorists there, so we don't have to face them in America. And we will help transform

Iraq into an example of progress and democracy and freedom that can inspire change and hope throughout the Middle East.

Thank you for listening.

Source: http://www.whitehouse.gov/news/releases/2003/09/20030913.html

NOTES

1 *The Oxford English Dictionary.* 2nd ed. CD-ROM. Oxford: Oxford University Press, 1992; s.v. "Fantasy."
2 The questions are drawn from Bormann's essay, "Fantasy and Rhetorical Vision: The Rhetorical Criticism of Social Reality." We have taken Bormann's questions and reorganized them somewhat for ease of use, but we encourage you to examine them in the context of the original essay.

WORKS CITED

Bales, Robert F. *Personality and Interpersonal Behavior.* New York: Holt, Rinehart and Winston, 1970.

Bormann, Ernest. "Fantasy and Rhetorical Vision: The Rhetorical Criticism of Social Reality." *Quarterly Journal of Speech* 58 (1972): 396–402.

Bush, George W., Colin Powell, and John Ashcroft. "President Urges Readiness and Patience." Camp David Press Conference. September 15, 2001. The White House. Office of the Press Secretary. http://www.whitehouse.gov/news/releases/2001/09/20010915-4.html (accessed December 15, 2003).

———. "President's Remarks at the Pentagon." The Pentagon. September 11, 2002. The White House. Office of the Press Secretary. http://www.whitehouse.gov/news/releases/2002/09/20020911.html (accessed December 15, 2003).

Fisher, Walter. "The Narrative Paradigm: An Elaboration." *Communication Monographs* 52 (December 1985): 347–67.

Gergen, Kenneth. *The Saturated Self.* New York: Basic Books, 1991.

Lincoln, Bruce. *Discourse and the Construction of Society: Comparative Studies of Myth, Ritual and Classification.* New York: Oxford University Press, 1989.

Lupher, Antonio. *The Civil War Music Site.* http://www.civilwarmusic.net/songs/php (accessed July 24, 2001).

Mayer, George. "Republican Party." *Grolier Online Encyclopedia.* 2002. Grolier, Inc. http://gi.grolier.com/presidents/ea/side/rparty.html (accessed November 29, 2003).

Moseley, Catherine. "Irrepressible Conflict: Differences Between Northern and Southern Songs on the Civil War." *Journal of Popular Culture* 25 (1995): 45–55.

Taylor, William R. *The Yankee and the Cavalier: The Old South and American National Character.* New York: George Barziller, 1961.

SUGGESTED READINGS

Bormann, Ernest. "The Eagleton Affair: A Fantasy Theme Analysis." *Quarterly Journal of Speech* 59 (1973): 143–59.

———. "A Fantasy Theme Analysis of the Television Coverage of the Hostage Release and the Reagan Inaugural." *Quarterly Journal of Speech* 68 (1982): 133–45.

———. "Fantasy and Rhetorical Vision: Ten Years Later." *Quarterly Journal of Speech* 68 (1982): 288–305.

———. "Symbolic Convergence Theory: A Communication Formulation Based on Homo Narrans." *Journal of Communication* 35 (1985): 128–38.

Chesebro, James W. "Paradoxical Views of 'Homosexuality' in the Rhetoric of Social Scientists: A Fantasy Theme Analysis." *Quarterly Journal of Speech* 66 (1980): 127–39.

Mohrmann, G. P. "An Essay on Fantasy Theme Criticism." *Quarterly Journal of Speech* 68 (1982): 109–32.

———. "Fantasy Theme Criticism: A Peroration." *Quarterly Journal of Speech* 68 (1982): 306–13.

13

Burkeian Analysis

Have you ever wondered why very young children are fascinated with the word *no?* We've seen children make great use of the word, even when it hurts them. For example, here's a conversation overheard late one summer afternoon at a local zoo:

> *"C'mon, honey, it's time to go home."*
> *"No!"*
> *"Don't you want to see the puppy and have some juice to cool off?"*
> *"No! I don't want to go. I want to stay right here!"*
> *"The juice is nice and cool and it's your favorite kind."*
> *"No, I hate juice! I want to stay here!"*

And so it goes. Why do children (and adults) often persist in negating the will of others? One answer is that the use of *no* is a human action that extends our power in relation to others. *No* and *not* are words that give human beings a way of symbolically constructing experience that no other creature possesses. This rhetorical phenomenon provides a foundation for understanding the dramatistic approach we call Burkeian analysis or Burkeian criticism.

THE NEGATIVE AND HUMAN SPEECH

Starting from the premise that human beings are essentially "symbol using animals," Kenneth Burke, one of the titans of criticism, argued that language governs our understanding of and response to the world around us. Burke was extremely interested in language as a human action. For Burke, understanding the human condition necessitated an understanding of humans' defining characteristic: the capacity to use language. In order to outline some basic concepts of his approach to message analysis, let's begin with his extended definition of *man:*

> *Man is*
> *the symbol using (symbol-making, symbol-misusing) animal*
> *inventor of the negative (or moralized by the negative)*
> *separated from his natural condition by instruments of his own making*
> *goaded by a spirit of hierarchy (or moved by the sense of order)*
> *and rotten with perfection. (Burke 1966, 16)*

First, Burke makes clear that human beings possess the unique ability to use symbols. Other creatures may communicate, but they do so by signaling each other. For example, when a beaver senses danger, it signals the others by slapping its tail on the water. This is a signal that operates through a one-to-one connection between the recognition of danger and a physiological response. There is no ambiguity or discussion with a signal. The beavers, when safely in their lodge, do not discuss the recent events: "My, that was a close call! Perhaps we can establish a guard system to give earlier warning?" "No, we can't spare a single worker or the new dam will never get finished." Signal systems don't allow the kind of abstraction and ambiguity needed to create new ideas such as "past," "future," or "need." Those are ideas that can only be constructed via symbols, and human beings are the only creatures that can make and manipulate symbols (and misuse them, too).

THE NEGATIVE AND CREATION OF CATEGORIES

Being the "inventor of the negative" is an extremely important element of our human nature, according to Burke. There are two dimensions of the negative that you need to understand. The first use of the negative is the basic task of naming things. By naming what is and what is *not,* people are able to divide experience into segments that can be manipulated symbolically; this ability is unique to human beings since there is no natural state of the negative. The idea that the negative is not a natural thing may be a strange notion to you since you've always used negation to make sense of the world. (*No* may have been the first word you said!) But, nature, apart from human presence, exists as it is; trees are trees, rocks are rocks, and so on. Everything in nature only points to or indicates what exists. Conversely, nothing (notice how reliant we are on the negative to explain the concept itself) in nature gives any indication of what does not concretely exist. Conceiving of ideas or objects that do not exist is a purely symbolic, abstract human ability. As a result, we are as Burke noted, "separated from [our] natural condition by instruments of [our] own making." Therefore, we exist in a world of symbols that mediate or come between our experiences and our understanding of them.

The **negative** is *a powerful symbolic tool human beings use to create categories of experiences.* When a category is created some objects are defined as belonging in the category and others are excluded. For example, if we define message analysts as "people who consciously and creatively apply four specific kinds of thinking to messages in order to explain how the messages work," then anyone who does not exhibit those specific behaviors, by definition, is not a message analyst. The effect of the definition can be pictured as in Figure 13.1.

Starting with the definition of what some people are and others are not, you can make an argument that you are a person with a special set of skills that sets you apart from all other people if you can demonstrate that you possess the skills that define a message analyst. **Division**, then, is *a natural byproduct of the negative that permits reasoning.* Rhetorical use of the negative is for dividing, ordering, and structuring the world observed or experienced. But the technical

FIGURE 13.1

ability to create categories is not all the negative achieves. Burke notes that the negative is also used to create a moral order.

THE NEGATIVE AND MORAL ORDER

The second and more significant understanding of the negative is the "moral" use of the term in phrases such as "Thou *shalt* not . . ." (Burke 1966, 10). We use this version of the negative to create our social relations—all our laws, both civil and moral, grow out of this use of the negative. Burke points to the Ten Commandments of the Old Testament as exemplars of the moral use of the negative. For example, "You shall not kill. You shall not commit adultery. You shall not steal" (Exod. 20: 13–15; New American Standard Version). These commonly held values are basic to our legal codes regarding murder, marriage, and theft. Whether we use the Bible, the Koran, or the Analects of Confucius, we will find negative statements or statements of prohibition. Embedded in these statements are the guidelines for the shaping of our character and the criteria for judging the moral and ethical choices we make. So, by analyzing the choices people make as they talk about the world, we can assess the moral and ethical schemas of a rhetor. By examining the rhetorical choices of historic figures such as a Lincoln, Elizabeth Cady Stanton, Martin Luther King Jr., or Mahatma Gandhi we can discover their moral order; so too the language choices of William Jefferson Clinton or George W. Bush give us clues regarding their character and their ultimate motives for action.

As he further defines "man," Burke notes that human beings are "goaded by a spirit of hierarchy (or moved by the sense of order)." Notice that the division created by use of the negative (Figure 13.1) immediately created two classes of people who are able to identify with each other within the categories they occupy. Dividing and identifying are two very powerful human propensities that are exploited by rhetors to achieve their persuasive goals. Much advertising is based on the principles of identification and division. For example, as young men identify with Lebron James, they recognize or imagine some similarity with him; they often try to look and act like Lebron. Advertisers encourage audiences to identify with James by buying Nike products. As they identify with James and feel camaraderie with others who do the same, they simultaneously are divided from those who don't look or act like him. You can easily see these dynamics at work in political and religious discourse, as well.

IDENTIFICATION AND PERSUASION

Identification, for Burke, is the essential nature of persuasion. *To identify is to seek to be "consubstantial" or perceived to be "substantially one" with the person you are attempting to persuade* (1969b, 20–21). Burke states, "Here is perhaps the simplest case of persuasion. You persuade a man only insofar as you can talk his language by speech, gesture, tonality, order, image, attitude, idea, *identifying* your ways with his" (55, emphasis added). He uses the metaphor of "courtship" to describe identification (176–77). For example, if you've ever done something like reading about ballet because the person you want to date loves ballet, you have a good idea of what identification is. So, the central means of persuasion is to find the substantial (via symbols) likenesses between you and your audience.

On the other hand, when people identify with some person or group, they automatically divide from others (22). We constantly negotiate our group memberships. Some people like what we like and fear what we fear; we experience identification with such people. At the same time, others may strongly dislike what we like or they may embrace what we fear; in those cases we experience division (49). Identification and division are not always so easy to see, nor are they unchanging conditions or relationships once established. As contexts and conditions change in our lives, those who are our friends or enemies can become clouded. For example, this can happen in marriages wherein, over time, people change and no longer identify with each other; they may go from loving to hating each other (a courtship gone bad). In truth, those ambiguous or changing relationships of identification or division spark a great deal of rhetoric (25). When we are not sure where we fit in the web of human relationships, we talk about the situation with others to reduce our uncertainty and reorder our world. At its most basic level, that's what rhetoric is about. The ambiguity of identification and division in much of our talk invites clear thinking message analysts to understand and explain how people make sense of their life experience.

HIERARCHY, GUILT, AND MEANING

Not only does the negative foster identification and division but it inherently creates **hierarchy**, which is *ranking of categories*. Burke suggests that people, by nature, are organizers—once we create categories, we rank them. For example, if you listen to kids on a playground, you may hear them arguing about whose heroes are best: one argues Sammy Sosa is the greatest all-around hitter while another lobbies for Mark McGuire and another for Barry Bonds. One names Madonna as the best pop singer ever, but another argues that Michael Jackson merits the title. It's as if they cannot bear to have two equally great heroes. As they create categories, they rank them. Constructing hierarchies is also related to the next clause in Burke's definition: man is "rotten with perfection," which, in turn, is a source of guilt.

According to Burke, human beings are in a perpetual state of guilt because they are not perfect; they are not at the top of whatever hierarchy they or others feel they occupy. For all of us, no matter how successful we are, there seems to be someone more successful who prevents us from being at the top of whatever hierarchy is most important to us. Students struggle to get good grades in an effort to move up the academic hierarchy, employees attempt to move up organizational hierarchies, and so on. However, we never completely succeed and we remain "guilty." Among those who do succeed at achieving pinnacle positions, many find it is a temporary state. Former President Bill Clinton, once the leader of the free world, is now "the husband of the senator from New York"; his presidency will be compared to other presidents and he will be ranked as less than the best because of his imperfections; Jesse Jackson's position as preeminent civil leader of people of color has been damaged because of his marital indiscretions. Andrew Lloyd Webber's music has fallen out of style; no one reads the pop psychology of M. Scott Peck or Thomas Harris anymore; sales of the new Ford Thunderbird are lagging; and Structure clothing is passé. The point is that we make sense of our experience by naming and organizing (i.e., ranking) categories. As circumstances, values, and behaviors change over time, so do our hierarchies. We adapt social symbolic constructs for ourselves and others through rhetoric.

VICTIMAGE AND SALVATION

Burke argues that since we cannot achieve perfection ourselves, we must do what the Judeo-Christian tradition demands—provide a sacrifice to atone for the sin and guilt of imperfection. *The demand for a sacrifice* is known as **victimage.** There are two options for enacting victimage: (1) **mortification,** which is *sacrificing oneself;* or (2) **scapegoating,** which is *placing the blame on someone or something other than oneself.* Martyrs of the Christian Church experienced mortification by choosing to die rather than deny their commitment to Jesus of Nazareth. In the ancient Jewish tradition, the people went through an annual ritual of purification by ceremonially placing their sins on a goat and driving the scapegoat into the wilderness to carry away the sin. Enactment of either form of victimage is intended to lead to purification or atonement for imperfection and to redemption (which is reestablishment of an appropriate position in a hierarchy). In short, as we tell our stories to each other, we can choose to purify ourselves of our sins of imperfection by blaming ourselves (mortification) or blaming someone else (scapegoating). As you listen to others and as you examine messages of all sorts, from news editorials to advertisements, you'll discover examples of both mortification and scapegoating.

Our examination of the concepts of the negative and its associated concepts of identification and division, of hierarchy, guilt, and victimage, focuses attention at the word level of any text. By examining word choices we are able to draw inferences about the moral foundations from which rhetors operate. Larger slices of the text may also provide significant insights about any text. Burke provides a set of complementary concepts by which we can do this.

THE PENTAD

According to Burke, any rhetorical event can be described using five inter-related and overlapping dramatic concepts called the *pentad.* Here's how Burke himself lays it out:

> *We shall use five terms as generating principles for our investigation. They are: Act, Scene, Agent, Agency, Purpose. In a rounded statement about motives, you must have some word that names the* act *(names what took place, in thought or deed), and another that names the* scene *(the background of the act, the situation in which it occurred); also, you must indicate what kind of person* (agent) *performed the act, what means or instruments he used* (agency), *and the* purpose. *(1969a, xv)*

The **pentad** is a *search model that provides a ready-made set of topics or starting points to get us thinking systematically about the dramas embedded in all messages.* Burke believed that all messages are essentially dramas. He created the pentad as a way to examine the dramatic elements present in messages that on their faces don't appear dramatic. By identifying the act, agent, agency, scene, and purpose of a message, we start to see the component parts of the rhetorical event. The pentad is especially useful because its application facilitates both critical *and* creative thinking. That is, the pentad allows you to distinguish specific elements of the message while experimenting with different frames of analysis relative to the message. You'll see how this works in our examples coming up.

A word of caution is appropriate here. There is a powerful temptation to apply the pentad to a text like a meat cleaver, chopping a message into the components of the pentad. But Burke makes clear that the terms are purposely ambiguous.[1] They are meant to spark thinking, not make final, decisive declarations; the terms enable you to look at a text in different ways in an effort to determine not necessarily what is exactly right, but "more nearly right" regarding rhetorical motives (1969a, xvii). Here's Burke's advice:

> *When they [the terms of the pentad] might become difficult, when we can hardly see them, through having stared at them too intensely, we can all of a sudden relax, to* look at them as we always have, lightly, glancingly. *And having reassured ourselves, we can start out again, once more daring to let them look strange and difficult for a time. (1969a, xvi, emphasis added)*

TWO EXAMPLES OF THE PENTAD APPLIED

What we need to do is try out what Burke is suggesting—using the terms in more creative ways than just naming the parts of the pentad as if we were writing a newspaper story about the text. For example, a critic could use the pentad to describe the Gettysburg Address from a journalistic perspective (this is purposely the meat-cleaver approach), and the terms would look like this:

Act: a brief ceremonial speech

Agent: Abraham Lincoln

Agency: public speech

Scene: a civil war battlefield

Purpose: to honor dead Union soldiers

Each of the designations is a legitimate completion of the pentadic terms. What this array will stimulate is essentially a report about the event; a synopsis of a eulogy. This frame provides little new theoretical or interpretive understanding of the text.

The pentad, however, allows us to play with other frames. For example, we suspect, in part from what we know about how Lincoln struggled with composing the speech, and given the public response over time, this was more than a common eulogy. The speech, following Edward Everett's two-hour opus, strikes us as being like the benediction of a church service. So, for example, we can try reframing the speech as a "priestly benedictory prayer" for the nation. We could try out the pentad like this:

Act: a prayer of humility, forgiveness, and hope

Agent: the president as priestly intercessor for a national congregation

Agency: "prophetic" language

Scene: a ritual of consecration to create a "holy" site

Purpose: to heal the nation's psychological and spiritual wounds inflicted by the great battle fought at Gettysburg

Clearly, this application of the pentad is quite different from the preceding one, but it is equally legitimate. It is also more interesting and provocative than the first, we think. This conception of the Gettysburg Address raises new and more complex options for understanding Lincoln's motives in doing what he did. By shifting the frame, the focus is now on the purpose of the speech. He was expected to offer a lengthy dissertation, as did the previous speaker, Edward Everett; the battle was a horrible event and most listeners expected a lengthy speech to mark the occasion. However, if we frame this as a benediction, we have a better means of explaining its rhetorical power and appreciating Lincoln's insight into the meaning of the occasion and his motives. On the other hand, notice how the first version of the pentad actually inhibits discussion of anything but the meaning of the message.

The pentad facilitates analysis of the elements of the rhetorical event while allowing us, as critics, to explore a variety of possible approaches to the message. As we try out different frames, different dynamics of the message come to light. As you can see, the creative change in frame substantially changes the kinds of insights that may be generated about the message.

The terms of the pentad are extremely useful because they are so flexible in application. That is also what makes them difficult for new critics to use. Using the pentad, you can identify message parts in different ways, depending on the context and nature of the message you are analyzing. In the analytical process, feel free to play with the pentad, as we did, to find an application that provides insight about what constitutes or makes up the message and what internal dynamics seem to govern the message's impact or lack of impact on its audience.

A second word of caution is necessary here. Although we are encouraged by Burke to play with the terms, it is essential that the terms are always logically consistent with each other. Burke cautions against using concepts "merely slung together" (1969a, 128). He argues that your work loses its logical power and insight if you just grab this term and that concept without carefully examining their theoretical relationships. Consistency is essential for you to be able to make a sensible case for what you are seeing in any text. Let's use the preceding examples to understand this point. If you named the act as "a brief ceremonial speech," it would make no logical sense then to define the scene as "a ritual of consecration to create a 'holy' site." The definition of the act doesn't connect with the scene because there is no common logical thread. Either both must be in the frame of a common eulogy (the first example) or in the frame of a high priestly prayer (the second example), but mixing the frames is confusing and will limit the insight provided by an inconsistent analysis. To use the pentad well, you must be rigorous and consistent in your application of the elements of the pentad while exercising your creativity in choosing a starting point for your application of it. That is, once you choose a frame for applying the pentad, be consistent in how you develop and apply it.

Using Pentadic Ratios

Recall that knowledge about how a message works is created only when a critic is able to explain how the parts interact with each other. Simply naming the elements of the pentad does little to generate any substantive understanding of the communicative or rhetorical dynamics of the message. Stopping at that point leaves us with a laundry list of ideas that do nothing to answer the question, "So what?" In other words, we must always be searching for relationships between the most functional parts of the message. Burke's approach recommends a search for the most meaningful ratio between parts of the pentad. *Ratio* is a complex term, but the *Oxford English Dictionary* gives us some useful insights about it. One definition is "The corresponding relationship between things not precisely measurable."[2] The key word in the definition is *relationship* because what we, as critics, are trying to learn about are the invisible dynamics or interactions of rhetorical elements in a message. We want to know, "What works with what to make the message effective?" A second definition of *ratio* is "the reason or rationale upon which a juridical decision is based."[3] The key words are *reason* and *rationale*. We conclude that a **pentadic ratio** *(relationship between message parts) explains or provides a rationale for how a message works.*

There are a total of twenty combinations and permutations of the elements of the pentad. Selection of an appropriate ratio requires some "play" on your part to see which one seems to provide you with a perspective on the message that is interesting. Here it is important to note Burke's observation that within a ratio, the first element controls its interpretation.[4] For example, one possible ratio we might consider from our first ("journalistic") pentadic analysis of the Gettysburg Address is a *scene/purpose* ratio. In this ratio, scene controls how we interpret the purpose of the message. From the journalistic version we laid out earlier, the existence of the battlefield (scene) required honoring those who died there (purpose). This configuration of the ratio makes more sense than its converse, *purpose/scene,* which suggests that honoring the soldiers (purpose) somehow created the battlefield (scene). Obviously, that was not the case, so the purpose/scene ratio can be discarded.

This example tells us that a ratio is not a neutral or unbiased lens. The configuration of the ratio has a logic that must be recognized. In our second version of the pentad, which framed Lincoln's speech as a priestly prayer, we may conclude that an important ratio is *agent/act.* The focus in this ratio suggests that Lincoln (agent) was the only person capable of offering a benediction (act) for the battle. Given the circumstances of the times, we can think of no other person who was "called" to perform the act. Certainly, none of the other speakers that day seem to have been so called; few people know that Edward Everett, not Lincoln, had been asked to deliver the main speech, or that Everett's Gettysburg Address lasted two hours (Van Doren and Carmer 1946, 39). In spite of all efforts by others to consecrate the battlefield, it was Lincoln who among them all, performed the act of consecration. It seems the motive for the address is an idealistic attempt to give meaning to the bloodshed that occurred there and complete the mourning for the casualties.

In this case, the converse, *act/agent,* is interesting as well, suggesting that by "coming up to the task" (performing the act), Lincoln assumed a new role of secular priest (agent) for the country. The logic of this ratio leads us to see the motive for the address as an act of redefinition performed by an officeholder as part of the office, and by doing it, expanded the role of the office. Knowing that Lincoln was not much wanted by those organizing the ceremony, the conclusions we may draw from this ratio are consistent with the context. What we learn about rhetoric is that exemplary performance of some rhetorical acts can change the meaning of the agent in the mind of the audience.

In this case, both configurations of the ratio, agent/act or act/agent, provide some incentive to closely examine the message and the context of it in order to explain the motive, effect, and staying power of that brief but notable discourse. (Notice, too, how much more potential for interesting ratios grow out of a creative application of the pentad.) However, the pentad is not all there is to Burke's system.

DISCOVERING MOTIVES

Numerous times in the preceding discussion we've used the term *motive*. For Burke, discovering motives of rhetorical acts was the goal of criticism (1969a, xxii–xxiii, 57–58). Motive is a tough concept to deal with because motives are difficult to know with any certainty. We often treat the idea of motive as if it is a lever or tool or some objective cause of human action. However, in rhetorical studies, a direct cause of any human action in relation to a message is hard to know with any certainty. Burke suggests that an analyst can piece together motives for discourse by examining the text itself (57). What a person says gives indications of a person's values. In other words, the choices made when inventing a message are traceable to the person's basic philosophy. Burke's hypothesis is that our words reflect our beliefs; **motives** are *traces of our philosophies* (xvi–xvii).

Recall that for Burke rhetorical analysis is accomplished by application of the pentad to the selected text. Burke posits that each element of the pentad can be associated with a basic philosophy. Ironically, these simple associations then allow us to interpret and evaluate discourse in very sophisticated ways. We discover that motives for rhetorical actions are directly connected to the language choices of a message maker since language is our basic tool for both thought and action. Burke associated the pentadic terms and philosophies like this: agency is associated with pragmatism; agent, with idealism; act, with realism; scene, with materialism; and purpose, with mysticism (1969a, 128). It may be helpful to know just a bit about each of the philosophies.

According to the *Oxford Dictionary of Philosophy,* "the driving motivation of **pragmatism** is *the idea that belief in the truth on the one hand must have a close connection with success in action on the other hand"* (Blackburn 1994, 297). For the pragmatist, whatever leads to good ends is itself good. For example, if breaking a treaty (agency) that the United States signed many years ago with another country allows it to reach valued goals such as greater perceived safety of the U.S. population or an increase in domestic jobs, a pragmatist would say breaking the treaty is sensible and good. The goods of safety or prosperity validate the means, which was breaking a treaty. Here's a second example: let's imagine that a powerful government official in the face of a crisis purposely lied to the public to maintain calm. Once that fact about the message was discovered, the agency of the lie would certainly be featured. Most likely, a pragmatist would argue that misleading the public is acceptable, if by lying, a speaker prevents a panic among the population and maintains public safety. When agency is featured in discourse, pay special attention to the connections made between the message and its effects.

Next, agent is associated with idealism. **Idealism** is *a doctrine "holding that reality is fundamentally mental in nature"* (Blackburn 1994, 184). There are different versions of idealism but the one most relevant to our work is **linguistic idealism.** *This version says that "we 'create' the world we inhabit by employing mind-dependent linguistic and social categories"* (184). This definition is very compatible with present beliefs in the field of communication studies that our world of experience is socially constructed. When one person says to another, "Look at events like this . . . ," the speaker is attempting to construct reality from the mental operations of symbols and signs; that is, the speaker is attempting to construct or reconstruct interpretation of experience in the mind of the audience. So, when agent is featured in a text, focus your attention on how that agent describes an ideal world; the description will clue you in to the motives of the message. For example, on September 20, 2001, when George W. Bush said, regarding the war on terrorism, "This is not, however, just America's fight. And what is at stake is not just America's freedom. This is the world's fight. This is civilization's fight. This is the fight of all who believe in progress and pluralism, tolerance and freedom." Through these statements, Bush makes quite clear his ideals. He describes a world in which pluralism, tolerance, and freedom are ideals that should be privileged over all others. (We often forget that these are not the preeminent values of many countries around the world.) Bush's words provide insight regarding his motives for his actions in response to the terrorist attack on the World Trade Center and the Pentagon. When agent is featured, look carefully at the rhetor's personhood; look for clues to the nature of the agent's psychology (mind), theology (religion), axiology (beliefs), and epistemology (knowledge).

Realism is associated with the act. **Realism** is *"a theory to the effect that entities of a certain category or kind exist independently of what we think"* (Mautner 1996, 358). Realism is a complicated philosophy and, like its counterpart idealism, numerous versions of realism are in use. The one that is most relevant to our concerns is **semantic realism** *in which we use language to describe the world in ways that are understood to be true or false* (358). When act is featured, the rhetoric tends to point to commonsense understandings of experience wherein "common" sense joins people in substantial ways. This needs to be understood as a creative quality of rhetoric (Burke 1969a, 249). The rhetorical act serves to create new ways of experiencing, understanding, and valuing human experience. The act of rhetoric is to say, "Here is X phenomenon and this is the (new) meaning you should attach to it." Rhetoric is an action in the form of argument that invites us to see the world in similar ways. For example, let's reconsider President Bush's September 20 address as act. Bush is creating the concept of "war on terror." His effort is to describe experience in a verifiable way—to state our condition in terms the audience will perceive as true. He is overtly redefining and reinterpreting experience with an aim to joining the audience into a "tribe" (Burke 1969a, 250). Notice how the president uses the passive form, "is," in order to describe the condition of "fighting." He states, "This *is* the world's fight. This *is* civilization's fight. This *is* the fight of all who believe in progress . . ." (emphasis added). He is creating a state of being that features potential action over present action. Such statements at that moment were easily accepted by almost everyone as true. The tribe was unified in its future.[5] When act is featured in a ratio, look at what rhetorical resources the rhetor draws upon to create a particular interpretation of experience among audience members. Look particularly at the nouns used to name aspects of reality, as well as descriptors selected to feature specific characteristics of those things named. However, it is important to examine the verbs, too, because verbs name actions. Even passive verb forms imply actions.[6]

A focus on scene, according to Burke, is associated with materialism. **Materialism** *views the world as entirely composed of matter* (Blackburn 1994, 233). Featuring scene in discourse focuses attention on the material conditions of all involved—rhetor and audience. According to Burke, scene is especially important to rhetoric because all messages occur in some context. A materialist motive would tend to feature scene or scenic elements to persuade via appeals to the nature of things, often, but not always, using "scientific" arguments that appeal to material conditions or events. (Recall Perelman's appeal to the real discussed in Chapter 10.) For example, much post-9/11 talk about the terrorist attack on the World Trade Center and the Pentagon has featured scene. An example of this can also be found in President Bush's September 20, 2001, address to a joint session of Congress and the nation. The speech begins, "In the normal course of events, Presidents come to this chamber to report on the state of the Union. Tonight, no such report is needed. It has already been delivered by the American people." A bit later he announces, "Tonight we are a country awakened to danger and called to defend freedom. Our grief has turned to anger, and anger to resolution. Whether we bring our enemies to justice, or bring justice to our enemies, justice will be done." The speech features scene and makes efforts to describe the scene, explain it, and anticipate how it will change. This is not surprising since the terrorists attacked the material wealth and military strength of the country. When scene is featured, notice how the material dimension of life is central to the discourse.

Finally, purpose is associated with mysticism. **Mysticism** *maintains "that one can gain knowledge of reality that is not accessible to sense perception or to rational, conceptual thought"* (Audi 1999, 593). As a result, mystical discourse is "characterized by metaphor and simile" (593). However, this does not mean that all discourse that uses metaphor and simile as tools or tropes is mystical. What it does suggest is that metaphorical texts as such tend to feature purpose. A good example is *The Pilgrim's Progress* by John Bunyan. Bunyan's story is an allegory designed to teach spiritual truths. Bunyan even includes a prologue that states his purpose is not to lay out an argument per se for Christian living, but rather to present truths that cannot be made rationally. His purpose is decidedly mystical. When purpose is featured, look carefully at the metaphors employed by the rhetor to explain or justify seemingly unexplainable or ineffable truths. If you determine the controlling element of any ratio is purpose, you should be able to discern a transcendent and intuitive motive in the rhetoric.

So, according to Burke, the elements of the pentad are associated with philosophical predispositions as noted in Table 13.1. As you use these associations, keep in mind that the pentadic elements are ambiguous and fluid, and that the philosophies associated with them are complex and variable. Use these ideas to assist you in interpreting rhetorical events and the findings of your analyses. Bringing to bear a discussion of the apparent motives of rhetoric helps to illuminate the nature of the response any message is shooting for.

TABLE 13.1

Act	⟶	Realism
Agent	⟶	Idealism
Agency	⟶	Pragmatism
Scene	⟶	Materialism
Purpose	⟶	Mysticism

The Burkeian approach is certainly complex with many dimensions to it beyond just the negative, its related concepts, and the five elements of the pentad. As part of your apprenticeship in message analysis, let's try applying it to a complex message and see some ways that we can put Burke's ideas to work.

BURKEIAN CONCEPTS APPLIED TO WWF SMACKDOWN!

For purposes of this example, we're going to examine a specific segment of the episode we treated in Chapter 12. Such a focus is particularly important because of the segment's central place in the plot of the show, because of the time devoted to it, and because of its nature. The specific segment is the culmination of Vince McMahon's plotting to humiliate his wife.

DESCRIPTION

Early in the episode, we are allowed to overhear Vince McMahon talking on the telephone to an unidentified individual. McMahon first proudly recounts how he recently humiliated Trish Stratus, who now happens to be his mistress. He then promises the listener that during this evening's show he will humiliate another person and "this humiliation is more personal!" At that time, Debra Austin enters the room to ask McMahon if she can resign as "Lieutenant Commissioner" in order "to do what I do best—managing." She quickly adds, "If that's OK with you." McMahon assigns her the task of managing The Rock, who is the archrival of Debra's husband, Stone Cold Steve Austin. McMahon then explains in patronizing and ingenuous tones, "I've always thought of you as a career woman. I've always thought of you as someone who is goal-oriented" (and by implication not the bimbo that she appears to be); he says he "has the utmost respect for women" so he's given her significant responsibility in managing the top wrestler. Thus, we learn in this exposition that McMahon intends to humiliate someone close to him and that he is completely ingenuous and untrustworthy.

About midway through the evening's card all the wrestling action stops. McMahon is introduced to make some comments, and he takes the stage with a microphone in hand. The scene is gradually built to resemble that of a televangelist—McMahon is the center of attention and his delivery is a kind of mocking sermon in which he punctuates his talk with ecstatic shouts, and the audience responds to him as if in a church revival meeting. He relates some of his recent marital history, reminding the audience (or informing newcomers) that some months earlier he had demanded a divorce from his wife in front of the crowd, and she had refused. In spite of her refusal, she has since had a nervous breakdown, is incapacitated, and, according to McMahon, "overmedicated." He then has his wife brought onstage in a wheelchair by his mistress, Trish Stratus. Linda McMahon's face is without expression; her eyes are blank, her head is tilted slightly to the side, and her hands lay limply on the blanket covering her legs. The scene looks increasingly like televangelism in which the sick are brought to the preacher/healer for release from disease. However, the scene constructed by McMahon is not for displaying miracles of God but for degradation of one person by another. McMahon approaches his wife and in extremely sarcastic tones inquires about her condition. He then tells her he has something for her to see. Stepping directly in front of her, he gropes Trish Stratus, licking her tongue while looking at Linda. The audience, particularly the men, revel in the event, cheering loudly, laughing, and pumping their fists in the air. Michael Cole, one of the commentators, claims to be shocked at this humiliation. His partner, Tazz, shouts, "The key word, Cole, is 'humiliation!' " and he laughs loudly, and shouts, "What do you know about morals or couth?"

ANALYSIS

The act is shocking in spite of the fact we know that all are in collusion in this drama. Viewing this event from a Burkeian perspective, the connection between act and scene is striking. The act is the controlling element here in that it is so carefully and self-consciously performed. Everything about the scene, as suggested in the preceding description, is designed to mock or negate what is a deeply rooted ritual of healing played out in theaters, halls, tents, and churches every night across the country as well as on our televisions. Rather than experience restoration of her health and relationship with her husband, Linda McMahon is attacked psychologically by him. McMahon's act is shocking and immoral from the perspective of mainstream society. The act is profoundly cold-hearted, making it a significant element in the drama McMahon is constructing. The act turns the scene on its head, creating a moment of pure rejection of all civility and social structure; it radically redefines the nature of human relationships from opportunities for commitment to another and self-sacrifice for the other's well-being to sources of physical pleasure and personal power derived from another.

The act serves its purposes of shocking and entertaining the audience, while challenging social values. The scene constructed here is purely material in its concerns and negative in its nature. McMahon's remarks as addressed to the audience and his wife are consistent in that he describes his relationship with her in scientist terms (such that there is no moral dimension to their relationship but purely material). This is a world of hyperphysicality in which all internal states are displayed and enacted physically. There is no sense of "thou shalt not," which implies moral limitations; rather, all discourse among the participants is constantly couched as "You are not . . ." (e.g., "You are not worthy of my attention"; "You are not tough enough to defeat me"). Given these examples, it appears that the negative has the dual function of creating categories and hierarchies allowing participants to best opponents physically in order to win a title or psychologically to gratify one's desire for psychological control over others. The world created in the WWF arena is simple and elemental. As commentator Cole stated at one point, "It's all about survival; it's that simple."

INTERPRETATION

WWF Smackdown! is an interesting and ambiguous event. It is simultaneously anarchic and conservative. While it very consciously rejects the rules of sport and society (in both literal and figurative ways), it shamelessly promotes a conservative Darwinian and capitalist value of survival of the fittest.

As we saw from the preceding analysis, accepted and expected social and interpersonal rules are flaunted and mocked. Breaking the rules of the sport is basic to the spectacle since, in spite of the constant presence of the referee, illegal moves are the staple of the competition. The bouts rarely, if ever, are confined to the ring and its implicit rule-governed boundaries, but the action shifts outside the ring, away from its confines, rules, and referee. On the other hand, when action moves back into the ring, objects from outside the ring like chairs and tables are brought in, or wrestlers not related to a particular bout find their way into the ring. It is a chaotic world that requires pure muscle and grit and an apparently high pain threshold to survive. The events replicate, in an exaggerated fashion, the individualism and derring-do of American pioneers, soldiers, and adventurers (as well as the transgressions of the misfits and sociopaths who also headed west) all of whom were nonconformists unconfined by conventional rules of polite and civilized society.

The constant promotion (sale) of upcoming events and products such as highlight videos, coupled with the consistent victory of the toughest competitor (presently embodied in the character of The Rock), is a conservative, capitalistic behavior. The capitalist value of competition is reflexively used in both the content of the program and against alternative programs to which the audience could give its time and attention.

In sum, the motives of the rhetoric of *WWF Smackdown!* seem to be grounded in a materialist perspective that reveres the physical dimension of existence and getting what one wants. By powerfully foregrounding the material, more abstract notions like obedience to rules, civility in behavior, or altruism are blocked from the audience's view—out of sight, out of mind. What is left is the simple and titillating fantasy of one going it alone against a chaotic and threatening environment and triumphing in spite of the odds. Perhaps Vince McMahon has recognized that the complexity of the real world the audience faces is more troubling than they would like. The drama he offers invites the audience to enter a world they could control or at least experience the glory of trying.

SUMMARY

In sum, Burke's dramatistic search model is grounded in the pentad, which allows us to describe and analyze rhetorical events with a vocabulary that permits explanation of rhetoric in a systematic and insightful manner. As Burke suggests:

> Surrounding us wordy animals there is the infinite wordless universe out of which we have been gradually carving our universes of discourse since the time when our primordial ancestors added to their sensations of words for sensations. When they could duplicate the taste of an orange by saying "the taste of an orange," that's when STORY was born, since words tell about sensations.
>
> . . . when STORY comes into the world there enters the realm of true, false, honest, mistaken, the downright lie, the imaginative, the visionary, the sublime, the ridiculous, the eschatological . . . , the satirical, every single detail of every single science or speculation, even every bit of gossip–for although all animals in their way communicate, only our kind of animal can gossip. There was no story before we came and when we're gone the universe will go on sans [without] story. (1985, 90)

As we discovered, at the outset of this discussion, people are symbol users who use those symbols to create categories (via the negative) in order to control the environment in which they find themselves. People aspire to perfection as they compare themselves constantly to others and use talk or rhetoric to deal with the guilt they experience by not being perfect. People are motivated by their symbolic constructions, that is, their philosophies, which were made to help them make sense of experience. In effect, the stories we tell each other take over and become our reasons for behaving, thus controlling us, when we created them to control what is around us.

Burke's dramatism is a useful tool for looking at any kind of symbolic action of human beings. It differs substantially from the narrative paradigm and fantasy theme analysis in many ways but is complementary to them in its focus on dramas, stories, or fantasies that are unique to us as human beings. Keep in mind the freedom of application that Burke believes is so valuable for discovering what is meaningful and for discovering how messages work to persuade us to think, believe, or behave in certain ways.

EXERCISES

To complete the exercises, you first must read the following reprinted "Radio Address of the President to the Nation" delivered by George W. Bush, September 15, 2001.

THE PRESIDENT: Good morning. This weekend I am engaged in extensive sessions with members of my National Security Council, as we plan a comprehensive assault on terrorism. This will be a different kind of conflict against a different kind of enemy.

This is a conflict without battlefields or beachheads, a conflict with opponents who believe they are invisible. Yet, they are mistaken. They will be exposed, and they will discover what others in the past have learned: Those who make war against the United States have chosen their own destruction. Victory against terrorism will not take place in a single battle, but in a series of decisive actions against terrorist organizations and those who harbor and support them.

We are planning a broad and sustained campaign to secure our country and eradicate the evil of terrorism. And we are determined to see this conflict through. Americans of every faith and background are committed to this goal.

Yesterday I visited the site of the destruction in New York City and saw an amazing spirit of sacrifice and patriotism and defiance. I met with rescuers who have worked past exhaustion, who cheered for our country and the great cause we have entered.

In Washington, D.C., the political parties and both Houses of Congress have shown a remarkable unity, and I'm deeply grateful. A terrorist attack designed to tear us apart has instead bound us together as a nation. Over the past few days, we have learned much about American courage—the courage of firefighters and police officers who suffered so great a loss, the courage of passengers aboard United 93 who may well have fought with the hijackers and saved many lives on the ground.

Now we honor those who died, and prepare to respond to these attacks on our nation. I will not settle for a token act. Our response must be sweeping, sustained and effective. We have much to do, and much to ask of the American people.

You will be asked for your patience; for, the conflict will not be short. You will be asked for resolve; for, the conflict will not be easy. You will be asked for your strength, because the course to victory may be long.

In the past week, we have seen the American people at their very best everywhere in America. Citizens have come together to pray, to give blood, to fly our country's flag. Americans are coming together to share their grief and gain strength from one another.

Great tragedy has come to us, and we are meeting it with the best that is in our country, with courage and concern for others. Because this is America. This is who we are. This is what our enemies hate and have attacked. And this is why we will prevail.

Thank you for listening.

When using the pentad as a search model, it is important to play with possible frames for the text. Keeping in mind Burke's admonition to treat the pentadic elements consistently, try finishing the following two arrays. Once you have completed the arrays, compare your answers with those we suggest in the boxes that follow.

1. Complete this array:
   Act: Report of actions taken by the Bush administration in response to the 9/11 attack
   Agent: President Bush
   Agency: A radio address to the nation
   Scene:
   Purpose:
   Suggested answers to exercise 1:

> **Scene:** A frightened and angry U.S. population
>
> **Purpose:** Assurance to the population that retaliation is planned and praise of citizens' responses

   Briefly discuss the effect on your ability to see the rhetorical dynamics of the message after framing the speech as a report of presidential action.

2. Complete this array:
   Act: A "prophecy" of future conditions and deeds
   Agent: The president *as* Oracle
   Agency: augury or divination based on the signs observed in the rubble and behavior of the people
   Scene:
   Purpose:
   Suggested answers to exercise 2:

> **Scene:** Unexpected conflict with a deadly, unique, and as yet unseen enemy
>
> **Purpose:** Assure the population that forces are marshaled to attack terrorism

   Briefly discuss here the effect on your ability to see the rhetorical dynamics of the message after framing the speech as a prophetic oracle.

3. Choose any two of the following Burkeian concepts and explain how they are working in the radio address: identification, division, hierarchy, guilt, victimage.

4. Using the pentadic description from exercise 1 or 2 (or construct your own), determine what ratio you feel is most powerfully operating in the speech. Using that ratio, explain what rhetorical motives emerge from your analysis of the radio address.

NOTES

1 The slippery and sometimes confusing nature of pentadic terms is explained and celebrated by Burke as he writes:

> We take it for granted that, insofar as men cannot create the universe, there must remain something essentially enigmatic about the problem of motives, and that this underlying enigma will manifest itself in inevitable ambiguities and inconsistencies among the terms for motives. Accordingly, what we want is *not terms that avoid ambiguity, but terms that clearly reveal the strategic spots at which ambiguities necessarily arise.* (1969a, xviii)

Rhetoric must use and *reuse* the common signs and symbols of language, organizational structures, topics, and tropes in order to create new and unique ideas. If the resources of communication were not ambiguous and fluid, if they were not able to be shifted and transformed, we would be left with denotation only. We would need a word for every single object in the world. Imagine, if you will, all language being like the bar codes on products you buy. There is no ambiguity in the bar code or we'd be hearing the dreaded, "Price check on register 2!" so often all commerce would stop! Bar codes are not poetic; they are useless beyond their single, specific, unambiguous, inflexible denotative job of "naming" a product. To communicate new ideas or respond to our constantly changing environment and experience, we must use an ambiguous, flexible code that is adaptable in meaning. Burke is arguing that his approach is designed to fit the necessarily ambiguous nature of speech.

2 *Oxford English Dictionary.* 2nd ed. CD-ROM. Oxford: Oxford University Press, 1992; s.v. "Ratio," definition 1b.

3 Ibid., definition 1a.

4 The order of pentadic elements in a ratio is an artifact of a "grammar" of motives. Burke writes:

> We want to inquire into the purely internal relationships which the five terms bear to one another, considering their possibilities of transformation, their range of permutations and combinations—and then to see how these various resources figure in actual statements about human motives. Strictly speaking, we mean by a Grammar of motives a concern with the terms alone, without reference to the ways their potentialities have been or can be utilized in actual statements about motives. Speaking broadly we could designate as "philosophies" any statements in which these grammatical resources are specifically utilized. Random or unsystematic statements about motives could be considered as fragments of a philosophy. (1969a, xvi)

A grammar amounts to rules of organization that guide how one assigns meaning to symbols within any code. So, for example, we must follow the rules of grammar in English (or any language) in order for our message to be understood and meaningful. Burke is arguing that there is a larger grammatical structure in discourse, a kind of meta-grammar that can be made visible by applying the pentad. Which pentadic elements are associated and which element is primary in the associated pair reflects an implicit rhetorical grammar. According to Burke, these pentadic relationships have philosophical (or explanatory) meanings that are activated by the grammar of motives.

5 If President Bush had chosen to describe circumstances in another way, those descriptions may have proven too divisive for the circumstances. For example, consider what responses could have obtained if Bush had said, "The world fights terror-ism. Civilization fights it. All who believe in progress fight it." The first sentence would have been much disputed since the 9/11 attack was "proof" that the world was not fighting terrorism. The second sentence may have alienated Muslim coun-tries known to be the bases of terrorist operations. Certainly, Saudi Arabia considers itself a civilized society in spite of the presence of terrorists on its soil. The third sen-tence may simply enrage those who believe that progress is not defined in material terms, as we are wont to do in the West, but in spiritual terms.

6 For example, saying, "Frank is generous" equates Frank's essence with generous acts. Implicit in the sentence is a cue that Frank must have performed one or more gen-erous acts in order to merit being described as generous.

Works Cited

Audi, Robert, ed. *The Cambridge Dictionary of Philosophy.* 2nd ed. Cambridge: Cambridge University Press, 1999.

Blackburn, Simon. *The Oxford Dictionary of Philosophy.* Oxford: Oxford University Press, 1994.

Burke, Kenneth. "Dramatism and Logology." *Communication Quarterly* 33 (1985): 89–90.

———. *A Grammar of Motives.* Berkeley: University of California Press, 1969.

———. *A Rhetoric of Motives.* Berkeley: University of California Press, 1969.

———. *Language as Symbolic Action: Essays on Life, Literature and Method.* Berkeley: University of California Press, 1966.

Bush, George W. "Address to a Joint Session of Congress and the American People." September 21, 2001. The White House. http://www.whitehouse.gov/news/releases/2001/09/20010920-8.html (accessed December 12, 2003).

———. "Radio Address of the President to the Nation." September 15, 2001. The White House. http://www.whitehouse.gov/news/releases/2001/09/20010915.html (accessed December 19, 2003).

Mautner, Thomas. *A Dictionary of Philosophy.* Oxford: Blackwell Reference, 1996.

Van Doren, Carl, and Carl Carmer. *American Scriptures.* New York: Boni & Gaer, 1946.

Warnick, Barbara. "The Narrative Paradigm: Another Story." *Quarterly Journal of Speech* 73 (1987): 172–82.

Suggested Readings

Blakesley, David. *The Elements of Dramatism.* New York: Longman, 2002.

Brummett, Barry. "A Pentadic Analysis of Ideologies in Two Gay Rights Controversies." *Central States Speech Journal* 30 (1979): 250–61.

Burke, Kenneth. "Definition of Man." *Language as Symbolic Action: Essays on Life, Literature, and Method.* Berkeley: University of California Press, 1966.

Gusfield, Joseph R., ed. *Kenneth Burke: On Symbols and Society.* Chicago: University of Chicago Press, 1989.

Meister, Mark. "Meteorology and the Rhetoric of Nature's Cultural Display." *Quarterly Journal of Speech* 87 (2001): 415–28.

Shultz, Kara. "Every Implanted Child a Star (and Some Other Failures): Guilt and Shame in the Cochlear Implant Debates." *Quarterly Journal of Speech* 86 (2000): 251–75.

Solomon, Martha. "The Rhetoric of Dehumanization: An Analysis of Medical Reports of the Tuskegee Syphilis Project." *Western Journal of Speech Communication* 49 (1985): 233–47.

SOCIOPOLITICAL APPROACHES

The next three chapters form a unit because they all present theories that draw our attention to human power struggles evident, more or less obviously, in rhetorical messages. The twentieth century made imminently clear that humans are in constant struggle for power and domination over one another because of class, race, ethnicity, sex, sexual preference, age, and more. The start of the twenty-first century has been marked by power struggles between Middle Eastern countries and the United States, power struggles between national and state legislatures, and power struggles in organizations and interpersonal relationships. Some rhetorical messages explicitly advocate for some sort of domination—take, for example, Hitler's speeches on the necessity of a pure Aryan race, KKK rituals of lynching in the Jim Crow era, or speeches debating the role of the United States in countries like Iraq and Afghanistan. Those messages obviously advocate morals that disturb us, and when conducting an analysis, we would likely evaluate them as unethical; but we might focus our analysis on how their rhetoric was so effective, and we would use classical or dramatistic tools to find out.

Other messages, however, perpetuate unjust distributions of power in subtle, even unintentional ways. Mediated messages are particularly good examples. When 1950s television shows like *Leave It to Beaver* and *Father Knows Best* were aired, no one observed that the characters and plots in those shows represented a particular, privileged population of the United States or that the shows perpetuated gender ideals that bound women to domestic spheres of life. Our culture's television media, speeches, newspapers, literature, and institutions often serve to sustain social structures that keep some people and ideas in domination over others. Unlike a classical or dramatistic analysis of Hitler's speeches that might focus on the rhetorical strategies he used to convince white Austrians of their superiority, a sociopolitical analysis of *Leave It to Beaver* or more currently, *Seventh Heaven,* would look for the more subtle mechanisms by which the shows, perhaps unintentionally, perpetuate dominant ways of thinking about race, class, and gender. The approaches in Chapters 14, 15, and 16 assume that the critic using them starts with an explicit concern about power and domination. In a sense, the critic carries a somewhat specific ethical agenda into the critique, but the critic is still responsible for getting into the balcony to see the text and context in an informed, emotionally distant, and intellectually responsible manner. In other words, in using these approaches, the critic may be concerned explicitly with the representations of race or class or gender in a text, but the critic is not permitted to simply spout opinions and reactions to the texts based on those concerns. Careful description, analysis, and interpretation are still required.

The first approach, in Chapter 14, we call *ideological* because it focuses most broadly on the ways that messages sustain and often discourage audiences from questioning dominant beliefs about how the world is and ought to be. This approach is rooted in Marxist thinking, though its focus is less on economics per se and more on how messages are created to make people believe that the systems they operate in (government, education, capitalism, religion, etc.) are good for them, even though they may better serve the interests of those who are in positions of power. In reading this chapter you'll learn to look for some mechanisms by which messages often unintentionally perpetuate unquestioned beliefs that benefit a few at the expense of many.

Then, in Chapter 15 we narrow the kinds of questions raised in the ideological approach to focus specifically on social concerns related to gender, sex, and sex relations. This chapter suggests ways to examine a text from a *feminist* perspective, which is directly related to the ideological approach in Chapter 14. Specifically, you will see that there are a variety of wide-ranging perspectives among feminists, and you can decide which perspective, if any, you most agree with and would find useful in helping you analyze the way women and men are represented in all kinds of messages.

The final chapter in this section, Chapter 16, focuses even more specifically on the question of how our language—words, signs, symbols—shapes our thought patterns, our cultural patterns, our assumptions about reality, our politics, our religions, our education . . . everything. Several theories are presented in this chapter. We call these theories *postmodern* because they start from the presumption that everything we experience, think, and do is filtered and thus affected by the language we use. We are, in fact, trapped in our language (we cannot not use it), but we need to reflect on that language to see how it directs and often limits our assumptions about the world.

Whereas the classical and dramatistic approaches focus a critic's attention on *how messages are crafted* to convince audiences of particular ideas, the sociopolitical approaches focus a critic's attention on *how power itself communicates.* As with the other units, this unit merely introduces you to a host of theories. To use them well, you will need to expand your understanding through additional reading.

IDEOLOGICAL APPROACHES

As the largest retail and entertainment complex in the United States, the Mall of America in Bloomington, Minnesota, is quite a consumer phenomenon. Each year over 42 million people come to the mall, which is visited more than any other attraction in the United States. The mall has three floors, each of which is over half a mile in walking distance, and it holds nearly 530 stores, more than fifty restaurants, and fourteen movie theaters. The Bloomington Convention and Visitors Bureau boasts that seven Yankee Stadiums would fit inside the mall and that if visitors spent ten minutes in every store, it would take them more than eighty-six hours to complete their shopping ("Mall of America" 2003). We would like to suggest at least two ways a person could experience the Mall of America. The first way is as a consumer, completely in awe of the magnitude of the mall and the number of stores, restaurants, and entertainment options. Experiencing the mall as a consumer, one would shop with the satisfaction of knowing that most anything desired could be found in the mall, and one would bask in the pleasure of being entertained through amusement rides, movies, and endless food choices.

A second way to experience the mall is as a critic, particularly a critic with an eye toward the social power relations at work in the mall. The critic concerned with power relations would walk through the mall, conscious of things the designers of the mall hope the average consumers never think too hard about. For example, the critic might pay attention to how the architecture of the mall encourages unnecessary spending for the benefit of profit-seeking storeowners. Specifically the critic might note that escalators only take shoppers from one level to another, but never to all three levels. To go from the first to the third level, one must ride an elevator, get off, and walk some distance to find the next elevator going up. A critic interested in power relations would view this as a strategy of domination in which those making a profit maneuver the consumers to make sure they see more stores and items than what they really need. Thus, the interests of the profit makers are served at the potential exploitation of the consumers. The critic concerned with power relations might also examine how issues of race and class are played out in the mall by paying attention to whom she does or does not see shopping and working at the mall, what kind of people are and are not represented in the advertising throughout the mall, and what race and class of people are and are not represented in the entertainment offered in the mall. Such observations might tell the critic something about how the Mall of

America systematically sustains certain race and class relations in mainstream America.

This second way of experiencing the Mall of America reflects an approach to analysis that is ideological in its focus. The term **ideology** refers to *the culturally shared beliefs about how the world is (created, structured, ordered, etc.) and how it ought to be.* Many ideological approaches to the study of messages originally stem from Marxist theory, which responded to the rapid substituting of capitalism for feudal systems in the nineteenth century. **Marxism** held that *all of human experience, from religion to politics to morality to art to entertainment, was ultimately determined by a culture's economic base, rooted in its "mode of production."* Consequently, how materials that become valued commodities are produced and distributed impacts all else in a culture. Modes of production determine social class, conditions of health, accessibility of products for the generation of art, science, religious practice, education, and more. The "superstructure" or social relations recognized as government, art, science, organized religion, education, and so on are all bound by the necessary perpetuation of the economic base. As Marx and Engels write in their *Communist Manifesto,* "man's ideas, views and conceptions, in one word, man's consciousness, changes with every change in the conditions of his material existence, in his social relations and in his social life" (1968, 43). Lenin elaborates this way, "Just as a man's knowledge reflects nature . . . which exists independently of him, so man's *social knowledge* (i.e., his various views and doctrines—philosophical, religious, political and so forth) reflects the *economic system* of society" (1968, 24). All our worldviews—political, religious, philosophical, and so on—are affected by the economic system we participate in. Without the economy, for example, no synagogue could run as is. The synagogue relies on its members, who earn their money by working in industries that produce and distribute material goods, to provide money and materials that sustain the building and its contents and to meet the material needs of rabbis and other religious leaders. Building materials, computers, candles, and rabbi's robes, for example, all must be produced, distributed, and bought. By making those material provisions, the people ultimately sustain the organizational structure. So the entire religious institution is dependent on and determined by the perpetuation of the cultural economic base. The religious teachings must somehow support that economic base or the synagogue itself would cease to exist in its present state. The "message" of the church is never detached from the economic cycle of production, Marx would argue. In fact, the message perpetuates beliefs that keep that economic order in place.

According to Marx, the economic base and those who benefit from it are sustained by an ideology that he believed to be a set of illusory ideals that justify that base, even though many are exploited by it. Marx and Engels state, "[The bourgeoisie] has drowned the most heavenly ecstasies of religious fervor, of chivalrous enthusiasm . . . in the icy water of egotistical calculation. . . . In one word, for exploitation, veiled by religious and political illusions, it has substituted naked, shameless, direct, brutal exploitation" (1968, 16). The working class, they argue, go through stages in which they unite against the bourgeoisie but then end up competing against one another, keeping the upper class (bourgeoisie) in place (26–32). For example, as a McDonald's employee Ralph may work for low wages while the storeowner makes an impressive profit each year (what Marx considered reality), but Ralph accepts his condition because he buys into an ideology that masks the economic forces arrayed against the poor. Ralph has been taught through a host of structures and institutions (school, business, movies, television, newspapers, and more) that if he works hard and is willing to start at the bottom, he will eventually be as rich as he wants or, at least, climb the corporate ladder. So Ralph stays content with his position and sees value in his contribution to the general economic base, competing with his fellow employees for raises, better hours, and increased hours. By accepting the ideology (what Engels called a "false consciousness") Ralph fails to perceive the reality that he is no more than an instrument for someone else's wealth. In Marxist thought, there are no ideals, just illusions that support the prevailing modes of production and those whose interests it serves.

CRITICAL THEORY

Critical theory, *an offshoot of Marxism that developed in the Frankfurt School founded in Germany in 1923, argues that the modes of material production impact ideology and its ensuing social relations, and purports that no knowledge (science, history, theology, etc.) exists objectively apart from the material conditions of its authors.* While critical theorists seek to dismantle the distortions in knowledge that stem from ideology, they also recognize the role that language, media, and other types of visual representations play in the creation of ideology. To look at material conditions apart from the way we interpret the world through our symbols is a mistake. Ideological domination of particular classes, races, genders, and so on is not only a function of economics but also a function of our symbol systems, say the critical theorists. In other words, to free people from oppressive conditions, critical theorists believe, we must analyze not just economic systems, but the many forms of public communication that perpetuate economic and other oppressive systems.

In what follows we offer a few key terms from various ideological approaches and suggest ways you might use those terms in your analysis of rhetorical texts.

HEGEMONY AND MARGINALIZATION

Two central terms one encounters in ideological theory are *hegemony* and *marginalization*. The term **hegemony**, as used by Marxist Antonio Gramsci (1971), refers to *the everyday means by which a dominant belief system, practice, custom, or people prevails within a culture.* By contrast, **marginalization** refers to *those beliefs, practices, and customs that are often overlooked, discarded, ignored, or explicitly oppressed.* Think of a piece of notebook paper and how you use it.

What you write in the center is considered the important matter to read. The real meat or essence of your thoughts, for example, is written in that space. That's what we might call the hegemony: the dominant, prevailing ideas, practices, and people that get public attention. What goes in the margins? Notes, subsidiary comments, ideas less important or merely in reference to the important material between the margins. That which is in the margins is, in fact, marginal. On a broader scale, in any culture we can identify those customs, behaviors, beliefs, practices, even people that are hegemonic and those that are marginalized. For example, what some call "hegemonic masculinity" is idealized in our culture (Messner 1992, 18).[1] One might characterize hegemonic masculinity as the condition of being physically strong, aggressive, athletic, heterosexual, handsome, and economically stable. Hegemonic masculinity is perpetuated through all sorts of male images, verbal and nonverbal. Crying wrestlers are never the heroes in WWE episodes; only aggressive fighters are the heroes. Gay men are never the subjects of beer commercials aired during a football game. Men who garden are never the subjects of after-shave commercials. Men with multiple sclerosis are never the heroes in action/adventure films. Men who openly weep, men who enjoy horticulture, men with serious physical disabilities, or men who are gay are typically marginalized in the dominant cultural representational systems.

Those people, ideas, and practices that are marginalized are often invisible in the media or shown as an aberration to mainstream culture. Consequently, these people and ways of being are ignored or misunderstood by powerful cultural institutions like legislative bodies, the courts, religious institutions, and educational institutions. Those in power often make decisions that sustain the comfort and welfare of those within the margins, ignoring (sometimes inadvertently) the needs and conditions of those outside the margins.

A critic analyzing a message from the point of view of critical theory examines how messages perpetuate or subvert prevailing hegemonies. You might ask in what subtle ways a message accomplishes persuasive purposes on one level, but at another level reinforces social relations and beliefs that sustain the power of some over others. A presidential campaign speech, for example, might successfully persuade audiences to vote for a candidate because he or she will cut taxes, but when you carefully examine the metaphors, allusions, and phrases of the speech you might discover that the candidate reinforces a hegemonic belief in individualism that serves the interests of CEOs more than working-class families. Or, conversely, you might discover that the speech relies on images and language that subvert the ideals of individualism, calling attention to the virtues of interdependence, thus challenging the American ideals presumed necessary to sustain a capitalist economy. Individualism and interdependence may very well never have been mentioned explicitly by the speaker; after all, the subject of the speech was tax cuts. But an observant critic might attend to these underlying ideologies, recognizing that all symbol use is situated in power (including economic) struggles.

Critical theorists have given us some specific ideas about (rhetorical) strategies often used, consciously or not, to sustain a hegemony. Two terms that might help you identify these strategies are *legitimation* and *naturalization*.

LEGITIMATION

German theorist Jurgen Habermas defines **legitimation** as *the process whereby a political order's worthiness is recognized as just and right* (1976, 178–79). That which is legitimate is presumed to be in the general public's interest. Habermas encourages critics to question the way capitalistic accomplishments are represented (in a capitalistic economic system) as being in the general public's best interest. How are the discoveries, advancements, products, and services that are produced and exchanged in a capitalistic society presented to the public so that the public perceives them to be in their best interest even though, in fact, workers may be exploited in their making, natural resources may be abused in their making, and the public who seems to receive the benefits may be exploited? Here you as a critic may be asking how the accomplishments of capitalism are represented in public messages so people believe those accomplishments are for their benefit.

Take, for example, the case of advancements in medical research, which are partially a function of a capitalistic society that still maintains a competitive and profit base for medical development despite the current controls of HMOs. Let's say the medical community conducts research leading to the discovery of more effective treatments for breast cancer. Those discoveries are first reported to the medical community in medical journals. Then those discoveries are picked up by journalists who write about them in newspapers and magazines, which may receive advertising money from pharmaceutical companies that sponsored the research. Additionally, HMOs may put together a public service campaign encouraging women to be aware of these new treatments and seek diagnosis early. Each of these venues constitutes a rhetorical act as each attempts to shape others' beliefs, attitudes, and behaviors related to breast cancer and medical research. Each rhetorical act also represents the issue of breast cancer in particular ways that cause the reader to view the medical development as beneficial to women. However, a critic carefully examining those messages may discover that those medical developments help only a small percentage of the population (perhaps primarily white middle- and upper-class women), but bring considerable profits to a pharmaceutical company. Perhaps the critic may see that the representation of the medical discovery validates the *treatment* as a benefit to white, middle-/upper-class women, ignoring alternative *causes* of cancer, which might require more radical changes that pose threats to the current capitalistic system (e.g., dietary alterations that might lead to the death of junk food industries; environmental changes that might threaten the automobile industry, etc.). Or the critic may discover that the messages lead women to believe that the advancements are for their own good when many animals were killed in the process, though that fact was never reported. No doubt many would argue that lives of women are worth the cost of killing some animals. But the point the critic might make is that the way the messages represent and celebrate the "discovery" as "saving of (human) lives" keeps at bay the philosophical debate about the relationship between humans and animals.

In these examples, the scientific methods, the profit interests of the pharmaceutical companies and HMOs, and the assumption that medical treatment is preferable to radical holistic health and environmental alterations are all legitimized by rhetoric that portrays the medical development as beneficial to women. After all, who would deny or really want to oppose the development of a treatment that might save a valued friend or family member's life? By preventing rather than inviting such discussions, these rhetorical messages legitimate the dominant political (power) base and dominant ideology.

As a critic, you might consider examining the visual and verbal images in a message to see how the representations of ideas, developments, products, services, rules, or legislation lead audiences to assume their interests are most valued. This requires you to look beyond the explicit arguments made to the audience. An advertisement or magazine article may very well contain an explicit argument for why a medical development is advantageous to you. Or a politician might make an explicit argument for why a new tax policy is beneficial to you. Looking at those arguments would require you to use classical or argumentation tools for analysis, but to look at the legitimation is to look at how the symbols cause the audience to believe that the dominant political order is legitimate or concerns itself with the common good of the people and their world. Keep in mind that "dominant political order" does not just refer to a government system or political party. Your academic institution and work organization sustain (legitimize) certain power structures. Religious institutions engage political (power) struggles both within and among themselves. Even a social unit as informal and small as your family manages power struggles whereby family members use rhetorical symbols to legitimize or challenge dominant political orders.

When analyzing legitimation, you may ask questions like this of the message(s) at hand:

- How do the symbols in this message represent the accomplishments of capitalism or our democracy as offering the best possible satisfaction of a collective good?
- How do the symbols in this message represent the accomplishments of an authoritative institution (governmental, religious, academic, etc.) as serving the common good of people?
- How does the configuration of symbols in this message invite or prevent questions that might shake up the current economic, political, social, or religious order?
- How do the symbols in this message prevent audiences from rejecting the presumed American values of accumulation and wealth?
- How do the symbols in this message prevent audiences from shaking up the presumed values of _____ institution?
- How do the symbols in this message represent the accomplishments of my work organization as serving the common good?
- How is authority established to legitimize the apparent "good" done by that organization?

NATURALIZATION

A more specific symbolic mechanism whereby hegemonic beliefs, customs, practices, institutions, and so on are given legitimacy is through what might be called **naturalization** (or **normalization**); that is, *the portrayal of beliefs, customs, practices, and so on as coming from nature, the "natural way."* In some cases, naturalization stems from an implicit philosophy of social Darwinism, which argues that who or whatever was "on top" of a biological or social hierarchy deserves "by inexorable design" to be there (Donovan 1992, 43). Anything that exists in nature, we often assume, must be true and ultimately good. Moreover, we cannot argue with, control, or change nature. It's just "the way things (naturally) are," or "the natural order of things." To represent our ideas and practices as the way things (naturally) are is to present them as nondebatable. Nature (the natural), and perhaps by implication the supernatural (super-nature), are ultimate authorities that cannot be fought. Historically, naturalization was a symbolic strategy used by eighteenth-century antisuffragists to argue that women ought not have the right to vote. Notice the nonitalicized language in the following excerpt of this 1887 antisuffrage speech by Senator Joseph E. Brown:

> *I believe that* the Creator intended *that the sphere of the males and females of our race should be different . . . and that each sex is equally well qualified* by natural endowments *for the discharge of the important duties which pertain to each, and that each sex is equally competent to discharge those duties.*
>
> *We find an abundance of evidence,* both in the works of nature and in the Divine revelation, *to establish the fact that the family properly regulated is the foundation and pillar of society. . . . In* the Divine economy *it is provided that the man shall be the head of the family, and shall take upon himself the solemn obligation of providing for and protecting the family.*
>
> *Man,* by reason of his physical strength, *and* his other endowments and faculties, *is qualified for the discharge of those duties that require strength and ability to combat with the sterner realities and difficulties of life. . . . These are some of the active and sterner duties of life to which the male sex is by nature better fitted than the female sex. (94)*

By suggesting that women's emotional sensitivity and men's rational capacity were "natural," even Divinely assigned, Senator Brown's argument was implicitly afforded more authority. Who can argue with nature or God (especially in the nineteenth century)?

A more contemporary example of naturalization can be found in an infomercial for Rogaine. The video, entitled "Taking Control of Your Hair Loss: Man's Struggle with Nature," portrays six men who like to "take on the challenges of nature" on a river rafting/camping trip. Male pattern baldness is represented as natural, and the men are represented as doing what men naturally do. The narrator tells us, "A lot of men enjoy meeting challenges, overcoming obstacles, the feeling of success and taking control of the world around them."

The visual imagery suggests that men are, by nature, rugged, athletic, heterosexual, thereby sustaining the hegemonic view of masculinity and marginalizing those who do not fit this created image. In just the opening scenes, the idea of "taking control" is made natural: what men, by nature, do. Throughout the video, the men talk about their successes with Rogaine. One states that he knows hair loss is inevitable, but he wants to "slow down" the inevitable. Another argues that "a hairpiece is artificial. I particularly don't want anything artificial on my head." His comment implies that Rogaine, unlike a hairpiece, is natural, not artificial. In fact, this man explicitly states, "If I have to go bald, if that's what nature gives me, then I definitely want to go bald gracefully. Rogaine is not artificial; it's my own hair." The men all discuss their use of Rogaine as a way to overcome the challenges of nature just as they are shown to overcome the challenges of white water rapids. Fighting baldness with Rogaine is part of that challenge men should, by virtue of their nature as men, take on. So while the infomercial admits that baldness is natural (something we normally argue cannot be fought), it subjects that natural process to a superior natural activity in men: challenging, dominating, overcoming nature. Ironically, the fighting of nature is itself naturalized and thus legitimized as a superior natural act.

Symbols that naturalize are sometimes more subtle. In films, for example, we often see animals represented with humanlike characteristics, causing us to feel toward them as we would toward humans. We go to animal parks that are symbolic representations of natural environments and habitats, but not the animals' natural habitats. We watch animals perform for us, developing implicit beliefs that they are naturally our entertainers. The naturalized environment helps us forget the profit motive behind the park. In essence, we naturalize their environments and behaviors, allowing ourselves to believe that it is perfectly normal for them to perform for our own gratification. Unfortunately, when by surprise a mother whale unexpectedly consumes her dying young in front of an audience, our naturalized conception of our dominant and friendly relationship to animals that entertain us is shattered.

Sometimes messages themselves contain implicit critiques of naturalization. In 1854 abolitionist Frederick Douglass delivered a speech titled "The Claims of the Negro Ethnologically Considered" in which he acted as a rhetorical critic, questioning two claims of nineteenth-century white ethnologists and anthropologists: first, that the African American was, by nature, "not a man" and, second, that the white and black races did not descend from a common ancestry. In so many words, Douglass critiqued the racist rhetoric that naturalized the differences between African Americans and Euro-Americans. He pointed out that once it is "granted that the human race are of multitudinous origin, *naturally* different in their moral, physical and intellectual capacities . . . you make plausible a demand for classes, grades and conditions . . . and a chance is left for slavery, as a necessary institution" (1950, 295, emphasis added). He noted the severe social and political consequences for his people when the differences between the races are "naturalized." Although naturalization can distort perceptions and lead us to make heinous generalizations and stereotypes, the strategy also can be used for good. While critiquing

his opponents' naturalizations of racial differences Douglass himself naturalized the common ancestry of the races, something he admitted could not be
proven empirically. He argued that "all mankind have [by nature] the same
wants, arising out of a common *nature*" (307, emphasis added). That common
nature is "registered in the Courts of Heaven, and is enforced by the eloquence
of the God of all the earth" (308). Here he referred to a biblical passage stating,
"'that God has made of one blood all nations of men for to dwell upon all the
face of the earth'" (293). Douglass himself relied on the authority of nature to
represent the common humanity among the races.

Making that which is not necessarily of nature appear to be natural is a
powerful rhetorical strategy used both for good and for ill. A wise critic carefully examines the way symbols naturalize that which we commonly take for
granted. When analyzing the use of naturalization, you may ask questions like
this of the message(s) at hand:

- How do the symbols in this message make the rhetor's position appear to be
  of nature or the natural course of things?
- What does the rhetor(s) say to make the natural condition seem authoritative? What authorities are used to make the audience believe in the rhetor's
  view of the natural condition?
- How does the naturalization of the rhetor's position give authority to that
  position?
- How does the representation of the rhetor's position as natural limit the
  audience's criticism of his/her position?

Let's try applying the concepts of an ideological critique. In the following
paragraphs we attempt to look at two popular films from an ideological perspective, asking questions about the way the plots, characters, and settings of
both films challenge and also sustain hegemonic structures of race and class.
We've selected these films because they are, indeed, popular and because their
animation and assumed audience of children, youth, and families give them a
quality of innocence that we often fail to examine critically. Take note at how
our analysis uses constructs from narrative analysis (e.g., plot, characters, setting) to name precisely the mechanisms by which ideologies are evident in the
two films.

IDEOLOGICAL CONCEPTS APPLIED TO BEAUTY AND THE BEAST AND SHREK

L et's apply some concepts from an ideological perspective to analyze the two
popular animated fairy-tale films: Walt Disney's *Beauty and the Beast* (1991)
and PDI/Dreamworks' *Shrek* (2001). Keep in mind that what you will read is
not a final report that argues our interpretation or evaluation. Rather, you will
read our descriptive and analytical process guided by ideological concepts.

First we briefly describe Disney's version of the plot in *Beauty and the Beast*. The heroine, Belle, is the daughter of a poor, eccentric inventor, Maurice, who lives in a small province in France. Early in the film we learn that Belle is considered by herself and others to be a misfit in her village because although she is the town beauty, she is antisocial, preferring to spend her time reading books and dreaming of "more than this provincial life." The antagonist, Gaston, who is considered by himself and others to be the most desired single man in the village, decides that he wants Belle to be his wife. After Belle refuses his marriage proposal, he devises a plot to blackmail her father so she will be forced to marry him. In the meantime, Belle's father leaves the village to enter his most recent invention into a neighboring village competition. On his way to the competition he loses his direction and encounters dangerous wolves that scare away his horse, forcing him to seek refuge in a dark and mysterious castle. In the castle lives the Beast, a prince who in his youth was turned into a beast because of his cruelty to an unattractive beggar woman. His spell would be broken only if, by the time he entered adulthood, he earned the love of a woman despite his ugliness.

Ashamed of his appearance, the Beast has secluded himself, refusing contact with all humankind. When he discovers Maurice, he is enraged, imprisoning him for life. When Belle discovers her father is missing, she begins her search and eventually finds him in the castle. She, too, is discovered by the raging Beast and begs him to let her sick father go, offering to serve out his sentence. The Beast agrees to the offer, knowing that she might be the one to break his spell. Over time, he comes to love Belle and she him as his intimidating demeanor softens. One night, after a romantic evening of dancing in the grand library, the Beast asks Belle if she is happy. She says yes, but expresses her longing for her father. When the Beast permits her to go see her father (the indication of his love for her), she leaves to go nurse her father back to health. In the meantime, Gaston carries out his plot to send Maurice to an insane asylum so Belle will be forced to marry him. Once Gaston learns about the Beast, he turns his energy away from Belle and her father and, instead, decides to conquer the fearsome Beast so he can become the hero. Ultimately, the Beast and Gaston battle over Belle (the beautiful object of desire). Of course, the Beast wins and when Belle confesses her love to him, the spell is broken and he transforms into a handsome prince.

Embedded in the plot of *Beauty and the Beast* are several ideological assumptions about social class relations. After all, Belle comes from a poor, working-class family while the Beast is an aristocrat, born into the wealthiest of wealthy families. The plot seems to naturalize the appropriateness of existing class differentials. Several points of the plot indicate this.

Early in the film Belle walks through her French province, describing the poverty of her people and characterizing her poor village life as banal. She dreams of "more than this provincial life," though we're never told what, specifically, she hopes for. She tells the bookshop owner how she loves the books about dungeons, dragons, and handsome princes. When her father promises that his latest invention "will be the start of a new life for us," we can only assume that the life they dream of is one of wealth and opportunity ("adventure") that comes with financial stature, which would legitimize a move from provincial to aristocratic life.

Because Belle is already made out to be a flawless heroine whose motives are pure (compared with Gaston's), her desire for the better life of the upper class is made acceptable and desirable, indeed legitimate. Yet an ideological perspective draws to our attention the fact that Belle seems to want out of her provincial life for herself, not to be an activist for the people of her class. Thus, she is willing to leave her people to assimilate into a higher social class position within the existing structure rather than to seek change in the structure to benefit others in her class. In fact, while a prisoner of the Beast in the castle, Belle rather quickly forgets the class of people from whom she comes (remembering only her individual loss of her father) and is enticed by the comforts and luxuries of aristocratic life. She initially resists the Beast's offer of elegant clothing and fine dining, but before long, curiosity gets the best of her and she wanders into the palace kitchen where she is swept away by the dazzling dances of the kitchen utensils who sing "Be Our Guest," convincing her that she is not a prisoner, but a guest. In fact, Lumiere, one of the characters she befriends, corrects Mrs. Potts, who characterized Belle as having lost her freedom. Lumiere explicitly states, "She's not a prisoner; she's our guest." In subsequent scenes, we see Belle wearing the elegant gowns and feasting with the Beast. Convinced that she is not oppressed, Belle becomes a social passivist, uninterested in political or economic freedom, and complacent in economic comfort afforded by her love for the Beast.

For a fleeting moment the film offers a sense of awareness of social justice when Gaston leads the villagers in a revolt, attempting to overthrow the Beast. But even that subplot reinforces the perceived benevolence of the power structure. Gaston's motives for overthrowing the Beast are self-interested, and he cannot see that the Beast is actually kind and gentle. Consequently, as the battle unfolds, the palace staff members (all of whom were transformed into dishes and other household items when the prince was transformed into the Beast) become victims of the uprising. Viewers are made to side with those in the palace, again reinforcing their faith in the class differential. The ending of the story functions still further to legitimize the class hierarchy. Upon marrying the Beast, Belle does escape her class. She and her father, by virtue of her marriage to the Beast, acquire wealth, thus perpetuating the illusion, the sustaining glimmer of hope that those who are good enough or lucky enough will rise above their class into a dreamland of wealth and prestige. In sum, the plot subtly naturalizes then legitimizes class difference and, thus, sustains the system that keeps the wealthy in their place, and the poor in theirs.

On the other hand, PDI/Dreamworks' 2001 release, *Shrek*, is a contemporary fairy tale that offers a critique of the racial and class ideologies typically upheld in traditional fairy tales like *Beauty and the Beast*. First, we briefly describe the plot.

The character Shrek is a large, ugly ogre who lives a secluded life near a swamp outside the city of Duloc, led by the selfish and greedy Lord Farquaad. In the opening scene, we find Shrek reading a fairy tale about a princess who is locked in a castle tower and finds her "true love" in her rescuer. Shrek immediately expresses doubt in the ideology of romance as he closes the fairy-tale book and sarcastically concludes, "As if that would happen."

In subsequent scenes we see various fairy-tale characters (the three little pigs, the seven dwarfs, the big bad wolf, Pinocchio, and others) being sold to Farquaad's knights as "freak" commodities. Those who are considered worthless are threatened some hideous punishment. A group of characters escape and go to Shrek's swamp, much like a refugee camp. There they hope to persuade Shrek to help them seek justice and safety. One character who is sought for captivity because of his value in having unique freakish qualities is the talking Donkey. In running away from his captors, Donkey stumbles into Shrek, who scares the pursuing knights away with his fearsome behavior and appearance. Grateful to Shrek for saving his life, Donkey seeks Shrek's companionship, though Shrek offers none. The two return to Shrek's swamp only to find all the exiled fairy-tale creatures. Wanting the creatures off his land, Shrek and Donkey go to Lord Farquaad, seeking relief. When they enter the castle, they find Farquaad overseeing a contest among the knights to see who is most fit to journey on his behalf to rescue Princess Fiona who is trapped by a fearsome dragon in a faraway castle surrounded by lava and fire. After Shrek interrupts to request that the fairy-tale creatures be removed from his swamp, Farquaad decides that whichever knight kills the ogre is the one to make his trek to rescue the princess. To Farquaad's surprise, however, Shrek and Donkey defeat all the knights. So Farquaad offers to remove the fairy-tale creatures from the swamp if Shrek rescues the princess.

Shrek and Donkey journey to the castle where they find and rescue Princess Fiona. Expecting her rescuer to be her true love, Fiona is surprised to discover that her rescuer is an ugly ogre and is confused that Lord Farquaad did not come for her himself. But because of his self-interest in getting his swamp back, Shrek insists that the princess be delivered to Lord Farquaad. Reluctantly, she complies. As the three characters journey back to Duloc, Shrek and Fiona develop an affection for each other. But we discover that Fiona is under a spell whereby she is beautiful by day and ugly by night until she is kissed by her true love (whom she assumes will be Lord Farquaad). Each evening at dusk, her body transforms into an ogrelike appearance. Each night of the journey she strategically hides from the ogre and Donkey so they will not learn of her condition. But one night Donkey seeks out the princess to tell her of Shrek's love for her. He finds the princess in her nighttime state and she confesses her love for Shrek but her belief that she must be kissed by Lord Farquaad for her spell to be broken. Donkey vows to keep her secret, though Shrek is left thinking that Fiona refuses to love him because of his appearance.

When the three reach Duloc, Fiona meets Lord Farquaad and though disappointed that he is not her true love, she urgently requests a wedding that day so her spell might be broken and her secret not be known to Lord Farquaad. In the meantime, Shrek learns from Donkey that Fiona does love him and they decide to stop the wedding so she might be with Shrek instead. The two successfully interrupt the wedding, and Shrek publicly confesses his love for Fiona. The sun begins to set, and Fiona transforms into her ugly appearance. Lord Farquaad is repulsed, but Shrek tells her she is beautiful, and he, her true love, kisses her. The spell is broken, but Fiona permanently retains her nighttime appearance rather than her daytime appearance. So (in contrast to the Beast who turns into a handsome prince in *Beauty and the Beast*), Fiona is not transformed into a physical beauty, thus requiring Shrek and the viewer to truly accept Fiona for who she is (and vice versa).

Four aspects of plot and character development in *Shrek* lead the viewer to a more critical view of class and race relations. First, the plot makes explicitly evident the social injustice experienced by the fairy-tale citizens. Early in the film we find them being exploited as they are sold like slaves, according to their potential market value. The creatures are lined up and sold as Lord Farquaad's knights determine their worth. One might argue that the film draws attention to the fact that fairy-tale figures are, in fact, bought and sold for the financial prosperity of others. In any case, it is apparent that those without value are exiled to what becomes a sort of refugee camp or squatters' camp on Shrek's swampland. They are clearly depicted as an oppressed group of people in need of a Moses, a Gandhi, a Nelson Mandela, to lead them out of bondage.

The second indicator of a critical view of class ideology is that Lord Farquaad is clearly depicted as a greedy, upper-class oppressor, interested only in his political gain. He refers to his city Duloc as "my perfect world," "a perfect place," not to be contaminated by the imperfections of poor, freakish fairy-tale characters. Whereas the dreamland of aristocracy is legitimized in *Beauty and the Beast,* in *Shrek,* the dreamland is exposed as artificial, cruel, and unjust. Farquaad's cruelty is especially evident as we see him torturing the Gingerbread Man in order to find out where the fairy-tale creatures are. Though the scene has comedic elements, it leaves no doubt in the viewer's mind that Farquaad's greed is unacceptable. Additionally, Duloc is portrayed as a replication of Disney's Magic Kingdom in Walt Disneyland and Walt Disney World. The horses and carriages are parked in a lot with character markers to indicate where one is parked. The entrance to the city mimics the entrance to the Disney theme parks, complete with back-and-forth roped lines and turnstiles to count the number of visitors. Upon entering the city, one immediately sees a large flowerbed that depicts the image of Lord Farquaad, much like the flowerbed that depicts the image of Mickey Mouse in the Magic Kingdom entrance. Lord Farquaad's description of Duloc as "a perfect place" echoes the self-ascribed characterization of Disneyland as "The Happiest Place on Earth." The mocking of Disney in *Shrek* subtly requires the viewer to recognize the Disney Corporation as "dominator" and to question its corporate profit motives.

A third ingredient of the film's critical nature is that the oppressed characters do, at some level, revolt against the oppressor. In the end, Lord Farquaad is defeated, and the fairy-tale characters are shown celebrating their apparent freedom, dancing and singing at the end of the film. So whereas Belle fails to act in the interest of liberating her people, Shrek succeeds. In *Shrek,* the fantasy dreamland of the upper class is not naturalized as "how things are." It is critiqued as an ideology that perpetuates social injustice motivated by (corporate) greed, and overthrow of that system is what the viewer is made to celebrate.

Finally, whereas *Beauty and the Beast,* like many traditional fairy tales, makes no reference to race and portrays only a white Eurocentric cast, one of *Shrek*'s major characters is voiced as and by an African American. Actor Eddie Murphy, who is the voice of Donkey, uses black English as well as humor common to the African-American culture in his development of the character Donkey. Although one might argue that the African American is once again subjugated to the role of sidekick or "the fool" (in this case, even referred to as the "ass"), it is important to note Donkey's critical roles in the overall plot. For example, Donkey is much more aware than Shrek of the importance of liberating the fairy-tale characters. His motivation for rescuing Princess Fiona is not as self-interested as Shrek's. Additionally, Donkey has the empathic ability to offer deep psychological insight into Shrek's character. Donkey is the one who forces Shrek to confront his fear of people and his loneliness. Donkey even forces Shrek to acknowledge his mistreatment of Donkey (the Euro-American mistreatment of the African American) as he pronounces, "Guess what? Now it's my turn, so you just shut up and pay attention. You are mean to me. You insult me, and you don't appreciate anything that I do. You're always pushing me around or pushing me away." Donkey plays the critically important role of delegitimizing the prevalence of racism.

Although, from an ideological perspective, this analysis suggests that *Shrek* functions to delegitimize unjust social, class, and race relations, the film is limited in the extent to which it is willing to radically change the existing system. For example, although Shrek and Princess Fiona are instrumental in the liberation of the fairy-tale creatures, their motivations were nevertheless self-interested. Shrek wanted his swamp back and, in the end, Shrek and Fiona wanted each other. While those motivations are not, of themselves, evil, the plot ends with a focus on their happiness with each other, leaving ambiguous (and, thus, unimportant) the question of what happens to the fairy-tale creatures. Though they are shown celebrating in the final scene, they are singing not about their freedom, but about Shrek's love for Fiona. The viewer is left to wonder whether the political and economic system was actually dismantled when Lord Farquaad was destroyed (eaten by a dragon). By placing the plight of the oppressed in the backdrop, the social justice concerns are made less important. To do otherwise would delegitimize the very production of *Shrek* itself.

Finally, it is worth noting that the film critiques the exploitation of fairy-tale characters for economic gain, and it critiques the Walt Disney Corporation for its construction of a false ideology ("The Happiest Place on Earth") that masks its enormous profit gains. But the characters of Shrek, Donkey, Princess Fiona, and Lord Farquaad are themselves marketed and exploited for profit. Aisle upon aisle of *Shrek* paraphernalia can be found in toy stores and video stores, on cereal boxes and candy wrappers, in magazines and newspapers. It appears that although the plot of *Shrek* attempts to critique the very industry of entertainment, it is unwilling to critique or sacrifice itself as a participant in that economic system.

SUMMARY

In essence, critical approaches to analysis cause the critic to focus on how symbols, often masked or creatively modified, function to legitimize and sustain social systems wherein the interests of some are held in dominion over the interests of others. Do note that critical approaches are not looking at or for propaganda per se or subliminal advertising, both of which imply a kind of intentionality and self-awareness of manipulative symbol production. The kinds of subtle mechanisms of maintaining power explored by critical theorists are more often than not unintentional and unintentionally masked by both those in power and those not in power. The very absence of intentionality and awareness is what keeps the power struggle a struggle, as we see in the case of *Beauty and the Beast.* Those who appear out of power sometimes have a sort of power by seeing the entrapment of those who are seemingly in power. Those who appear out of power may unknowingly create symbols that recreate the domination, or those in power may unknowingly offer ways for the oppressed to critique the political order. Theorist Michel Foucault writes that individuals "circulate between [powers'] threads; they are always in a position of simultaneously undergoing and exercising this power" (1980, 198). So, the rhetorical critic looks not only for the way those symbols create or reinforce injustices but also for the ways those symbols offer avenues for resistance and liberation. Our analysis of *Shrek* illustrates this.

You should also note that this kind of analysis often works in conjunction with other analytical perspectives. Because we examined two films with clear narrative structures, we needed to use the language of narrative analysis to help focus our analysis on the types of symbols in the films that helped legitimize and naturalize certain socioeconomic positions. We looked at how the characters (e.g., Donkey and the fairy-tale creatures in *Shrek* and servants in *Beauty and the Beast*) represented race and class conflicts; and we looked at how the plots (e.g., the liberation of the fairy-tale creatures in *Shrek* and Belle's concern only for herself rather than her social class) challenged and reinforced class conflicts and differentials. We also looked at how the settings (e.g., the mimicry of Disneyland and Disney World) drew attention to the exploitative relationship between consumers and profit makers in the Disney Corporation. The questions asked in the ideological approach may require you to use additional tools to help explain *how* power relations are represented in a message.

When would a critic choose to use this approach? Because power relations are everywhere (in families, in corporations, in nonprofit organizations, in politics, in education, in religion), we would argue that it is always good for a critic to be conscious of how any message wields or challenges power. However, you will likely find this approach most interesting and useful if the message gives you a particular reason to be concerned with how problematic power relations are reinforced in a message, especially if it is subtle—something the audience is likely to overlook because of some other personal appeal in the message. It is important to recognize, too, that in using this approach you are leading yourself to an evaluation that will be based on beliefs about the importance of equity in all kinds of contexts. If you do not hold those beliefs (e.g., if you believe in the authority of a priest over his parish), you likely would not find the representation of power in a message to be problematic. It may also be the case that although you find the representation of power interesting in a message, you may find more interesting the way the message maker uses classical strategies to accomplish his or her ends or the way the message maker uses dramatic strategies to convince the audience of his or her position. In other words, you may find that other elements of the message are more compelling to you and better help you explain how the message functions. In that case, you should rely on more traditional analytical approaches.

The next two approaches we discuss, feminist and postmodern, are close affiliates of ideological approaches, but with slightly different emphases. The problem of subordination and power, however, remains central.

EXERCISES

1. Go to a fast-food restaurant not to consume, but to observe. Study the displays of food, the arrangement of tables, the décor, the advertising on the walls and windows, and the direction and pacing of traffic throughout the restaurant. Consider all of these elements to be symbols.

2. Analyze the "rhetoric" of the restaurant by answering these questions:

   - How do the symbols in the restaurant suggest that the good of the people is being served?
   - How is "junk food" legitimized symbolically?
   - How do the symbols discourage the consumers (audience) from raising questions about their experience, and whose interests are being served by their consumption in that restaurant or by questions about the value of the fast-food industry?
   - How do the various symbols make the fast-food experience appear to be part of the natural course of daily American life?
   - How is the representation of daily American life given authority in the symbols?

3. Write a short essay in which you first describe the experience of that restaurant from the perspective of a consumer. Then analyze the experience in terms of the domination of the industry over the consumer. Expose what the consumer, in his or her haste, is unlikely to see about how the restaurant symbols legitimize the fast-food industry despite its known health hazards.

NOTES

1 For a thorough analysis of hegemonic masculinity, see R. W. Connell, *Gender and Power* (Stanford: Stanford University Press, 1987) and R. W. Connell, "An Iron Man: The Body and Some Contradictions of Hegemonic Masculinity," in *Sport, Men and the Gender Order: Critical Feminist Perspectives,* edited by Michael A. Messner and Don F. Sabo, 83–96 (Champaign, IL: Human Kinetics, 1990).

WORKS CITED

Brown, Senator Joseph E. (Ga.). "Speech Opposing a Constitutional Amendment for Woman Suffrage, January 25, 1887." In *History of Woman Suffrage,* IV, 1883–1900, edited by Susan B. Anthony and Ida Husted, 93–100, 105–108. New York: Arno & *The New York Times,* 1969.

Connell, R. W. "An Iron Man: The Body and Some Contradictions of Hegemonic Masculinity." In *Sport, Men and the Gender Order: Critical Feminist Perspectives,* edited by Michael A. Messner and Don F. Sabo, 83–96. Champaign, IL: Human Kinetics, 1990.

———. *Gender and Power.* Stanford, CA: Stanford University Press, 1987.

Donovan, Josephine. *Feminist Theory: The Intellectual Traditions of American Feminism.* New York: Continuum, 1992.

Douglass, Frederick. "The Claims of the Negro Ethnologically Considered." Speech delivered at Western Reserve College in Rochester, NY, July 12, 1854. In *The Life and Writings of Frederick Douglass,* edited by Philip S. Foner, Vol. 2, 289–309. New York: International Publishers, 1950.

Foucault, Michel. *Power/Knowledge: Selected Interviews and Other Writings 1927–1977.* Edited and translated by Colin Gordon. New York: Pantheon, 1980.

Gramsci, Antonio. "The Intellectuals." In *Selections from the Prison Notebooks,* translated and edited by Q. Hoare and G. N. Smith, 3–23. New York: International Publishers, 1971. *Marxist Internet Archive,* April 5, 2002. http://www.marxists.org/archive/gramsci/editions/spn/problems/intellectuals.htm (accessed November 20, 2003).

Habermas, Jürgen. *Communication and the Evolution of Society.* Translated by Thomas McCarthy. Boston: Beacon Press, 1976.

Lenin, V. I. "The Three Sources and Three Component Parts of Marxism." In *Karl Marx and Frederick Engels: Selected Works,* 23–27. New York: International Publishers, 1968.

"Mall of America." *Destination Bloomington Minnesota.* Bloomington Convention and Visitor's Bureau. http://www.bloomingtonmn.org/mallofamerica.asp (accessed October 22, 2003).

Marx, Karl, and Frederick Engels. *Communist Manifesto.* Authorized trans. Ed. Frederick Engels. New York: New York Labor News, 1968.

Messner, Michael, A. *Power At Play: Sports and the Problem of Masculinity.* Boston: Beacon Press, 1992.

SUGGESTED READINGS

Cloud, Dana. "Hegemony or Concordance? The Rhetoric of Tokenism in 'Oprah' Winfrey's Rags to Riches Biography." *Critical Studies in Mass Communication* 13 (1996): 115–37.

Jordan, John W. "Sabotage or Performed Compliance: Rhetorics of Resistance in Temp Worker Discourse." *Quarterly Journal of Speech* 89 (2003): 19–40.

McKerrow, Raymie E. "Critical Rhetoric: Theory and Praxis." *Communication Monographs* 56 (1989): 91–111.

Mechling, Elizabeth Walker, and Jay Mechling. "The Campaign for Civil Defense and the Struggle to Naturalize the Bomb." *Western Journal of Speech Communication* 6 (1989): 61–80.

Vavrus, Mary Douglas. "Domesticating Patriarchy: Hegemonic Masculinity and Television's 'Mr. Mom.'" *Critical Studies in Mass Communication* 19 (2002): 352–75.

Wander, Philip. "The Ideological Turn in Modern Criticism." *Central States Speech Journal* 34 (1983): 1–18.

15

FEMINIST APPROACHES

Think for a moment about the college classes you are currently attending. Whether you are male or female, the presence of women in these classrooms probably seems nothing unusual to you. If you saw any of them in a voting poll booth next to you, you would probably think nothing of it. And if after college you and one of those women landed the same entry-level job with your local newspaper, whether you are male or female, you would probably assume that you would both earn the same salary. Indeed we find it difficult to imagine today that less than a hundred years ago women could not vote and that just over a hundred years ago women were not permitted to attend college with men or not permitted to attend college at all, since higher education was believed by many to be wasted on women. Assuming you agree that women should be permitted to attend college (with men), vote, and earn salaries equivalent to those of their male counterparts, you are a person who holds some feminist beliefs. If someone were to come to your college campus and protest the presence of women, you probably cannot imagine yourself making a sign and joining the protest. Your resistance, whether active or passive, is grounded in thinking that is in some way feminist. In fact, you might find yourself interested in the protest rhetoric not only to learn how the protesters attempt to appeal to passersby, but you might find yourself interested in and troubled by the content of their messages, particularly how their discourse portrays women and men, and their relationship to one another.

In the discipline of communication, the study of women and rhetoric began with the study of women orators, specifically those who spoke on behalf of women's rights in the nineteenth and early twentieth centuries. Traditional approaches (e.g., classical and dramatistic) were used to study these texts, but many scholars began to recognize that the study of messages by feminist rhetors, using traditional approaches, was not the same as examining *any* text using a feminist approach (Dow 1995, 106). In fact, as feminists began to recognize the impact of culture on gender relations, they became increasingly interested in the portrayal and representation of women in not only public speech but also media and mediated images, and they became increasingly interested in the possibility that traditional analytical approaches like the classical and dramatistic approaches implicitly devalued a type of rhetoric more common to women. Scholars became interested, for example, in a "feminine style" in speeches on all kinds of topics (Dow and Tonn 1993, 286). Others became interested in the representation of women in popular films, like *Thelma and Louise* (e.g., Cooper 2000), or by popular celebrities, like Princess Diana (e.g., Rushing 1998), and in advertising (e.g., Rakow 1992). So today a feminist approach may be useful in examining a wide variety of texts; the determining factor is whether you, the critic, are interested in the dynamic of gender in those texts. If, for example, you watch reality TV shows like *The Bachelor, The Bachelorette,* or *Average Joe* and take interest in the way the shows portray women and men and their relationship to one another, you would find a feminist approach useful. You may be even more inclined to use a feminist approach on some occasions as you come to understand the variety of feminist perspectives that critics take.

Unfortunately, the term *feminism* is frequently misconstrued, misused, and simply avoided by many. Feminism is a complex concept, evident by the fact that women and men who proclaim to be feminist themselves disagree about its meaning. One can safely say that all feminists recognize the historic social injustices suffered by women from **patriarchy**, which is *the domination of men and male thinking and speech in the political, social, and economic structure of a culture*. All feminists believe that because of the patriarchy, women have been denied certain rights assumed to be natural and inalienable for men, and that because of the patriarchy, women have been denied certain privileges enjoyed by men, including an equal voice and participation in social, political, and economic life outside the domestic sphere of the home. Although all feminists generally share a concern about the implications of patriarchy for women, they do not all agree about the nature and causes of women's conditions, nor do they agree on the changes necessary to achieve gender equality. They disagree about the issues of concern to women, about the causes of women's oppression, about what constitutes women's oppression, and about the ideals and goals for women as a political group. Because of these disagreements, a host of philosophical feminist perspectives have evolved over the years. Some focus on the ways in which men and women are similar, arguing that equity lies in the recognition of our basic common nature, whereas others emphasize presumed differences between men and women, arguing that gender inequities stem from the devaluing of women's differences from men.

In what follows we present three broad strands of feminist thought: liberal feminism, cultural feminism, and postmodern feminism.[1] Although there are more than these three feminist perspectives[2] and not all theorists agree on the labels for these categories (liberal, cultural, and feminist), we find these three terms and constructs to be sufficiently comprehensive and comprehendible for novice critics. As we briefly describe each orientation, we will demonstrate how those philosophies might assist in an analysis of rhetorical messages. Male or female, you will likely find yourself agreeing *and* disagreeing with various parts of these philosophies, and, male or female, you will find each of these philosophies relevant to your experience. It is important to remember that when analyzing a text from a feminist perspective, whichever of the three you use, you keep clear in your mind the general feminist concern about whether the text is progressive or regressive for the cause of women and men. You might consider which, if any, of the following three perspectives *the text* suggests, but, more important, your interpretation and evaluation of the text will depend on which of these three perspectives (or some combination) *you personally* uphold.[3]

LIBERAL FEMINISM

Liberal feminism was the dominant philosophy of the early women's rights and suffrage activists of the nineteenth and early twentieth centuries. *This perspective argues that women are entitled to the same inalienable, "natural" rights as men because they are, essentially, the same as men: reasoning, independent, autonomous human beings* (Donovan 1992, 8). Drawing from abolitionist arguments of the nineteenth century and civil rights arguments in the 1960s, still today liberal feminists argue that all humans, men and women of all colors and creeds, are created equal and that, on those grounds alone, women deserve the same basic rights as men: the right to vote, the right to equal representation in the government, and the right to divorce, for example. By the twentieth century, liberal feminist thinking motivated women to pursue other equalities as well: equal pay, equal access to jobs and careers, equal representation in education, and equal representation in popular culture, the arts, and more.

In America, the liberal feminist position accepts the existing political and economic structure as it is, but demands that women be assimilated fairly and equally into that structure. The argument is similar to those made by mainstream civil rights activists like Frederick Douglass and the Reverend Dr. Martin Luther King Jr. who argued that black Americans are essentially (by nature) the same as white Americans and are, therefore, entitled to the same *natural rights* afforded to white Americans, rights such as voting, ownership of property, and representation in government. These activists argued for the assimilation of black Americans into the white American culture, economy, and political structure. Liberal feminists argue the same for women.

In the 1960s and 1970s academics began paying attention to the ways in which women were not equally represented in various disciplines. Just as they were not equally represented in the workforce, women were not equally represented in popular culture, scientific studies, medical studies, and more. In the field of communication, scholars noted that men's speeches had been studied, but not women's (Campbell 1989, 1). Feminists began to argue that scholarly attention ought to be paid to women's oratory as well as men's. So the very act of studying women's oratory was, in a sense, a liberal feminist critique, but the approaches to analysis were not necessarily *feminist* in nature (Dow 1995, 106). Over the past thirty years feminist scholars not only have studied women's oratory but also the representation of women in rhetorical texts, analyzing the way symbols are used to enhance or deter efforts toward sexual equality. Such an approach is more explicitly feminist. For example, scholar Martha Solomon studied the rhetoric that Equal Rights Amendment (ERA) opponent Phyllis

Schlafly used to convince women of the evils of the ERA. Solomon's analysis of Schlafly's messages suggests her concern that the antifeminists have a more persuasive appeal in their message than feminists do, because of their representation of women as mythic heroes. Solomon (1979) argues, for example, that whereas the feminist persuasive techniques of the 1970s urged women to discover individual truths about themselves as women through in-depth self-analysis, Schlafly offered "conveniently discovered truths and simplistic answers guaranteed to produce fulfillment and happiness" (273). Solomon clarifies her concern about the more effective STOP ERA rhetoric over the feminist rhetoric when she states, "Schlafly's ability to create a myth which so effectively taps the cultural reservoirs is almost certainly one critical factor in her success. The inability of her opposition [feminists] to create such a compelling vision may be the source of much of their political frustration" (274). Solomon's evaluative position springs from a liberal feminist orientation. She observes with frustration the way Schlafly portrays the "Positive Woman" as achieving her goals and fulfillment "not through courage or daring active qualities, but through cheerfulness in adversity and faithfulness to tradition—passive virtues" (264). In other words, Schlafly affirms traditional assumptions about woman's unique characteristics and responsibilities that are different from man's: nurturing her home and family, supporting and encouraging her husband, weaving the moral fabric of society. For Schlafly, women "are defined by the group, and are encouraged to define themselves in terms of these roles" (269). By contrast, argues Solomon, the feminist orientation was (and should have been) focused on the individual personalities of women—viewing women as people, like men, rather than as women, different from men. Ultimately Solomon judges Schlafly's rhetoric as effective, but she makes that claim not so much in praise for Schlafly as in concern from a liberal feminist perspective about the problem of viewing women as naturally different from men and, thus, necessarily designed for traditional roles and behaviors (274).

A critic with a liberal feminist perspective might examine a presidential candidate's campaign speeches, asking whether his or her representation of women makes them seem different and thus inferior to men, or whether the representations portray women as essentially the same as men, sharing the same rights, goals, concerns, and needs. Similarly, a liberal feminist critic may analyze the way women's roles have changed over the course of time on a television series like *Star Trek*. Such a perspective would note the praiseworthy move of including a black female, Lieutenant Uhura played by Nichelle Nichols, on the crew of the first *Star Trek* series. But the critic would be still more interested in the development of female characters on subsequent *Star Trek* series, probably praising the progressive positioning of women in traditionally male roles. For example, in *Star Trek: The Next Generation,* the ship's physician is female (Dr. Beverly Crusher). More progressive still is *Star Trek Voyager* in which the ship's captain is a woman (Captain Kathryn Janeway) as is the ship's chief engineer (Lieutenant B'Elanna Torres). A liberal feminist analysis would examine the characterization of these women to see how a television series implicitly advances the goal of assimilating women into existing sociopolitical and economic structures.

In analyzing a message from a liberal feminist position, the following questions can help guide your thinking:

- How does the message represent women, implicitly or explicitly?
- Does the representation of women suggest that women are essentially the same as or different from men?
- If women are portrayed as being different from men, how are their differences valued or devalued?
- How are the goals of assimilating women into the existing economic and sociopolitical structures advanced or hindered by the text? Do the representations of women perpetuate their exclusion from the mainstream economic and social systems? Or do the representations encourage their inclusion?

While liberal feminist arguments are agreeable to many, others have challenged two primary assumptions of liberal feminist thought: (1) that men and women *are* essentially the same and (2) that true equality for women can be attained in the existing sociopolitical and economic system. Alternative feminist viewpoints address these concerns.

CULTURAL FEMINISM

Whereas liberal feminists believe that women can achieve equality through the liberal democratic ideals of natural human rights, cultural feminists believe that the causes of inequality for women are rooted in complex ideologies about gender that are enmeshed in our culture and perpetuated more subtly through institutions like religion and mass media. **Cultural feminism** is *skeptical of the assimilation strategy, believing that more fundamental cultural and ideological changes are necessary if women are to attain true equality. Perhaps most pertinent to cultural feminism is the belief that while women are the same as men insofar as they are moral equals deserving of natural rights, they are also fundamentally different from men.* Donovan writes:

> Instead of emphasizing similarities between men and women, [cultural feminists] often stress the differences, ultimately affirming that feminine qualities may be a source of personal strength and pride and a fount of public regeneration. These feminists imagined alternatives to institutions the liberal theorists left more or less intact—religion, marriage, and the home. (1992, 31)

Cultural feminists argue that women do exhibit feminine qualities that are typically devalued in a patriarchal, capitalistic society. Such feminine qualities include women's concern about social connectedness and their inclination (perhaps because of their historical experience as mothers) to be life-affirming, creative, cooperative, and peaceful in contrast to the masculine qualities of dominance, forcefulness, competition, and individualism. For example, theorist Carol Gilligan argues that women's morality differs from men's, which is apparent in their rhetoric. Men make moral decisions based on principles of fairness, rights, and rules, all of which emphasize "separation rather than connection" and "consideration of the individual rather than the relationship as primary" (Gilligan 1982, 19). Women, however, process the immediate context and people's stories about that context, caring for the responsibilities and relationships at stake in a decision. The ethic of care motivates the feminine orientation toward responsibility and relationships, whereas the ethic of fairness motivates the masculine orientation toward justice.

In the field of communication studies, scholars have taken cultural feminist positions to examine women's discourse, highlighting the differences between women's style of speech and men's style of speech, both in the podium and in interpersonal relations. In studying the rhetoric of the contemporary women's movement, Karlyn Kohrs Campbell discovered that women participating in consciousness-raising groups in the late 1960s and early 1970s used what she called a "feminine style" that strategically adapted to the norms of femininity. The feminine style entailed these basic characteristics: (1) using a personal tone; (2) speaking from a position of peer rather than authority; (3) using examples, testimony, and enactment as evidence; (4) using inductive structure; and (5) making efforts to stimulate audience participation (Campbell 1973, 83; 1983, 106). In other words, the rhetorical style most suitable for women in that context focused on personal experience rather than distant abstraction; relied on concrete, personal evidence in the form of testimony and example; reasoned inductively from concrete (personal) case to concrete (personal) case; and assumed the connection of peers rather than the distance and domination of an authority. In studying the speeches of Texas governor Ann Richards, Bonnie Dow and Mari Boor Tonn discovered that Richards exemplified a feminine style that was not just appropriate for disempowered female audiences, but appealed widely to male and female audiences (1993, 298). Moreover, Richards's use of the feminine style (including concrete examples, personal anecdotes, and inductive reasoning) enabled her to advance a political philosophy governed by the ethics of care and empathy (294–96). Dow and Tonn recognize the importance of a feminine style not only in advancing women's causes, but in advancing a feminine orientation to politics more broadly (298–300).

Elsewhere Dow makes clear that Dow, Tonn, and Campbell all view "the feminine style as a *strategic* approach for some female rhetors, not as an *innate* characteristic" (Dow 1995, 108). Other scholars, however, perceive those differences to be innate. Feminist scholar Sally Miller Gearhart, for example, argues that women and men are biologically different and those differences are reflected in their communication. She argues that because of their biological capacity for reproduction, women are natural "nurturers, incubators, holders, enfolders, listeners" (Gearhart 1982, 197) and more concerned than men with the collective good. Thus, their communication features care and respect rather than persuasion and influence. Gearhart suggests that if we are to become a nonviolent society, the definition of rhetoric needs to focus on creating a caring, respectful environment in which change can occur rather than the traditionally male-oriented definition of rhetoric as persuasion and influence (1979, 198–99). For Gearhart, the feminist standard upon which messages are judged is not whether they are persuasive, but whether rhetors "feel love, care, connection, and warmth as a result of their interactions with others. . . . if, on the other hand, they feel disconnected, angry, and frustrated, their rhetoric is not effective" (Foss, Foss, and Griffin 1999, 288–89).

Other scholars are less clear about whether women's communication styles are a function of nurture or nature. Nonetheless they agree that women's modes of communication, more than men's, are relational in focus and purpose—concerned with equality, personal and concrete, among participants (Hall and Langellier 1988, 123; Treichler and Kramarae 1983, 119–21). Cheris Kramarae, for example, focuses on linguistic differences among men and women. Some of the differences she notes are about the cultural expectations of men's and women's talk. Women, for example, are urged not to talk too much and not to interrupt (Kramarae 1974, 16–17). More important, Kramarae points out that language is central to the social construction of reality, and the reality about women created through common daily language is generally subordinating. For example, the titles for women of "Mrs." and "Miss" reveal their marital status, a male interest, according to Kramarae (West, Lazar, and Kramarae 1997, 121). "Mr." reveals nothing of marital status, making clear that men have held control in constructing a language system toward their interests, whereas women have not had the same role in constructing the language system they live and operate in. Language systems often fail to account for the experience of women, according to Kramarae. Her theory, then, urges the critic to pay close attention to how language perpetuates male domination or constructions of gender, both masculine and feminine, that discourage the growth and interconnectedness of those participating in the language. Ideal rhetoric would be that which offers language in which women are comfortable (Foss, Foss, and Griffin 1999, 63).

Arguments about the differences between men and women inevitably give rise to questions about whether those differences are social or biological. As you can see, cultural feminists have different leanings on that question, but what binds them together is their concern that feminine qualities (specifically feminine forms of speech), whether socially or biologically derived, are less valued than masculine qualities. According to cultural feminists, this discrepancy cannot be resolved merely by assimilating women into the existing culture. The culture itself, particularly its ideologies regarding gender, must change. Voting rights, for example, do not solve the problem of how women are required to speak in traditionally and predominantly male environments. For many years women have struggled with the double bind they face in sometimes needing and choosing to behave assertively in their jobs yet being shunned by colleagues who expect women to be pleasant, gentle, and compliant. Cultural feminists doubt the ability of basic equal rights to address these deeper, more disturbing undercurrents of sexual politics that perpetuate a patriarchal culture.

A critic examining a message from a cultural feminist position examines how gender is portrayed in the message. Specifically, the critic analyzes how women and men are portrayed differently, whether they are portrayed as essentially the same or essentially different. If men and women are depicted as holding different gender orientations, the critic looks for cues as to whether feminine *and* masculine qualities are valued or whether one is valued over the other. Additionally, the critic questions whether the message presumes that equality can be achieved within the status quo or whether some more radical ideological, economic, or political change is necessary. For example, in 1992 critic Bonnie Dow published an analysis of the television show *Murphy Brown,* a series that featured a female television news anchor, Murphy Brown. Her analysis carefully examined Murphy's character: what she said, what she wore, what she did. By using the principles of both liberal feminism and radical feminism, Dow was able to demonstrate how the show celebrates the liberal feminist value of Murphy having equal career opportunities and having competed successfully with her male colleagues (1992, 144–47). At the same time, Dow discovered that the character of Murphy rejects traditional femininity by enacting a competitive, aggressive, and interpersonally insensitive personality. Dow demonstrates how the audience is made to poke fun at Murphy's enactment of masculinity, thereby overlooking the central social problem that to be successful she must behave as a man in a man's world (1992, 151–52). Dow argues from a cultural (what she calls radical) feminist orientation that Murphy herself devalues feminine qualities, suggesting that women must abandon their femininity if they are to assimilate successfully into the male-dominated workforce. After analyzing the representation of the construct of "woman" on the show, Dow ultimately offers a negative evaluation of how the show celebrates liberal feminism. She suggests that in fact the show actually illustrates the limitations of liberal feminism (1992, 152–53).

When analyzing messages from a cultural feminist position, you might ask yourself the following questions:

- Does the message portray men and women as essentially the same or as qualitatively different?
- Does the portrayal of differences between men and women serve to value one gender over another? If so, how? With what consequences?
- Does the message suggest that sexual equality can be attained within the dominant sociopolitical and economic structure? Or does the message challenge the status quo? What are the consequences of this challenge (or lack thereof) for women and men?
- What styles of communication are evident in the message? Masculine? Feminine?
- How does the style of communication in the message fit with the presumed audience of the message? Who might be welcomed or distanced by the style?
- How does the language of the message diminish women's experiences or type of speech? Or how does the language of the message affirm women's experiences or speech? How comfortable would women be with the type of speech used in the message?
- Does the message create an environment of care, cooperation, and respect or does it emphasize persuasion, influence, and assertion?

A critic using this approach might analyze presidential debates, comparing the town hall style of debate to the traditional podium-speech style of debate to see if one is more likely to balance feminine and masculine styles. A critic might also analyze the messages of the debaters to determine whether their styles are more or less masculine or feminine. Or the critic might seek to determine whether the content of their arguments implicitly sustain a male-dominated orientation that is competitive and individualistic, or whether the arguments imply an orientation that values collaboration and interdependency.

In sum, the cultural feminist perspective highlights some underlying belief systems, assumptions, and cultural systems that make it difficult for men and women to live in absolute equity. The cultural feminist perspective chooses to feature the ways in which men and women are different in an effort to celebrate and value that which is feminine and has, historically, been devalued. However, when analyzing rhetoric from a cultural feminist perspective, one must be careful of the temptation to overgeneralize (or naturalize) the qualities of men and women. The foremost limitation of this perspective is the potential for the critic to assume that all men or all women share certain characteristics. Such an assumption is dangerous. First, individual psychological and physiological differences may render such assumptions erroneous. Second, women are all enmeshed in other social and historical contexts that challenge the assumption that the notion of womanhood is universal. African-American women may have different styles than Euro-American or Asian women. So generalizing among African American or Asian women might lead to erroneous assumptions. Third, the naturalization of the qualities of men and women can be used against a feminist cause, giving opponents reason to discriminate. If a feminist asserts, for example, that women are naturally caring and nurturing and men are naturally invasive and aggressive, a military official has grounds for arguing that women ought not be allowed in combat units of the military. *This tendency to assume that all women, men, or any other grouping are "essentially" the same* is referred to as **essentialization** and is something critics look out for in the messages they examine as well as in themselves (Wood 1992, 5). The problem of essentialization is the basis for the third feminist philosophy we examine: postmodern feminism.

POSTMODERN FEMINISM

The term **postmodernism** is highly complex and loaded with many varied and conflicting connotations, but for our purposes it may be defined as *a general contemporary skepticism of objectivity, absolutism, universality, and precise rationality*. What does that mean? Postmodernist thinkers question the assumptions born of the seventeenth-century Enlightenment that through careful objective observation we can discover the absolute, universal patterns of nature in order to control it. Postmodernist thinkers believe that one can never be fully objective, and so there is no perfectly objective knowledge. They doubt the existence of universal truths, particularly universal truths about the nature of humanity. A postmodern perspective on religion, for example, might conclude that religion is not a representation of any absolute spiritual truth but is always a construction of spiritual reality that is limited by the political structure of religious institutions, the cultural norms of those within the religion, the language used to discuss and convey the religion, the historical time period for any given religious practices, and so forth. A postmodern thinker may or may not necessarily reject religion altogether because of these conditions, but he or she would be skeptical of its claims to absolute truth.

Given the concerns we just raised about the inclination for cultural feminist thinking to assume universal truths about men and women, it is not surprising that many feminists have taken on a postmodern perspective and rejected the cultural feminist emphasis on a universal, stable, and definable notion of womanhood. Kramarae anticipated this concern back in the 1970s when she wrote that although it is important to investigate how women speak and how people think women should speak, "it must be realized that women are individuals. Researchers interested in studying the speech of women as women . . . must be careful not to make the error of grouping all women together" (1974, 24). **Postmodern feminism** *insists that feminists themselves hold different perspectives or standpoints because of the variations in their experience due to age, race, ethnicity, class, or sexual preference, and it expresses doubt that the differences between men and women are permanent or universal.* Postmodern feminist thinking often relies on "standpoint theory," which urges feminists to focus not just on women, but on "how women understand and represent their lives," which will differ from woman to woman (Wood 1992, 14). Differences may also be a function of the culture men and women live in, the time in history in which they are speaking and acting, or their political and economic conditions. For example, one might find that the communication style among black slave women of the antebellum period was quite different from that of upper-class white women. In fact, postmodern feminism argues that to make claims about the nature of woman or womanhood is merely to make claims about the experience of a few women, more likely than not, white women. So postmodern feminists urge critics to more carefully represent the specific or distinctive concerns, experiences, and interests of women—women of color, women of varied sexual orientation, women of different religious belief, women of different classes—and to question assumptions about essential differences between men and women or essential similarities among women. Moreover, critics must question whether these claims privilege some groups of people over others. The postmodern feminist warns of the constant danger of essentializing any category of women. Not all Hispanic or Asian or lesbian women, for example, can be lumped together. The postmodern orientation keeps the critic cautious of this problematic inclination.

Feminists of color have been particularly instrumental in raising these questions. Black feminist theorist bell hooks writes:

A central tenet of modern feminist thought has been the assertion that "all women are oppressed." This assertion implies that women share a common lot, that factors like class, race, religion, sexual preference, etc. do not create a diversity of experience that determines the extent to which sexism will be an oppressive force in the lives of individual women. Sexism as a system of domination is institutionalized, but it has never determined in an absolute way the fate of all women in this society. (2000, 5)

Hooks encourages critics to examine television and film because they impact how society perceives oppressed people. She encourages the critic to examine all forms of domination in texts and to look for ways in which texts allow audiences to hear the particular experiences or perspectives of those outside the margins, including women of color, poor women, elderly women, lesbians, and others. The representation of a wide variety of "standpoints" becomes the basis for a critic's judgment. If few standpoints are offered in a text, the critic must judge that text negatively insofar as it suggests an essentialized view of women that overlooks important needs and conditions of women from different walks of life.

A critic analyzing a text from a postmodern feminist position might ask the following kinds of questions about a text:

- Does the message, via its words, dialogue, or visual representations, portray women as being "one of a kind"? If so, how is that portrayal problematic for women of a different experience?
- If the representation of women in the message is progressive, for whom is it progressive? How does the advancement for women suggested by the message play out for women of different races, classes, sexual orientations, or ages?
- If the representation of women in the message is not progressive, what relationship does that negative representation have for women of different races, classes, sexual orientations, or ages?
- Does the message represent men as being "one of a kind"? If so, how is that representation problematic for men of a different experience?

As a critic you might, for example, analyze a senator's speech on abortion, asking how women are represented in the speech. Are they portrayed as having different experiences, coming from different social, racial, and economic backgrounds? Are they portrayed as having a unified moral outlook on the problem of abortion and the same ethical approach to the problem? Are men portrayed as essentially the same? Having the same moral orientation and experience? The critic looking for these essentializations is also concerned with which hegemony and whose dominant position the essentialized portrayal represents. For example, in analyzing the senator's representation of men and women, the critic might find that men are, in fact, portrayed as being essentially the same. Moreover, that sameness might be representative of the hegemonic masculinity that corporations want men to enact (aggressive, competitive, successful, heterosexual, and in domination over women). The critic might find that representation not only inaccurate but also oppressive to men. In analyzing the media representations of former Texas baseball star

Nolan Ryan, scholar Nick Trujillo explains that through sport, masculinity is reinforced in hegemonic ways that essentialize the features of a "real man" as one who (1) exercises physical force and control, (2) pursues occupational achievement, (3) reinforces familial patriarchy, (4) demonstrates frontiersmanship, and (5) is heterosexual (1991, 291). Television, newspaper, and magazine articles on Nolan Ryan repeatedly represent him in terms of these five features, reinforcing the cultural hegemonic view of the real man, who is thus essentialized. Trujillo writes that these media "castigate individuals who do not" conform to these qualities and "depict alternatives . . . as unconventional or deviant" (293). Of course, not all men are masculine in these ways, but one would not see those variations in the mainstream media.

Although a postmodern feminist perspective wisely recognizes the inappropriateness and injustice of assuming all women or all men have the same experience, the perspective potentially creates the problem of making unity among women, in particular, difficult. To achieve political action, leaders of any cause must rally their supporters to unite around a perceived shared cause. When feminists focus on the differences in women's experiences, they risk losing the cohesion necessary to mobilize people toward action and political impact. The critic must also recognize this limitation when judging a text from a postmodern feminist perspective.

To better understand a feminist approach to message analysis, let's reexamine *Beauty and the Beast* and *Shrek,* both of which offer interesting representations of women and men and their relationship to one another.

FEMINIST CONCEPTS APPLIED TO BEAUTY AND THE BEAST AND SHREK

The animated films *Beauty and the Beast* and *Shrek* share a similar moral theme; both challenge the common cultural value of physical appearance, suggesting that people are not as they appear and we must look past physical appearances to love another person. The overarching moral might be considered the same, but when these films are viewed from a feminist perspective, they appear quite different. By comparing these two films we can see what might be gained from an analysis using different feminist orientations.

Disney's version of the Beauty and the Beast fairy tale does, in fact, challenge the cultural value of physical appearance. One might even note that this particular rendition of the story offers a liberal feminist portrayal of Belle. She is portrayed as having intellectual interests and abilities traditionally presumed to belong to men. When she enters the village bookshop, she asks what new books are in, suggesting she has read them all. The shop owner's reply "Not since yesterday!" tells us that Belle is not only a reader, but a voracious one. In the song "Belle" the villagers describe her as beautiful but "peculiar," "odd," "always having her nose in a book." When wooed by Gaston he makes the sexist remark, "It's about time you got your head out of those books and paid attention to more important things . . . like me." Then he adds, "It's not right for a woman to read. Soon she starts getting ideas, and thinking." By contrast, the Beast offers Belle all the books in his vast library. As the villain, Gaston's sexist remarks are to be read as foolish, suggesting that this feminist Belle can do what men can do, read what men can read, think what men can think. In short, Belle is portrayed as an autonomous individual capable of rational thought, just as any man.

Although we see some progressive feminist depictions in the characterization of Belle in Disney's version, the way the plot challenges the value of physical appearance ultimately reinforces patriarchal ideology that, according to radical feminist Shulamith Firestone, (1) insists on an ideal feminine beauty and (2) is perpetuated through the ideology of romance (Donovan 1992, 148–49). The ideology of romance tells women that they should, ultimately, live for men, romance, and sex through which they will attain happiness. Men, romance, and sex, then, become the ends of their existence. Consequently, women become love objects that must be physically adorned as the male pleases (hence, the ideal feminine beauty). And as objects, women are devalued as a class. This insistence on an idealized feminine beauty is evident in the very naming of the heroine "Belle" (French for "Beauty"). Belle's feminine beauty is exceptional and gets attention from the other characters in the film. The villagers sing, "It's no wonder that her name means beauty. Her looks have got no parallel." Both Gaston and the Beast are attracted to her beauty, and though she must learn to love the Beast for his internal beauty, her external beauty is never brought into question. No male is required to do the same of her: a "truly loving," gentle, and kind female is also a physical beauty.

Additionally, the ideology of romance is reinforced throughout by the plot's conclusion as the Beast becomes a handsome prince and the two live "happily ever after" in a romantic, upper-class condition. Ultimately, as the Beast is transformed into a handsome prince, the cultural (and perhaps oppressive) ideals about romance and gender roles stay in place. Belle doesn't really have to love a beast, and certainly the Beast doesn't have to love an "unattractive" woman. True love (characterized in the film as heterosexual, involving physically attractive and wealthy as well as inwardly attractive people) is the ultimate life conclusion (happily ever after). In a sense, the patriarchal values that rely on romantic ideology are reinforced by the plot of *Beauty and the Beast.*

Shrek, by contrast, challenges the cultural value of physical appearance by framing that value as part of a patriarchal ideology that needs to be dismantled. To a certain extent, *Shrek* functions as a radical feminist critique of patriarchal ideologies. By analyzing *Shrek* in terms of cultural feminist concepts, we see at least five ways in which the plot and characters offer a more radical/ cultural feminist perspective on patriarchal systems.

First, the alteration of the plot from the expected fairy-tale story line in which the beast (or other ugly frog, etc.) is turned into a handsome/beautiful body challenges the ideology that makes women into objects of beauty and challenges the ideology of romance noted by Firestone, which ultimately requires women to uphold a false ideal of physical perfection. The viewers are directly encouraged to question their own assumptions of the romantic ideal and ensuing gender relations as Fiona herself states what the viewer might be thinking when she discovers she has been rescued by an ogre: "But this can't be right. . . . You know how it goes. . . . Everyone knows what happens when you meet your true love." Suddenly, what's "right" about gender relations is no longer certain. The altered ending itself critically draws the viewer's attention to the way in which *Beauty and the Beast* reinforces a patriarchal gender ideology.

Second, not only does the unique transformation of appearance challenge the ideology of romance, but the fact that Fiona does not become a princess at all challenges that ideology. Part of the gender stereotype in the ideology of romance is that a woman achieves social status only through a man. Here we see a woman who chooses against such social status.

Third, the fact that the story's hero remains an ogre challenges the patriarchal ideology that perpetuates stereotypes not only about women but also about the ideal male. Scholars refer to ideologies that perpetuate macho idealism as *hegemonic masculinity* (Messner 1992, 18). In *Beauty and the Beast*, Gaston embodies this ideal masculinity as he is praised for being "burly" and "hairy," for having large biceps, for being "the size of a barge," for his ability to wrestle, shoot guns, and even for decorating his home with antlers. Although the film pokes fun of that excessive masculinity, in many ways the Beast upholds the same qualities. He uses brute force when necessary (though he also learns gentility); as the handsome prince he is strong, young, virile looking, his head enshrouded in thick long golden hair. Certainly he is not ugly, small, bald, or unathletic. While Shrek is a big, burly, strong ogre, those masculine qualities are portrayed as protective layers to cover his awareness of feelings of inadequacy and loneliness. Shrek describes himself to Donkey as having "layers" like an onion. Later, Donkey poignantly forces Shrek to confront his fears of intimacy, asking him who he is trying to keep out by secluding himself in his swamp. Donkey probes, "You're afraid of your own feelings." Such a discussion among male characters is not typical of fairy tales, much less most portrayals of hegemonic masculine characters.

Fourth, in contrast to the male hero who ultimately resists the patriarchal traps of the ideology of romance and hegemonic masculinity, the villain, Lord Farquaad, embodies those ideological traps, and because he is the villain, the viewer is made to find those qualities repulsive. Lord Farquaad is portrayed as sexist and misogynistic. He desires domination and control. In fact, his primary interest in Fiona is not her or true love, but the fact that marrying her will give him the status of king. In fact, he selects Fiona as his wife-to-be (a commodity) when she is presented to him in a mock version of the old television show *The Dating Game*. He is permitted to choose from Cinderella, Sleeping Beauty, and Fiona. All three princesses are presented as objectified commodities and the viewer is made to view this process as part of an unacceptable patriarchal social structure.

Finally, a few additional twists on the *Beauty and the Beast* narrative further dismantle patriarchal gender ideologies that keep women and men in unequal relation to one another. For example, Fiona is the princess of this story, thus she is the equivalent of Belle in *Beauty and the Beast*. But she is also the Beast insofar as she is the one upon whom the spell has been cast. She hides this masculine self in her and must be liberated to embrace it. Shrek and the audience are required to accept a woman whose appearance does not meet the cultural standard, which is perhaps more challenging than accepting an "unattractive" male. Fiona, like the Beast, must be accepted for who she is. But unlike the Beast, she must also accept the ogre for who he is, despite her expectations. The Beast does not face this challenge.

Shrek is, in many ways, the equivalent of Beast in that he is the unlovable male who has isolated himself because of his appearance. But Shrek is also the "Belle" who must accept Fiona for who she is, even when her appearance is no longer the cultural ideal. Just as Fiona must be liberated from gender stereotypes to embrace her masculine self, Shrek must be liberated from gender stereotypes that cause him to hide his feminine self that feels deeply.

In *Beauty and the Beast,* the princess must accept her dominator, her oppressor, in order to be happy. The teapot, Mrs. Potts, notes that Belle is a prisoner when she says, "The girl lost her father and her freedom all in one day." But in *Shrek,* the princess must accept herself and reject her oppressor (Lord Farquaad), who wants to use her for his own personal and political gain. From a cultural feminist position we might say that *Beauty and the Beast* reinforces the existing patriarchal system by convincing women they must love their oppressors in order to be happy. *Shrek,* by contrast, suggests that women must reject their oppressor and enter a self-accepting, egalitarian relationship in order to be free and happy.

Although *Shrek* appears to be a more radical critique of gender assumptions from a cultural feminist perspective, the film is limited in the extent to which it challenges patriarchy. For example, a cultural feminist perspective seeks to affirm feminine qualities as a source of strength. Radical/cultural feminist Roxanne Dunbar argues that women have been socialized to be caring, flexible, noncompetitive, and cooperative, but she advocates that women see these traits as necessary for a humane moral society. In fact, she argues for a dismantling of the existing, generally competitive democratic and economic system in order to establish a system governed by the feminine qualities just listed (Dunbar 1970, 53). In applying that perspective to an analysis of *Shrek,* one might see patterns of behavior in Fiona that suggest she co-opts masculine ideals rather than celebrates the virtues of feminine behavior. While making the trek back to Duloc, for instance, Fiona, Shrek, and Donkey suddenly encounter Robin Hood and his Merry Men who attack Fiona. Admirably and autonomously, Fiona defends herself with her martial arts skills, rather than depending on Shrek to rescue her. Then, when strolling along, Shrek and Fiona engage in a belching contest. Clearly Fiona can behave like a man. Although her autonomy is celebrated, we never see Fiona engaging in or celebrating any traditionally "feminine" behaviors that cultural feminists wish to celebrate as strengths. She never connects with other women, for example, and never aligns herself with her oppressed sisters, Cinderella and Sleeping Beauty. In fact, those two women are shown in the final scene fighting with each other over the dwarfs, rather than uniting in sisterhood against their oppressive conditions.

Perhaps most important, we see Fiona enacting her life's goal by finding true love. While she may be freed from some of the explicit oppressive patriarchal forces, one might argue that she still succumbs to the ideology of romance, which Donovan interprets from Firestone as an "opiate that keeps women drugged" (Donovan 1992, 148). In fact, we hear the lyrics in the closing, celebratory song, "I thought love was only true in fairy tales." "But I saw her face, now I'm a believer." So although the film is progressive with its feminist goals, it stops short of questioning the ideology of romance altogether.

SUMMARY

The three feminist orientations outlined here, liberal, cultural, and postmodern, merely scratch the surface of the depth and breadth of feminist thought. Our intent is to give you a sense of the different ways feminists think about the problem of sexual politics and to offer you some ways to critically examine the symbols you see in messages, as those symbols relate to men and women. We urge you to read further about these and other perspectives on feminism. In the meantime, however, when analyzing a message using the perspective of feminism, you must consider your own position about the power struggles between men and women. Then, depending on the perspective(s) you are concerned with in the message(s) you are analyzing, you must ask yourself a host of questions about the ways in which symbols, visual and verbal, are used to represent the experience of men and women, and their relationship to one another. As you begin to use this tool, you will be surprised at how many messages that don't, on their surface, appear to have anything to do with gender, in fact have a significant, subtle impact on how we come to think of ourselves as male or female.

EXERCISES

1. Study the article "Jewel Tones Return for the Holidays," from the Hispanic magazine *La Buena Vida* found at the end of this exercise section. Examine the text, focusing on the various techniques through which women are represented.

2. For this exercise you must take on perspectives about gender that you may not necessarily agree with; but try it for the sake of enhancing your understanding of what a feminist critique can illuminate.

   ■ First, adopt a liberal feminist point of view (even if it is not your own). Use the bulleted list of questions in the "Liberal Feminism" section of the chapter to analyze and interpret the article "Jewel Tones Return for the Holidays."
   ■ Second, analyze and interpret the article from a cultural feminist point of view, using the bulleted list of questions in the "Cultural Feminism" section of the chapter.
   ■ Third, analyze and interpret the article from a postmodern feminist point of view, using the bulleted list of questions in the "Postmodern Feminism" section of the chapter.

3. Write a brief, two-page essay explaining how your perceptions of the article differ depending on the feminist position you adopt. Which feminist position are you in most agreement with? Why?

Jewel Tones Return for the Holidays
by Linda Pliagas

There was little to celebrate last year. The country's focus on the events of Sept. 11 turned the mood—and the fashion—gloomy. But now it seems the nation is once again eager to take on the holidays in full force and ready to dress up for the occasion.

"We're ready to heal and take the steps to appreciate the life we're living," says Colleen Quen, a San Francisco–based fashion designer.

This year's holiday fashion shows just how much we want to start living again. Gone are last season's somber black gowns in subdued styles. This year, even Santa will be stunned by the sultry cuts and variety of colors available. "This is a time to start wearing color so that we can feel better about ourselves," Quen says. "When you wear black there is a certain psychological feeling that goes along with it, but when you wear color, it brings back your spirit." Nova Lorraine, an East Coast–based couturier with a master's degree in psychology, agrees: "Color makes a big difference in our aspect and our mood."

For the most part, people generally seem to shy away from color, says Lorraine, explaining that most consumers are not aware of which hues look best for their skin tone. Plus she adds that store buyers don't help consumers add spunk to their wardrobe because they tend to view basic colors as safer, more "sellable" items. So even if a woman wanted a vibrant gown, in prior seasons, the color she desired was usually difficult to find.

"My clients are frustrated by the lack of colors that are available," says Lorraine. Her designs are geared toward ethnic women—ladies who want more extravagant styles and shades than their Caucasian counterparts. "Women of color gravitate toward more colorful items. Color is just part of our culture."

It seems retail executives are finally listening to the pleas of ethnic women and finally adding more variety to their selections. Quen predicts that orange, red, yellow and chocolate brown will be the colors of choice for holiday socialites. Black will make a cameo, but it won't be a headliner. "If it is going to be black, there will be color in the print," she explains.

For holiday get-togethers, Lorraine's color preference is anything in metallic. Whether it is silver or gold, metallic colors will shimmer throughout the season. Metallics compliment [sic] bronzed skin tones wonderfully, an added bonus for darker-skinned Latinas, like salsa queen Celia Cruz. Cruz sparkled at the Third Annual Latin Grammy awards in Los Angeles wearing a striking long gold gown, which made her dark tone glow.

Marcie Pérez, a shopping expert for Marshalls, one of the nation's leading off-price retailers, says that all things sparkly are making a comeback. Nights will be lit up with shimmery flecks of gold, bronze and platinum incorporated into everything from off-the-shoulder tops to long taffeta gowns.

Lorraine also likes deep, rich colors, which she feels look great on a variety of skin tones, especially those of ethnic women. "My muse is the woman of color, so I tend to gravitate toward a lot of very earth tone colors—your rich burgundies, greens and blues."

Cuts will also play an important role this merry season. Whether a gown is sheered in all the right places, as shown by Alejandra Guzmán's spider-woman gown at the Grammy Awards, or plunged on the backside, like Roselyn Sánchez's how-low-can-you-go feminine lilac cocktail dress, sexy gowns will be provocatively slashed. The look will not be trashy, just titillating.

Skirt length will vary from mini and knee-length to floor sweeping. The appropriate measure will vary according to the event's dress code and the partygoers' age. "You're going to have your younger customers, probably under 35, gravitating toward the cocktail length. And then you are going to see your older clientele gravitate towards your full-length gown," Lorraine predicts.

Also popular among avant-garde socialites are pantsuits. "They're classic and depending on how they're cut, they can still be very sexy," Lorraine says. Quen predicts dressy pantsuits will become more relaxed and less tailored this holiday. She particularly likes pants with fuller legs so that it looks like a feminine skirt. It's clear that tailored, unisex dressing is definitely a thing of the past. This year, 'tis the season to be sexy.

NOTES

1 The terms *liberal feminism* and *cultural feminism* are adapted from Josephine Donovan's excellent overview of feminist thought in her book *Feminist Theory,* 2nd ed. (New York: Continuum Publishing, 1992). In her chapter entitled "The Eighties and Beyond," she describes the kind of thinking that we have categorized as postmodern liberalism. Others who use this term include Jane Flax in *Thinking Fragments: Psychoanalysis, Feminism, and Postmodernism in the Contemporary West* (Berkeley: University of California Press, 1990) and various authors in Linda Nicholson, ed., *Feminism/Postmodernism* (New York: Routledge, 1990).

2 One important feminist stance not included among these three is *socialist feminism.* Socialist feminism is rooted in Marxist philosophy and argues that the root cause of women's subordination is their material condition, which has been bound, historically, by their reproductive function. Socialist feminists argue that as long as women continue to be the primary caretakers of children, of the elderly, and of domestic life generally, they will continue to suffer injustices and subordination since, in a capitalistic society, the domestic (reproductive) sphere is qualitatively less valuable than the capital-seeking (productive) sphere and is, in fact, designed to provide the resources necessary for capitalism. For socialist feminists, assimilation of women into the existing system is an inadequate solution. Instead, they argue, the economic system must change if women are to gain true equality and social value. We have chosen to focus on the other three feminist philosophies because few feminist critics in the field of communication feature a socialist orientation in their judgment of texts and because we treat the topic of economic injustice more thoroughly in Chapter 14.

3 While your interpretation is based on your admittedly subjective feminist preference, the process of analyzing the text still requires you to maintain a balcony stance. That is, you must still try to see everything you possibly can see about the text in its context with as much emotional distance as possible, but once you are certain that you have seen the patterns as clearly as possible, you can explain and judge them according to the logic of the feminist perspective you adopt. You must use that perspective consistently and with clarity of reason and understanding. In sum, the feminist approach does not excuse critics from adopting a balcony stance in relation to a message.

WORKS CITED

Campbell, Karlyn Kohrs. "Femininity and Feminism: To Be or Not to Be a Woman." *Communication Quarterly* 31 (1983): 101–08.

———. "The Rhetoric of Women's Liberation: An Oxymoron." *Quarterly Journal of Speech* 59 (1973): 74–86.

———. *Man Cannot Speak for Her: A Critical Study of Early Feminist Rhetoric.* Vol. 1. New York: Greenwood Press, 1989.

Cooper, Brenda. "'Chick Flicks' as Feminist Texts: The Appropriation of the Male Gaze in *Thelma and Louise.*" *Women's Studies in Communication* 23 (2000): 307–37.

Donovan, Josephine. *Feminist Theory: The Intellectual Traditions of American Feminism.* New York: Continuum, 1992.

Dow, Bonnie J. "Femininity and Feminism in *Murphy Brown.*" *The Southern Communication Journal* 57 (1992): 143–55.

———. "Feminism, Difference(s), and Rhetorical Studies." *Communication Studies* 46 (1995): 106–17.

Dow, Bonnie J., and Tonn, Mari Boor. "'Feminine Style' and Political Judgment in the Rhetoric of Ann Richards." *Quarterly Journal of Speech* 79 (1993): 286–302.

Dunbar, Roxanne. "Female Liberation as a Basis for Social Revolution." In *Notes from the Second Year,* edited by Shulamith Firestone and Anne Koedt, 48–54. New York: Bantam, 1970.

Flax, Jane. *Thinking Fragments: Psychoanalysis, Feminism, and Postmodernism in the Contemporary West.* Berkeley: University of California Press, 1990.

Foss, Karen A., Sonja K. Foss, and Cindy L. Griffin. *Feminist Rhetorical Theories.* Thousand Oaks, CA: Sage, 1999.

Gearhart, Sally Miller. "Womanpower: Energy Re-sourcement." In *The Politics of Women's Spirituality: Essays on the rise of Spiritual Power within the Feminist Movement,* edited by Charlene Spretnak, 194–206. Garden City, NY: Anchor, 1982.

———. "The Womanization of Rhetoric." *Women's Studies International Quarterly* 2 (1979): 195–201.

Gilligan, Carol. *In a Different Voice: Psychological Theory and Women's Development.* Cambridge, MA: Harvard University Press, 1982.

Hall, Deana L., and Kristin Langellier. "Storytelling Strategies in Mother-Daughter Communication." In *Women Communicating: Studies of Women's Talk,* edited by Barbara Bate and Anita Taylor, 197–226. Norwood, NJ: Ablex, 1988.

hooks, bell. *Feminist Theory: From Margin to Center.* 2nd ed. Cambridge, MA: South End Press, 2000.

Kramarae, Cheris. "Women's Speech: Separate But Unequal?" *Quarterly Journal of Speech* 60 (1974): 14–24.

Messner, Michael, A. *Power At Play: Sports and the Problem of Masculinity.* Boston: Beacon Press, 1992.

Nicholson, Linda, ed. *Feminism/Postmodernism.* New York: Routledge, 1990.

Rakow, Lana F. "'Don't Hate Me Because I'm Beautiful': Feminist Resistance to Advertising's Irresistible Meanings." *The Southern Communication Journal* 57 (1992): 132–42.

Rushing, Janice Hocker. "Putting Away Childish Things: Looking at Diana's Funeral and Media Criticism." *Women's Studies in Communication* 21 (1998): 150–68.

Solomon, Martha. "The 'Positive Woman's' Journey: A Mythic Analysis of the Rhetoric of STOP ERA." *Quarterly Journal of Speech* 65 (1979): 262–74.

Treichler, Paula A., and Cheris Kramarae. "Women's Talk in the Ivory Tower." *Communication Quarterly* 31 (1983): 118–32.

Trujillo, Nick. "Hegemonic Masculinity on the Mound: Media Representations of Nolan Ryan and American Sports Culture." *Critical Studies in Mass Communication* 8 (1991): 290–309.

West, Candace, Michelle M. Lazar, and Cheris Kramarae. "Gender in Discourse." In *Discourse as Social Interaction,* edited by Teun A. van Dijk, 119–43. Thousand Oaks, CA: Sage, 1997.

Wood, Julia. "Gender and Moral Voice: Moving from Woman's Nature to Standpoint Epistemology." *Women's Studies in Communication* 15 (1992): 1–24.

SUGGESTED READINGS

Foss, Karen A., Sonja K. Foss, and Cindy L Griffin. *Feminist Rhetorical Theories.* Thousand Oaks, CA: Sage, 1999.

Campbell, Karlyn Kohrs. "The Rhetoric of Women's Liberation: An Oxymoron." *Quarterly Journal of Speech* 59 (1973): 74–86.

Cooper, Brenda. "Unapologetic Women, 'Comic Men' and Feminine Spectatorship in David E. Kelley's *Ally McBeal.*" *Critical Studies in Mass Communication* 8 (1991): 416–35.

Dow, Bonnie J. "Feminism, Difference(s), and Rhetorical Studies." *Communication Studies* 46 (1995): 106–17.

Dow, Bonnie J., and Mari Boor Tonn, "'Feminine Style' and Political Judgment in the Rhetoric of Ann Richards." *Quarterly Journal of Speech* 79 (1993): 286–302.

Hayden, Sara. "Family Metaphors and The Nation: Promoting a Politics of Care through the Million Mom March." *Quarterly Journal of Speech* 89 (2003): 196–215.

Trujillo, Nick. "Hegemonic Masculinity on the Mound: Media Representations of Nolan Ryan and American Sports Culture." *Critical Studies in Mass Communication* 8 (1991): 290–308.

POSTMODERN APPROACHES

16

If you've ever been in a courtroom, you know that many things in life are a matter of interpretation. In a child custody dispute, for example, a husband and wife interpret their marital conflict differently. The wife contends that her husband neglected her and their children with his frequent work-related travel and his emotionally distant attitude upon his return from business trips. The husband argues that, to him, the travel (albeit unfortunate) was a way for him to provide well for his family financially, and what seemed like emotional distance was exhaustion and a natural response to his wife's anger upon his return. The judge's response, too, is a matter of interpretation. She must interpret the legal definitions of neglect and the legal requirements for child custody, determining what interpretations of this conflict are most accurate and how the law should be applied. Although things have always been a matter of interpretation, we live in a world today where many people are hyperconscious of the fact that there are seemingly few absolutes in life and much that is a matter of interpretation.

In part, this hyperconsciousness is a function of the postmodern condition that we described in Chapter 15. Recall our definition of **postmodernism**: *a general contemporary skepticism about the existence of objectivity, absolutes, universality, and precise rationality*. Postmodern thinkers doubt the possibility that there is one absolute, objective interpretation of much of anything, and much of that doubt, philosophically, stems from a focus on language: how we assign meanings to things and experiences through our use of language and how our language constrains the meanings we assign.

In Chapters 14 and 15 we saw how critical theorists challenge the way ideas come to have meaning when they are portrayed as having their foundation in nature, and we saw how postmodern feminists question the meaning of *womanhood*, wondering whether the term really refers to anything true at all. Many contemporary scholars have been inspired by the Marxist question of what ideologies are real and what ideologies are false, just as the judge must ask whether the husband or wife offers the most real interpretation of their marital conflict. Many who study the process of interpretation would conclude that a host of factors are at issue in determining what we believe about how the world is and ought to be: language, rules of speech, and rules for knowledge development, among others. While postmodern philosophers place their focus in different areas, what they share is an adamant *dis*belief that any ideology is derived

Vocabulary

➤ postmodernism
➤ postmodern approaches
➤ semiology
➤ signs
➤ signifier
➤ signified
➤ polysemic
➤ deconstruction
➤ referential truth
➤ binary oppositions
➤ ideographs
➤ discursive formation
➤ rules of formation
➤ archaeological method

from pure, objective rational thought. There's more to it than that. This chapter examines three approaches to the question of how we create meanings and develop our interpretations of the world. The first approach, which we label "deconstruction," is a way to challenge the presumption that language offers meanings that are constant and shared. The second approach focuses on "ideographs," which help us challenge the way political ideologies prevail in a culture through language. The third approach looks at "discursive formations," which encourage us to examine and challenge the unwritten cultural rules of speech and discourse. We refer to these as **postmodern approaches** *wherein they all focus on how meanings are constructed through language and its rules, denying the preexistence of a single truth or meaning that language simply reflects.* They are *post*modern because the modernist beliefs in our scientific ability to objectively measure, predict, and control natural phenomena are being replaced by this tentative, critical, skeptical belief system.

DECONSTRUCTION

Consider the first approach, which we call *deconstruction.*

SIGNS, SIGNIFIERS, AND THE SIGNIFIED

Many contemporary scholars purport that no meaning exists prior to our use of language to express it. There would be no notion of "love," for example, without language. Theorists also argue that no pure meaning exists separate from our material conditions of history, race and ethnicity, sex, economics, organizations and institutions, political systems, language, and so forth. That is, all of our meanings for symbols are influenced by history, race, sex, economics, and more, even though we rarely stop to think about it. In other words, we create our meanings for things based on a host of conditions that surround and define us. This sort of study comes from a practice derived from linguistics known as **semiology**, *the study of how signs mean in a culture (rather than the study of what signs mean)*. Semiology originates primarily from the works of Ferdinand de Saussure (1959) and Charles Sanders Peirce (1966). De Saussure's basic model of **signs** suggests that *they are made up of two parts: a signifier and that which is signified.* The **signifier** is *the symbol or icon, the word or drawing or media technique (e.g., camera angle or lighting), that refers to something*—the **signified** (de Saussure 1959, 65–67). So if you hear someone say "Stop!" the signifier is the actual word (its sound or its letter construction and combination) and the signified is the meaning of a request or command that you no longer continue what you are doing. That is simple enough on its face, but what de Saussure and other semiologists have drawn to our attention is that signs and the sign systems we use are not natural or in any way independent of the ideologies and values of the users (de Saussure 1959, 115–17). Furthermore, what we assume to be reality is a construction of meaning that is constrained by the signs we use, and those signs are never neutral or value-free. As critic and theorist John Fiske says,

> *"reality" is always encoded, or rather the only way we can perceive and make sense of reality is by the codes of our culture. There may be an objective, empiricist reality out there, but there is no universal, objective way of perceiving and making sense of it. What passes for reality in any culture is the product of the culture's codes, so "reality" is always encoded, it is never "raw." (1987, 4–5)*

Let's take, for example, the concept of "marriage." What, one might ask, does marriage *mean*? Certainly the term distinguishes those who are in some particular way connected to another human being from those who are not, that is, those who are single. But to be sure, the word *marriage* means different things to different people. In fact, until recent years, the meaning of the term in Western culture was presumably agreed upon and fixed. But we now contend with the struggle between a host of meanings, recognizing the inevitable cultural baggage of the sign related to ideological, political, and religious beliefs. For some, it means a union (what does *union* mean?!) between a man and a woman to establish a mutually beneficial economic unit. For some, it means a woman and a man living together in the same dwelling, in a monogamous relationship. For some, it means two people of either sex living together in the same dwelling, in a monogamous relationship. For some, it means two people who do not necessarily dwell together in a monogamous relationship. The point is that there is no universal meaning that precedes or stands fixed and permanent outside the signifier *marriage,* nor is there an empirical reality called marriage whose meaning is free of political, ideological, and/or religious value. The signifier *marriage* hardly is neutral, nor does it signify something that is empirically objective. Meanings, then, are unstable, dynamic, always changing between and even within people. And so, by implication, symbols are **polysemic**; that is, *they have many (poly) meanings (semy).*

Many semiologists since de Saussure have emphasized the activity of the reader of signs (what we might call the audience) in making meaning. Some, like philosopher Jacques Derrida, argue that we who make meaning are ourselves structured by that language. Who we are is a function of the sign system we participate in, and, consequently, we can never get outside of language to understand ourselves or our reality. For poststructuralists like Derrida, the critic's goal is to draw attention to and analyze the way we assume we are operating from a position of objectivity with stability and singularity in our meanings when, in fact, we are operating from the confines of our sign systems (e.g., our language). This process, called **deconstruction**, involves *questioning or breaking down (deconstructing) the presumed meanings of a message or symbols to expose the limitations of assuming a single, stable meaning.*

THE ABSENCE OF REFERENTIAL TRUTH

Derrida, well known for his theories on deconstruction, argues that signs refer not to some particular material reality, but simply to other signs (1976, 43, 49–50). So language is not referential per se. It does not refer to a thought or a reference, though we use it as if it does in fact refer to some *underlying know-able truth of reality, a presumed* **referential truth**. What we say a sign points to is merely another set of signs, which themselves acquire meaning from yet another set of signs and so on in an infinite process of making meaning. Chandler explains that "no sign makes sense on its own but only in relation to other signs. Both signifier and signified are purely relational entities" (2001). Although we may think that a single sign (e.g., a word like *cup*) has a defini-tion that we can understand separate from other signs, the very definition itself is a set of signs. If someone were to ask you what "independence" means, you would not point to an object that holds its meaning. Instead, you would use a string of signifiers to give meaning to the sign *independence*. You might use the signifiers "to be free from the constraints of others" or "to be free to act without the consent of others." Those signs you use, themselves, have mean-ing from a collection of other signs. Your inquisitor might then ask what "free" means, and you would refer to yet more signs. Because signs have an infinite and dependent relationship to one another, the location of a single, stable meaning is impossible, according to Derrida (1982, 15). Consequently, we are never "outside" of our sign systems in our effort to understand the world. Derrida's often quoted statement, "There is nothing outside of the text," sug-gests that the signs in a text refer to nothing (of meaning) but other texts, which are compilations of signs (1976, 158). At best, at any given moment we hang on to a temporary, partial meaning from which to operate.

BINARY OPPOSITIONS

Additionally, Derrida critiques the assumption that our language tends to drive us to talk about things in terms of **binary oppositions** *(e.g., light/dark, good/evil, successful/unsuccessful, free/oppressed). These oppositions assume a hierarchical rela-tionship (light being better than dark, good being better than evil) based on a belief that there is an underlying "center" or sense of order that is real and reliable.* Derrida and others are skeptical of that belief, urging critics to question the truthful-ness of binary oppositions that appear in discourse. In fact, Derrida writes that when one plays with the multiple meanings "between" bipolar oppositions, one "dislocates [the] oppositions. It carries them off, impresses upon them a certain play that propagates itself through all the text's moving parts, con-stantly shifting them" (1981, 236). In other words, for the critic to explore the possible nuances of meaning between apparent binary oppositions in a text is to dismantle the presumed certainty and stability of those opposed concepts. For example, it is easy for Americans to accept the binary oppositions between good and evil posed in the speeches of President George W. Bush after the ter-rorist attacks of September 11, 2001. In referring to the terrorists as evil, the president implies that the United States is good. But the very term *evil* is merely a signifier whose meaning is generated by infinite references to other signs. There is, according to Derrida, no actual evil to which the signifier refers. Even the attacks on the World Trade Center are behaviors to which different people in the world attach different meanings. Osama Bin Laden's and his close per-sonal followers' meaning for that event differs from that of most Americans.

For Derrida, the very presence of these multiple meanings breaks down the certainty of the opposition between good and evil.

This dynamic perspective of meanings has important implications for our understanding of rhetorical messages. Most important, it suggests that a message cannot contain a single meaning or a "hidden meaning." We often hear students say that the goal of their critique is to reveal a rhetor's hidden meaning. Many interpretive theorists would retort that such a goal is impossible to achieve because no message has *a* hidden meaning. Messages have many meanings to their makers and their audiences, meanings that may change from reading to reading, viewing to viewing. Rhetors are not "covering up" the real meaning or truth with their message; they are creating a momentary truth or meaning that they themselves may interpret differently from minute to minute. This does not mean that any meaning is valid or believable. Rather, it suggests that we must be cautious not to hold onto or be deceived by meanings that do not hold the truth that we think they do.

From this analytical perspective the critic's job is to analyze the assumptions about what signs mean (to both rhetors and audiences) in rhetorical messages, helping others take a more critical look at those meanings. Taking this perspective into account, then, as a critic conducting analysis you are looking not for hidden or subliminal messages but for what is *assumed* (by rhetors and audiences) to be the referential truth to which the signs refer. You also might list as many viable interpretations of the message from as many different perspectives as possible, asking yourself how people of different social classes, genders, ethnic backgrounds, or religious backgrounds might interpret the message or particular symbols in a message. You might discover that what appears oppressive to some may be liberating in another way to others.

Some questions you might ask are as follows:

- What reality do the rhetors and/or audiences assume, as made evident by the signs they use in the message?
- How, then, do the signs reinforce or challenge the assumption of that reality?
- Is that truth in any way real or is it a construction of other sign uses?
- How do some signs (words, images, gestures, colorings, etc.) give meaning to other signs in a text, shaping the audience's perspectives?
- What are the many possible meanings in the message? How are those meaning consistent? Contradictory?
- How might people of different social classes, genders, ethnic backgrounds, or religious backgrounds interpret the message or particular signs?
- What artificial binary oppositions (e.g., male/female, light/dark, good/evil, strong/weak, independent/dependent) are assumed or challenged in the message?
- How closed or open are the binary oppositions? Do they emphasize polarity or do they play with the range and nuances of meaning between the oppositions?

Scholar Barbara Johnson wisely points out that this kind of analysis is not aimed at pointing out "the flaws or weaknesses or stupidities of an author, but the *necessity* with which what [the critic sees] is systematically related to what [the critic] does not see" (1981, xv). That is, the critic is looking at how the structure of language (its *suggestion* that it represents reality) relates to what does not appear in a text (e.g., the nuances of meanings between binary oppositions) rather than attempting to point out foolish omissions on behalf of the rhetor.

This approach can be valuable in analyzing WWE dramas because the characters and plots are driven by binary oppositions and because the dramas are very postmodern insofar as they play with, twist, and turn traditional notions of good and evil. In fact, a deconstructive approach to your analysis might reveal that the WWE drama itself challenges the audience's assumptions about "real" morality. In each episode the wrestlers battle over the principles of good and evil (binary opposites). At face value, one might assume to know what constitutes good and what constitutes evil, who are good characters and who are evil characters. The Rock is a hero, a good character, while The Undertaker is an evil villain. But what if we see The Rock suddenly beating Triple H's girlfriend in the name of justice? Much of the thrill of WWE to fans is the fact that good characters break the "rules" of "good behavior." Suddenly our assumptions of what constitutes goodness and what constitutes evil are challenged. Contrast this to an old John Wayne western movie where the meaning of good and evil was assumed to be constant, clear, and attainable. Everyone, we assumed, knew what made the bad guys bad and the good guys good. Moreover, the bad guys were all bad and the good guys were all good. They never crossed the line; their goodness or badness was never questionable. But in WWE, the characters challenge all kinds of assumptions of meaning by breaking the assumed rules that accompany those meanings. The meanings of good and evil are no longer clear when the heroes are caught and even applauded for beating a woman. The rules, and thus the meaning, of wrestling are broken as the characters use techniques, costumes, and speech that would be shunned in a serious Olympic wrestling match. Even the meaning of the wrestling ring is called into question as the characters step beyond the bounds of the ring, carrying their fights into the stands and even to the dressing rooms. Where we once presumed a stable meaning of the ring as a boundary within which the dramatic play occurs, now the boundary is crossed and the line between what is acting or play and what is real becomes blurred. In short, a deconstructive analysis of WWE suggests that in contemporary Western culture, the old meanings of good/evil and play/reality are no longer distinguishable as clear-cut opposites.

IDEOGRAPHS

Although Derrida and other poststructural linguists doubt the existence of any real, fixed meanings, other scholars do contend, in a critical theoretical fashion, that there may be some difference between real and false ideologies. One such scholar in communication studies is Michael McGee, who acknowledges the importance of language (more than economics) in sustaining a dominant ideology. McGee rejects the traditional Marxist position that the elite dominate a society solely through economics by intentionally creating a false ideology that the proletariat buy into, but instead McGee argues that even the elite of a society are conditioned to a social "vocabulary of concepts" or words and phrases that "function as guides, warrants, reasons, or excuses for behavior and belief" (1980, 6). In other words, the whole of society is well trained to be guided by a language that signifies a dominant political ideology. In fact, McGee believes that political ideology is rarely argued in philosophical terms but, rather, is apparent in what he calls **ideographs**: *slogans or single words that are used freely and frequently in a society, are often mistaken for the technical language of a political philosophy, and influence each person's "reality"*(5).

Some examples of ideographs are words or phrases like *liberty, world peace, tolerance, equality, rule of the law, human rights, freedom,* or *pluralism*. If you think about it, those terms refer to ideas that are made up of propositions about how the world is and ought to be. The word *liberty* actually stands for a whole philosophy (different philosophies depending on the philosopher) constituted by a series of arguments about what constitutes freedom in what circumstances. But we use the word casually without each time pronouncing its philosophical nuances, none of which are purely agreed upon in the realm of philosophy anyway. Most people who use the term lack the skills necessary to participate in the philosophical debate over the meaning of the term. Instead, we rely on cultural uses of the term, historically and in context with other ideographs, to construct our sense of reality about the term. As McGee argues, the meanings are always "clouded, hindered, made irrelevant" by prior uses of the term in the culture (9). We use the ideographs, assuming that people fill in those propositions and share a commitment to them.

Ideographs are powerful in their ability to guide, warrant, or excuse behavior and beliefs. McGee argues that no one "is permitted to question the fundamental logic of ideographs" (6). Everyone is conditioned to think of the ideographs as a reasonable commitment "just as one is taught to think that '186,000 miles per second' is an accurate empirical description of the speed of light even though few can work the experiments or do the mathematics to prove it" (7). Accepting the ideographs is a necessary prerequisite for belonging to the society (15). Not to accept the vocabulary of ideographs is to be a menace to society, and punishment is likely to ensue in some fashion. The vocabulary is what we are committed to and what helps conform our behavior and beliefs.

Because we are conditioned to believe that ideographs have obvious, self-evident, undebatable meanings, we often become unconscious of how those terms are used to justify behaviors and decisions that may or may not necessarily be in the best interest of the whole and may or may not be grounded in sound logic. We allow ourselves to assume that the use of the terms equals a logical argument, but that is often not the case at all. Take, for example, the prevailing ideographs in President George W. Bush's national address on March

17, 2003, in which the president issued his ultimatum, demanding that Saddam Hussein leave Iraq within forty-eight hours. In nearly every paragraph of that twenty-six-paragraph speech, Bush uses at least one of the following four ideographs: "disarmament," "threat" or "danger," and "peaceful." The meanings of these terms are made to appear self-evident as in the following passage:

> *The Iraqi regime has used diplomacy as a ploy to gain time and advantage. It has uniformly defied Security Council resolutions demanding full* **disarmament.** *Over the years, U.N. weapon inspectors have been* **threatened** *by Iraqi officials, electronically bugged, and systematically deceived.* **Peaceful** *efforts to* **disarm** *the Iraqi regime have failed again and again—because we are not dealing with* **peaceful** *men. . . . The* **danger** *is clear. (Bush 2003, "President Says," emphasis added)*

Paragraph upon paragraph contains these ideographs, and it is assumed that the listener is committed foremost to the eradication of threats and danger of any sort, the maintenance of peace, and disarmament as a means toward the ends of peace and safety. Moreover, it is assumed that the listener will assign meaning to those terms from the vantage point of American welfare. Yet never does the speech examine the complexities of the meanings of those terms. What, for example, does threat or danger really mean? Political philosophers (as evident even in the discord among members of the UN Security Council) disagree as to what constitutes a threat to the United States from Iraq, and they disagree as to what constitutes appropriate measures and timing for the insistence on disarmament. In just a few months after the conflict in Iraq began, the media reported that weapons of mass destruction had yet to be found, let alone in the magnitude the president described. The phrases "peaceful efforts" and "peaceful men" seem self-evident, but their meanings vary greatly between the Iraqi and American cultures.

Perhaps more enlightening than the ideographs in this speech alone is what we find by comparing these ideographs to those in a speech given by President Bush to the nation six months later, September 7, 2003, in which he intended to "keep [Americans] informed of America's actions in the war on terror." Although the general subject of this address is the war on terrorism, much of its particular focus is the war in Iraq. The ideographs "disarmament," "peace," and "threat/danger" rarely are mentioned in this speech. Instead we find the ideographs "freedom," "democracy," and "liberty" as evident in the following passage:

> *Our enemies understand this. They know that a* free *Iraq will be* **free** *of them—***free** *of assassins, and torturers, and secret police. They know that as* **democracy** *rises in Iraq, all of their hateful ambitions will fall like the statues of the former dictator. And that is why, five months after we* **liberated** *Iraq, a collection of killers is desperately trying to undermine Iraq's progress and throw the country into chaos. (Bush 2003, "President Addresses," emphasis added)*

Because the war efforts failed to produce evidence of the eminent danger Bush spoke of, a new set of ideographs are used to justify the continued presence of the United States in Iraq. Once again, these ideographs assume a certain commitment to a presumably shared set of ideas about what freedom, democracy, and liberty mean, operating as a warrant for the public belief about and response to the administration's decisions regarding the war. Indeed, no good American is "permitted" to question the logic of freedom, democracy, or liberty, and yet what those ideographs mean to Iraqi people in the cultural context of their political and religious history is likely quite different from what those ideographs mean to Americans. Because previous persuasion has conditioned Americans to rally in support around the terms *freedom, democracy,* and *liberty,* the American audience and those in power using these terms are unlikely to question the influence and actions justified through the dominant ideology signified by these ideographs, nor are they likely to debate their meaning.

As a critic you may be interested in analyzing the ideographs in a message anytime you see evidence-based propositions supplanted or embellished by ideographs. As McGee says, words of this sort "used as agencies of social control may have an intrinsic force" (1980, 6). As a critic, your social, political, and moral conscience may drive you to look for how ideographs exert that force in a particular message or set of messages. Some questions you might ask when conducting that analysis include these:

- What ideographs pervade the message(s)?
- How does the use of the ideographs discourage questioning of the rhetor's goals and agenda?
- What are historical uses of the ideograph (by that or other rhetors) that shape its meaning for the nonphilosophical public?
- How do the ideographs in the message(s) work together? Are they contradictory? Consistent? If they are inconsistent, how is the conflict between them worked out to justify the behaviors or beliefs advocated by the rhetor?[1]
- What philosophical deliberations about the ideas signified by the ideographs are ignored in the message?
- What behaviors and beliefs do the ideographs justify, guide, or excuse?

Analyzing ideographs is a good way to make yourself conscious of the power language has over the way we think and act and a good way to make you pause to ask, now what does that *really* mean?

DISCURSIVE FORMATIONS

Another interpretive focus comes from French philosopher Michel Foucault. He was concerned with the broader question of how a concept or idea originates or forms as an "object of discourse" in the first place. He asks how certain concepts come to be subjects a culture can legitimately discuss. He calls this *complex process and system of influences on the origination of a concept for social discussion* **discursive formation** (Foucault 1969, 40–42). Take, for example, the notion of emotional abuse. Such is an object of contemporary discourse that did not exist twenty-five years ago. Foucault would ask the question, how did emotional abuse (not the practice thereof, but the object of discussion) come into play? He argues that objects of discourse don't just randomly appear. The concept of emotional abuse did not suddenly appear because the practice of emotional abuse suddenly appeared. Rather, objects of this sort form as a function of cultural rules about what, where, when, how, and by whom various subjects can be discussed. Foucault would urge the critic to understand the term *emotional abuse* by examining the **rules of formation**: *the unwritten rules that constrain and direct social discourse, ultimately controlling what is and is not spoken about and in what way* (50–53). Rules you might inquire about include the following:

- Who is permitted to speak on a subject and who is not? (People emotionally abused are only as of recent allowed to speak on the matter, in part because of media [talk shows, etc.], developments and increasing legitimacy of social work and psychology, and so on. Only "scientifically based experts" are allowed to name a phenomenon as emotional abuse.)

- In what context (oral or written) is one permitted to speak of a subject? (Historically, children of all ages could never speak of emotional abuse because of unwritten rules about parental authority. Over time, such speech was permitted in a doctor's, psychiatrist's, or counselor's office. Now it is permitted in casual relationships, even on national television.)

- What rules of speech/writing must one follow to be considered legitimate and authoritative? (One is most authoritative on the subject for public discourse if one has conducted scientific research or has been trained in social sciences and practices within the disciplines of social science. Legitimate knowledge-producing writing on emotional abuse must be scientific in tone. References to Yahweh, the Holy Spirit, Tao, or practices of clairvoyance are not considered legitimate in such discourse.)

- What can be said about a subject? What cannot be said?

- How must we speak about a subject? What type of style, vocabulary, and evidence is required for the discourse to have legitimacy?

- What procedures, policies, political relations, economic conditions, legal conditions, and social conditions control the discourse around a subject? (Economic interests around the process of publication influence what writings on emotional abuse get published. Economic advantages to commercial television stations, advertisers, and so on influence the topics selected for discussion on popular TV talk shows like *Oprah*. Availability [or not] of grant money often impacts whether research on something like emotional abuse is conducted.)

Foucault refers to *the analytical process of examining these rules and relations that impact formation and discussion of a subject* as the **archaeological method** of analysis. Just as an archaeologist digs under the surface to discover a complex network of historical economic, political, geographical, and environmental conditions, the critic digs past the outer layers of discourse to find an underlying complex and dynamic network of political, economic, material, and procedural relations that constantly shape meaning and produce what we assume to be "knowledge" (Foucault 1969, 44–46).

By digging around in the rules of discourse the critic is able to reveal to a culture the limitations of what it assumes to be truth. For example, a critic might discover the mechanisms by which certain ways of knowing are delegitimized in a culture. In a January 8, 2002, interview with actor-director-screenwriter Billy Bob Thorton on National Public Radio, interviewer Terry Gross inquired about Thorton's mother, who was a psychic. Generally speaking, the term *psychic* is not a legitimate object of discussion about ways of knowing in academic, government, or theological arenas. The ideas of a politician, priest, history professor, or scientist would be dismissed, even shunned from their respective communities of discourse, if it were announced that those ideas were inspired by meetings with a psychic. In the interview, Thorton noted the mocking he and his siblings received as children about their mother's profession. Yet he also noted that while most of his community members mocked his mother, most of them also came to her (in secrecy, of course). Foucault urges us to take interest in the (unwritten) rules that prohibit someone like a psychic from having an authoritative, legitimate voice in a culture. He urges us not necessarily to abandon our rules of discourse, but to question our rules by asking whose interests, power, and status are sustained by maintaining the rules, and what discursive mechanisms are used to keep the rules in place. For example, a critic might ask, who is considered a legitimate psychologist? What language must he use to prove his legitimacy with his clients and the psychological community? (Can he call upon the deceased?) What language can he not use? In what sort of space must she practice her counseling to gain legitimacy? What limitations are there on how she shapes her space? (Can she use incense? Candles? Wine?) What institutions, economic conditions, or political relations shape her practice? (What do insurance companies require to support her practice? How much money is considered "standard practice" for her to maintain legitimacy? What legal practices limit the techniques of a psychiatrist?)

The critic who examines rules of discourse through the archaeological method typically does not study a single, isolated message like a speech or essay. While a single text may be of interest and value to the critic, the challenge is to see that text as a small piece of a much larger and complex network of relations between the rules of discourse, rules of authority, economic/political/legal conditions, and so on, all of which continuously shape and reshape what people consider to be legitimate truth. From this analytical perspective the critic is interested in the multifaceted relations (between institutions, practices, rules, customs, economics, politics, etc.) that influence the use of symbols in a society.

USING THE POSTMODERN APPROACHES

The postmodern approaches we've described here—deconstruction, analyzing ideographs, and analyzing discursive formations (the archaeological method)—can be useful when you encounter a text that causes you to question its meanings or how the text comes to mean anything for the rhetors and audiences. It may be useful when you find yourself troubled by the assumptions rhetors and audiences make about their circumstances. The deconstructive approach may be helpful if you observe strong binary oppositions in a text or if you doubt the stability or singularity of meaning suggested by a rhetor in his or her language. The ideograph approach might help you if you notice a patterned use of terms that stand for complex political ideologies and you are concerned that the use of those terms may serve to justify undesirable political ends. You may choose to use the archaeological method if you are looking at a body of texts and are curious less about the use of words in those texts per se, but more about how the concepts they signify came into our social consciousness, what rules control their usage (and, thus, our social consciousness), and what network of factors shape their meanings.

In a sense, you would use these approaches when you share the postmodern skepticism about the existence of fixed, shared, absolute meanings that are objectively identifiable. In what follows we take a text that is packed with American cultural tradition, the song "America," and deconstruct its ideographs. While an examination of a collection of patriotic songs might allow us to use the archaeological method, for the purposes of illustration we model deconstruction as method.

POSTMODERN CONCEPTS APPLIED TO "AMERICA"

Each year in the United States, perhaps on the Fourth of July, Memorial Day, Labor Day, Veterans' Day, or at a ball game, we hear and sing patriotic music. After the terrorist attacks on September 11, 2001, many Americans joined in chorus around such familiar tunes as "America the Beautiful," "God Bless America," "The Star-Spangled Banner," and "Stars and Stripes Forever." One tune that many of us learn as children, "My Country, 'Tis of Thee" (actually titled "America"), is generally representative of the content of most American patriotic songs. Let's look at how the lyrics of "America" present a rather unified, coherent image of America and its freedom. Then, we'll apply some deconstruction and ideograph concepts to analyze the presumed meanings and implications of those lyrics. First, take a look at all the verses of the song.

AMERICA
By Samuel F. Smith

My country, 'tis of Thee,
Sweet Land of Liberty
Of thee I sing;
Land where my fathers died,
Land of the pilgrims' pride,
From every mountain side
Let Freedom ring.

My native country, thee,
Land of the noble free,
Thy name I love;
I love thy rocks and rills,
Thy woods and templed hills,
My heart with rapture thrills
Like that above.

Let music swell the breeze,
And ring from all the trees
Sweet Freedom's song;
Let mortal tongues awake;
Let all that breathe partake;
Let rocks their silence break,
The sound prolong.

Our fathers' God to Thee,
Author of Liberty,
To thee we sing,
Long may our land be bright
With Freedom's holy light,
Protect us by thy might
Great God, our King.

Our glorious Land to-day
'Neath Education's sway,
Soars upward still.
Its hills of learning fair,
Whose bounties all may share,
Behold them everywhere
On vale and hill!

Thy safeguard, Liberty,
The school shall ever be,
Our Nation's pride!
No tyrant hand shall smite,
While with encircling might
All here are taught the Right
With Truth allied.

Beneath Heaven's gracious will
The stars of progress still
Our course do sway;
In unity sublime
To broader heights we climb,
Triumphant over Time,
God speeds our way!

Grand birthright of our sires,
Our altars and our fires
Keep we still pure!
Our starry flag unfurled,
The hope of all the world,
In peace and light impearled,
God hold secure!

The song "America" is sung over and over because it represents America as more than just a body of land. The song endows that land with meaning that is presumed to be real, authoritative, and coherent. The geographical space within and upon which we function is assigned meanings through this song. The meaning of America is framed as part of a unified natural and supernatural system, the center of which is God. America is referred to symbolically as "Liberty" and "Freedom," which are authored and protected by God (the central source and sustainer). While God is the author and protector, the system is technically sustained by "Education," which teaches Right and Truth. Education is referred to as the mechanism by which we assure ourselves of the continuation of liberty ("Thy safeguard, Liberty, the school shall ever be") and human progress ("The stars of progress still our course do sway"). Progress is the purpose to fulfill by way of our freedom. This unified system is mapped visually in Figure 16.1.

As we presume to share and understand the meaning of the symbols within which this system is constructed, it seems logical, coherent, stable, and "right." But let's stop for a moment to deconstruct some of the assumptions of meanings assigned to these symbols. First, notice the words in the poem that are given the status of proper noun: *America (Thee), Land, Liberty, Freedom, God, King, Education, Nation, Right, Truth, Heaven, Time.* Proper nouns, by definition, refer to things that are unique, including specific or particular people, animals, places, events, languages, or religions (Rivers and Rodriguez 1995, 176–77). More than other nouns, proper nouns convey the presence of an actual, identifiable, and real reference. No doubt we are accustomed to seeing "God" and "America" as proper nouns as these symbols typically convey a unique, presumably agreed upon reference. But we are not accustomed to seeing "Education," "Freedom," "Liberty," "Right," and "Truth" as proper nouns. The adjustment of the first letter from lower- to uppercase conveys the presumption that there is a single conception of or practice of education that is definable, identifiable, and fixed. Similarly, this symbolic alteration presumes the existence of a single notion of what is right and true. Yet the more we examine such symbols as education, right, and truth, the more we may become

FIGURE 16.1

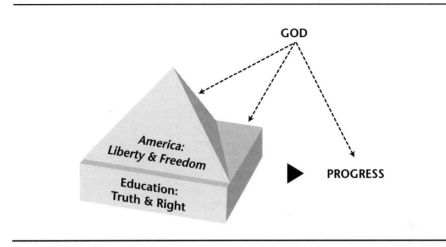

skeptical of any singularity in their meaning. Education, for example, is in no way a clearly identifiable referent for which we share a single meaning. The meanings of education are multiple, bound up in the relationships among those who participate in behaviors and discourse in its name: students, teachers, administrators, parents, politicians, nonprofit agencies, corporations, and so on. When the song was written, only privileged Americans received an education. The rights of slaves, women, and immigrants were not protected by education. Moreover, the past thirty years have made abundantly clear the fact that no single truth is or can be taught in schools. We have discovered, for example, that history is a product of human construction and therefore limited by the political, social, and economic perspective of those doing the writing of history. History is not truth per se; it is the construction of a particular people's truth at a particular time. Given this condition, we cannot claim that education is a stable, reproducible condition, event, or institution that ensures the reification of that which is definitively right or true.

Consider the terms *Liberty* and *Freedom*. By assigning these terms the status of proper noun, the concepts are made to appear as if there is little or perhaps no question as to what they refer. But liberty, as a term, has meaning only against something else: liberty from _____. Liberty "means" only as a binary opposition to something from which one is not liberated. Perhaps the original reference was to America's liberty from the rule of King George in England or any other tyrant, as mentioned in the sixth stanza. But that meaning was only true for some Americans, mostly white males who owned property. At the time, those who owned slaves, for instance, were not assigned the meaning of "tyrant." What, we might ask, does liberty mean for those today who are discriminated against on the basis of race, appearance, disability, or sexual orientation? What does liberty mean for those enslaved to addictions? To those who are homeless? To those who are enslaved to work? Is America, specifically what we have assigned it to mean, really the equivalent of liberty? The very fact that we seem unable to agree about the conflicts embedded in these questions is indicative of the absence of any singular, stable, identifiable referent for liberty and freedom.

So too, the terms *liberty* and *freedom* are ideographs signifying and arousing commitment to a series of propositions about government that are, of course, not articulated in song. In fact, song and poetry play a significant role in perpetuating an ideology throughout a culture, ensuring that the people of a culture learn the vocabulary of the ideology. The repetition, rhyme, and meter of poetic form sweep its singers up emotionally, further distancing the citizenry from the philosophical propositions and debate that constitute the "real," contested meanings of the terms. What American is likely to stop to question the meaning and appropriateness of liberty and freedom while singing that song?

Another ideograph in this song is the word *Land.* While the word *land* is not the usual ideograph that is abstract (e.g., "liberty," "diversity," "rule of the law"), it is used in this text metaphorically, thus referring to a concept more than the literal land of America. It is the "Land of Liberty" and the "Land of the noble free," a land we want to "be bright with Freedom's holy light." The term *land* signifies space and people who embody that space, practicing their "freedom." Yet again, we are missing the philosophical query as to what that land is physically and who those people are. In our mind's eye we perhaps imagine the geographical territory of the United States as we sing the song, but where and who is that land at the Mexican American borders where illegal immigrants come daily? Where and who was that land when African Americans were slaves? The land is claimed in the song as "our land" and "my land," and is, in some stanzas, described in terms of its physical beauty:

> *My native country, thee,*
> *Land of the noble free,*
> *Thy name I love;*
> *I love thy rocks and rills,*
> *Thy woods and templed hills,*
> *My heart with rapture thrills*
> *Like that above.*

Yet the portrayal of land ownership ("my country," "our country") in terms of physical beauty masks the complex philosophical question of what land ownership means and how it is acquired. Specifically, it overlooks the debate of ownership between Native Americans and the Euro-Americans who came to dominate the land. The ideograph of "land" in the song focuses just enough on physical beauty and richness to discourage the singer from considering the larger philosophical debate over the meanings of land ownership. When we sing the song repeatedly, starting in our youth and in conjunction with other patriotic songs, we grow increasingly committed to the vocabulary and conform our allegiances accordingly.

Notice how the deconstruction of the symbols and an analysis of the ideographs in the song "America" lead us to question the assumptions of meanings, particularly the assumptions of stable singular meanings that, when examined closely, we find full of contradiction and uncertainty. This kind of analysis does not necessarily need to bring us to the conclusion that important cultural concepts like God, freedom, liberty, and education have no meaning or that their meanings are so unstable as to be useless or that their usage is entirely unjust or motivated by evil. To function socially without complete chaos, we *must* at any given moment assume a certain stability and truthfulness to our symbols. However, at the same time, the process of deconstruction and the examination of ideographs encourage us to keep a skeptical eye open and willing to scrutinize those meanings, because only when we check our assumptions are we able to see potentially destructive errors in our thinking and behaviors.

SUMMARY

Postmodern approaches start from the presumption that truth is created through communication, that is, the interactive use of symbols among human beings. These approaches discard the traditional presumptions that truth, ideas, thoughts, or meaning exist prior to language. Rather, it is believed that reality is what we interpret it to be, and our interpretations are constrained by the language we have available, our political/economic/legal/social/historical conditions, our individual perspectives, and the very symbols we use to talk about our realities. Beyond the material world (and even that we construct and assign meanings to), no meaning exists. We create it in order to function as social beings. This perspective is the basis for what many identify as postmodern thinking, and it is a perspective that has profoundly impacted contemporary Western culture.

This analytical approach is bold insofar as it requires you, the critic, to challenge assumptions that perhaps you yourself have held. The process can be rewarding and valuable, however, in helping raise our consciousness to critique the beliefs and behaviors that may stand in the way of our ability to serve the interests of all, not just the privileged few.

EXERCISES

1. Write out the Pledge of Allegiance so you can study its words. Then, using a different color pen (to remind yourself that what you are writing is not "text" per se), make some notes about the gestures we use when reciting the Pledge and contexts in which the Pledge is recited.

2. Analyze the ideographs in the Pledge and the signifiers in both the written text and the gestures and contexts for reciting the Pledge. Use the following questions to prompt your thinking:

   - What are the prominent ideographs in the Pledge?
   - What philosophical deliberations about the ideas signified by the ideographs are ignored in the Pledge?

- What behaviors and beliefs (good and bad) do the ideographs in the Pledge encourage or excuse?
- How do the ideographs in the Pledge relate to one another? Do they conflict in any way? If so, how is that conflict resolved in the reciting of the Pledge?
- What do the "signifiers" in the Pledge "signify"? What other signs do the signifiers in the Pledge refer to?
- What reality or meaning could be considered doubtful upon tracing the signifiers that refer to one another in the Pledge?
- What are the many possible meanings in some of the signs (including gestures and contexts for reciting the Pledge)? How are those meaning consistent? Contradictory?
- How might people of different social classes, genders, ethnic backgrounds, or religious backgrounds interpret particular signs differently?
- What, if any, binary oppositions (e.g., male/female, light/dark, good/evil, strong/weak, independent/dependent) dominate the message? What nuances of meaning between the binary oppositions are closed or explored by the other signs of the Pledge?

3. Look over your answers to the preceding analysis questions and consider the implications of your answers for Americans who recite the Pledge faithfully, often as young children. Write a paragraph in which you teach a group of high school students something about the Pledge that they would otherwise not consider. What does your analysis urge us to question or think about what the signs and ideographs in the Pledge (and its accompanying gestures and contexts) "mean" for Americans and their government leaders? What are the strengths and limitations of the Pledge in building allegiance to America?

NOTES

1 The second and third questions in this list are derived from McGee's recommendation that the critic look at the diachronic structure of the ideograph (i.e., its historical usage and the development of the ideograph over time) and the synchronic structure of the ideograph (i.e., an ideograph's usage in relation to other ideographs in a text or set of texts). For more details on these two directions of analysis, see Michael McGee, "The 'Ideograph': A Link Between Rhetoric and Ideology," *Quarterly Journal of Speech* 66 (1980): 1–16.

WORKS CITED

Bush, George W. "President Addresses the Nation." The White House. September 7, 2003. http://www.whitehouse.gov/news/relseases/2003/09/20030907-1. html (accessed November 10, 2003).

———. "President Says Saddam Hussein Must Leave Iraq Within 48 Hours." The White House. March 17, 2003. http://www.whitehouse.gov/news/releases/2003/03/20030317-7.html (accessed November 10, 2003).

Chandler, David. "Signs." *Semiotics for Beginners.* February 19, 2001. http://www.aber.ac.uk/media/Documents/S4B/sem02.html (accessed November 20, 2003).

De Saussure, Ferdinand. *Course in General Linguistics.* Trans. Wade Baskin. Eds. Charles Bally, Albert Sechehaye, and Albert Reidlinger. New York: Philosophical Library, 1959.

Derrida, Jacques. *Dissemination.* Trans. Barbara Johnson. Chicago: University of Chicago Press, 1981.

———. *Of Grammatology.* Trans. G. Sprivak. Baltimore: Johns Hopkins University Press, 1976.

———. "Difference." In *Margins of Philosophy,* translated by Alan Bass. Chicago: University of Chicago Press, 1982.

———. "Signature Event Context." In *Margins of Philosophy,* translated by Alan Bass. Chicago: University of Chicago Press, 1982.

Fiske, John. *Television Culture.* New York: Methuen, 1987.

Foucault, Michel. *The Archaeology of Knowledge and the Discourse on Language.* Trans. A. M. Sheridan Smith. New York: Harper, 1969.

Johnson, Barbara. Translator's Introduction. *Dissemination,* by Jacques Derrida. Trans. Barbara Johnson, vii–xxxiii. Chicago: University of Chicago Press, 1981.

McGee, Michael Calvin. "The 'Ideograph': A Link Between Rhetoric and Ideology." *Quarterly Journal of Speech* 66 (1980): 1–16.

Peirce, Charles Sanders. *Selected Writings.* New York: Dover, 1966.

Rivers, William L., and Alison Work Rodriguez. *A Journalist's Guide to Grammar and Style.* Boston: Allyn and Bacon, 1995.

Smith, Samuel F. "America." ScoutSongs.com. 2003. http://www.scoutsongs.com/lyrics/america.html (accessed November 21, 2003).

SUGGESTED READINGS

Ceccarelli, Leah. "Polysemy: Multiple Meanings in Rhetorical Criticism." *Quarterly Journal of Speech* 84 (1998): 395–415.

Edwards, Janis L., and Carol K. Winkler. "Representative Form and the Visual Ideograph: The Iwo Jima Image in Editorial Cartoons." *Quarterly Journal of Speech* 83 (1997): 289–310.

Fiske, John. "Television: Polysemy and Popularity." *Critical Studies in Mass Communication* 3 (1986): 391–408.

Grossberg, Lawrence. "Is There Rock after Punk?" *Critical Studies in Mass Communication* 3 (1986): 50–74.

McGee, Michael Calvin. "The 'Ideograph': A Link Between Rhetoric and Ideology." *Quarterly Journal of Speech* 66 (1980): 1–16.

Schwichtenberg, Cathy. "Madonna's Postmodern Feminism: Bringing the Margins to the Center." *Southern Communication Journal* 57 (1992): 120–31.

VISUAL COMMUNICATION

When you hear the words "One small step for man, one giant leap for mankind," what comes to mind? Most likely your brain conjures up an image of Neil Armstrong descending a ladder from the lunar module and gingerly hopping onto the moon's surface. When you hear the words "I have a dream!" most likely you see in your mind an image of Martin Luther King Jr. on the steps of the Lincoln Memorial speaking to a crowd of over two hundred thousand people. Now, when you hear the date September 11, most likely you see in your mind images of the World Trade Towers imploding. In this age of information, seldom are significant verbal rhetorical efforts separated from some form of visual communication. Whether you are surfing the Net, watching TV, driving your car, or attending a sports event, you are confronted with visual messages that often merit some analysis. As a communication professional you need to be able to analyze visual communication just as you will always need to be competent in making sense of verbal messages.

This chapter introduces you to some tools that you can use to analyze visual communication. As a result of studying the chapter, you'll be better able to analyze most visual texts you encounter, and you will have some ideas about which theorists and theories you may want to explore in order to create more sophisticated approaches than we offer here. This chapter differs from the previous eight chapters in a substantial way—it does *not* present a theoretical approach to messages. Rather, the concepts herein are intended as tools to complement analyses using any of the previous search models. The analysis we model at the end of the chapter illustrates how concepts of visual communication work. The product is more technical in focus than theoretical. As you read it, think about how use of a search model could add to the power of the analysis to inform readers about how rhetoric works.

VISUAL MESSAGES AND ARGUMENT

As you have discovered in reading this book, rhetoric is action that is carried out by creating messages that are delivered to particular audiences in order to achieve some purpose or goal. In the study of communication, the larger class of such purposes is "persuasion." Rhetors want audiences to feel a particular way or see things like they do; they want audiences to believe something or do something. Persuasion can be accomplished in many ways, which may or may not entail providing a good argument for action. Sometimes, however, a message maker must provide a rationale or an argument to move an audience. So, an argument is a kind of, or a subset of, persuasion. Visual communication is different from verbal communication, and its role in arguing and persuading is not as well understood. Since visual communication usually is connected in some way to verbal messages, we have to be able to discern its specific role and function in relation to verbal messages when analyzing, interpreting, and evaluating persuasive effects.

Since the time of Aristotle the study of argument has focused on words. In recent history, visual communication has proved influential, but can visuals be *arguments*? To answer the question, let's first review some ideas about the structure of arguments. First, at minimum, an argument must make a claim (part 1) and provide a reason or rationale for the claim (part 2) (Fleming 1996, 13). That is, arguments "are propositional because claims and reasons have to be propositions [statements]" (Blair 1996, 25). So, to make a reasoned claim about something, we must use words to describe and explain the relationships of the elements of those experiences, events, or objects that concern us.

For example, imagine this: a defense attorney tries to convince a jury of the defendant's innocence by doing nothing more than silently laying a rusty gun on a table for the jury to see. The attorney steps back, points to the gun, and nods to the jury. How would you feel about the quality of defense if you were the defendant? You would most likely want to shout, "Say something! Don't just let the gun lay there!" You perceive that the object (the gun, or a photo of it) alone is too ambiguous to allow the jury to make any inferences about its meaning. Words are necessary to guide interpretation of it. The defense attorney must make statements that describe and explain the relationships between the gun, the client, and the claim that the client is innocent. The attorney must say things like: "We agree that this is my client's gun. Notice, however, that the gun is rusty both outside and *inside* the barrel. Since a gun this rusty cannot be fired, my client's gun cannot be the weapon used in the crime." As you can see, claims and reasons must be verbal, so visual communication, as part of an argument, must be connected with the verbal channel.

In the preceding hypothetical case, the visual element was important. It provided information that was relevant to the argument, but it did not provide a claim or any reason to reject the prosecution's contention that the defendant had committed an assault. The visual played a significant role in the argument, but its role is difficult to pin down—the visual is **indeterminate** (Messaris 1997, xiii), which means *it lacks specific definition or guides for interpretation; it is vague or uncertain*. This "indeterminacy about visual expression" (Blair 1996, 27) is exactly what limits the ability of a visual, in and of itself, to present an argument. Visual communications may invite interpretation, but they cannot *control* interpretation to the same degree that a verbal argument can. Someone has to talk about or write about how to make sense of the information provided visually.

FIGURE 17.1

Some visuals, of course, act very much like words. For example, Figure 17.1 substitutes for the words *handicapped* or *disabled*. Figure 17.2 substitutes for "No U-turns allowed here." Figure 17.1, due to its indeterminacy, can be verbally extrapolated to mean different things depending on its context. For example, if you encounter this visual on the door of a restroom, it means "This restroom is *equipped* with devices to accommodate disabled users." If you see it on a sign in a parking lot, it means "This space is *reserved* for disabled drivers or passengers." In both contexts, the "statement" made by the image must be verbally constructed by the observer. Notice, too, how the nature of any concept presented visually changes as the associated verbs draw attention to very different natures of the places indicated by the signs.

The visual in Figure 17.2 is confined to a single context, the highway, and is therefore a bit less ambiguous, but it is still indeterminate. The sign is not clear about whether (1) the prohibition of a U-turn is restricted to the specific place the sign marks, or (2) it is a notice of a general prohibition for the length

FIGURE 17.2

of this particular highway (or a segment of it), or even (3) it suggests a prohibition of U-turns in a geographic area irrespective of the type of road on which you may be driving. Since the visual message is ambiguous, you are posed with a problem in getting to your destination. The nature of the message suggests numerous questions to you as you barrel down the road. You may ask yourself, "If I drive on, will I be able to turn at the next intersection or not? If not, how far will I have to go to reverse my direction? What happens if I make another wrong turn and I can't make a U-turn anywhere?" (If you've driven in a foreign country, the question of the breadth of the prohibition is one you definitely want answered!) In either case, though, you must understand that the best these visuals can do is to make declarative statements.[1] What they cannot do is make claims, which are statements put forward to be accepted or rejected by an audience. So, to function rhetorically, visual messages, must be "translated" into linguistic form, as we learned from the earlier hypothetical court case and discussion of Figures 17.1 and 17.2. Since visual messages are indeterminate, the statements they provoke may be different and mean different things given the context and the person interpreting the visual message.

Does what we've learned so far mean that visual communication cannot be used in *making* an argument? Not at all. Although a photo, painting, graphic, or object alone cannot make an argument, when placed in the context of language, visuals can be powerful elements of arguments. In print advertising in magazines, newspapers, and even webpages, visuals "serve up the affective, psychological identification, and thus do a real selling job" (Blair 1996, 33). Here's how Blair sums up the discussion:

> *What makes visual messages influential . . . is not any argumentative function they perform, but the unconscious identifications they invoke. . . . The difficulties [visual messages] do present are practical ones of . . . interpretation. Moreover, we have to translate them into verbal arguments in order to analyze and criticize them. So verbal arguments retain their position of primacy. (1996, 34)*

So far, we've discovered that visual messages don't make traditional arguments because they cannot make specific claims. On the other hand, visual messages may be useful as a part of an argument or as a means of persuasion.

Persuasion can be accomplished in many ways—some of which do not entail words. For example, if you are on a strict diet and we offer you a plate of homemade tortellini Alfredo, your first response may well be a resounding, "No, thank you!" However, you may be persuaded to eat if we slowly pass the dish under your nose while vocalizing "Mmmmm . . . ahhhh. . . ." If you *choose* to eat, we have persuaded you. Persuasion merely necessitates influencing your will. Such influence need not be rational or symbolic. We discuss this issue more in the next section. We need to remember at this point that visual messages cannot function *as* arguments because they are indeterminate and so cannot express statements of claim. However, they can be used to provide support for arguments as in our hypothetical courtroom example. Next, let's look at how visual messages may affect persuasion.

THE NATURE OF VISUAL MESSAGES

Taken as a whole, visual messages are indeterminate and, as you will see, usually quite complex in nature. This section provides some starting points for your analyses of visual communication as persuasion. It would take the space of many chapters or even books to thoroughly discuss all that could be discussed about visual communication. As a complement to further research, your greatest resource in dealing with visual communication is your own experiences with it. You will need to reflect on your experiences and creatively apply the concepts presented in the next few pages; you will also need to adopt a balcony stance to see more clearly how these complex messages, which are so easy to consume, are constructed.

THREE BASIC CONCEPTS

Since we are dealing with visual messages as rhetoric, we need to understand where they fit in the scheme of humanly created representations. In the early part of the twentieth century, Charles W. Morris (1938), in studying the problems associated with systems of human symbolic communication, identified three dimensions: syntactics, semantics, and pragmatics. Briefly, **syntactics** has to do with *the rules of organization and ordering of symbols*. A major factor in understanding a language is knowledge of the ordered patterns of the words. For example, read this: *messages this apprenticeship book is an in critically analyzing*. If it makes no sense, that is because it violates the rules or patterns of English syntax. To understand this group of words, you employ your experience in speaking the language, and (where there were multiple possibilities for organizing the sentence) you draw upon your knowledge of the formal rules of syntax to properly order the words. We assume that every competent reader probably came up with the appropriate organization: *this book is an apprenticeship in critically analyzing messages*. The uniformity of conclusion by different readers is due to the well-developed and familiar rules of ordering verbal symbols (i.e., grammar). However, for visual messages (as is the case in nonverbal communication, in general), there is no codified body of syntactical or grammatical rules. At best, we may have habits or conventions for structuring visual messages, but there are no set rules for constructing or interpreting them. That's why they are indeterminate. Different people, due to different perceptual acuities, experiences, and even cultural backgrounds, may order the elements of a visual differently, which leads them to assign different meanings to the same messages.[2] Syntactics features the relationships among signs, symbols, and their parts.

Deriving meaning from messages is the ostensible goal of any communication event. In Morris's taxonomy, **semantics** is *concerned with the process of assigning meaning to or interpreting communications*. This is a very complex and problematic area—one that has merited substantial and diverse study by many scholars. However, in its simplest form, there exist two fundamental forms of symbolism: discursive and presentational (Langer 1951, 237). **Discursive symbols** are *words (and nonverbal emblems[3])* while **presentational symbols** correspond to *visual communication (which includes photos, films, drawings, diagrams, maps, etc.)*. How each of these kinds of messages means can be quite different. For example, a presentational message such as a map can be a scaled-down literal description of some locale, or like those from the Middle Ages, a fanciful, artistic, even theological, interpretation of reality. A discursive form, such as a poem, may be meaningful as an artistic, nonliteral expression of experience or as a practical pneumonic device to remember a formula. Symbols of all sorts may not only have figurative and literal meaning but also carry emotional freight in the form of connotative meanings. Photos of firefighters who died in the line of duty may elicit a powerfully devastating emotional response for one person, while to another person the same photo may only indicate the one-time physical presence in the world of an unknown person. Given the presentational nature of visual communication, and its inability to assert a proposition, visuals tend to function either as information or as triggers of emotional responses.

Finally, **pragmatics** is *concerned with the behavioral effects of symbol use*. These effects may be related to the psychological, biological, or sociological nature of symbol users (Morris 1958, 30). In the preceding example of the photos of firefighters, the behavioral effect of eliciting a paralyzing emotional response is quite different from the effect of a cognitive response. One viewer responds biologically (emotionally) while another responds psychologically. The question that researchers in communication, linguistics, advertising, psychology, and other related fields want to answer is how visual communications can elicit specific behaviors or responses. Lacking a syntax for visual messages and lacking a lexicon of meanings to determine specific meanings, we must look for patterns of behaviors in people associated with particular kinds of visual messages within similar contexts. Attributions of meaning and conclusions about effects of visual communication must be tentatively constructed by critics who thoughtfully and carefully examine patterns of human symbolic action. There is no final arbiter like a dictionary of visual communication you can go to for answers. You have to rigorously and creatively examine the particular visuals in which you are interested by taking into account their sometimes complex structure (syntax) and potential meanings (semantics) within the specific context they exist in order to comment about their effects (pragmatics).

SEMANTICS AND VISUAL COMMUNICATION

To understand the nature of visual communication more fully, we draw on the work of C. S. Peirce who posits three categories of semantics: icon, index, and symbol.

An **icon** *means by similarity to that which it is representing*. For example, ——————— is an icon for the idea of a line, which, in geometry, is the

FIGURE 17.3

object being represented. The horizontal marks are *like* a line; it has meaning stemming from its similarity to its object. Another example in Western culture is the classic icon of the crucifix (Figure 17.3). The crucifix means by similarity—the carved figure on the cross presents the person of Jesus of Nazareth in his passion, which is what the crucifix means. This is a literal rendition of the object for which it stands; it means by mimicking its referent.

However, icons can be much more complex than the preceding examples. Peirce argues that a diagram, even one composed primarily of words, functions as an icon. For example, a diagram like Figure 17.4 means by picturing theory as a likeness of the relationships between its conceptual parts (Peirce 1955, 107). Regarding this example, keep in mind that what is being represented (pointed to) here is the *relationship* of the concepts—the diagram was constructed in order to feature the relationship. (When we discuss symbol, we'll learn that each of the words in the diagram is a symbol.) Peirce's point is that meaning is conveyed iconically by re-presenting an object. In this example, the object is conceptual relationship.

An index is quite different from an icon. An **index** has no resemblance to its object, but rather *means by its association with the object*. Think of an index like a clue or a symptom of something. When you see plastic, glass, and metal fragments at an intersection, they indicate an accident occurred; if you have a cut on your hand that gets red and hot, those qualities indicate infection. Footprints in snow indicate someone preceded you in that place; and a diamond ring on the hand of a model in an advertisement for a stockbroker indicates prosperity. According to Peirce, indices work by calling "upon the hearer [or viewer] to use his powers of observation, and so establish a real connection

FIGURE 17.4

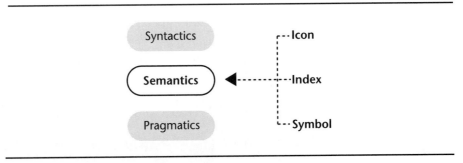

between his mind and the object" (1955, 110). Since, as we noted previously, visual messages cannot make claims or assertions themselves but must be "translated" into a verbal form, indices are essentially imperative statements saying, "Look at this!" (Peirce 1955, 111). In visual communication, much of what you see is intended to do just that—direct your attention to this or that; to hint at a connection between the index and an unseen object that the message maker wants you to bring to mind. You are actually quite adept at using indices, but you use them so often and effortlessly that it is sometimes hard to become conscious of that skill. For example, when Mark wears a tie to class (a rare occasion almost always prompted by the need to wear a tie to another venue immediately after the class), inevitably a student will comment the moment Mark walks in the classroom. The student notes the tie and associates it with some other context. The tie indicates a more formal context than the classroom. The students recognize a pattern, and although it is indeterminate, they attribute some meaning to the tie.

Let's try a slightly more challenging task. Take a look at Figure 17.5. Any meaning you can make of the image is based entirely on indices. Is the person in the red scarf hiding or guarding a child? Is that person male or female? Where is the person? What are his/her circumstances? The kind of head covering *indicates* a female. That conclusion may be drawn because the complexion of the subject and the apparent design of the cloth indicates a Middle Eastern or West Asian culture. Women's head coverings in that region are flowing or draped whereas men's head coverings may be missing or of various sorts from hats to turbans. Since the person seems to be wearing a skirt (men tend to wear Western pants under long shirts or baggy pants that fit tight around the ankles), most likely the subject of the photo is female. The rubble in the background indicates destruction such as we associate with a bomb blast or some other catastrophic event as opposed to what we would expect to see from mere lack of maintenance. However, we can't know from indices whether a bomb or an earthquake did the damage. We can make some sense of the visual from the indices, but who exactly is pictured here, and where, when, and what has happened, are still indeterminate.

In the next few days, practice becoming conscious of your sensitivity to indices. For example, as you look at advertisements in the magazines you read,

FIGURE 17.5

look for all the hints or clues being presented by those elements of the image we can now call indices. You'll discover that they are pervasive—a critical part of our communication environment.

The third category of semiotics is that of symbols. **Symbols** *mean by an arbitrary agreement that such and such a sign will mean such and such.* That is, there is no necessary connection between the symbol and the object of reference. An icon means by similarity, an index means by association with the object, but a symbol is connected to a referent or object only by agreement among users of the language. The words we use are symbols. Some gestures are symbols—applause, for instance—and some visual messages are symbols. Visual symbols are equally arbitrary. For example, look at Figure 17.6, which is the logo for the Information Center for the Environment (ICE) at the University of California, Davis. This visual acts as a symbol for the center because there is no necessary relationship between signifier (the blurred cubes) and the referent, which is the ICE. The logo is not a representation of anything having to do with maps or data sets of environmental information about California. Neither is it associated with the center's mission as we would expect of an index. The figure is a symbol because we have to be informed that it stands for the ICE at UCD. Once we know this, we can make the connection in our minds. What makes symbols so important is that they may "grow" and change (Peirce 1955, 115). The kind of shift and adaptation that can happen with symbols cannot happen with icons and indices because those signs are "frozen" in their relationships with the referent. A crucifix will always represent Jesus; the broken pieces of glass on the road will always indicate a colli-

FIGURE 17.6

sion. However, symbols are not so tightly connected to referents. Words change in meaning over time. To change a meaning of a symbol users must simply agree to connect the symbol with a new or different referent. Visual symbols can change meaning just as verbal symbols do. For example, Enron Corporation (Figure 17.7) has shifted from being North America's largest electricity marketer and darling of Wall Street to a bankrupt company whose shares are essentially worthless. At one time the Enron logo meant "prosperity, power, and security" for those who worked for and invested in the company. Today, as Enron is discussed in the news media, new terms surround the symbol that serve to redefine it. Now this symbol means "deception, greed, and irresponsibility" to thousands of former employees and their dependents, retirees, and investors. As Peirce noted, symbols change as they are related to other symbols. It is important to pay attention to the context of visual messages that you may encounter as a critic because the context of other symbols (both in words and images) may have much to do with how you make sense of the visual message you are examining.

So far, we've looked at the *nature* of visual messages. In examining visuals in arguments, we found that their indeterminate nature precludes the making of claims or other logical statements by them. Visual messages may be used as data for claims or backing for warrants, but they cannot make an argument or logical case by themselves. Visual communications are certainly meaningful, but how they mean is much different from how words mean. Although they are useful in argument in a limited fashion, they are ubiquitous in persuasive messages. In the next section, we look at two general functions of visual communication within persuasion. The model for this discussion is adapted from Paul Messaris's work in visual persuasion.

FIGURE 17.7

FUNCTIONS OF VISUALS IN PERSUASION

According to Messaris (1997), visuals serve two primary functions in persuasive communication: *attracting attention* and *stirring emotions*. We first look at how these functions are accomplished via the design of various visual messages. Then we apply them to a case in which visual communication is central to a persuasive effort.

As you no doubt learned in your basic public speaking course, to get your message across to an audience, you must first get the audience's attention. Certainly, no message is worth much without a receiver or audience. Visual communication is a powerful tool for attracting attention since most human beings are primarily visually oriented. Our eyes deliver one hundred times as much data to our brains as do our ears (Norretranders 1998, 143). There seem to be four common means of attracting attention visually: (1) violating reality, (2) visual metaphor, (3) parody, and (4) point of view.

VIOLATING REALITY

Messaris argues that in a medium that can reproduce the look of reality, the best way to get attention is to violate it (1997, 5). **Violating reality** is accomplished by *presenting an unexpected, odd, or confusing image that grabs our attention*. Anomalies are interesting to us because they provide information or "news of difference" (Bateson 1988, 72), and we are naturally attracted to anomalies because they may be important to our needs or interests. Messaris states, "Because of iconicity, we experience the [anomalous] image as a warp in reality, not just the manipulation of a symbol. It gives us a jolt, and it gets us to look" (1997, 7). For example, if you were browsing a magazine, Figure 17.8 would be difficult to pass without spending some time examining it. Certainly, the image herein is sufficiently like a person (an icon) that is burning and becoming a flaming bird such that this strikes us as a "warp in reality" and "gives us a jolt." If an attention-getting visual needs to violate reality, this image accomplishes the task just as Messaris suggests.

VISUAL METAPHOR

A second means of attracting attention is via **visual metaphor**, which attempts *to illuminate a familiar target or idea by juxtaposing it with an unfamiliar one*. If you recall the television advertisements for the release of Microsoft's new XP operating system, people were seen floating/flying effortlessly from place to place—a visual metaphor for the notion of effortless transportation of information via the built-in features of XP. Something as simple as the image in Figure 17.9 also grabs attention via visual metaphor. Replacing the computer with the earth not only provides the vehicle for the metaphor, but the image also violates reality, grabbing attention while stirring the emotional response of feeling in control. Messaris contends that as a result, the main impact of visual metaphors beyond getting attention is emotional impact. The presenta-

FIGURE 17.8

tional message form is instantaneous, eye-catching, and emotionally stimulating. When coupled with a well-crafted, complementary verbal message appealing to the audience's reason, visual metaphors can be quite powerful.

PARODY

A third means of attracting attention and striking an emotional chord is through parody. This is quite different from metaphor. Whereas metaphor works by featuring apparent differences between elements, **parody** works by *imitating some object wherein a key element of the original is made ridiculous through distortion*. The effect is to draw attention to a significant element of a message and, by doing so, create a sense of absurdity. The emotional effects can be varied, but often parodies serve to point out foibles or shortcomings in ideas, behaviors, institutions, habits, practices, and so on. In recognizing shortcomings in the object, the receiver experiences a sense of superiority or insight and identifies with the parodist while distancing him- or herself from the target.

FIGURE 17.9

However, if the receiver identifies with some part of the target image, feelings of embarrassment or shame may be experienced. Take a look at Figure 17.10.

This is a parody of the Marlboro Man advertisement series presented by Philip Morris, Inc. The image taken as a whole is not a metaphor, but an imitation of the kind and style of picture used to advertise Marlboro cigarettes. The lone cowboy gazing off into the sun, setting his mind to accomplish the difficult and manly tasks of a rancher, and quietly smoking a cigarette are common elements of those ads. The single distorted element, the flaccid cigarette, makes the seriousness of the cowboy's pose ludicrous. Presumably, the target audience is smokers or those thinking about taking it up. Smokers who identify with the image (a cigarette in one's mouth is sufficient) may feel disparaged or shamed. Nonsmokers may feel confirmed and supported. Interestingly, the specific appeal is sexual. To the extent that the dangling cigarette is like an

FIGURE 17.10

WARNING: SMOKING CAUSES IMPOTENCE

impotent penis, that element of the entire image works metaphorically. This shows us that images are complex in their rhetorical dynamic. In this case, the kind of approach is parody, but within the image visual metaphor is also operating.

POINT OF VIEW

The final means of getting and directing attention, according to Messaris, is point of view. There are five points of view we quickly examine in this section: **direct gaze**, *wherein the subject of the visual is gazing directly at the viewer*; **rear view**, *where the viewer is placed behind the subject*; **close-up**, *generally featuring from the shoulders up*; **distant**, *showing the entire subject*; and finally the **subjective** point of view, *where the image is as if through the eyes of the viewer*. Our interpersonal experiences provide the resources for analyzing and interpreting many visual messages. Visuals "re-present" reality, and we have few means[4] by which to respond other than applying the rules and habits of decoding real-world experience to images (Gombrich 1980, 185, 202).

In understanding gaze, look back at Figure 17.10. The subject of the image is gazing off to some point in space to his left. When you are in proximity to another and he or she adopts such a posture, it usually indicates that the person does not want to interact because the person is thinking about something else. It is a solitary position. The Marlboro Man, which this image is parodying, embodies the strong, solitary, tough, self-made individualist. It suggests a kind of unassailable self-containment that Americans have always valued. Interestingly, the device is not just for men. What is the effect of the indirect gaze in the image in Figure 17.11?

FIGURE 17.11

This woman is also looking away as if lost in thought. She is beautiful and she seems relatively close to the viewer, but she maintains her distance and power by averting her gaze. She is not demure, shy, or troubled; if so, her eyes would be cast down. Rather like the cowboy, her level gaze suggests thoughtfulness and willingness to confront reality alone. Notice the difference in effect when the gaze is direct, as in Figure 17.12. The characters in this image directly engage the viewer. Interestingly, the emotional effect of each is a study in contrast—the lady's eye contact is pleasant and reassuring, while the man's is deadpan and somewhat threatening. You can see the lady's eyes as she peers over her reading glasses while the man's eyes are dark and difficult to "read." The effect in the photo of the man with his inaccessible eyes is similar to talking with someone wearing dark sunglasses. It's disconcerting because you can't see what the person is really attending to or what his or her own emotional responses are while you remain exposed. Having your eyes covered is a position of interpersonal power while showing them is an invitation to interaction and equality.

FIGURE 17.12

Images from behind the subject have a very different effect. Since turning the back is a common way of creating distance or breaking relationship, visuals that use this form generally direct attention to the context. Messaris notes that travel advertisements often use this perspective, which draws attention to the surrounding environment (1997, 24–27). Figure 17.13 illustrates that point of view: the model in the picture draws less attention to herself than to the context—a dark tunnel-like staircase that emerges into bright light. The ambiguity of the picture invites us to think about the image: is the woman a distant ideal to be pursued or is she leaving the viewer? Is she leaving early in the evening portending an evening alone or is she leaving in the morning after a night with another? The rear view is ambiguous, suggesting romance, love unrequited or fulfilled; it suggests mystery and potential, even power as the turn away from another denotes decision and action. Since the action is unclear, we tend to turn to the context for clues to guide our interpretation and reduce our uncertainty regarding the meaning of the image.

The perception of distance is an important cue to us. Whether we are near or far from the subject has much to do with our emotional responses. Look at the next two images and assess your responses to both. The apparently close proximity of the crocodile in Figure 17.14 elicits more of a sense of dread or fear than the distant perspective in Figure 17.15. Our experience tells us that the farther we are away from danger, the safer we are and the more relaxed we feel. When makers of visual messages want to increase involvement between viewer and the subject of the image, creation of a perception of a short distance between them is effective (Messaris 1997, 29).

FIGURE 17.13

FIGURE 17.14

FIGURE 17.15

Finally, we are sometimes presented with a subjective view of some object. A subjective view places you directly in the position of observer. Figure 17.16 exemplifies the subjective view. The hands in the picture appear to be coming from your own arms; the effect is as if you were looking through a lens at objects immediately in front of you. It's like being in someone else's skin— sometimes an interesting thought, sometimes a terrifying one. In either case, the perspective is involving. This device is often used in thriller films to induce in the audience the sort of emotional rush that a character in the film must be experiencing. For example, this is often done in the film thriller *What Lies Beneath*. In one particular scene, the camera (which makes *you* vicariously the voyeur) looks through a knothole in a fence into the neighbor's yard to spy on the neighbor suspected of murder. Suddenly, an eye appears looking directly into the lens (and at you). The effect is a powerful shock, and you feel as if you've been caught.

Given the devices we've just examined, violating reality, visual metaphor, parody, and point of view, we can see how images serve to get, control, and limit audience attention. Such control is extremely important for it serves the persuasive purposes of the message maker by "re-creating" reality in the way the message maker wants us to see it. The often iconic nature of the visual channel is powerful because we instantaneously grasp the message. The speed and complexity of that encounter can override our ability to sort through the mes-

FIGURE 17.16

sage parts and analyze their persuasive dynamics. By contrast, a purely discursive message, due to the relatively slow rate at which we construct the sentences, allows us to reflect on what we're being asked to do by the writer, which often makes assessment and counterargument easier.

AN APPLICATION

Visual messages are very complex, as we have seen. They serve powerful argumentative and persuasive functions. To better understand how the specific rhetorical elements we've discussed work together, let's briefly examine the sort of visual and textual message that we often encounter in daily life. Figure 17.17 will serve as the "text" for our summary discussion. Take a few minutes and study the poster.

As you can see, the poster relies equally on both discursive and presentational forms. Imagine the poster with just the copy. Without the pictures the argument would be substantially diminished in power. The headline would

FIGURE 17.17

make no sense, and the balance of the argument at the bottom would be robbed of the emotional punch the pictures provide. Now, imagine the poster with just the pictures. The pairing of Martin Luther King Jr. and Charles Manson would make little or no sense without verbal commentary or context. Viewers could construct their own interpretations, but there is only a small chance that any viewer would connect the two in the way intended by the message makers. The images, without context, are indeterminate and do little or nothing persuasive. Now, imagine the poster as it is, but with a distant shot of King, with his back to the camera, locked arm in arm with others in a civil rights march, and a distant shot of Manson sitting alone in a prison exercise yard. A distant shot would diminish the power of both subjects. Finally, imagine the man on the left as an anonymous African American and the man on the right as an anonymous Caucasian. Without the stories brought to mind by the notable subjects, the images would have much less to add to the discursive argument. The choices of images certainly make a difference, and the images and words are tightly woven together in this message. The faces chosen are necessary to maximize both audience attention (creating curiosity about why these are in such proximity) and the emotional impact of the argument.

The form of the visual message is a parody of a wanted poster like those tacked on walls in the Wild West. The suggested stucco or adobe wall, hastily driven nails, and the paper discolored by exposure to sun and rain are all cues of the message form that it is imitating and parodying. This wanted poster parodies the present practices of the justice system that the ACLU argues are flawed and unfair. In a complementary way, the poster serves as a metaphor for racial profiling by placing King and Manson in the position of "vehicle" for the metaphor—they stand in for all minorities and whites, respectively. Profiling makes little sense since the net it casts would allow a Manson to pass through untouched while a King would be caught in it.

The choice of these particular faces is important in that they both have come to symbolize love of others versus hate of others. Their images have become symbols because our social narratives in news and history have associated love and hate with them. Neither is *inherently* connected with either meaning. Consequently, to some subgroups in our country, their meanings are quite different and almost exactly reversed in the emotional effect they have on audiences in those groups. Within the verbal argument presented, however, these images are complementary. If King's image was replaced by, say, Mahatma Gandhi, and Manson's replaced by Adolf Hitler, the same meanings of love and hate may be triggered, but the pictures would not direct attention to the specific social problem of racial profiling by police in modern America.

The syntax of the faces in a parallel form is significant because it demands comparison and contrast. One person deserves to be on a wanted poster; the other does not. The photos minimize contextual distractions by cropping, and they immediately highlight the single specific element of the face that the verbal argument is featuring—the color of skin and ethnicity. If nothing else was known about them, the black man would be a target and the white man would not; the irony of exactly who these men are works to show the ludicrous nature of profiling and invites an emotional reaction of disdain for it.

Finally, the point of view of the photos is significant. The images place you "in front of" the faces so you can get a good look at who they are. Their gaze is not directed at you but at a slight angle, allowing you to view them without confronting them eye to eye. If you were so engaged, it would be difficult to maintain a position of judge of the argument presented. If King was looking directly into the camera, and you are white, the effect would be accusatory and potentially intimidating or annoying (if you are already in agreement with the conclusion of the argument). Some distance is necessary to allow you to involve yourself in controversy as judge. If Manson was pictured as looking directly at you, most likely the effect would be intimidation or repugnance toward Manson alone. The placement of gaze permits the viewer to treat the faces both as symbols and as specific individuals. As a result, the argument against profiling is grounded in both specific cases and general probability, which makes it compelling.

EXPANDING THE ANALYSIS

As we noted at the beginning of the chapter, this collection of concepts about visual communication is not the same as a search model or theory, which raises questions about a message. These concepts don't raise questions, but they do help you to answer some that may be raised by any particular theory of rhetoric. These concepts help you to point out elements of the visual dimension of the text and explain how they work, but they don't prod you to critique rhetorical motives or the quality of the argument presented, for example. Using just visual concepts can lead to some knowledge about a message, but that knowledge is limited to the technical nature of the images themselves. We urge you to use these tools as a way of developing a more comprehensive rhetorical study of any text that is controlled by a well-developed theoretical approach. The outcome will be a much more interesting, useful, and insightful product.

SUMMARY

In this chapter we have briefly explored some of the dynamics of visual communication. We found that the rhetorical purposes of argument cannot be handled by visual communication alone due to its inherent ambiguity and indeterminate quality. Visuals alone cannot make claims. Due to their tendency to be iconic or indexical they often get stuck at a too specific, concrete, or limited level of reference to allow logical manipulation. Conversely, due to their tendency to replicate reality, visuals serve well as support for arguments. In persuasive communication, visual communication has at least two important pragmatic functions: to get audience attention and to elicit emotional responses.

How audiences decode visual messages is often variable since visuals are not governed by formal syntactical rules. Visuals can be organized in all sorts of ways and still be meaningful. To interpret visual messages, consumers and critics must rely on generic patterns of visual or life experience. Thus the semantic function of visuals is indeterminate or ambiguous because no rule book or reference exists to say exactly what a visual means. Meaning is dependent on the acuity, knowledge, and experience of the receiver within a context that guides interpretation.

Visual messages exist on a continuum from iconic through indexical to symbolic. Most visual messages operate iconically, representing their objects and meaning. You must keep in mind the complicated indexical relationship a visual may have with its object since an index means by association with its object. These associations must be treated as clues to meaning, not direct representations.

Symbols constitute a broad class of visual messages. Anything from a red light, to the Nike "swoosh," to a single letter (e.g., "The Scarlet Letter") can act as symbol. Keep in mind the ability of symbols to evolve and change meanings. When working with visuals that you suspect are symbolic, it is important to consider the context as a guide to their meanings.

Finally, we explored some specific structural characteristics of visual messages. Some are absurd or violate reality in order to get attention and stimulate emotions; others do so as visual metaphors or by parody. We saw too how the point of view of the visual may have significant meaning and effects.

Visual messages are quite complex, inviting rigorous and creative analyses. Since we are generally visually oriented creatures, it is important that as critics we don't allow our quick responses to presentational messages to overwhelm us; nor can we allow our familiarity with the visual channel to lull us into thinking that we can easily and correctly make sense of visuals without investing effort into a thoughtful analysis. This chapter provides basic tools for asking relevant and potentially significant questions about any visual text you encounter. Just as you must control responses to verbal texts, and just as the search models help you to more impartially query any written message worth analyzing, the concepts in this chapter should initiate analysis of visual communication. Use these ideas and your own experience as tools to develop and elaborate any theoretically grounded analysis, interpretation, and evaluation of messages that are both presentational and discursive in nature.

EXERCISES

Each of the following exercises is related to Figure 17.17. Before attempting the exercises, spend some time studying it.

1. Using classical approaches (Chapters 9 and 10), create a list of at least five significant critical questions about the poster. Explain what concepts from this chapter would be most useful for answering any of the questions you created, and explain how they will augment your understanding of the poster as rhetoric.

2. Using dramatistic approaches (Chapters 11, 12, and 13), create a list of at least five significant critical questions about the poster. Explain what concepts

from this chapter would be most useful for answering any of the questions you created, and explain how they will augment your understanding of the poster as rhetoric.

3. Using sociopolitical approaches (Chapters 14, 15, and 16), create a list of at least five significant critical questions about the poster. Explain what concepts from this chapter would be most useful for answering any of the questions you created, and explain how they will augment your understanding of the poster as rhetoric.

NOTES

1 Visual messages do not have the capacity for negative messages. All they can do is represent reality (or what appears to be reality). Language, on the other hand, has the capacity to say what is *not* present or what is *not* in existence. Sally cannot, for example, give you a photo of her not being somewhere. Even if the photo does not contain her image, the photo cannot convey the message, "Sally was not here." The photo necessarily presents an image of who *was* there (a declarative statement). Neither can a photo convey the secondary message, "And Sally did not take this photo of the group." Those negative statements can only be conveyed linguistically. Therefore, a visual message is positive or declarative in what it is able to communicate.

2 Tor Norretranders recounts the following story regarding the Me'en people of Ethiopia: "The anthropologists gave them a picture and asked what it was. 'They felt the paper, sniffed it, crumpled it, and listened to the crackling noise it made; they nipped off little bits and chewed them to taste it.' The pattern on the paper did not interest the Me'en, because pictures as they knew them were painted on cloth. (Presented with Western pictures on cloth, the Me'en had trouble seeing what they were meant to see by our standards.)" (1998, 187–88). Here is a significant case wherein the culture and the mental schemas shaped by the culture actually affected the perceptual apparatus of the Me'en. As a result, the syntax of Western photos made no sense to them whatsoever.

3 Emblems are a special class of nonverbal messages that function as words. That is, their meaning is agreed to by the users of the language. An emblem can be an iconic symbol such as when someone drags his or her index finger across the throat. It is iconic in that it mimes the cutting of a throat with a knife. It is symbolic in that when we see it, we don't really think of cutting a person's throat. Rather, we treat it like a symbol that we've learned means an emphatic, "Stop! Desist!" Finally, a nonverbal emblem can be symbolic such as when someone shows the middle finger to another. This code switching across channels is something that is important to keep in mind when examining visual messages.

4 Earlier in the chapter when we discussed Figures 17.1 and 17.2, we noted that our imagination is necessary for making sense of visual communications. Due to the incomplete nature of any visual message, we use our imagination to construct context, add in missing information, or translate the message into a verbal form. Of course, we draw upon experience as the raw material for our imagination. What we want to make clear is primacy of experience in the process of interpreting visual messages.

WORKS CITED

Bateson, Gregory. *Mind and Nature: A Necessary Unity.* Toronto: Bantam Books, 1988.

Blair, J. Anthony. "The Possibility and Actuality of Visual Arguments." *Argumentation and Advocacy* 33 (1996): 23–39.

Fleming, David. "Can Pictures Be Arguments?" *Argumentation and Advocacy* 33 (1996): 11–22.

Gombrich, E. M. "Standards of Truth: The Arrested Image and the Moving Eye." In *The Language of Images,* edited by W. J. T. Mitchell, 181–217. Chicago: University of Chicago Press, 1980.

Langer, Susanne K. *Philosophy in a New Key: A Study in the Symbolism of Reason, Rite and Art.* New York: Mentor, 1951.

Messaris, Paul. *Visual Persuasion: The Role of Images in Advertising.* Thousand Oaks, CA: Sage, 1997.

Morris, Charles W. "Foundations of a Theory of Signs." In *International Encyclopedia of Unified Science,* edited by Otto Neurath, Rudolph Carnap, and Charles W. Morris, vol. 1, 1–59. Chicago: University of Chicago Press, 1938.

Norretranders, Tor. *The User Illusion: Cutting Consciousness Down to Size.* New York: Viking, 1998.

Peirce, Charles Saunders. "Logic as Semiotic: The Theory of Signs." In *Philosophical Writings of Peirce,* edited by Justus Buchler, 98–119. New York: Dover, 1955.

SUGGESTED READINGS

Barbatsis, Gretchen S. "'Look and I Will Show You Something You Will Want to See': Pictorial Engagement in Negative Political Campaign Commercials." *Argumentation and Advocacy* 33 (1996): 69–80.

Finnegan, C. A. "Social Engineering, Visual Politics, and the New Deal: FSA Photography in *Survey Graphic.*" *Rhetoric and Public Affairs* 3 (2000): 333–62.

Messaris, Paul. "Visual Literacy v. Visual Manipulation." *Critical Studies in Mass Communication* 11 (1994): 181–203.

Scott, Linda M. "Images in Advertising: The Need for a Theory of Visual Rhetoric." *Journal of Consumer Research* 21 (1994): 252–73.

Van Leeuwen, Theo, and Carey Jewitt, eds. *Handbook of Visual Analysis.* Thousand Oaks, CA: Sage, 2001.

SAMPLE ANALYSIS OF "SHE'S LEAVING HOME"

Directions: We suggest that you first read the text of the study, which is in the left column, in order to see what a finished product of criticism looks like. As you read, look for description of content and context; analysis using specific theoretical concepts; interpretation of the rhetors' choices; and evaluation of the song as rhetoric. Make sure you study the essay's structure—look for how we have constructed the arguments; pay attention to the pathway we use to help a reader see something about the song that provides insight into how it works as rhetoric.

Once you have studied the essay (left column), then read the commentary (right column) and highlight statements that help you understand how a critic thinks about a message and explains that thinking to others.

"Can't Buy Me Love," but You Can Buy Me Fun[1]

TEXT OF THE STUDY	COMMENTARY ON THE STUDY
Description of Context The decade of the 1960s was a watershed of change in Western culture. While one may argue that the changes seen during that time were developing well before 1964 and continued well after 1970, this seven-year span was a period of articulation of deep changes in values. In America, the effects of the rhetoric were powerful, approaching the kind of discursive power of the rhetoric that spurred the American Revolution of the 1700s or the abolition movement of the 1800s. Interestingly, it was the Beatles, a British rock group that provided the youth of the '60s with a means to speak their minds via the lyrics of the Beatles' songs. The wake of the Beatles phenomenon pushed aside the insipid ballads of hot rods, teen romances, and adolescent problems and replaced them with songs that extolled the virtues of drugs, free sex, and political revolution. The Beatles themselves underwent a metamorphosis beginning with songs expressing rather traditional values, "I Want to Hold Your Hand!" (1963) and "Can't Buy Me Love" (1964), and moving to "Lucy in the Sky With Diamonds," (1967), "I Am the Walrus" (1967), and "Revolution" (1968) to name a few. The album entitled *Sgt. Pepper's Lonely Hearts Club Band* (1967) was a turning point for the group and for rock music in general. The album was groundbreaking in form and content from the cover art to the parenthetical structure of the album's first and penultimate tracks, and lack of discrete breaks between songs. One of the most interesting songs on the album, "She's Leaving Home," is an apparently mournful ballad that, at first, seems to tell a common story of youth misunderstood. However,	The introduction is designed to help the reader contextualize the message under analysis. These first few lines identify the historical setting and the rhetorical focus of this study. At this point we begin a brief argument that the period of time we are examining is important historically and culturally. This discussion is necessary to connect the Beatles, who are British, with the American cultural changes we described above. We also need to introduce the idea that their music is rhetorical. To be reasonable, we need to show here that the evolution of culture is facilitated by people who are themselves changing; the Beatles were not devils who appeared in a puff of smoke; they were part and parcel of the cultural revolution of the 1960s. Their unique contribution was their ability to articulate what was happening socially. Our task here is to logically zero-in on the specific message we are analyzing, showing that it is in fact a *significant fragment* of a larger rhetorical phenomenon (The Sgt. Pepper album) that was *centrally placed in time and circumstance*. In other words, we argue that a song that is often overlooked articulates essential values of the cultural wave that crested in 1967 breaking over Western culture through the rest of the decade and beyond.

TEXT OF THE STUDY (cont.)	**COMMENTARY ON THE STUDY** (cont.)
upon close examination of the narrative, it appears that the Beatles were pursuing a revolution of traditional understandings of relational expectations and moral obligations. *This song employs the presentation of characters in a struggle for self-satisfaction in order to mock the traditional moral purposes of significant relationships.* This analysis is important because it provides some insight into the effects of the rhetoric of popular music on the development of social values and behavior. By unmasking the subtle narrative devices employed in this seemingly innocuous song, we learn something about the persuasive dynamics of a medium that served as the voice of a generation.	At this point, we are leading the reader to our claim, which we created after spending considerable effort in characterizing and analyzing the song. From that we learned how communication was used to effect cultural change. We attempted to articulate in the claim the essence of what we discovered. Notice that the claim features the rhetorical means used to accomplish a specific outcome. If we fail to mention the narrative element, the claim is reduced to saying what the song meant: "traditional moral values no longer hold." However, by including "presentation of characters" we introduce a rhetorical explanation for how the Beatles accomplished their apparent rhetorical goals.
Description of Text "She's Leaving Home" is a simple story of a young lady who abruptly leaves her home and her parents. We are presented a glimpse of her life and activities from early on a Wednesday morning when she leaves a note for her parents, quietly moves to the backdoor and "stepping outside she is free." Her parents find her letter that "she wished would say more" and they struggle to understand her actions. By Friday she is far away, with a man, completing a rendezvous that she had previously, and apparently secretly, made.	For readers unfamiliar with the song, we describe it with an eye to pointing out those characteristics most relevant to understanding the song as narrative. We chose to begin by describing the plot. Notice that we don't try to account for every detail. We include only those that will matter for the reader later. We also give the reader a taste of the message by providing appropriate snippets of it in the description/characterization.
The song presents two voices: that of an omniscient narrator describing the young lady's actions and feelings and the voices of the parents' echoing refrains of what have come to be clichéd parental perspective: "We gave her most of our lives/Sacrificed most of our lives"; "We never thought of ourselves/Never a thought for ourselves." Through these two voices Lennon and McCartney create the characters and their relationships. Using these elements, the composers manage to re-create traditional familial moral expectations.	Here we show that the story structure and characters are interwoven. The parents, as a single character, are so constructed by what they say and by placement in the refrain. The effect of the interaction of these two elements of the message is to distance them from their daughter and the listener. The last two sentences in the paragraph transition from description to analysis.

TEXT OF THE STUDY (cont.)	**COMMENTARY ON THE STUDY** (cont.)
Analysis The use of a song in the form of a narrative is a powerful rhetorical tool because the poetic dimension of the story is simple and seductive. The narrative is a powerful mechanism for effecting changes in values since it is through the interaction of the logic and poetic of narratives that societies create and maintain moral structures for social organization.[2] In effect, societies manage their moral constructs by using stories as a kind of public language that provides common understandings of experience and commitment. According to Celeste Condit, "Social discourse units [narratives] carry moral import beyond individual interest, in part, because they indicate shared commitments and prescribe what each person as a member of a collectivity is obliged to do within a collectivity."[3] It is not difficult to classify popular music as a form of public rhetoric, and "[p]ublic rhetoric can therefore be viewed as a process in which basic human desires are transformed into moral codes."[4] In other words, popular music functions as rhetoric by negotiating and arguing for particular social mores and norms, and the Beatles, among others, provided sophisticated narratives challenging or re-creating traditional relational expectations and obligations. Within the story of "She's Leaving Home," two specific characters are presented: a female who has been living with her parents for "so many years" and the parents—who act as a single moral entity. The narrator describes the woman's behavior as furtive; she leaves before dawn, "silently," and "quietly"; and purposeful; "Waiting to keep the appointment she made/Meeting a man from the motor trade." Although she seems to be saddened by the leaving, as she is described as "clutching her handkerchief," the listener's certainty of that emotion is later called into question by her goal as presented by the narrator. As the song	This section begins a brief discussion of rhetorical theory—specifically the ability of narratives to make logical arguments via poetic or artistic means. Fisher's article that we cite here explains that human beings use stories to make sense of the most important issues in life [review our discussion in Chapter 11]. A clear, concise explanation of theory is foundational to both analysis and interpretation of the text. It is worth spending the time developing your understanding of theory because it provides the tools needed to explain how a message works in language that is outside of your personal experience. At this point, we develop theory related to the second part of our claim. Condit's work helps us argue that the "basic human desires" expressed in the song are the ground for moral codes by which we can judge our interpersonal behavior. At this point, we turn the focus from theory to specific analysis of the text itself. Here we apply the narrative concept of character (which was central to our claim) to the content of the song. Notice how we develop our case by citing evidence from the song itself. We signal that we have a perspective on the message ("that emotion is *later* called into question"). We are not just marching through

TEXT OF THE STUDY (cont.)	COMMENTARY ON THE STUDY (cont.)
unfolds, the moral commitments of the daughter become increasingly ambiguous. The second character, the parents, is characterized ambiguously, too. The parents' character is first presented as an echo in the mind of the daughter, "We gave her most of our lives/Sacrificed most of our lives/We gave her everything money could buy." Again, at the end of the song the parents appear as echoes or wraiths haunting the daughter: "What did we do that was wrong?/We didn't know it was wrong." In the middle stanza of the song, the mother (speaking for "Daddy," too) says, upon discovering her daughter's note, "Daddy, our baby's gone!/Why would she treat us so thoughtlessly?/How could she do this to me?" With this structure, Lennon and McCartney create a story that at some level is experienced by everyone in the process of maturation. Everyone experiences specific needs for independence and dependence, and the negotiation of those needs is central to family life. Such relational dilemmas are fraught with moral obligations that have traditionally been resolved by applying traditional moral demands such as "loving others more than ourselves," by "doing unto others as we would have them do to us," and so on. However, "She's Leaving Home" provides a different moral rule: the relationship is defined by one's degree of satisfaction and one's obligation is to making oneself happy within or without the relationship. In other words, the existence of the family relationship cannot, in and of itself, make moral demands on the participants. The only obligations presented here are to achievement of self-satisfaction. **Interpretation** What is striking about the relationship of the characters is the lack of connection or interaction between them. Lennon and McCartney, by using an omniscient narrator and the echoing voices of the parents keep the auditor	line by line but are trying to teach our reader something about how the message is structured as whole. Interesting and useful statements about messages require a perspective that contextualizes any *particular* element of the message within the message as a *whole*. Rhetoric is for uncovering and expressing truth. Narratives are valuable to the degree that they articulate life experience with "fidelity." Lennon and McCartney start their case by creating identification between their listeners' experience and that portrayed by the daughter in the story. Once identification is achieved, they turn the moral obligations of traditional relationships upside down. This is the heart of our argument—the point of stasis. If we convince our readers that moral obligations have been redefined by how the rhetors realign relationships in the narrative, then we have taught them something important about how discourse can be used to reshape our perceptions, beliefs, values, and behaviors.

TEXT OF THE STUDY (cont.)	**COMMENTARY ON THE STUDY** (cont.)
distant from the characters, avoiding too much identification with either one. As a result the composers are able to depict the relationship as one disconnected. The daughter as she fled her home left a note of explanation that "she hoped would say more." She was either unable to find the means to express her feelings or did not care to exert the effort to manage the task fully. The actual reason is not as important as the fact that the message was incomplete.	Here we elaborate our argument. We are trying to take our readers deeper into the dynamics between the parts of the narrative that function subtly to change reality for listeners.
The character of the parents is depicted as equally self-involved. The echoing voices feature the parents' interest: "We gave . . ."; "[W]e sacrificed . . ."; "We gave . . ."; "We never thought of ourselves." They look for absolution for mistakes, "We didn't know it was wrong," rather than worry about where their daughter was and what her condition may be. The characters are portrayed as self-interested, self-involved, and seeking self-satisfaction.	At this point we are elaborating our earlier contention that the daughter's behavior is self-involved (this is central to our claim).
Relationships lacking communication of substance are essentially nonexistent. Silence due to disinterestedness evaporates any sense of mutual obligation. As Condit suggests, when parties in a relationship converse, they do so in order to persuade each other about how to see and understand the world; they must listen to each other and adjust their ideas and actions to each other, even if they disagree. However, when they reach a point where disagreement is so great that persuasion cannot occur, the hope of moral resolution is suspended.[5] When one is not in relationship with another, no moral obligations exist, and one is free to behave however one wants. Consequently, the daughter need not take the time to craft a note to say all that was necessary to explain her behavior because she does not "owe" that to the parents; the parents don't feel they owe their daughter any greater attention or assistance in her development because they have already given "her everything money could buy." The	In a complementary fashion, we show how the parents are characterized by Lennon and McCartney as being self-involved as well.
	To make our case, we must at this point take on a slightly riskier argument. This section makes a rather large inference about the nature of relationships based on our knowledge of communication systems. We conclude that people who do not communicate (think of the word *commune*), even if they live under the same roof and are related by birth, are not actually in relationship.

TEXT OF THE STUDY (cont.)	COMMENTARY ON THE STUDY (cont.)

relationship was never allocentric and personal, but was economic and impersonal.
 	
What this narrative argues is that relationships such as the one depicted here (and one with which most youthful auditors could identify more or less), relationships that only *look* like relationships but do not truly exist since they lack the communion born of communication, lack the moral purposes and obligations of *actual* relationships. Lennon and McCartney, by creating recognizable characters in a recognizable story suggest that all such relationships are without substance and where there is no love, no traditional obligations exist. The conclusion to the argument is presented in the refrain of the last stanza, and its surprising conclusion calls into question the expected words most auditors have in mind as a taken-for-granted conclusion to the story.
 	
The final stanza is:
 	
She
(What did we do that was wrong?)
  is having
(We didn't know it was wrong.)
  Fun
(Fun is the one thing money can't buy.)
  Something inside that was always denied for so many years.
(Bye-Bye)
  She's leaving home.
(Bye-Bye.)
 	
Unless one listens to or reads the lyrics very carefully, the *expected* words to describe the daughter after meeting the man (assuming that love was requited there) are:
  She
(What did we do that was wrong?)
  is having
(We didn't know it was wrong.)
  Fun
(*Love* is the one thing money can't buy.)
	This clinches our case about the central messages of the song—if no relationship exists, then no moral obligation to others exists.
	
	This section summarizes the part of our case that deals with how the rhetors use characters and their problematic relations to redefine moral obligation, but we have one more thread to tie up—how the message structure was used to subtly accomplish revolutionary goals.
	
	When we were engaged in the process of criticism we noticed that the message structure changed in the final stanza. We assumed such a change was intentional on the part of the rhetors so we had to investigate the consequences of the decision by Lennon and McCartney to disrupt the pattern they had previously established.

TEXT OF THE STUDY (cont.)	COMMENTARY ON THE STUDY (cont.)
But the expected subject, love, is not the lyric. The composers, by substituting the lesser value, fun, for the greater value, love, turn the purpose of significant relationships upside down. Fun is the daughter's motive for leaving and for meeting the "man in the motor trade." The admittedly clichéd statement "Love is the one thing money can't buy" is mocked by the narrator by so matter-of-factly substituting "fun." Not only is the listener confronted with a surprising and therefore attention-grabbing and possibly persuasive alternative to the morally grounded "glue" of significant relationships, the listener is also presented a statement that is patently not true. The story suggests our present relational expectations are all a joke, since fun is something purchased constantly. The song mocks the traditional expectations of the listener as the song calls for a postmodern response to the listener's situation. The call is to forget the constraining moral baggage that society has laid upon individuals and experience life in the carnival or burlesque where Sgt. Pepper's Band is playing.	Note here that in this section of our argument, our voice becomes louder. We are slightly less objective because we are drawing on our personal experience as a touchstone in understanding its effects. Since we have worked hard to present an impartial perspective earlier, it seems legitimate at this point to speak as people who have dealt with the message like most everyone else to flesh out the argument.
Evaluation The question that arises, then, is this rhetorical effort a good one? Does it achieve its implicit goals of drawing attention to our relational expectations and obligations and reconfigure those expectations? Within the context of the times, from which the song clearly draws, we believe it does accomplish those goals, and does so in a way that is consistent with its revolutionary message, and it does this by purposely violating narrative fidelity. In Walter Fisher's terms, this song exhibits narrative probability wherein the "probable" story is marked by coherence, consistency, and noncontradiction. The story exhibits "fidelity" or "rings true" when compared to similar stories as well as with life experience.[6] In the	We are concluding our argument that began with the claim. The characteristic of message structure that is important here is the switch of words that shift our perceptions of reality. This is the same dynamic that makes a joke funny. A humorist sets us thinking along one track and by using a single word, gesture, or image re-creates our understanding of a situation. We laugh because we've been tricked. While "She's Leaving Home" doesn't make us laugh, it does create a visceral response in the same way a joke does. Our final task as critics is evaluation of the message as a persuasive effort. The questions we pose here are fairly standard evaluative questions. (What other questions come to your mind?)

TEXT OF THE STUDY (cont.)	COMMENTARY ON THE STUDY (cont.)
case of "She's Leaving Home," the *story* line moves in a simple and expected chronology wherein the story elements are coherent, consistent, and noncontradictory.	
However, the final stanza of the song features not plot but morality. This concluding stanza does not move the listener in time or space but shifts attention from action to interpretation. That is, the listener's attention is grabbed by the statement that "Fun is the one thing money can't buy," which is a statement that does not ring true; society has never said that, and the testimonies of individuals who have tried hedonism attest to the fact that fun is not the path to personal meaning and value. That violation of fidelity, however, seems to be a conscious choice of the composers—it was no mere slip of the pen; it was not demanded by the meter of the song. The violation of fidelity is essential to the goals of the song because fidelity is about the truth of matters and the composers were attempting a significant shift in our understanding of "the way things are."	Since we used narrative theory for the analysis, it makes logical sense to draw evaluative criteria from it.

The first criterion is set out by Fisher—narrative probability. When we applied this concept to the story, we concluded that the events of the plot followed one because of another; the plot was probable. That's good.

The second criterion Fisher lays out is that of narrative "fidelity," which, as we noted above, has to do with the degree to which the story presents the "truth of the matter." |
| *If Lennon and McCartney had chosen words that exhibited complete fidelity to audience expectations, they would have undermined their own revolutionary project because they would have assented to and verified society's norms. The song would have been just one more pop ballad among the thousands before it. | Given the shift in structure of the last stanza, which masks the core claim of the song, and given the absurd affirmation of "fun" as one's ultimate moral obligation, we concluded that the message does not exhibit fidelity. We could simply end with the easy evaluation that the message was good and bad—Lennon and McCartney just made a mistake as storytellers. But we were compelled to rethink that since the first part of the song was so masterfully constructed. Certainly, the composers didn't go to lunch between stanzas and return to the job without skill! |
| **Conclusion**
In sum, this song is a powerful message that marks a significant turn away from traditional relational values. By employing the compelling logic of a story well told within the musical medium and by purposely violating moral expectations, the Beatles were able to create a subtle and powerful attack on the traditional moral purposes of significant relationships. By saying you can't buy love, but you | If we assume they chose to do what they did (as we must with any rhetor until there is reason to believe otherwise), there had to be a reason for their choice. (The reason is explained in the left column starting at *.)

This paragraph serves to bring together the various threads of our argument. Since we are |

TEXT OF THE STUDY (cont.)	COMMENTARY ON THE STUDY (cont.)
can buy fun, they call their audience to a whole new moral and relational code, the effects of which we still feel decades years.	trying to teach our readers something about how the message worked, we felt it was important to review the main ideas, putting them as close together as possible so they

NOTES

1 The title is intended to connect one of the Beatles' early traditional songs, "Can't Buy Me Love," to what was a newer value of self-orientation that we think is central to "She's Leaving Home." The title has value as it provides an abstract of the main argument. It is intended to be playful and interesting as well.

2 Fisher, Walter R. "The Narrative Paradigm: In the Beginning." *Journal of Communication* 35 (1985): 75.

3 Condit, Celeste Michelle. "Crafting Virtue: The Rhetorical Construction of Public Morality." *Quarterly Journal of Speech* 73 (1987): 82.

4 Ibid., 84.

5 Ibid., 80.

6 Fisher, Walter. "Narration as a Human Communication Paradigm: The Case of Public Moral Argument." *Communication Monographs* 51 (1984): 8.

SAMPLE STUDENT PAPER*

Barbara Jordan's Keynote Address at the 1992 Democratic National Convention: A Neutral Approach to a Partisan Task
by Toby Mitchell

APPENDIX
2

CONTEXT DESCRIBED

1 In 1991, the United States was mired in a recession. The deficit was high,
2 taxes were high, losses were huge and unemployment was skyrocketing.
3 Things were so bad that in a December 1991 article by Frank Grimshaw
4 entitled, "The Economy Running on Empty," in *U.S. News and World*
5 *Report* it was stated, "In three months, 107 firms have announced 212,407
6 job losses, bringing the 1991 total to 544,000" (29).
7   In the presidential election, Bill Clinton, the Governor of Arkansas,
8 was running on a platform of change and federal stimulation of the econ-
9 omy to defeat George H. W. Bush, the incumbent. Clinton had credibil-
10 ity problems due to some of his personal financial dealings and several
11 accusations from women who said Clinton had sexually harassed them.
12 So, his selection of Barbara Jordan to deliver the keynote address at the
13 1992 Democratic National Convention was important because she had
14 the credibility to overshadow some of Clinton's credibility problems and
15 could therefore endear her audience, undecided voters, to Clinton. Also,
16 she had been the keynote speaker at the 1976 Democratic National
17 Convention, the last time a Democratic candidate had been elected
18 President.

TEXT DESCRIBED

19 Jordan's speech was an optimistic look at what the Democratic Party
20 could do for itself and the country to solve public ills which were cause
21 for major apprehension at the time. Using inclusive language, the speech
22 implored the Democratic Party and the country to join together as one
23 and make the necessary sacrifices to improve the situation. Attacks on the
24 opposition party were veiled and subtle, and were often left as an unspo-
25 ken contrast to the positive attributes of the Democratic Party listed by
26 Jordan.

*This essay was one of the first finished critical essays written by a student in an introductory criticism course. This student writer drew from the principles of criticism we have been discussing in the text. In this case, the writer also chose to apply concepts from search models discussed in the text.

The lines of the text are numbered to faciliate in-class discussion about what the writer was doing or trying to do at specific points in the essay.

27
28
29
30
31
32
33

Through her examination of the word "change," Jordan eroded the credibility of Republicans, making Clinton look like the best solution to the problems of the time. Using the Aristotelian and Burkeian search models, I intend to prove that Jordan's speech, through the use of carefully crafted arguments which garnered credibility while skewering the opposition, appeased the most liberal of Democrats, avoided offending undecided mainstream voters, and helped generate the momentum that swept Clinton into the White House.

ANALYSIS

34
35
36
37
38
39
40
41
42
43
44

The task of crafting and delivering a keynote address is not an easy one. In Craig R. Smith's (1975) essay, "The Republican Keynote Address of 1968: Adaptive Rhetoric for the Multiple Audience," he states that when Daniel Evans "was called upon to deliver the [1968 Republican] keynote address, he was forced to balance three audiences: the conservative audience of delegates, the general American audience who were more conservative than he, and the voters in Washington who were more liberal than the general American audience" (32). Jordan was likewise forced to balance between audiences that were very liberal (the delegates at the convention) and more moderate, if not conservative (the mainstream, undecided voting-age population watching on television).

45
46
47
48
49

Keeping this in mind gives one a frame of reference to use when applying the Aristotelian search model. First of all, Jordan's speech was both deliberative and forensic, in that it described the problems that had come about in the past four to 12 years and sought to ascertain what the best course of action for the country would be.

50
51
52
53
54
55
56
57
58
59
60
61
62
63
64
65
66
67
68
69

The invention of the speech came from the author's desire to promote her party and cause voters to cast their votes for her party's candidate. An important part of her speech was her credibility as a politician. Ethos, which "refers to the establishment of the credibility of the speaker," was addressed by Aristotle when he wrote that a "speaker with ethos is considered a person of good character, good sense and good will for the audience" (Stoner and Perkins 150). A rhetor might bolster his or her image by associating him or herself "with something or someone the audience perceives as credible" (150). Jordan referred to her keynote address at the 1976 Democratic National Convention, and reminded the audience that the Democrats had won that election. Also, she referred to areas where the Democratic Party had been the agent of change in education, human and civil rights, and the environment. These were both examples of comparing herself with things the audience perceived as credible. Further, she used a quote from "our 19th century visitor from France, de Toqueville," which stated that America's strength was in its women. Using this quote must have made her look credible, because Jordan was comparing herself to something considered positive. Finally, she used a quote by FDR in which he talks about the relation a good leader must have with the nation in times of trouble. This was comparing herself to a politician with a very favorable image among senior citizens, as well as anyone who has studied the Great

70
71
72
73
74
75
76
77
78
79
80
81
82
83
84
85
86
87
88
89
90
91
92
93
94
95
96
97
98
99
100
101
102
103
104
105
106
107
108
109
110
111
112
113
114
115
116

Depression, and therefore couldn't have done anything but make Jordan look more credible to these groups.

"Pathos refers to the rhetor's efforts to stir the audience's emotions" (Stoner and Perkins 150). A rhetor might "appeal to the audience's feelings of guilt, fear, pride or patriotism," or "values of family, health, appearance, youth, money or education" (150). By painting pictures of the hardships endured by many minorities in the country, the author appealed to the audience's feelings of guilt and values of health and education. She pointed out that to fix the problems that had been hurting minorities, changes needed to be made from the characteristic norms of the eighties. She implied that the way to do this was through an increase in government involvement to correct the course of events.

The arrangement of the speech made strong use of comparison and contrast, where the author contrasted the policies of the Republicans and those of the Democrats. This may have been one of the reasons why she was successful in balancing her message between audiences. She let the contrast between the two parties do the arguing for her. Her message was topical, moving from a description of the necessity for change to specific possibilities for change to descriptions of hardships caused by the Republicans' "trickle-down" economics. The author used repetition of the phrases "change" and "trickle-down" economics throughout the speech. While going to great length to define what "change" meant, however, she never made any attempt to describe what "trickle-down" meant. This may indicate a desire to use the effect of a popular phrase without getting mired in an actual definition, which may have lessened the effect she was trying to have. Also, this was in keeping with her mandate as a keynote speaker to not offend mainstream voters, since "trickle-down" is essentially a nice way of saying that Republicans give the lion's share of wealth to the rich, who let little bits of it "trickle-down" to the majority of the country.

It is interesting that she not only sought to pump up her party's candidate, but also looked at what her party needed to change within itself. "A message maker might also establish ethos by building identification between him or herself and the audience" (Stoner and Perkins 150). By saying that the entire country, including the Democratic Party, needed to change, Jordan was identifying with the audience.

Her contrast of the Republicans' "trickle-down" policies and her own party's willingness to change seems to be the key relationship between elements of the text. After describing the problems, she established that her party wished to fix those problems by changing its own philosophies, if necessary. A key part of the speech came when Jordan stated that diversity was America's strength and implied that her party supported diversity, while leaving unspoken the implication that the other party did not. This is an enthymeme. An enthymeme "is a line of deductive reasoning (moving from a general premise to a particular conclusion)" (Stoner and Perkins 149). For example, an enthymeme looks like a syllogism (Jason is human + All humans are mortal ∴ Jason is mortal), but an enthymeme is composed of probable premises instead of absolute ones, whereas a syllogism uses absolute premises. By leaving part of the argument unspoken, Jordan encouraged the listener to reach his or her

117
118
119
120
121

own the conclusion that the Republican Party was against diversity and limited it. In fact, by leaving out any other groups who had suffered besides minorities, she encouraged the audience to conclude that other groups had not suffered under Republican policies and that minorities were particular targets for conservative policies.

122
123
124
125
126

Another enthymematic device employed by Jordan is that she started the speech with the need for change and then went right into the problems of Republican policies. This again provided probable premises (change is needed + Republican policies caused the status quo) that led the audience to a probable conclusion (∴ change from Republican leadership is needed).

127
128
129
130
131
132

She did nothing to define how the Republican Party had caused minorities to suffer; she didn't describe any ways that the Republican Party had specifically caused the economy to crumble, and she didn't go into any detail about what a conservative Supreme Court Justice did to "burden" the economy. Further, she did not go into any detail about the philosophy of the Republican Party or what exactly she meant by "trickle-down" economics.

133
134
135
136
137

This may indicate that the true audience of the speech was composed of minorities, or that she thought the popular terms she was using (trickle-down, moral bankruptcy, mega-mergers, debt-overhang, burden) were sufficient to place a doubt in the minds of undecided listeners, while actually defining the terms would have lessened the effect they would have.

INTERPRETATION

138
139
140
141
142
143
144
145
146
147
148
149

In any case, Jordan was merely remaining true to the purpose of a keynote address, which is to encourage the partisan delegates at the convention without offending moderate, undecided voters who were watching on television. It can be noted here that by doing the above, she actually held fast to the tenets used by the Democrats in 1972 for their keynote address. In Sara Arendall and Thomas R. King's (1974) essay entitled, "The Keynote Address of the Democratic National Convention, 1972: The Evolution of a Speech," the "ghost writers" of that speech sought to achieve four goals as they went through their numerous revisions: "find a common denominator," "[n]egativisms . . . were dropped," (349), "ideas were added or eliminated in order to emphasize or de-emphasize campaign issues," (350) and the authors "added and eliminated ideas to promote reactions from the audience" (351).

150
151
152
153
154
155
156
157
158
159
160

Jordan found a common denominator with the theme of diversity. Further, she avoided offending undecided mainstream voters through negativity by using subtle, enthymematic arguments and never mentioned any Republicans by name, using instead vague catch phrases (trickle down, etc.). This pleased those in her own party while she abstained from offensive name-calling that would have alienated the general public. Also, she emphasized campaign issues (again with the use of the phrase "trickle down"), provoking positive reactions from the audience with the quotes and anecdotal arguments mentioned above. Jordan also identified with her audience well through the use of a few principles found in the Burkeian model of rhetoric: drama and mortification. Victimage refers to the apparent human need to have someone atone for individual or communal "sins" or mistakes. There are two ways that these mistakes can be atoned for: mortification (blaming one's self), and scapegoating (blaming another). In the speech, she admitted that everyone needed to take responsibility for the situation and implied that her party also had to change in order to solve the problems the country was facing. This was mortification. The majority of the blame, however, she heaped on her scapegoat, the Republicans, saying that the country needed to change from the ways of the recent past, namely greed, debt-overhang and mega-mergers. Again, Jordan remained true to her responsibility as a keynote speaker, encouraging her partisan audience without offending her undecided one.

EVALUATION

Her choices stand up well to scrutiny because the other choices she could have made would have involved more overt finger pointing at the opposition party, and that is something a good keynote address avoids. She could have been more negative, but the positive messages she used were intended to give people some hope, while making the opposition look dark and menacing in contrast. Her choices indicate that she was an optimist and that she was willing to look at problems from all angles to determine what was necessary to fix them. As much as her use of partisan terms made the speech a decidedly liberal one, her focus on the basic concept of change and the usefulness of diversity kept her from offending the mainstream audience with partisan accusations. Wayne N. Thompson states that Jordan succeeded in 1978 because "her method—seemingly objective and high-minded—won the respect of the latter [television audience] and set off no adverse reactions; while her conclusions, favorable to her own party, pleased the delegates, alternates and spectators" (274).

As a person who believes in conservative economic policies, I was and remain against the use of government to solve problems every time the national economy takes a downturn. However, the rhetorical choices made by Barbara Jordan in this speech were masterful in that she appeared to take the moral high ground while still slipping in attacks against the opposition with the skill of a saboteur.

Her credibility with every group was established beyond question and the picture she painted of the Democratic Party was of a modest servant, humble, good-natured and ready to accommodate when called upon. Barbara Jordan's speech primed the delegates at the convention and an undecided television audience for a new and different solution to the status quo, Bill Clinton.

Works Cited

Grimshaw, Frank. "The Economy Running on Empty." *U.S. News & World Report* 30 December 1991: 29.

Newell, Sara Arendall, and King, Thomas R. "The Keynote Address of the Democratic National Convention, 1972: The Evolution of a Speech." *Southern Speech Communication Journal* 39 (1974): 346–58.

Smith, Craig R. "The Republican Keynote Address of 1968: Adaptive Rhetoric for the Multiple Audience." *Western States Speech Journal* 39 (1975): 32–39.

Stoner, Mark and Sally Perkins. *A Critical Apprenticeship: Making Sense of Messages* Unpublished manuscript, 1999.

Thompson, Wayne N. "Barbara Jordan's Keynote Address: Fulfilling Dual and Conflicting Purposes." *Central States Speech Journal* 30 (1979): 272–77.

SAMPLE STUDENT ESSAY*

A Response to the Death of a Princess: The Form and Function of a Eulogy
by Camille Priselac

CONTEXT DESCRIBED

1 Princess Diana was viewed by many people throughout the world as a
2 great humanitarian. Through the charities she helped and by the per-
3 sonal accounts of people who met her, this view was reinforced. That is
4 why when she tragically died in the early hours of August 31, 1997 the
5 world fell into a state of shock, overwhelmed by grief. Her life began like
6 a fairytale and in the end was a tragedy that the whole world would
7 mourn.
8   It seemed to an outsider looking in on Princess Diana's life that at
9 first she had it all. She was a beautiful woman married to the Prince of
10 Wales with whom she shared two sons, both of whom she loved very
11 much. It was a life that most people could only dream of. However,
12 things changed in the Princess' life as the years went by. She was faced
13 with her husband's rumored infidelity and this led to a string of eating
14 disorders. There were also the incessant photographers that seemed to
15 follow her every move. Through all of this turmoil the Princess never lost
16 her ability to captivate the world with her genuine sense of self. That is
17 why when she died that early morning the world lost its "queen of
18 hearts" and needed something from the royal family to reinforce the
19 longstanding belief that she was irreplaceable.
20   At first when the news of the crash that killed Princess Diana became
21 public there was an extraordinary outpouring of grief. People came from
22 all over Britain to show their remorse. They filled the gates to her home
23 with flowers and cards, and also the place itself. People around the world
24 made makeshift memorials and cried for the Princess. After the initial
25 shock wore off people began to question why the royal family was not
26 showing a public display of grief. They began to ask questions, as
27 Montalbano reports: "'Where Is Our Queen? Where Is Her Flag?'

*This essay was one of the first finished critical essays written by a student in an
introductory criticism course. This student writer drew from the principles of criticism we have been discussing in the text. In this case the writer also chose to construct a unique search model by adapting concepts from sources not discussed in the
textbook. While there are strengths and weaknesses in the analysis, we feel it is
important to see an example of how a critic can expand theoretical options for
analysis.
    The lines of the text are numbered to facilitate discussion about what the writer
was doing or trying to do at specific points in the essay.

28
29
30
31
32
demanded the Sun. 'Show Us You Care,' said the Express. 'Your People Are Suffering. Speak to Us Ma'am,' said the Mirror" ("Criticism" A1). All of this criticism did not go unnoticed by the royal family. After a week of silence the Queen decided to eulogize Diana to the world in hopes that maybe her words would offer some comfort to the grieving.

MESSAGE DESCRIBED

33
34
35
36
37
38
39
40
41
42
43
44
45
46
The message was broadcast to the world the night before the funeral was to take place. With the palace in the background, the Queen, dressed in black, appeared very stoic as she talked. The message begins with the Queen paying tribute to Diana. "First, I want to pay tribute to Diana myself. She was an exceptional and gifted human being. In good times and bad, she never lost her capacity to smile or laugh, nor to inspire others with her warmth and kindness" (*The Times* 2) The Queen also talks about how she admired and respected her, "I admired and respected her for her energy and commitment to others, and especially for her devotion to her two boys." The rest of the message contains statements that refer to the other families whose loved ones were involved in the crash as well as a statement to the many people who were grieving for Diana. One of the Queen's last statements is, "I hope that tomorrow we can all, wherever we are, join in expressing our grief at Diana's loss, and gratitude for her all-too-short-life."

ANALYSIS

47
48
49
50
51
52
53
This eulogy was given out of a demand by the people to have some sort of acknowledgment from the royal family. The situation demanded attention, and the people were waiting for the Queen to give it to them. Lloyd Bitzer calls what the Queen faced an exigence of a rhetorical situation. He states that "In any rhetorical situation there will be at least one controlling exigence which functions as the organizing principle: it specifies the audience to be addressed and the change to be effected" (7). Bitzer's theory helps one realize why the Queen spoke out the way she did.

54
55
56
57
58
59
60
Karen Foss states that eulogies tend to follow certain structural patterns (187). Her theory along with Bitzer's helps us explain the effects of the Queen's rhetorical choices in her speech. Exposing the choices made by the Queen makes it easier to understand why the message was constructed the way it was. I intend to show that, considering the public's expectations for a more heartfelt speech, the Queen's rhetorical choices were not a fitting response to Princess Diana's death.

61
62
63
64
65
66
67
68
69
Lloyd Bitzer defines any exigence as an "imperfection marked by urgency; it is a defect, an obstacle, something waiting to be done, a thing which is other than it should be" (6). I believe that the Queen felt the pressures of the situation and knew if she didn't respond that it would mean disaster for the royal family. The Queen had a rhetorical exigence on her hands. The rhetorical choices that she made in the speech show the presence of this exigence. One rhetorical choice she made was to exclude examples from Diana's life to support her statements. In the following sentence the Queen suggests that Diana's life was important but she leaves out why. "I for one believe that there are les-

sons to be drawn from her life and from the extraordinary and moving reaction to her death." The lessons that should be drawn are unclear. Should we draw lessons from her family life or from her charity work? The rhetorical choice that the Queen made of not giving examples is deliberate not only in the example but as a pattern throughout the eulogy. The Queen was challenged into saying something by the circumstances. Bitzer states that "rhetorical discourse comes into existence as a response to a situation . . . or a solution in response to a problem" (5). His theory outlines exactly what the Queen did, she responded to the situation. The Queen said the eulogy to accomplish a task, but it was not heartfelt, and it definitely was not fitting.

Borrowing a model from Kathleen Jamison, Foss asserts that eulogies generally are assumed to serve four basic functions. The functions are: "(1) to make real the death to the shocked audience; (2) to lessen the personal fears of mortality with the descriptions of how the deceased 'lives on'; (3) to allow the audience to reorient themselves to the deceased; and (4) to reassure the audience that the community will continue despite death" (187). These four functions are not all operating in the Queen's eulogy of Diana. The Queen chose not to make the death real to the audience. Throughout the message there is no mention of the fact that Diana is gone and is never coming back. Surprisingly, the Queen never addresses Diana herself; she never gives an interpersonal goodbye. This is why the Queen fails at the very first function. The Queen chose not to say something like "Goodbye, Diana, we will miss you." This choice is a clear indicator of an ill-fitting response to the death of Diana.

The second function that Foss lists is that "the speaker should lessen the audience's fears of mortality" (187). The Queen gives no examples of this function throughout her eulogy. She does not mention how Diana's two sons will carry on her spirit. This is something I feel the audience was looking for. Also, there is no mention of how the organizations that Diana campaigned for will keep her memory alive. Clearly, these missing elements weaken the effectiveness of the eulogy.

The third function of a eulogy is to "allow the audience to reorient themselves with the deceased" (187). This function is where the Queen shows some sign of acknowledgment but is still lacking in content. The Queen states in the eulogy that, "No one who knew Diana will ever forget her." In this sentence the Queen begins to orient us with Diana and then ends the sentence abruptly. This would have been the perfect opportunity for the Queen to talk more with the public and address why they felt such a deep connection to her.

The last function that eulogies serve is to "reassure the audience that the community will continue despite the death" (187). At the beginning of the eulogy the Queen states that, "We have all been trying in our different ways to cope. It is not easy to express a sense of loss, since the initial shock is often succeeded by a mixture of other feelings: disbelief, incomprehension, anger and concern for those who remain."

I believe a statement of continuity would have been much more appropriate in this paragraph. It would have lifted the spirits of the audience and would have given the eulogy an uplifting feel. The continuity would have also filled the last function, and made the eulogy have a more heartfelt appeal.

117 Any rhetorical situation, such as the situation faced by the Queen, invites
118 a response (Bitzer 8). However, the response demanded of the Queen needed
119 to be a fitting one. As illustrated, the eulogy by the Queen failed to function
120 properly because of poor rhetorical choices. The missing elements I pointed
121 out support the argument that the Queen's message was not a fitting response.
122 The people were tired of waiting. Even before the Queen's eulogy, efforts by the
123 royal family were seen as insufficient. "On Wednesday, four days after the 36-
124 year-old princess died in a Paris car crash, the royal family issued a three-line
125 communiqué from a vacation castle in Scotland thanking people for their
126 affection. . . . For many, Wednesday's gesture from a royal family with which
127 Diana fought repeatedly seemed too little, too late" ("Royals" A1). The words
128 "too little, too late" suggest the public's need for a more appealing response
129 from the royal family.
130

INTERPRETATION

131 The rhetorical choices made by the Queen in response to the exigence she
132 faced make clear the missing attributes of the eulogy. These elements ranged
133 from the lack of emotional attachment to the lack of examples from Diana's
134 life. The audience was expecting a tribute to the late Princess and instead they
135 received an oversimplified message.
136 The Queen had many choices to make when preparing this eulogy for the
137 world. In the end the choices she did make were not wise, and could be viewed
138 as unfair. The world wanted a tribute to their dead Princess, and instead they
139 received an unfitting response to someone whom they cherished.
140 Lloyd Bitzer's theory of rhetorical exigence and Karen Foss' theory of the
141 functional aspects of a eulogy have a significant relationship between them.
142 Together they help explain how the Queen's message and the rhetorical
143 choices she made were not a fitting response to Diana's death. The Queen's
144 eulogy did not follow function well because it was not shaped to meet the sit-
145 uation or the expectations of the audience.

WORKS CITED

Bitzer, Lloyd. "The Rhetorical Situation." *Philosophy and Rhetoric* 25 Supplementary
    Issue (1992): 1–14.

Foss, Karen. "John Lennon and the Advisory Function of Eulogies." *Central States
    Speech Journal* 34 (1983): 187–194.

Montalbano, Wm. D. "Royals Bow to Public, Extend Funeral Route." *Los Angeles
    Times* 4 September 1997, home ed: A1+.

———. "Criticism Spurs Windsors to End Silence, Isolation." *Los Angeles Times* 5
    September 1997, home ed.: A1+.

Queen Elizabeth II. "Queen's Heartfelt Tribute to 'Gifted Human Being'." *The Times*
    6 September 1997: 2.

INDEX